your
pregnancy™
after 35

your
pregnancy™
after 35

THIRD EDITION

GLADE B. CURTIS, M.D., M.P.H., OB/GYN

JUDITH SCHULER, M.S.

Da Capo
LIFE
LONG
A Member of the Perseus Books Group

Your Pregnancy™ is a registered trademark of Da Capo Press
Set in 11-point Minion Pro by The Perseus Books Group

Library of Congress Cataloging-in-Publication Data
Curtis, Glade B.
    Your pregnancy after 35 / Glade B. Curtis, M.D., M.P.H., OB/GYN, Judith Schuler, M.S.—Third edition, first Da Capo Press edition.
        pages cm
    Revision of 2001 publication published under the same title; originally published as: Your pregnancy after 30. 1996.
    Includes bibliographical references and index.
    ISBN 978-0-7382-1648-5 (pbk.)—ISBN 978-0-7382-1649-2 (e-book) 1. Pregnancy in middle age.
I. Schuler, Judith. II. Curtis, Glade B. Your pregnancy after 30. III. Title.

RG556.6.C873 2013
618.2—dc23
                                                                                    2012044012

First Da Capo Press printing 2013
Published by Da Capo Press
A Member of the Perseus Books Group
www.dacapopress.com

Da Capo Press books are available at special discounts for bulk purchases in the U.S. by corporations, institutions, and other organizations. For more information, please contact the Special Markets Department at the Perseus Books Group, 2300 Chestnut Street, Suite 200, Philadelphia, PA, 19103, call (800) 255–1514, or e-mail special.markets@perseusbooks.com.

10 9 8 7 6 5 4 3 2 1

Contents

About the Authors

Glade B. Curtis, M.D., M.P.H., F.A.C.O.G., is board-certified by the American Board of Obstetrics and Gynecology and a Fellow of the American College of Obstetricians and Gynecologists. He has over 25 years of experience and has participated in more than 5000 deliveries.

Dr. Curtis is a graduate of the University of Utah with a Bachelor of Science and a Master's Degree in Public Health (M.P.H.). He attended the University of Rochester School of Medicine and Dentistry in New York. He interned and was a resident and chief resident in Obstetrics and Gynecology at the University of Rochester Strong Memorial Hospital, Rochester, New York.

Judith Schuler, M.S., has worked with Dr. Curtis for over 25 years as his co-author and editor. They have collaborated together on 18 books dealing with pregnancy, women's health and children's health.

Ms. Schuler earned a Master of Science degree in Family Studies from the University of Arizona in Tucson. Before becoming an editor for HPBooks, where she and Dr. Curtis first began working together, Ms. Schuler taught at the university level in California and Arizona.

Acknowledgments

Glade B. Curtis. In this, the third edition of *Your Pregnancy After 35*, I continue to draw upon the many questions from discussions with my patients and their partners, and my professional colleagues. I have gained new insights and a greater understanding of the joy and anticipation of impending parenthood. I have rejoiced in my patients' happiness and thank all of them for allowing me to be part of this miraculous process.

Credit must also be given to my understanding and generous wife, Debbie, and our family, who support me in a profession that requires much of them. Beyond that commitment, they have supported and encouraged me to pursue the challenge of this project. Thanks to David Stevens, D.D.S., for his dental expertise. And my mother has always offered her unconditional love and support.

Judith Schuler. Thanks to my son, Ian, for his continued support and encouragement. Special thanks to Bob Rucinski for his help and computer expertise with every book I write or revise. And thanks to the pregnant couples who, through the years, have inspired us. Our books are for you.

Chapter 1

Welcome to Your Pregnancy

Pregnancy is an exciting time, and more women every year are happy to find they are pregnant in their 30s or 40s. Older mothers are giving birth to more than 675,000 babies a year.

During the 1980s, births to women in the 30- to 44-year-old age range nearly doubled. First births to women in their 30s in 1990 accounted for about 25% of all births to women in that age group. In 2008, it was reported nearly 15% of *all* births were to women 35 and older.

If you waited to start a family, you aren't alone. Many couples choose to postpone having children until careers are on track or relationships are firmly established. Births to older couples may occur because they married late or a couple is in a second marriage and starting a new family together. Other couples have experienced infertility and do not achieve a pregnancy until they have gone through major workups and testing or even surgery. Or a single woman may have chosen donor insemination to achieve pregnancy.

• •

Susan, a 38-year-old woman with two kids, recently married a man who had not fathered any children. Susan came to the office concerned about their chances of conceiving. I gave her a few suggestions and laid out a plan for the next few months. An ecstatic Susan called me 2 weeks later. She was pregnant and had probably been a few weeks along when we had discussed the possibility of infertility.

• •

Today, many healthcare professionals gauge pregnancy risk by a pregnant woman's health status, not her age. Pre-existing medical conditions have the greatest impact on a woman's well-being during pregnancy. For example, a healthy 39-year-old is less likely to develop problems than a diabetic woman in her 20s. A woman's fitness can also have a greater effect on her pregnancy than her age.

Most older women who become pregnant are in good health. A woman in good physical condition who has exercised regularly may go through pregnancy as easily as a woman 15 to 20 years younger. An exception—women in a first pregnancy who are over 40 may have more problems than women the same age who have previously had children. But most healthy women will have a safe delivery.

Some health problems are age related, and the risk of developing a condition increases with age. You may not know you have a problem unless you see your healthcare provider regularly.

Genetic Counseling May Be a Wise Choice

If either you or your partner is over 35, genetic counseling may be recommended; see the discussion in Chapter 10. Two risks that increase for older pregnant women are chromosomal abnormalities and miscarriage. The risk of chromosome problems exceeds 5% for the over-35 age group. The risk of miscarriage is about 50% at age 42. Genetic counseling may help answer questions you have about these and other problems.

Genetic counseling brings together a couple and professionals who are trained to deal with the questions about the occurrence, or risk of occurrence, of a genetic problem. With genetic counseling, information about human genetics is applied to a particular couple's situation. Professionals interpret this information so the couple can make informed decisions.

When a mother is older, the father is often older as well; a father's age can affect a pregnancy. It can be difficult to determine whether the mother's age or the father's age matters more. More research is needed before we definitely know the effects of a father's age on pregnancy.

Will Your Pregnancy Be Different if You're Older?

As an older pregnant woman, your healthcare provider may see you more often or you may have more tests. You may be advised to have amniocentesis or chorionic villus sampling (CVS) to find out whether your child has Down

Benefits of Pregnancy

- The natural steroids produced during pregnancy may reduce symptoms of allergies and asthma and may help reduce inflammation, a common symptom of rheumatoid arthritis, systemic lupus erythematosus, inflammatory bowel disease and other autoimmune disorders.
- Pregnancy may protect you from breast cancer or ovarian cancer later in life.
- Migraine headaches often disappear during the second and third trimesters of pregnancy.
- Menstrual cramps are a thing of the past during pregnancy. An added benefit—they may not return after baby is born!
- Pregnancy stops the growth of endometrial tissue when ovulation stops and may help relieve moderate endometriosis. Endometriosis is the condition in which endometrial tissue attaches to parts of the ovaries and other sites outside the uterus; it causes pelvic pain, heavy bleeding and other problems during menstruation for some women.

syndrome or some other problem. Even if you would never terminate a pregnancy, this information helps you and your healthcare team prepare for the birth of your baby.

If you're over 35, you do have a greater chance of having problems. You may be watched more closely during pregnancy for signs of those problems. Some can be troublesome, but with good medical care, they can usually be handled fairly well.

Pregnancy when you're older can take its toll. You may gain more weight, see stretch marks where there were none before, notice your breasts sag lower or feel a lack of tone in your muscles. Attention to nutrition, exercise and rest can help a great deal.

Because of demands on your time and energy, fatigue may be one of your greatest issues. It's a common complaint of many pregnant women, no matter their age! Rest is essential to your health and to your baby's. Rest and nap when possible. Don't take on more tasks or new roles. Don't volunteer for any big projects. Learn to say, "No." You'll feel better!

Moderate exercise can help boost energy levels and may ease some discomforts. However, check first with your healthcare provider before starting an exercise program.

Stress can also be a problem. Exercising, eating healthfully and getting as much rest as possible may help relieve stress. Take time for yourself.

Some women find that a pregnancy support group is an excellent way to deal with difficulties they may experience. Ask your healthcare provider for further information.

Through research, we know labor and delivery for an older woman may be different from a younger woman's labor. Labor may last longer. Older women also have a higher rate of Cesarean deliveries. After baby's birth, your uterus may not contract as quickly; postpartum bleeding may last longer and be heavier.

Your Health May Be
More Important Than Your Age

Pre-existing medical conditions are the most important indicator of a woman's well-being during pregnancy and the health of her developing baby. Most women who become pregnant in their 30s and 40s are in good health. A woman in good physical condition who has been exercising regularly may go through pregnancy as easily as a woman 15 to 20 years younger.

Some health problems are age related—the risk of developing a condition increases with age. High blood pressure and some forms of diabetes are age related. These conditions can complicate a pregnancy and should be brought under control before pregnancy, if possible.

I'm 40 and just found out I'm pregnant. Am I considered high risk?
No, you are not high risk because of your age, although being pregnant at 40 is different from being pregnant at 20. You may do some things differently, such as have amniocentesis or seek genetic counseling. If you're concerned about your risk, talk to your healthcare provider about it.

Age affects fertility, which begins to decline faster after age 35. Couples older than 35 may take twice as long to conceive a child as a younger couple. A woman older than 40 may take longer to conceive because of the declining number and quality of eggs in the ovaries and because ovulation is less frequent. The good news is that advances in fertility and reproductive technology have helped women conceive who might never have conceived before. Your healthcare provider can learn more about your ovulatory cycle by administering a test called the *clomiphene challenge,* which involves administering a drug to test the ovaries.

Other factors can affect fertility. One study showed drinking even one alcoholic beverage can lower a woman's chances of getting pregnant. Caffeine can also affect a woman's ability to conceive.

You may be advised to use a home ovulation-predictor kit, which can help confirm if and when ovulation occurs. A variety of over-the-counter tests are available. A kit works by measuring the increase or surge of luteinizing hormone (LH) in a woman's urine. This hormone is made in the brain and promotes maturation of the ovarian follicle, resulting in ovulation. LH increases and can be detected 24 to 40 hours *before* ovulation. Kits range in price from $20 (a one-time-use test) to a few hundred dollars (kit can be used repeatedly).

Some older couples turn to assisted reproductive technology (ART) to achieve pregnancy. ART includes in-vitro fertilization (IVF) and gamete intrafallopian transfer (GIFT), in which a donor egg is paired to the partner's sperm. Success relates to the woman's age. For women at 34, the success of in-vitro fertilization is about 20% per menstrual cycle. At 44, a woman can expect a 5% success rate per cycle with the procedure.

The Older Couple

As an older pregnant woman, you can take many positive steps to help ensure your pregnancy will go as smoothly as possible for you and your baby. Reading this book and our other pregnancy books can help you; see page ii for a current list of all the titles in our series.

If either you or your partner is older than 35, genetic counseling may be advisable. The risk of chromosome abnormalities exceeds 5% in this situation. For further information on genetic counseling, see Chapter 10.

Some researchers recommend men father children before they are 40. This is a conservative viewpoint, and not everyone agrees with it. More data and research are needed before we can make definite statements about a father's age and its effect on pregnancy.

> You will find many boxes in each weekly discussion that will provide you with information you will not find in the text. Our boxes do not repeat information contained in a discussion. Each box is unique, so read them for specific information.

Chapter 2

First-Time or Repeat Pregnancy?

Being pregnant can be wonderful and a little nerve-racking at the same time. It's a time of learning and can also be a time of spiritual, intellectual and physical growth. It's important for you to be open about your concerns.

When a woman discovers she is pregnant, she may feel many emotions— excitement, anxiety, joy. You may be surprised by your emotions when you learn you're pregnant. Even if you and your partner have been anticipating a pregnancy, you may not feel the way you thought you would.

If you aren't immediately thrilled about pregnancy, don't feel alone. It's common to feel conflicted about the news and to question your condition. Some of this may be attributed to the anxiety you feel if you're not sure what lies ahead.

Your First Pregnancy after 35

If you've never been pregnant before, you may feel overwhelmed thinking about the next 9 months. A lot will be happening in your life, and many changes will be taking place. We're not talking only about the physical changes you will experience. They are certainly a big part of pregnancy, but changes will be occurring in other areas of your life, such as changes in your professional life, changes in your life with your partner and changes in the relation-

> With a repeat pregnancy, you may feel baby move sooner than with a first pregnancy. Part of this may be because you already know what baby's movements feel like, so you identify them sooner.

ships you share with family and friends. It's a lot to take in right now, but having some time to deal with these various situations—you have many months ahead of you—may make your tasks easier.

On the physical and emotional side, you may experience fatigue and emotional mood swings. You must adjust to your changing body. People will give you advice and share stories about their own pregnancies, labors and deliveries. You will receive lots of attention, sometimes unwanted.

You can't avoid some of these experiences. However, knowing the facts about pregnancy can prepare you to accept or to ignore advice. Knowing how the female body reacts to pregnancy can help you understand the changes you experience and help you make intelligent choices as the need arises. If you're willing to adapt and adjust your lifestyle for the sake of your health and that of your growing baby, you can do a lot to make your pregnancy a happy, fulfilling experience.

You'll Receive a Lot of Attention

A positive (sometimes negative) aspect of a first pregnancy is the attention you receive. At times you may be irritated by people who ask how you feel and what you're experiencing.

. . . .

Debbie was tired of inane questions and wisecracks from co-workers about her pregnancy. She turned it back on them by asking them the same questions. When asked about her weight gain, she would reply with a grin, "My healthcare provider says I'm doing great with my weight gain. What has your healthcare provider said about yours?" Her co-workers took it in good humor and soon got the message.

. . . .

Allow people to help you and do things for you. Some women don't appreciate how much others are willing to do for them during their first pregnancy until they become pregnant again. Helpful attention is a luxury not always offered in subsequent pregnancies, so take advantage of it now!

Sharing the News

You may feel a little awkward telling family members, friends and co-workers you're pregnant. Some people thoughtlessly offer their advice or opinions on "being an older mother."

If others are critical or do not have your best wishes in mind, ignore them! Focus your attention on staying healthy and having a happy pregnancy. Your pregnancy is your business—you don't need the good opinion of anyone else to make it a positive experience for you.

When you announce to co-workers and supervisors you're pregnant, be prepared for a range of reactions. Be clear you have made the right decision for you. Assure co-workers your pregnancy is just one aspect of your life (a very important aspect), and you plan to continue your job as long as you are able, if this is what you choose.

Repeat Pregnancy

With a first-time pregnancy, every experience is a new one for you. In later pregnancies, things are different. Many women assume their second pregnancy will be just like their first. Often it isn't—your emotions in a repeat pregnancy may not be the same as in a first pregnancy. However, you may feel more relaxed.

In a repeat pregnancy, you are often seen as a "pregnant mother"; in other words, you should know what's going on. You may be reluctant to ask for extra attention, although you may need it more. A second pregnancy can be more stressful because of the extra demands on your time and energies. You must attend to your family's well-being, take care of yourself and maybe a career as well. You may wonder where you will find the energy to satisfy everyone else's needs. Physical discomforts may bother you a bit more. If you experienced various problems in your first pregnancy, you're more likely to have those same problems in subsequent pregnancies. Some repeat pregnancy problems include gestational diabetes, premature labor and some placenta problems.

On the plus side, women usually have a shorter labor with their second child, often only about half as long as with a first baby. Pain may not lessen, but because labor is usually shorter and you know more about what's going to happen, it may be easier to handle.

Physical Changes

With a repeat pregnancy, you may show sooner. Some women think they are further along than they really are because they look pregnant sooner than they did the first time. Be realistic about your body. If this is a repeat pregnancy or if it's been a while since your last pregnancy, you may notice changes sooner. Most women's bodies *will* show the results of having more than one baby. Pregnancy, combined with the natural effects of being older, takes its toll. Attention to diet and exercise can help a great deal.

You may experience backaches more frequently because your first pregnancy stretched the ligaments that hold the uterus in place. You may carry your second pregnancy lower, which puts pressure on your back and sometimes on your bladder.

Carrying lower with your pregnancy can be beneficial in a lot of ways, including breathing more easily and eating more comfortably. However, when you carry lower, you may feel the need to go to the bathroom more often and more urgently. In addition, you may feel greater strain in your lower back, which could result in more back pain or discomfort.

Be careful when lifting, especially lifting young children. Bending over to pick up a toddler can cause back strain. To help with backache, practice the exercises you learn in childbirth-education classes. A hot-water bottle or a light maternity girdle also helps relieve backache. Exercising may also help; see the exercises we provide in Chapter 13.

It may be harder to determine when you actually go into labor

> ### Time-Saving, Energy-Saving Tip
>
> If your toddler is hanging on to his pacifier, you may want to help him give it up before the new baby is born so you don't have to keep track of more than one child's pacifier. An easy way to help your older child is to cut off the pacifier tip (end of the nipple part) with scissors. It's no fun for a child to suck on air, so he may quickly give up the habit.

with a second or repeat pregnancy when you're older. You may have more false labor pains this time around.

I was in my 20s when I was pregnant before. Now that I'm 36, will pregnancy be different?
Every pregnancy is unique. There are more possibilities for issues or problems to occur when you're older, but that may not necessarily be the case. You may take better care of yourself now. At 36, you may eat better, exercise more regularly or get more sleep than when you were younger. Taking good care of yourself will help you have a healthier pregnancy.

Some Challenges with this Pregnancy

Fatigue is a pregnant woman's most common complaint. Feeling tired sooner with a second pregnancy is a common complaint. Not only are you older, but you also have children to care for and interact with, and these can add stress and strain to your life, resulting in fatigue. Rest and nap whenever you can. Nap when your child does, or put up your feet.

You may start to feel guilty because you can't do everything you want as your pregnancy progresses. Evaluate a situation, do what you can, let the rest go, then relax and enjoy life! Keep things simple and in perspective—the health of you and your baby are most important.

Moderate exercise can boost your energy level and may eliminate or alleviate some discomforts. When you exercise, your heart pumps faster; this helps move oxygen throughout your body, resulting in feeling more energetic. It's a great way to help wake you up when you're feeling tired. Consider an activity you can do with your child, but check with your healthcare provider before starting any exercise program. See Chapter 13 for an in-depth discussion of exercise before and after pregnancy.

Stress can also take its toll on you. To alleviate stress, eat healthfully, exercise and get as much rest as possible. Take time for yourself. Don't let mood swings control you. If you feel one coming on, remember it won't last forever.

Involving Your Children

Being pregnant when you already have children may raise some concerns for you. You'll probably feel anxious about how the new baby will affect your older children and your relationships with them.

Explain to children, in simple terms, how pregnancy affects your body. Try to help your children understand any problems you may experience, such as morning sickness. If you're too tired to do some regular activities with your children, let them know it's because of how you're feeling, not because of them. Reassure them that as soon as you feel better, you will do as much as possible with them.

· ·

Kate didn't know how much to tell her kids about her pregnancy or how to explain things about it. She took Allison and Sam with her to the library to look for books in the children's section. She was amazed at how many excellent books were available, many with tasteful pictures and simple explanations. They took books home and spent time together going through them and talking about the new baby.

· ·

Let your children help prepare for the new baby. Older children might help choose the baby's name or decorate the nursery. A picture drawn by a big brother or sister adds color to the baby's room and can make an older child feel important.

Delay telling very young children about the baby until they can see for themselves it is growing inside you. Even then, it may be better to wait until close to the baby's birth to tell a very young child (under 3). Time passes much more slowly for young children, and a few weeks can seem like forever. If possible, use a familiar reference point for the birth, such as Thanksgiving or when school gets out.

Ask your healthcare provider if it's all right to bring one child with you to a prenatal visit so the child can listen to baby's heartbeat. Or take your child to the hospital nursery to see the new babies. Many hospitals offer preparation classes for siblings; choose one suited to your child's age.

When your child asks questions, keep answers simple. For example, if your young child wants to know how the baby eats while it's growing inside you, an explanation such as "the baby gets its food from Mommy" will probably suffice. To your young child, your pregnancy isn't very important.

You may need to provide older children with more information. Answer their questions honestly, but even with older kids, don't provide more information than they need. Most important, give them extra love and attention during this time, and plan time alone together with each of them after the baby is born.

Let your children know in advance who will be caring for them when you are in the hospital. If possible, include them in making this decision. If you can, allow them to stay at home, where things are familiar. This is a time of great upheaval for your children—make it as easy as possible on them.

Making Changes in Your Child's Life

Encourage your child's independence from you. Let your partner take over part of your regular childcare duties so they can spend time together without you. It'll help when you go to the hospital or are busy after the baby is born.

If you must make changes in your child's routine, such as putting her in a new room or taking away his crib, do it *before* baby comes. If the change occurs near the time of the baby's birth, your older child may feel displaced. Wait awhile to give your older child's toys, clothes or bottles to the new baby, or it could cause resentment.

Don't try to make life easier on yourself by pushing toilet training or making your child give up the bottle. It can cause more problems than it

Time-Saving, Energy-Saving Tip

If you have older children, now's the time to begin giving them additional responsibilities. You'll be glad you did when they can do some things for themselves, allowing you free time to rest or to care for the new baby. For example, a preteen child can begin doing his own laundry. A younger child can learn to sort her clothes and strip her bed.

resolves. Encourage your child toward independence in small steps at the appropriate times.

When You're Expecting More Than One Baby

As an older woman, you may be more likely to have twins. For older children, welcoming one baby into the family is hard enough; making room for two or more babies can be that much more difficult. Make sure the older child has her own familiar place and keeps her own things. Reassure him of your love frequently, and give him plenty of attention.

If you'll need help after the babies are born, especially with childcare, have the helper start work before the babies are born. Your older children can get to know the caregiver beforehand, which provides a sense of continuity after the babies come home.

Encourage your older child to express her feelings about the upcoming birth of the babies. Let your child know you understand why she might feel negative and help her find positive ways to deal with her feelings.

Establish a regular, uninterrupted time with your older child before the babies are born and continue it after their birth. This might be storytime in the evening or preparing for bed or bath time. These routines contribute to a child's sense of security. Tell your child this time is important to you and you will continue it after the babies are born. Then make every effort to do so.

> If you already have a child, the birth of a new baby may greatly affect him or her, especially if your child is a toddler. After baby's arrival, you may find she acts out more or has tantrums. Understand that your child is looking for comfort, and this is the only way she can express her fears.

Chapter 3

Your Career and Your Pregnancy

Working during pregnancy is not unusual today. In fact, more than half of all women work outside the home. Many women work almost until the day they deliver.

Whether you work throughout your pregnancy depends on your particular circumstances; it's a subject to discuss with your healthcare provider. No matter what kind of job you do or whether you work full- or part-time, expect to modify some daily activities. If your profession is especially demanding, set priorities and establish guidelines with co-workers about how much you can do during pregnancy.

> Vicki never had much to do with the human-resources person at her workplace. She decided to make an appointment with the woman to discuss her pregnancy. She found a friend and an advocate in Caroline. With her help, Vicki made a lot of changes at work, including her work hours and breaks, so she could lie down. With these changes, she was able to work through her entire pregnancy.

If you're concerned about whether your workplace is a safe environment for you during your pregnancy, talk to your healthcare provider and your human resources department. It may be difficult to know the specific risks of a particular job; the goal is to minimize as many risks as you can to you and your baby while enabling you to work. A healthy woman with an ordinary job should be able to work throughout her pregnancy.

Work Precautions during Pregnancy

If you work during pregnancy, keep in mind a few precautions. You will probably have to slow down and to lighten your duties. Expect to take things a little easier at work and at home—you may not be able to do some of the things you do when you aren't pregnant. Learn to ask for help when you need it.

•••

Heather had a demanding job as a vet; some days she worked 10 hours or more. She came to see me at the end of her sixth month, looking and feeling terrible. I told her what I tell others about work and pregnancy—I wanted her to be able to work, but her pregnancy had to come first. Her emphasis on work could have a negative effect on the health of her growing baby. She wouldn't last another week the way she was going. We decided she would set some boundaries at work and we devised a plan—8-hour days that would decrease to 4-hour days over the next 3 months. When she came in a month later, Heather reported things were much better at work.

•••

Making Changes

Your center of gravity is changing, so you may have to change the way you do certain tasks—lifting, for example. Do most of your lifting with your legs. Bend your knees to lift; don't bend at the waist. As your abdomen grows larger, don't lift anything heavier than 20 pounds.

Avoid activities that involve climbing and balance, especially during the third trimester. Talk to your supervisor about eliminating these activities. If you stand all day at your job, you may have to sit down for a period of time.

If you sit most of the time at your job, get up and move around regularly to stimulate circulation. Sit in a chair that offers good support for your back and legs. Don't slouch or cross your legs while sitting.

Work Risks Associated with Pregnancy

If your job includes two or more of the following risks, tell your healthcare provider. He or she may want to monitor your pregnancy more closely. Work-related pregnancy risks include the following:

- standing more than 3 hours a day
- working on an industrial machine, especially if it vibrates a lot or requires strenuous effort to operate

- strenuous physical tasks, such as lifting, pulling, pushing or heavy cleaning
- repetitious work, such as an assembly-line job
- environmental factors, such as high noise levels or extreme temperatures
- long working hours
- shift changes
- exposure to infectious diseases
- exposure to chemicals or toxic substances

Some substances in the workplace can pose a hazard to a developing fetus. If you think you may be exposed to hazardous substances, discuss it with your healthcare provider. Substances may be brought into your home on your work clothes or those of someone else in your family. A discussion of hazardous environmental substances can be found in Chapter 4.

Working at a Computer

We have no evidence working at a computer can harm a growing baby. However, be aware of how long you sit and the way you sit; keep good circulation in your legs. Get up and walk around frequently. Try to exercise a bit during the day to help keep you feeling tiptop.

Melinda was a cashier at a large department store. Before pregnancy, her legs ached after standing for an 8-hour shift. At her 6-month visit, she was miserable. She had just finished a shift and couldn't get her shoes off because her feet were so swollen. She needed to make some major changes. She did. Melinda changed to a 6-hour shift, with two breaks, during which she rested on her side on a couch for 30 minutes. She sat on a stool while she worked. Running shoes were more comfortable, and maternity support hose also helped a lot. Her boss was happy to work with her to make the changes possible.

Job Stress and Fatigue

Stress and fatigue are common during pregnancy. Fatigue may actually be an early sign of pregnancy. For some women, the feeling lasts throughout pregnancy. For others, stress on the job or at home can cause fatigue during the day or sleeping problems at night.

If possible, lie down during breaks or on your lunch hour. Even 10 or 15 minutes of rest can make you feel better. Do leg-stretching foot exercises several times each hour or whenever you can. Remove your shoes before doing the following exercise. Extend your legs in front, point your toes, then flex your feet. Repeat four or five times. Or write the alphabet with your toes by sitting in a chair and holding your feet off the ground. Using one foot, form the letters by moving your foot. Write the complete alphabet with each foot. These exercises help circulation in your feet and may prevent some swelling in your legs.

My mother-in-law says I'm selfish to want to continue working. Is she right?

Women often work through their entire pregnancy and do very well. You may need to make some adjustments, such as shorter shifts or less lifting, but it can be done. Discuss your situation with your healthcare provider, and if you get his or her OK, tell your mother-in-law not to worry and you've been given the green light to keep working.

Stress Relief

Two muscle exercises can help you relieve stress; you can do them at home or on the job.

1. Relax each muscle group in turn with a deep breath. Start with the feet, and work up through the legs, hands, arms, torso, shoulders, neck and face. Continue for 10 to 20 minutes. (This exercise also works when you're having trouble getting to sleep.)
2. Inhale slowly. Push your abdomen out as you breathe in. Count to 4 before exhaling. Let shoulders and neck relax as you slowly exhale while counting to 6. Repeat as often as needed.

Carpal Tunnel Syndrome during Pregnancy

Carpal tunnel syndrome is characterized by pain in the hand and wrist, which can extend into the forearm and shoulder. It is caused when the median nerve in the wrist is compressed. Symptoms can include numbness, tingling or burning of the inner half of one or both hands. At the same time, the fingers feel numb and useless. More than half of the time, both hands are involved.

The problem may occur during pregnancy due to water retention and swelling in the wrist and arm area. Up to 25% of all pregnant women experience mild symptoms, but treatment is usually unnecessary. The full syndrome, in which treatment may be needed, is less frequent; it occurs in only 1 to 2% of pregnant women.

Treatment depends on symptoms. In pregnant women, splints may be used during sleep and rest in an attempt to keep the wrist straight. Most often, symptoms disappear after delivery.

Occurrence of carpal tunnel syndrome during pregnancy does *not* mean you will suffer from this problem after baby's birth. In rare instances, symptoms may recur long after pregnancy. In these cases, surgery may be necessary.

Time-Saving, Energy-Saving Tip

Check out the possibilities of working part-time at home long before you anticipate taking maternity leave. Sometimes it takes a while to make arrangements or set up equipment in your home.

• •

When Tina's water broke at work, she went directly to the hospital. When she got there, she called her husband, Ross, and asked him to pack some things for her and to come right away. Tina's delivery went well. In her room later, she opened her overnight bag to look for a hairbrush. Was she surprised! She wished she'd taken the time to pack for herself. The nightgown Ross brought was one of her flimsiest, as was the underwear he had chosen. And he had forgotten her robe. Luckily the hospital provided her with a toothbrush, toothpaste and a comb. She was able to get her sister, Rayna, to bring her a robe, some makeup and other things she needed. At least the orange and apple Ross had packed came in handy after the delivery.

• •

Travel during Pregnancy

You may have to travel as a part of your job, which can be tiring and frustrating during pregnancy. If your pregnancy is normal, you should be able to travel in the first and second trimesters without too much trouble. Consult your healthcare provider if you're considering travel in your third trimester.

The best time to travel, if you can choose, is during the second trimester. You'll have more energy, and you'll feel better. Complications are less likely. In the first trimester, you may have morning sickness or feel tired. In the third trimester, you may find it hard to sit or stand for long periods, have difficulty getting in and out of tight spaces, and you may tire easily.

Travel Tips

The most important travel tip we have is *don't overdo it*. Pregnancy does impose some restrictions. Discuss any travel plans with your healthcare provider *before* you make final plans or buy tickets. Most will tell you it's fine to travel at certain times while you're pregnant, but each situation is different. Keep in mind the following general considerations about traveling during pregnancy.

- If your company requires you to travel, limit the amount of time you're away from home.
- Avoid areas in which good medical care is not available or where changes in climate, food or altitude could cause problems.
- Don't plan a trip during your last month of pregnancy.
- If you have any problems, such as bleeding or cramping, don't travel.

- If you're uncomfortable or your hands or feet swell, sitting in a car or on a plane, or walking a lot may make matters worse.
- Take a copy of your medical records with you.
- Keep your healthcare provider's name and telephone number handy in case of an emergency.
- If your pregnancy is considered high risk, don't travel during pregnancy.
- If you have problems with swelling, wear loose-fitting shoes and clothes. Avoid panty hose, tight clothes, knee-high socks or stockings, and tight waistlines.

If You Are Going to Fly

Avoid long flights, especially nonstop overseas or cross-country flights. It's difficult to make long journeys without being able to move around much.

When flying, preorder special meals if your flight includes food. Choose low-sodium or vegetarian if you want to avoid foods that might cause you problems.

Today many flights do not serve any food, so bring your own. Choose foods that travel well, such as cheese and crackers, fruit, a prepackaged salad or a sandwich made at home.

If you experience nausea when traveling, carry crackers or another bland snack food to nibble on. Prop up your feet when you sit for any length of time.

Bring your own empty water bottle through security, and fill it up before you board the plane. This allows you to have water or other fluid available whenever you need it.

Get up and move when you can during a flight. Try to walk at least 10 minutes every hour. Sometimes just standing up helps your circulation. Ask for an aisle seat close to the bathroom.

Observe seat-belt signs, and stay seated during most of the flight, especially during turbulence. Your balance may not be as good while you're pregnant.

If you're 36 weeks pregnant (or more), bring a letter from your healthcare provider saying it's OK for you to fly. Be advised: Even with a letter, a captain has the authority to keep you off the plane, but it doesn't happen very often.

Time-Saving, Energy-Saving Tip

Planning to fly during pregnancy? Find out about gate checking your bags and other equipment. If you have your child's stroller or bulky carry-on luggage, you may be able to check it in at the boarding gate before you get on the plane. The airline will place it in the cargo hold last and take it off first at your destination. It will be waiting for you at the gate when you get off the plane or transferred to baggage claim for you!

Ways to Travel

Flying should not present a problem. Consult someone at the airline about your condition *before* buying tickets. An airline can refuse to carry a pregnant passenger without the written consent of her healthcare provider. Many airlines allow preboarding for passengers who need extra time. Take advantage of the offer. Drink plenty of fluids, such as water and juice, because recirculated air in a plane can be extremely dry.

If you haven't considered train travel recently, now might be the time to do so. Trains have wide aisles and roomy seats, and the ride is smooth. Moving around may also be easier.

Bus trips and sailing on ships may not be good choices. On a bus, leg room is limited and the ride is jarring, which could make you uncomfortable. If you're unused to it, the rolling motion of a ship or boat can be unsettling. Seasickness could add to pregnancy discomforts you may already be experiencing. If you do sail, most healthcare providers believe Dramamine is safe against seasickness, but do not use a seasickness patch. Talk with your healthcare provider about other methods to deal with the problem.

Car travel may be comfortable or uncomfortable, depending on how far along you are. Limit car travel to no more than 5 hours a day (sitting longer slows circulation). Stop at regular intervals to take short walks and use the bathroom. When sitting in a car, tuck a pillow into the small of your back. Do ankle circles while riding to increase circulation in your feet and legs. Always wear your seat belt and shoulder harness (for more about lap belt and shoulder harness safety, see page 24).

Inconveniences and Risks to Consider

If you travel, your discomfort level is likely to increase, especially if you're cooped up in a car or plane for hours. You may have trouble sleeping in a strange bed. If you develop a complication while you're away from home, those who have been involved in your pregnancy and know your history will not be available to care for you.

It's best to avoid travel during the last month of pregnancy. Labor could begin at any time, your water could break or other problems could occur. Your healthcare provider knows what has happened during your pregnancy and has a record of tests you've undergone—important information. If you check into a hospital to deliver in a strange city, some healthcare providers won't accept you as a patient because they don't know your medical history. It doesn't make sense to take any chances.

Many women want to know if their healthcare provider can tell when they will go into labor so they can travel. Unfortunately, no one can predict when your labor will begin. Always discuss your travel plans with your healthcare provider before you finalize them.

Pregnancy in the Military

Are you pregnant and currently on active duty in the military? If you are, you have made the decision to stay in the Armed Forces. Before 1972, if you were on active duty and became pregnant, you were automatically separated from the military, whether you wanted to be or not!

Today, if you want to stay in the service, you can. Each branch of the service has particular policies regarding pregnancy. Below is a summary of those policies for the Army, Navy, Air Force, Marines and Coast Guard.

Army Policies

During pregnancy, you are exempt from body composition and fitness testing. You cannot be deployed overseas. At 20 weeks, you are required to stand at parade rest or attention for no longer than 15 minutes. At 28 weeks, your work week is limited to 40 hours a week, 8 hours a day.

Navy Policies

During pregnancy, you are exempt from body composition and fitness testing. You are not allowed to serve on a ship after 20 weeks of pregnancy. You are limited to serving duty in places within 6 hours of medical care. Your work week is limited to 40 hours, and you are required to stand at parade rest or attention for no longer than 20 minutes.

Air Force Policies

During pregnancy, you are exempt from body composition and fitness testing. Restrictions are based on your work environment. If you are assigned to an area without obstetrical care, your assignment will be curtailed by week 24.

Marine Corps Policies

You will be on full-duty status until a medical doctor certifies full duty is not medically advised. You may not participate in contingency operations nor may you be deployed aboard a Navy vessel. Flight personnel are grounded unless cleared by a medical waiver. If a medical doctor deems you are unfit for physical training or you cannot stand in formation, you will be excused from these activities. However, you will remain available for worldwide assignments.

Pregnant Marines will not be detached from Hawaii aboard a ship after their sixth month. If serving aboard a ship, a pregnant woman will be reassigned at the first opportunity but no later than by 20 weeks.

U.S. Coast Guard

During pregnancy, you are exempt from body composition and fitness testing. After 28 weeks of pregnancy, your work week will be limited to 40 hours. You will not be assigned overseas. Other duty restrictions are based on your job; however, you will not be assigned to any rescue-swimmer duties during your pregnancy.

You may not be deployed from the twentieth week of your pregnancy through 6 months postpartum. You will not be assigned to any flight duties after your second trimester (26 weeks), and you are limited to serving duty in places within 3 hours of medical care.

Some General Cautions if You're in the Military

We know women who get pregnant while on active duty face many challenges. The pressure to meet military body-weight standards could have an effect on your health; that's the reason these requirements are relaxed during pregnancy.

Work hard to eat healthy foods so your iron stores and folic-acid levels are adequate. Examine your job for any hazards you may be exposed to, such as standing for long periods, heavy lifting and exposure to toxic chemicals. Before receiving any vaccinations or inoculations, discuss them with your pregnancy doctor. Any of these factors can impact your pregnancy.

If you are concerned about any of the above, discuss it with a superior. Changes beyond those described above may have to be made.

Driving during Pregnancy

It is usually safe to drive during pregnancy, but it may become uncomfortable for you to get in and out of the car as pregnancy progresses. However, your increasing size shouldn't interfere with your ability to drive.

Many women are confused about whether they should wear seat belts and shoulder harnesses during pregnancy. These safety restraints are just as necessary during pregnancy as they are when you're not pregnant!

For your protection, and the protection of your developing baby, *always wear your safety belt/shoulder harness when driving or riding in a car!* There is no evidence that use of safety restraints increases the chance of fetal or uterine injury. You have a better chance of survival in an accident wearing a seat belt than not wearing one.

There is a correct way to wear your safety belt during pregnancy. Place the lap-belt part of the restraint under your abdomen and across your upper thighs so it's snug but comfortable. Adjust your sitting position so the belt crosses your shoulder without cutting into your neck. Position the shoulder harness between your breasts; don't slip it off your shoulder. The lap belt can't hold you safely by itself.

Health Insurance

Most employers offer some type of health insurance to their workers—private medical-and-hospitalization coverage, membership in a health maintenance organization (HMO) or a preferred-physicians plan (PPO). With private insurance, you can choose your own healthcare provider. With an HMO, you choose a healthcare provider affiliated with the group. With a PPO, you may choose any healthcare provider on a list of acceptable physicians and other healthcare providers.

Insurance-Coverage Questions

You will need answers to some important questions about pregnancy coverage under your insurance plan. Talk to the people in the personnel department or your employer's human-resource specialist. You may want your husband to ask these questions if you're covered through his employer.

- What type of coverage do I/we have?
- Are there maternity benefits? What are they?
- Do maternity benefits cover Cesarean deliveries?
- What kind of coverage is there for a high-risk pregnancy?
- Do I/we have to pay a deductible? If so, what is it?
- How do I/we submit claims?
- Is there a cap on total coverage?
- What percentage of pregnancy and birth costs are covered?
- Does coverage restrict the kind of hospital accommodations I may choose, such as a birthing center or a birthing room?
- What procedures must I follow before entering the hospital?
- Does the policy cover a nurse-midwife (if that is what you want)?
- Does coverage include medications?
- What tests during pregnancy are covered under the policy?
- What tests during labor and delivery are covered under the policy?
- What types of anesthesia are covered during labor and delivery?
- How long can I stay in the hospital?
- Does payment go directly to my healthcare provider or to me?
- What conditions or services are not covered?
- What kind of coverage is there for the baby after it is born?
- How long can the baby stay in the hospital?
- Is there an additional cost to add the baby to the policy?
- How do I/we add the baby to the policy?
- Can we collect a percentage of a fee from my husband's policy and the rest from mine?

Laws That Protect You during Pregnancy

The Pregnancy Discrimination Act

The Pregnancy Discrimination Act of 1978 requires companies employing 15 or more people to treat pregnant workers the same way they treat other workers who have medical disabilities and cannot work. The law prohibits job discrimination on the basis of pregnancy, childbirth or related disability. It guarantees equal treatment of all disabilities, including pregnancy, birth or related medical conditions.

Your employer can't fire you or force you to take mandatory maternity leave because you are pregnant. You are also protected in other ways.

- You must be granted the same health, disability and sick-leave benefits as any other employee who has a medical condition.
- You must be given modified tasks, alternate assignments, disability leave or leave without pay (depending on your company's policy).
- You are allowed to work as long as you can perform your job.
- You are guaranteed job security on leave.
- You continue to accrue seniority and vacation, and you remain eligible for pay increases and benefits.

If your company does not provide job security or benefits to other employees, it does not have to provide them to a pregnant woman.

Pregnancy Leave

Pregnancy leave is the period during which your healthcare provider states you cannot work. This can range from 4 to 6 weeks after a vaginal delivery to 6 to 8 weeks following a Cesarean delivery. (Fathers are not covered under this law, but see the *Family and Medical Leave Act* below.)

If you have problems obtaining these benefits from your employer, tell your healthcare provider. He or she may be able to direct you to someone who can help you.

The Family and Medical Leave Act

The Family and Medical Leave Act (FMLA) was passed in 1993. If you or your husband have worked for your present employer for at least 1 year, the law allows a new parent (man or woman) to take up to 12 weeks of unpaid leave in any 12-month period for the birth of a baby. To be eligible, you must work at your job for at least 1250 hours a year (about 60% of a normal 40-hour work week). In addition, if *both parents* work for the same employer, only a total of 12 weeks off between them is allowed. This act applies only to companies that employ 50 or more people within a 75-mile radius. States may allow an employer to deny job restoration to employees in the top 10% compensation bracket. In addition, any time you take off *before* the birth of your baby is counted toward the 12 weeks you and/or your husband are entitled to in any given year. You may take maternity leave intermittently or all at the same time.

••

Steve and Marianne were first-time prospective parents with busy careers. Marianne learned she could take 6 weeks off after delivery but wanted to go back to work after that. I suggested Steve ask about the policy for paternity leave at his job. He hadn't heard of it and was skeptical, but he learned his company's policy did cover leave for him. He got a week off after Marianne delivered, which he later reported to me was "the best week ever." He was able to get another 2 weeks when Marianne went back to work. Steve told me the time he had by himself with his new daughter, Jane, helped him get to know her better than he would have any other way. The time also helped him understand what Marianne was up against and eased the transition of leaving their daughter with a sitter.

••

Under this law, you must be restored to an equivalent position with equal benefits when you return. If you have questions that personnel in the HR department can't answer, check with your state's labor office.

If morning sickness causes you to be absent from your job, the FMLA states you do *not* need a healthcare provider's note verifying the problem. Nausea and vomiting in pregnancy is classified as a "chronic condition" and may require you be out occasionally, but you don't need a healthcare provider's treatment. Most healthcare providers will write a note, if necessary.

State Laws

Many states have passed legislation that deals with parental leave. Some states provide disability insurance if you have to leave work because of pregnancy or birth.

Laws differ, so check with your state's labor office or consult the personnel director in your company's HR department. You may also obtain a summary of state laws on family leave by sending a self-addressed mailing label to the following address:

Women's Bureau
U.S. Department of Labor
Box EX
200 Constitution Avenue NW
Washington, DC 20210 800–827–5335

Preparing to Leave Your Job

Whatever your plans—leaving work a few months early, working until the day you deliver—be *prepared* to leave by the end of your eighth month. You may need time to train your replacement to step into your job temporarily. You'll need to schedule times at which to call the office and to take care of other details.

Plan Ahead

Be prepared in case your water breaks or you have some other problem at work. Keep a towel and some sanitary pads available. Carry medical-information cards and identification with you. Check with your human-resources department to make sure paperwork for your maternity leave is in order.

Have your suitcase packed and ready at home, in case you need to go from your office to the hospital. Partners can pack some pretty weird stuff for the hospital when a woman doesn't have the chance!

Prepare Your Replacement

Save yourself problems by training the person who will handle your job to do the work the way you would. Initiate the relief worker to office procedures, rules and regulations, and particular ways to do your job efficiently. It's a good idea to have the person perform your duties while you're still on the scene so you can evaluate his or her work.

Before you leave, arrange to talk with your replacement, your boss and your co-workers one last time about details that must be taken care of while you're gone. Together, review the plans you have prepared.

Discuss with co-workers how to keep in touch with you. (Will you call them? When can they call you?) It's a good idea to schedule times to call the office. This enables your co-workers to have information available for you and have questions ready when you call. It can be annoying to have various people at your office call you every day asking questions when you are trying to concentrate on your baby! Letting them know in advance when you will call sets guidelines and puts you in control.

Chapter 4

Your Health and Medical History

Your health affects the health of your growing baby. Good nutrition, proper exercise, sufficient rest and attention to how you take care of yourself are all important to you *and* your baby.

When possible, visit your healthcare provider before you become pregnant to address any pre-existing medical problems and routine exams. If you know you're in good health before you get pregnant, you'll feel more secure about your growing baby. You'll know your Pap smear is normal, your breast exam is OK and any medical conditions are under control. You can have a mammogram if you need one. If a preconception consultation is not possible, make an appointment to see your healthcare provider as soon as you realize you're pregnant.

Prenatal Care

Prenatal care is the care you receive throughout your pregnancy. Special care from professionals during pregnancy can help identify pregnancy problems or conditions before they become serious. Always feel free to ask questions about your pregnancy at your prenatal appointments.

If you have confidence in your healthcare provider, you'll be able to relax and enjoy your pregnancy. Pregnancy is a special time in your life; good prenatal care helps ensure you do everything possible to make it the best 9 months possible for you and your growing baby.

Your First Prenatal Visit

Your first prenatal visit may be one of the longest. Your healthcare provider will ask questions, order lab tests and give you a physical examination.

If this is a new healthcare provider, you may be asked for a complete medical history. This can include questions about your menstrual periods, recent birth-control methods, previous pregnancies and other details. Tell your healthcare provider about any miscarriages or abortions you have had. Include information about hospital stays or surgical procedures.

Discuss any medications you take or those you are allergic to. Your family's medical history may be important, as in the case of diabetes or other chronic illnesses. Discuss any chronic medical problems you have. If you have medical records, bring them with you. Also see the discussion of your medical history that begins on page 59.

On your first visit, you will probably have a pelvic exam, which helps determine if your uterus is the appropriate size for how far along you believe you are in your pregnancy. You'll have a Pap smear if you haven't had one in the last year, and other tests may be necessary.

In most cases, you will visit your healthcare provider every 4 weeks for the first 7 months, then every 2 weeks until the last month, then once a week. You may be scheduled for visits more frequently if necessary. On every visit, your weight and blood pressure will be checked; they provide valuable information about how your pregnancy is progressing.

Taking Others to Your Office Visits

If you want to bring your partner with you to your prenatal visits, do so. These visits can help him understand what is happening to you and feel he's a part of your pregnancy. And it's nice for your partner and your healthcare provider to meet before labor begins.

It's all right to take your mother or mother-in-law. If you want to bring anyone else, discuss it with your healthcare provider first.

Many offices don't mind if you bring your children with you; other offices ask you not to bring children to office visits. Talking with your healthcare provider about a problem can be difficult if you're trying to take care of a young child at the same time. If you do bring children, observe the following rules of etiquette.

- Ask about office policy ahead of time.
- Bring only one child to a visit.
- Don't bring a child on your first visit, when you will probably have a pelvic exam.
- If you want your child to hear the baby's heartbeat, wait to bring him until after you have heard it.

- Bring something to entertain your child in case you have to wait. Not all offices have toys or books for kids.
- Be considerate of other patients; if your child has a cold or is sick, don't bring her.

Choosing a Healthcare Provider

You have many choices among healthcare providers to care for you during pregnancy. You can choose an obstetrician, a family practitioner, a certified nurse-midwife or a nurse practitioner to oversee your prenatal care.

An *obstetrician* is a medical doctor or an osteopathic physician who specializes in the care of pregnant women, including delivering babies. He or she has completed additional training in obstetrics and gynecology after medical school.

A *perinatologist* is an obstetrician who specializes in high-risk pregnancies. Only about 10% of all pregnant women need to see a perinatologist; your healthcare provider will refer you. If you see a perinatologist, you may still be able to deliver your baby with your regular healthcare provider. Or you may have to deliver at a hospital other than the one you had chosen because of its specialized facilities or the availability of specialized tests for you or your baby.

A *family practitioner* is a physician who provides care for the entire family. Many family practitioners have experience delivering babies. If problems arise, your family practitioner may refer you to an obstetrician or perinatologist for prenatal care.

A *certified nurse-midwife* is a trained professional who cares for women with low-risk, uncomplicated pregnancies and delivers their babies. These professionals are registered nurses who have additional training and certification in nurse-midwifery. Supervised by a physician, they will call him or her if care or delivery complications occur.

A *nurse practitioner* may also serve as your healthcare provider at office visits, if your pregnancy is normal. Nurse practitioners are registered nurses with advanced degrees in a specialty area. They are certified by national organizations in their specialty and practice under the rules and regulations of your state, under the supervision of a physician. They can provide prenatal care and family-planning services. At delivery, a nurse-midwife, obstetrician or family practitioner delivers the baby.

If you have a healthcare provider you like, you may be all set. If you don't, call your local medical society for a referral. Ask friends who recently had a baby about their healthcare providers. Sometimes another healthcare provider can refer you to someone to care for you during your pregnancy.

••

Ellie didn't fill out all of the forms at her first office visit; she left the family-history portion blank. She said she didn't realize it mattered. We discussed how her family history could affect her and her pregnancy. The next month, she told me she had spoken to her mother, and there was a family history of diabetes and twins, both important pieces of information for her pregnancy.

••

Make an effort to communicate with your healthcare provider so you can comfortably ask him or her questions about your condition. Read articles and books such as this one and our other books. They will help you prepare questions to ask your healthcare provider. However, never substitute information you receive from other sources for information, instructions or advice you receive from your own healthcare provider. Your healthcare provider knows you, your history and what has occurred during your pregnancy.

Don't be afraid to ask any question. Your healthcare provider has probably already heard it, so there is no need to be embarrassed. Check out even the smallest details. Your healthcare provider will be the first to tell you it's better to ask a thousand "silly" questions than risk overlooking a single important one.

Your Health Affects Your Baby

Your health directly affects your baby's health and well-being. Some illnesses, diseases and conditions women experience during pregnancy can affect their babies; it's a good idea to be informed about them.

Allergies

Allergy sufferers may notice their allergies change with pregnancy. They may improve or get worse. If you have allergies, drink plenty of fluid, especially during hot weather.

You may have to treat your allergy problems differently during pregnancy. Before taking *any* medication—whether it's prescription or over-the-counter—ask your healthcare provider or pharmacist whether it's safe to take during pregnancy. Don't just assume it's OK to take it. Asking before you use it is easier than fixing a problem it may cause later.

Nasal Congestion

Some women complain of nasal stuffiness during pregnancy, with allergies and even when they don't have allergies. We believe this congestion occurs because of circulation changes and hormonal changes that can cause mucous membranes of the nose and nasal passages to swell and to bleed more easily.

Don't use decongestants or nasal sprays to relieve stuffiness without first checking with your healthcare provider. Many preparations are combinations of several medications you should not use during pregnancy. To relieve congestion, use a humidifier, increase your fluid intake and use a gentle lubricant, such as petroleum jelly, in nasal passages. Discuss the problem with your healthcare provider if these remedies don't provide relief.

Anemia

Anemia is a common medical problem in pregnant and nonpregnant women. Women who are anemic don't have enough hemoglobin in their blood. Hemoglobin, the iron-containing pigment of red blood cells, is important because it carries oxygen to all the body's cells.

If you suffer from anemia, you won't feel well during pregnancy. You'll tire more easily. You may become dizzy. If you're anemic during labor, you may need a blood transfusion after baby is born. Pregnancy anemia increases the risk of preterm delivery, growth restriction in the baby (IUGR) and low birthweight.

> **Time-Saving, Energy-Saving Tip**
>
> Having pets is an enjoyable experience for a family; however, cleaning up unwanted animal hair can be time-consuming. Try this quick tip to help clear your furniture of the hair left by Spot or Tabby. Put on a clean pair of rubber gloves—those with texturing on the palms work best. Dampen the palms, and rub over furniture and clothes. Pet hair comes off quickly and easily.

Anemia is a serious but preventable condition during pregnancy. If you're anemic, your healthcare provider can prescribe a course of treatment to deal with the problem.

Iron-Deficiency Anemia

When you're pregnant, your baby uses some of the iron stored in your body. *Iron-deficiency anemia* is caused or aggravated by the fetus's demands on your iron stores. Your body makes red blood cells but not enough of them, and you become iron deficient. Several factors can cause iron-deficiency anemia:

- bleeding during pregnancy
- multiple fetuses

- recent surgery on your stomach or small bowel
- frequent antacid use
- poor nutrition

Iron-deficiency anemia is easy to control; most prenatal vitamins contain iron. If you can't take a prenatal vitamin, you may be given iron supplements. Eating foods high in iron, such as beef, turkey, liver, spinach, cooked beans, tofu, wheat germ, rice, and seeds and nuts, may also help.

Asthma

Asthma is a chronic respiratory disease that causes small airways in the lungs to narrow. It's characterized by attacks of labored breathing, wheezing, shortness of breath, coughing and chest constriction. The most common causes of asthma attacks include allergens, exercise, strong odors and cold air. Asthma is 40% more common in women than in men; about 8% of all pregnant women have asthma. The condition is one of the most common medical problems pregnant women face.

Most women with asthma can have safe pregnancies. If you have asthma, you may be able to use the medication you usually use, but discuss the matter with your healthcare provider before pregnancy or as soon as you have confirmed you are pregnant.

Many asthma sufferers have heartburn; heartburn may cause asthma symptoms to worsen. Upper-respiratory infections caused by the flu may also trigger an attack.

Many women feel better and have fewer problems with asthma if they increase their fluid intake during pregnancy. Try it—you should increase your fluid intake during pregnancy anyway.

Some women with asthma appear to get better during pregnancy, while others remain about the same. However, if you have severe asthma attacks when you aren't pregnant, you may also have severe attacks during pregnancy.

Studies show that if your asthma is under control throughout pregnancy, your pregnancy outcome can be as positive as a woman who doesn't have asthma. Controlling your asthma may help lower your risk of developing some pregnancy problems. We also know asthma symptoms often improve during the last month of pregnancy due to hormonal changes.

Treating asthma is important so baby can get the oxygen it needs to grow and to develop. During pregnancy, your oxygen consumption increases by about 25%. Untreated asthma can put you and baby at risk. If you have severe, uncontrolled asthma, baby may be deprived of oxygen during your asthma attacks. If you're not getting enough air, neither is baby.

Research shows it's better for you to take asthma medicine during pregnancy than to risk asthma attacks and their complications. Most asthma medicine appears to be safe during pregnancy. Terbutaline, and steroids, such as hydrocortisone or methylprednisolone, aminophylline, theophyline, metaproterenol (Alupent) and albuterol (Ventolin) can be used during pregnancy. Be sure to check with your healthcare provider before using your usual prescription medication.

Studies show inhaled steroids do not seem to affect baby's growth. Inhalers work directly on the lungs, so very little medicine enters your bloodstream. However, don't use Primatene Mist during pregnancy.

If your asthma is severe, you may be given an anti-inflammatory nasal spray, such as cromolyn sodium (Nasalcrom) or an inhaled steroid, such as beclomethasone (Vanceril). Discuss the situation at one of your early prenatal visits.

It's important to have a flu shot to reduce the risk of getting severe respiratory illness during pregnancy, which could make asthma attacks worse. Avoid cigarette smoke. Don't smoke, and keep away from others who do.

See your allergist regularly during pregnancy for a lung-function test. This helps determine whether your medication dosage needs to be adjusted. He or she may also suggest you monitor your breathing with a peak-flow meter to find out how open your airways are.

Asthma shouldn't be a deterrent to learning breathing techniques to use during labor. Talk to your healthcare provider about it.

Celiac Disease

Celiac disease is a digestive disease that affects the small intestine. If you have celiac disease, you have an allergy to gluten, which causes your intestines to absorb fewer nutrients. Symptoms include diarrhea, abdominal pain, bloating, irritability and depression.

The condition is hereditary and occurs more often in women than men. It's most common in Western Europeans. We believe celiac disease affects 1 in 100 people worldwide and 1 in every 250 Americans. It may be overlooked during pregnancy because symptoms can be the same as for other pregnancy problems. Many healthcare providers don't know much about the disease, and it can be difficult to diagnose. A blood test can determine if you may have celiac disease. A biopsy of the small intestine can confirm it.

If you have celiac disease, it's important to eat a gluten-free diet. You will probably need folic-acid supplements to ensure you receive enough folic acid.

Celiac disease may appear for the first time during pregnancy or after childbirth. If you have symptoms, talk to your healthcare provider. You may need to see a dietician during pregnancy to develop a nutrition plan.

Chicken Pox (Varicella)

Herpes is a family of viruses that includes the herpes-simplex virus, herpes varicella-zoster virus and cytomegalovirus. The word *chicken pox* is used interchangeably with *varicella*. (It is also used to describe the rash seen with chicken pox.) The term *herpes zoster* is used interchangeably with *shingles*.

When adults get chicken pox, they can become very ill. The most serious times for you to get chicken pox are during the first trimester and around the time of delivery. A baby can get the virus during delivery, which could cause a serious infection.

Cytomegalovirus (CMV)

Cytomegalovirus (CMV) is a member of the herpes-virus family and is transmitted in humans by contact with saliva or urine. Day-care centers are a common source of the infection; CMV can also be passed by sexual contact. Most infections do not cause symptoms; however, when symptoms occur, they include fever, sore throat and joint pain.

CMV is the most common virus passed from a mother-to-be to her baby during pregnancy. It infects about 1% of all newborns. Infection can cause low birthweight and other problems in a baby.

Diabetes

Diabetes is one of the most common medical complications of pregnancy. It occurs in 7 to 8% of all pregnancies. Today many diabetic women go through pregnancy safely.

Diabetes is defined as a lack of insulin in the bloodstream or a resistance to insulin by the body's cells. Pregnancy increases the body's resistance to insulin, and the body doesn't process insulin efficiently. If you don't have insulin, you will have high blood sugar and a high sugar content in your urine.

Pregnancy is well known for its tendency to reveal women who are predisposed to diabetes. Women who have trouble with high blood-sugar levels during pregnancy are more likely to develop diabetes in later life.

Some experts recommend screening pregnant women at risk for diabetes during the first trimester. Others recommend testing all pregnant women at 28 weeks of pregnancy. Tests used most often are the glucose-tolerance test (GTT) and/or a 1-hour glucose challenge test.

If you have diabetes or know members of your family have diabetes, tell your healthcare provider. This is important information.

Diabetes and Pregnancy

Diabetes can cause various problems during pregnancy. Birth defects may be more common. It's important to take care of diabetes *before* pregnancy. If your diabetes is not controlled during pregnancy, your baby is at greater risk.

If you take insulin, you may need to adjust your dosage or the timing of your dosage. You may also have to check your blood-sugar levels 4 to 8 times a day. You must balance your eating plan and your insulin at all times so your glucose levels don't climb too high. Avoid long-lasting insulin during pregnancy. It may also help if you take in more folic acid; discuss it with your pregnancy healthcare provider and endocrinologist.

Some women take diabetes pills; some oral antidiabetes medications taken during pregnancy may cause problems for the developing baby. (Metformin is not recommended during pregnancy.) There are safe oral medications for diabetes in pregnancy. You may have to adjust the amount of oral medication you take, or you may need to switch to insulin shots. Your healthcare provider can advise you. (Also see the discussion of pregnancy-induced [gestational] diabetes in Chapter 17.)

Diarrhea during Pregnancy

Diarrhea during pregnancy can raise concerns. If it doesn't go away in 24 hours or if it keeps returning, contact your healthcare provider. He or she may prescribe medication for the problem. Do *not* take medication for diarrhea without first discussing it with your healthcare provider.

One of the best things you can do for yourself if you experience diarrhea during pregnancy is to increase your fluid intake. Drink a lot of water, juice and other clear fluids, such as broth. (Avoid apple juice and prune juice because they are laxatives.) You may feel better eating a bland diet, without solid foods, until you feel better.

It's OK to avoid solid food for a few days if you keep up your fluid intake. Solid foods may actually cause you more gastrointestinal distress when you have diarrhea. Avoid milk products while you have diarrhea; they may make it worse.

Epilepsy

Epilepsy can be a serious problem during pregnancy. If you suffer from the disease and become pregnant, contact your healthcare provider immediately. It's important to control your disease during pregnancy because seizures can affect you and baby in many ways. During pregnancy, hormonal fluctuations can affect your epilepsy, and you may be at higher risk of some pregnancy problems.

One-third of women with epilepsy will see a decrease in the number of seizures they have during pregnancy. One-third will have more seizures, and one-third will see no change at all.

Seizures seldom occur during labor and delivery. More than 90% of all epileptic pregnant women give birth to healthy babies.

If you take medication for seizure control or prevention, tell your health-care provider before trying to get pregnant or at the beginning of pregnancy. Medication can be taken during pregnancy to control seizures, but some are safer than others.

There are concerns regarding use of anticonvulsant medications in pregnancy. There is also concern regarding *polytherapy*—when a woman takes several medications in combination. Ask your healthcare provider to put you on the lowest dosage of *one* anti-epileptic drug. Take your antiseizure medication *exactly* as it is prescribed.

Some medications may need to be avoided during pregnancy. Most studies show increased risk to baby when a mom-to-be takes valproate, especially in the first trimester. Dilantin is *not* recommended during pregnancy because we know it can cause birth defects. Phenobarbital may be used to control seizures during pregnancy, but there's some concern about its safety.

Lamotrigine therapy alone shows no increased risk of problems in baby. Ask about taking large doses of folic acid; it has proved helpful for some women.

If you have morning sickness, tell your healthcare provider. Nausea and vomiting can interfere with your body's ability to absorb your antiseizure medications.

During pregnancy, kidneys may remove greater amounts of anti-epileptic drugs from your system more quickly than usual. Drug levels could decrease by as much as 50%. It's important to see your neurologist every month for blood tests to check the levels in your blood. Any dosage adjustments can be made after test results are in.

Seizures during pregnancy can be serious; you may need increased monitoring. If you have questions or concerns about a history of possible seizures, talk to your healthcare provider about them.

Fifth Disease (Parvovirus 19)

Fifth disease, also called *parvovirus 19,* received its name because it was the fifth disease to be associated with a certain kind of rash. Fifth disease is a mild, moderately contagious airborne infection that spreads easily through groups, such as classrooms or day-care centers.

The rash looks like skin reddened by a slap. Reddening fades and recurs and can last from 2 to 34 days. There is no treatment for fifth disease, but it is important to distinguish it from rubella, especially if you are pregnant.

This virus is dangerous during pregnancy because it interferes with the production of red blood cells. If you believe you have been exposed to fifth disease, call your healthcare provider. A blood test will determine whether you had the virus before. If you have, you are immune. If you have not, your healthcare provider can monitor you to detect fetal problems. He or she may be able to deal with some problems before baby is born.

Group-B Streptococcus Infection (GBS)

Group-B streptococcus (GBS) is a type of bacteria found in up to 40% of all pregnant women. A GBS infection rarely causes problems in adults but can cause life-threatening infections in newborns. GBS passed to a newborn during birth can cause a blood infection, meningitis or pneumonia in the baby.

GBS can be transmitted from person to person by sexual contact but is not considered an STD. It is found in the mouth or lower-digestive tract, urinary tract or reproductive organs. In women, GBS is most often found in the vagina or rectum. If you have GBS in your system, you may not have any symptoms.

It is recommended that all women be screened for GBS between 35 and 37 weeks of pregnancy. If tests show you have the bacteria but no symptoms, you are *colonized*. If you're colonized, you can pass GBS to your baby.

The battle to eradicate GBS is one of the true medical success stories. Before the 1990s, 7500 newborns contracted the infection each year; 30% of those babies died. Today, fewer than 1600 cases are reported each year. Much of the success has been the result of healthcare providers following the 1996 Centers for Disease Control and Prevention (CDC) guidelines, which include the following:

- a late prenatal culture (35 to 37 weeks) for vaginal and rectal GBS colonization
- an earlier culture (earlier than 35 weeks), based on clinical risk factors
- antibiotics prescribed to all carriers—penicillin G is the antibiotic of choice, followed by ampicillin
- antibiotics prescribed for any woman who has given birth to a previous infant with proven GBS infection

If you're allergic to ampicillin or penicillin, other medications are available to treat the problem.

Medical experts have developed recommendations aimed at preventing this infection in newborns. They recommend all women with risk factors be treated for GBS. Risk factors include giving birth to a previous infant with GBS infection, preterm labor, ruptured membranes for more than 18 hours or a temperature of 100.4F (38C) immediately before or during childbirth. In addition, if you've had a bladder infection with a positive strep-B urine specimen during pregnancy, you should receive antibiotics at delivery.

Hepatitis

Hepatitis is a viral infection of the liver. It's near the top of the list of serious infections that affect a large percentage of our population every year and is one of the most serious infections that can occur during pregnancy. That's one reason all pregnant women are screened for hepatitis B at the beginning of pregnancy.

When people talk about hepatitis, it can be confusing. Six different forms of hepatitis have been identified—hepatitis A, hepatitis B, hepatitis C, hepatitis D, hepatitis E and hepatitis G. The most serious type of hepatitis during pregnancy is hepatitis B.

Hepatitis B is responsible for nearly half the cases of hepatitis in North America. It is transmitted by sexual contact and the reuse of intravenous needles. A woman with hepatitis B may experience flulike symptoms, nausea and pain in the liver area or upper-right abdomen. The person may appear yellow or jaundiced, and urine may be darker than normal. This form of hepatitis can be transmitted to the baby during birth or while breastfeeding.

If a mother tests positive for hepatitis B during pregnancy, the baby may receive immune globulin to treat hepatitis after birth. This is different from the hepatitis vaccine. Hepatitis vaccine is given to prevent hepatitis from occurring. It is now recommended that all newborns receive hepatitis vaccine shortly after birth. Ask your healthcare provider about it.

High Blood Pressure (Hypertension)

Blood pressure is the amount of force exerted by blood against arterial walls. When you have *high blood pressure*, your blood vessels narrow, which makes pumping blood through the body harder. It reduces blood flow to organs in the body. This is particularly unsafe during pregnancy because blood vessels in the uterus supply the developing baby with nutrients and oxygen. When uterine blood vessels are constricted, it can slow passage of nutrients and oxygen from you to your baby, which may slow fetal development.

If you have high blood pressure before pregnancy, you have *chronic hypertension*. Be sure your healthcare provider knows about it. Your condition will not go away during pregnancy and must be controlled to avoid problems. It can develop into a serious problem during pregnancy if left untreated.

Your healthcare provider will keep a close watch on you during your pregnancy to help avoid problems. High blood pressure is one of the most common chronic illnesses in older pregnant women; many older women enter pregnancy with the problem.

If you have chronic high blood pressure, you have a greater chance of having complications during pregnancy. Baby may be low birthweight and/or premature. High blood pressure also has other effects. About 20% of all women who have chronic high blood pressure before pregnancy develop pre-eclampsia.

If your blood pressure is high when you get pregnant, you may have more ultrasounds to monitor baby's growth. You may want to purchase a blood-pressure monitor to use at home so you can check your pressure any time.

Most blood-pressure medications are safe to use during pregnancy. However, ACE inhibitors should be avoided.

For a discussion of pregnancy-induced hypertension (PIH), see Chapter 17.

Influenza (Flu)

The flu seems to be a problem every year because different flu viruses come and go. When an outbreak of influenza occurs, it can have a greater impact on a pregnant woman because of her altered immune system.

If you are pregnant when a breakout occurs, you should receive any specific flu vaccine *and* the seasonal flu vaccine. You can be vaccinated any time during pregnancy. Studies show women who receive flu vaccines are less likely to give birth prematurely, their babies weigh more and infants are less likely to be hospitalized than those not immunized.

There are ways to protect yourself in addition to getting a seasonal flu shot. Avoid crowded areas, use a mask and wash your hands frequently (flu virus can live up to 2 hours on surfaces like doorknobs and telephones).

If you get the flu, follow your healthcare provider's guidelines regarding use of medication. Benefits of treatment outweigh any potential risk to the baby from medications. Treatment should begin as soon as possible; don't wait for lab results.

Pregnant women should receive antiviral treatment as soon as possible after symptoms appear—preferably within 48 hours. Tamiflu (oseltamivir) or Relenza (zanamivir) are prescription antiviral medications. These medications can shorten the course of the flu and help treat symptoms. Pregnant women who are suspected of having influenza should receive a 5-day course of Tamiflu or Relenza, preferably started within 48 hours of the onset of symptoms.

Lupus

Lupus is an autoimmune disorder of unknown cause that occurs most often in young or middle-aged women. It is a chronic inflammatory disease that can affect more than one organ system. The most common symptoms of lupus are arthritis, rashes and fatigue.

Over 1½ million people in the United States have some form of lupus. Women have lupus much more frequently than men—about nine women to every man. Nearly 80% of the cases develop in people between the ages of 15 and 45.

Lupus is diagnosed through blood tests, which look for suspect antibodies. Blood tests include a lupus antibody test and an antinuclear antibody test.

Steroids are generally prescribed to treat lupus. The most common medicines used are prednisone, prednisolone and methylprednisolone. A small amount of the medication passes to the baby.

If you use warfarin, contact your healthcare provider; it should be replaced with heparin as soon as possible. If you have high blood pressure, you may have to switch medicines. Don't take cyclophosphamide during the first trimester. Azathioprine and cyclosporin may be continued during pregnancy.

All lupus pregnancies should be considered *high risk,* although most lupus pregnancies are completely normal. "High risk" means solvable problems may occur during the pregnancy and should be expected. More than 50% of all lupus pregnancies are completely normal, and most of the babies are normal, although babies may be somewhat premature.

The risk of pregnancy complications is slightly increased in a woman with lupus. Protein in the urine may get worse. It's a good idea to see your rheumatologist every month during pregnancy. If you begin to have a flare-up or other problem, it can be dealt with.

If you had kidney damage from previous flare-ups, be on the lookout for kidney problems during pregnancy. Some women experience improvement in their lupus during pregnancy and breastfeeding.

Lyme Disease

Lyme disease is an infection carried and transmitted to humans by ticks. It crosses the placenta, which can cause complications for baby. The disease appears in stages. In most people, a skin lesion with a distinctive look, called a *bull's-eye*, appears at the site of the bite. Flulike symptoms appear next, and 4 to 6 weeks later, heart or neurological problems may develop. Arthritis may be a problem much later.

Treatment for Lyme disease includes long-term antibiotic therapy. Many medications used to treat Lyme disease are safe to use during pregnancy.

To avoid exposure to Lyme disease, avoid places known to have ticks, such as heavily wooded areas. If you can't avoid these areas, wear long-sleeved shirts, long pants, socks and boots or closed shoes. Keep your head and hair covered with a hat or scarf. Check your hair for ticks; they often attach to the hair or scalp.

MRSA

Methicillin-resistant Staphylococcus aureus (MRSA; sounds like *MERSA*) is a bacteria that causes difficult-to-treat infections because antibiotics often don't work against them. The bacteria (Staphylococcus aureus, also called *staph)* are resistant to many antibiotics; antibiotics that were effective in the past no longer work.

Methicillin is a strong antibiotic once useful in treating staph in the past, but it is less useful today. Other antibiotics ineffective against MRSA include dicloxacillin, nafcillin and oxacillin. A nickname used in the media for MRSA or Staphylococcus aureus is "super-bug."

MRSA is a serious infection and is passed from person to person, usually by poor hygiene. It can start as inflamed skin, with boils or pimples. The area may be red and hot to the touch. MRSA can spread through the bloodstream. When this happens, it can cause sepsis or septic shock. A very common location of MRSA is the nose or nostrils. Other possible sites are open wounds, I.V. catheters and the urinary tract.

Washing hands with regular soap, alcohol-based foams or hand sanitizers works well in preventing MRSA. Don't share towels, soap or other personal items. If you develop any pimples or boils, don't pop them. Keep the area tightly covered, and call your healthcare provider immediately.

Pregnant women may be at greater risk for MRSA. If either you or your partner work in a hospital or healthcare facility, prison or anyplace where you have a lot of contact with people, you could be at risk. Discuss any of your concerns with your healthcare provider. He or she can give you advice about your particular situation.

Take care of cuts and scratches. If you get a cut or scrape, keep it clean, dry and covered. Know what a MRSA infection looks like—it usually begins as a skin infection then develops small red bumps like pimples. This can be accompanied by a fever or a rash.

Call your healthcare provider if you believe you have been exposed to MRSA. Some antibiotics work well against MRSA, including TMP-SMZ (trimethoprim/sulfamethoxazole), vancomycin and doxycycline.

Your healthcare provider will probably lance and clean any infected area. Cultures or rapid tests of the skin may be done. A vaccine against MRSA is being developed.

There is no evidence to indicate MRSA during pregnancy causes increased risk of problems. It's very unlikely a mother would pass MRSA to her baby during delivery. In addition, breastfeeding is safe for a woman with MRSA.

Rheumatoid Arthritis (RA)

Rheumatoid arthritis (RA) affects 1 in every 1000 pregnant women. It's an autoimmune disease that can attack your body's joints and/or organs.

Many medicines used to treat RA are safe for a pregnant woman to use. However, some medications can be dangerous to use during pregnancy. Talk to your healthcare provider *before* you get pregnant about any medicine you take for your rheumatoid arthritis.

Acetaminophen is OK to use throughout pregnancy. However, NSAIDs should not be used in later pregnancy because they may increase the risk of heart problems in baby. Prednisone is usually acceptable, although methotrexate should *not* be used because it may cause miscarriage and birth defects.

Enbrel is one of the newer medications used to treat RA. Don't use this medication without checking first with your healthcare provider.

RA may not affect your labor and delivery; however, 25% of women with RA have a preterm birth. It may be harder to find comfortable labor positions if you have joint restrictions.

Rubella (German Measles)

Rubella is a viral infection that causes few problems in a nonpregnant woman. It is more serious during pregnancy, especially in the first trimester. There may be no symptoms, or you may have a rash (most common) or flulike symptoms. Rubella infection in a mother-to-be can increase the rate of miscarriage and cause birth defects, especially heart defects.

One of the blood tests you have at your first or second prenatal visit is a rubella titer. It determines whether you have been vaccinated against rubella or if you previously contracted the disease. Most women have had rubella, but if you haven't, you will be vaccinated after pregnancy to safeguard you in the future.

Sexually Transmitted Diseases

Sexually transmitted diseases (STDs) during pregnancy are serious because they can harm a developing fetus. STDs are contracted during sexual contact, including vaginal, oral or anal intercourse. If you have an STD, seek treatment as soon as possible!

Many pregnant women have an STD but don't know they are infected. Ask for a test or treatment if you think you have an STD. Your healthcare provider routinely offers tests for hepatitis B, HIV and syphilis.

Sexually transmitted diseases are more common in women than in men. A woman is more susceptible because her reproductive organs are inside her body, a fertile environment for infections to grow. This also makes diagnosis in women more difficult than in men.

Some STDs are transmitted when the baby comes in contact with the virus during birth. Others are passed to the baby through the mother's blood and infect the baby during pregnancy or birth. Left untreated, STDs can harm an unborn baby. Every year, thousands of babies are born early or suffer from infection because of undetected STDs passed to them by their mothers. Babies may suffer serious effects. In some cases, effects are not evident until years after birth.

The most common sexually transmitted diseases include monilial vulvovaginitis, trichomonal vaginitis, condyloma acuminatum (venereal warts; HPV), genital herpes simplex infection, chlamydia, gonorrhea, syphilis and HIV/AIDS.

Many sexually transmitted diseases can be diagnosed and treated during pregnancy. It's important to be tested for an STD if you believe you might have been exposed. Discuss this important subject with your healthcare provider.

HIV and AIDS

HIV (human immunodeficiency virus) is the virus that causes AIDS (acquired immune deficiency syndrome). About 1.2 million people in the United States are HIV-positive or have AIDS. Nearly 56,000 new HIV infections occur every year—20% of those infected don't know they are infected.

About 2 out of every 1000 women who enter pregnancy are HIV-positive, and the number of cases among women is rising. It's estimated that 6000 babies are born every year to mothers infected with HIV. In fact, the CDC now recommends all pregnant women be offered HIV testing. Home testing kits are available; most are very reliable.

Two tests are used to determine if someone has HIV—the ELISA test and the Western Blot test. The ELISA is a screening test. If positive, it should be confirmed by the Western Blot test. Both tests involve testing blood to measure antibodies to the virus. The Western Blot test is believed to be more than 99% sensitive and specific.

For those at high risk of HIV, experts suggest testing before pregnancy or as early in pregnancy as possible and testing again in the third trimester. Rapid HIV testing during labor is recommended if a woman's HIV status is unknown. With rapid HIV screening, results are available within 30 minutes.

After HIV enters a person's bloodstream, the body begins to produce antibodies to fight the disease. A blood test can detect these antibodies. When detected, a person is considered "HIV-positive" and can pass the virus to others. This is not the same as having AIDS. A person is HIV-positive before developing AIDS. The process can take many years, due to medications in use at this time.

Gynecological problems can be an early sign of an HIV infection, including ulcers in the vagina, yeast infections that won't go away and severe pelvic inflammatory disease. If you have any of these problems, discuss them with your healthcare provider. Early diagnosis and treatment are crucial. In most cases, antibodies can be detected 6 to 12 weeks after exposure. In some cases, it can take many months before antibodies can be found. Studies indicate taking over-the-counter multivitamins containing vitamins B, C and E every day may delay the progression of HIV and delay the need to start antiretroviral medications.

We know 90% of all cases of HIV in children are related to pregnancy—mother to baby during pregnancy, childbirth or breastfeeding. Research has shown an infected woman can pass the virus to her baby as early as 8 weeks of pregnancy. A mother can also pass HIV to her baby during birth. Breastfeeding is not recommended for women who are HIV-positive.

Research shows the chance of a woman infected with HIV passing the virus to her baby can be nearly eliminated with some medications. However, if an infection is not treated, there's a 25% chance a baby will be born with the virus. If a woman takes AZT during pregnancy and has a Cesarean delivery, she reduces the risk of passing the virus to her baby to about 2%! Studies have found no birth defects linked to the use of AZT. Other HIV medications have also been proved safe for use during pregnancy.

If you're HIV-positive, expect more blood tests during pregnancy. These tests help your healthcare provider assess how well you're doing.

The rate of AIDS among women has grown to 20% of all reported cases. AIDS can leave a person prone to, and unable to fight, various infections. If you're unsure about your risk, seek counseling about testing for the AIDS virus. Pregnancy may hide some AIDS symptoms, which makes the disease harder to discover.

There is some positive news for women who suffer from AIDS. We know if a woman is in the early course of the illness, she can usually have an uneventful pregnancy, labor and delivery.

Shingles

Shingles occurs when a type of herpes virus becomes active after having been dormant in nerve root ganglia. This can happen long after the primary infection has gone away. It occurs more often in people who are older, although it can occur in younger people as well.

Shingles occurs mainly in adults whose immune systems are compromised. During pregnancy, shingles can be a severe illness, with sharp pain and even breathing problems. The times of greatest concern for a pregnant woman are during the first half of pregnancy and around the time of delivery. Exposure during the first trimester, when major organs are developing in the fetus, can cause some birth defects. Fortunately, shingles rarely occurs during pregnancy.

Pain from shingles occurs in specific areas of nerve distribution. Treatment includes pain control with pain medications. If you think you have shingles, contact your healthcare provider, who can decide on treatment for you.

Sickle-Cell Disease

Sickle-cell disease is the most common inherited hemoglobin disorder in the United States. About 8% of Black/African-Americans carry the sickle-hemoglobin gene. However, it is also found in people of Arabic, Greek, Maltese, Italian, Sardinian, Turkish, Indian, Caribbean, Latin American and Middle-Eastern descent. In the United States, most cases of sickle-cell disease occur among Black/African-Americans and Latino/Hispanics. About one in every 500 Black/African-Americans has sickle-cell disease.

Normally, red blood cells are round and flexible and flow easily through blood vessels. In sickle-cell disease, abnormal hemoglobin causes red blood cells to become stiff. Under the microscope, they may look like the C-shaped farm tool called a *sickle*.

Because they are stiffer, these red blood cells can get stuck in tiny blood vessels and cut off the blood supply to nearby tissues. This causes a great deal of pain (called *sickle-cell pain episode* or *sickle-cell crisis*) and may damage organs. These abnormal red blood cells die and break down more quickly than normal red blood cells, which results in anemia.

A person who inherits the sickle-cell gene from one parent and the normal type of that gene from the other parent is said to have *sickle-cell trait*. Carriers of the sickle-cell trait are usually as healthy as noncarriers. Sickle-cell trait cannot change to become sickle-cell disease.

When two people with sickle-cell trait have a child, there is a one-in-four chance their child may inherit two sickle-cell genes (one gene from each parent) and have the disorder. There is a two-in-four chance the child will have the trait. There is a one-in-four chance the child will have neither the trait nor the disease. These chances are the same in each pregnancy. If only one parent has the trait and the other doesn't, there is *no* chance their children will have sickle-cell disease. However, there is a 50–50 chance of each child having the trait.

Sickle-cell disease can affect biracial children. To what degree depends on the ethnic group of each parent and his or her genetic makeup. A union of a Caucasian and a Black/African-American will not result in a child with sickle-cell disease because Caucasians are not carriers of the sickle-cell gene. However, the union of a Black/African-American and a person of Mediterranean or Latino/Hispanic descent *could* result in a child with sickle-cell disease if both parents carry the sickle-cell gene. In addition, if both parents are biracial, they could pass the disease to their children if each parent carries the gene. The risk of both biracial partners being carriers is lower, but the risk is still there and depends on each person's genetic background and makeup.

Pregnancy and Sickle-Cell Disease

A woman with sickle-cell disease can have a safe pregnancy. However, if you have the disease, your chances are greater of having problems that can affect your health and your baby's health. During pregnancy, the disease may become more severe, and pain episodes may be more frequent. You will need early prenatal care and careful monitoring throughout pregnancy.

Hydroxyurea is often used to reduce the number of pain episodes by about 50% in some severely affected adults. At this time, we don't recommend hydroxyurea for pregnant women.

A blood test can reveal sickle-cell trait. There also are prenatal tests to find out if a baby will have the disease or carry the trait. Most children with sickle-cell disease are now identified through newborn screening tests.

Thalassemia

Thalassemia, also called *Cooley's anemia,* is not just one disease. It includes a number of different forms of anemia. The thalassemia trait is found all over the world but is most common in people from the Middle East, Greece, Italy, Georgia (the country, not the state), Armenia, Vietnam, Laos, Thailand, Singapore, the Philippines, Cambodia, Malaysia, Burma, Indonesia, China, East India, Africa and Azerbaijan. It affects about 100,000 babies each year.

There are two main forms of the disease—alpha thalassemia and beta thalassemia. The type depends on which part of an oxygen-carrying protein (the hemoglobin) is lacking in red blood cells. Most individuals have a mild form of the disease. The effects of beta thalassemia can range from no effects to very severe.

A carrier of thalassemia has one normal gene and one thalassemia gene. Having the thalassemia trait doesn't usually cause health problems, although women with the trait may be more likely to develop anemia during pregnancy. Healthcare providers may treat this with folic-acid supplementation.

When two carriers have a child, there is a one-in-four chance their child will have a form of the disease. There is a two-in-four chance the child will be a carrier like its parents and a one-in-four chance the child will be completely free of the disease. These odds are the same for each pregnancy when both parents are carriers.

Various tests can determine whether a person has thalassemia or is a carrier. Chorionic villus sampling (CVS) and amniocentesis can detect thalassemia in a fetus. Early diagnosis is important so treatment can begin at birth to prevent as many complications as possible.

Most children born with thalassemia appear healthy at birth, but during the first or second year of life, they develop problems. They grow slowly and often develop jaundice.

Treatment includes frequent blood transfusions and antibiotics. When children are treated with transfusions to keep their hemoglobin level near normal, many complications of thalassemia can be prevented. However, repeated blood transfusions may lead to a buildup of iron in the body. A drug called an *iron chelator* may be given to help rid the body of excess iron.

Toxoplasmosis

Toxoplasmosis is a disease caused by the microbe *Toxoplasma gondii.* It is spread by eating infected raw meat, drinking infected raw goat's milk, eating infected raw eggs, eating food that has been contaminated by insects or by contact with an infected cat or its feces. You can pick up the protozoa from a cat's litter box, from counters or other surfaces the cat walks on, or from the cat itself when you pet it.

Infection in a mother-to-be can lead to miscarriage or an infected infant at birth. Usually an infection in a pregnant woman has no symptoms. An infected baby may appear normal at birth. Between 80 and 90% develop serious eye infections months to years later. Babies whose mothers had toxoplasmosis in the first trimester are usually the most severely affected. About 1 in 1000 babies is born with toxoplasmosis.

To prevent transmission of the microorganism, cook foods thoroughly and use hygienic measures in the kitchen. Get someone else to change the kitty litter. Keep cats off counters, tables and other areas where you could pick up the microbe. Wash your hands thoroughly after every contact with your cat or raw meat, and don't nuzzle or kiss your cat.

Urinary-Tract and Kidney Problems

A *urinary-tract infection (UTI)* refers to an infection anywhere in the urinary tract, which includes the bladder, urethra, ureters and kidneys. Your health-care provider may do a urinalysis and a urine culture for UTIs at your first visit. He or she may also check your urine for infections on subsequent visits.

UTIs are common during pregnancy because of increased pressure on the area. The uterus sits directly on top of the bladder and on the tubes, called *ureters,* that lead from the kidneys to the bladder. An enlarging uterus puts increasing pressure on the bladder and ureters.

Symptoms of a bladder infection include frequent or burning urination, the urge to urinate, though nothing comes out, and blood in the urine (if the infection is severe).

Pyelonephritis is an infection of the urinary tract that also involves the kidneys; it occurs in 1 to 2% of all pregnant women. Symptoms of pyelonephritis include many of those associated with a bladder infection. The infection may require hospitalization and treatment with intravenous antibiotics.

Kidney stones occur about once in every 1500 pregnancies. Symptoms usually include severe back pain and blood in the urine. In pregnancy, ultrasound is usually used to diagnose a kidney stone. A kidney stone in pregnancy is usually treated with pain medication and by drinking lots of fluid or receiving I.V.s to hydrate you so you can pass the stone.

Tay-Sachs Disease

Tay-Sachs disease is one of the most common Jewish genetic disorders. It is an inherited disease of the central nervous system. The disease occurs most

Do You Have a Fever?

Fever often accompanies illness. A fever, especially a high one, can be serious because your baby relies on you for its temperature control. A prolonged high fever, especially in the first trimester, may cause some birth defects. To bring down a high fever, drink lots of liquids (1 pint of fluid a day for every degree above 98.6F), take acetaminophen and dress appropriately to help you cool down. If your healthcare provider prescribes medication for an infection or other illness that may be causing the fever, take all of it as prescribed.

frequently in descendants of Ashkenazi Jews; about one out of every 30 American Jews carries the Tay-Sachs gene. Some non-Jewish people of French-Canadian ancestry (from the East St. Lawrence River Valley of Quebec) and members of the Cajun population in Louisiana are also at increased risk.

The most common form of the disease affects babies, who appear healthy at birth and seem to develop normally for the first few months of life. Then development slows, and symptoms begin to appear. Unfortunately, there is no treatment and no cure for Tay-Sachs disease at this time.

Babies born with Tay-Sachs disease lack a protein called *hexosaminidase A,* or *hex-A.* When hex-A isn't present, substances build up and gradually destroy brain and nerve cells, until the central nervous system stops working.

Tay-Sachs disease can be diagnosed before birth by amniocentesis and chorionic villus sampling (CVS). The disease is hereditary; a Tay-Sachs carrier has one normal gene for hex-A and one Tay-Sachs gene.

There are various types of Tay-Sachs disease. The classic type, which affects babies, is the most common. Other rare deficiencies of the hex-A enzyme are sometimes included under the umbrella of Tay-Sachs disease. These often are referred to as *juvenile, chronic* and *adult-onset* forms of hex-A deficiency.

Your Lifestyle May Impact Your Pregnancy

Your lifestyle and your environment can affect your health and your growing baby's health. Environmental poisons and pollutants that can harm a fetus include lead, mercury, PCBs (polychlorinated biphenyls) and pesticides.

Exposure to *lead* increases the chance of miscarriage. Lead is readily transported across the placenta to the baby; toxicity occurs as early as 12 weeks of pregnancy. Lead exposure can come from many sources, including water pipes, solders, storage batteries, some construction materials, paints, dyes and wood preservatives. Workplace exposure is possible; check to see if you are at risk.

Reports of *mercury* exposure have been linked to various problems in a baby. Exposure occurs with ingestion of contaminated fish; one report linked contaminated grain to mercury poisoning.

PCBs are mixtures of several chemical compounds used for industrial purposes. Most fish, birds and humans have small, measurable amounts of PCBs in their tissues. Typical exposure comes from some of the foods we eat, such as fish.

Exposure to *pesticides* during pregnancy is also held responsible for an increase in problems. Pesticides include a large number of agents. Human exposure is common because of the extensive use of pesticides; those of most concern include DDT, chlordane, heptachlor and lindane. Stop using pesticides in your home and around your work area during pregnancy.

You may not be able to eliminate all contact with pesticides. To protect yourself against these agents, avoid exposure when possible. Thoroughly wash all fruits and vegetables before eating them. If you know you'll be around certain chemicals, wash your hands thoroughly after exposure.

Substance Abuse

Every action you take during pregnancy may potentially affect the baby growing inside you. Substance abuse is never healthy for you; when you're pregnant, it can also harm your baby.

Many substances you normally use without adverse effects may adversely affect a developing fetus. Some substances readily cross the placenta and enter your baby's bloodstream, where they can cause problems. Cigarette smoke, alcohol and drugs are dangerous for the fetus.

Cigarette Smoking

Cigarette smoking can have serious effects on you and your growing baby. Over 10% of all pregnant women smoke; some experts put the number at 20%. Smoking is higher among pregnant women under 20 years old and those over 35. Stop smoking before or during pregnancy; fetal and infant mortality rates increase by more than 50% in first-time pregnant women who smoke more than a pack of cigarettes a day.

Tobacco smoke contains harmful substances; when you smoke, so does your baby! When you inhale cigarette smoke, it crosses the placenta to your baby and may harm the fetus. In addition, nicotine in a pregnant woman's

Nicoderm Patch/Gum, Zyban and Chantix

You may be wondering if you can use an aid, such as a patch, gum or a pill, to help you stop smoking during pregnancy. The specific effects on fetal development of these devices are unknown.

Nicotrol, available as an inhaler, nasal spray or patch, is sold under the brand names *Nicoderm* and *Nicorette*; it's also sold generically. All three Nicotrol preparations contain nicotine and are not recommended for use during pregnancy.

Nicotine-replacement therapy may be suggested if a woman can't stop smoking on her own. Studies show the benefits of these products may outweigh the risks during pregnancy, but some experts disagree. They state nicotine addiction cannot be stopped by using nicotine, which is contained in patches and gums. Discuss the situation with your healthcare provider if you have questions.

Zyban (bupropion hydrochloride) is an oral medication that is a nonnicotine aid to help with smoking cessation. This medication is also marketed as the antidepressant Wellbutrin or Wellbutrin SR. Zyban is not recommended for use by pregnant women.

Chantix (varenicline tartrate) is a prescription medication available to help someone stop smoking. It doesn't contain nicotine, but it is not recommended for pregnant women. Studies show it may reduce a fetus's bone mass and also cause low birthweight.

bloodstream interferes with the normal development of the major neurotransmitter systems in a baby's brain.

The problem is so serious that warnings for pregnant women appear on every cigarette package:

SURGEON GENERAL'S WARNING: Smoking by pregnant women may result in fetal injury, premature birth and low birthweight.

Some people mistakenly believe it's OK to use smokeless tobacco during pregnancy. It's not! Use of any smokeless tobacco product contributes to nicotine in the bloodstream.

In addition, if baby's *dad* smoked before conception and during pregnancy, the child has an increased risk of developing problems during childhood. If both parents smoke while a child is growing up, the child may have an increased risk of developing lymphoblastic leukemia.

Effects on the Fetus

A pregnant woman who smokes reduces her fetus's oxygen supply by as much as 50% because carbon monoxide in cigarette smoke displaces oxygen in the mother's bloodstream. Toxins in cigarette smoke narrow blood vessels. Smoking can damage the placenta and hamper baby's growth.

Smoking during pregnancy can increase the risk of many problems in a baby. Studies also show if you smoke during pregnancy, your child may have a much greater chance of being a smoker as an adult. The belief is that babies born to moms who smoke during pregnancy may be more susceptible to nicotine addiction.

Infants born to mothers who smoke weigh less than other babies, which can cause problems. When a woman smokes during pregnancy, the substances she inhales interfere with her body's absorption of vitamins B and C and folic acid, and increase her risk of pregnancy-related complications.

Effects on the Pregnant Woman

Serious pregnancy complications are more common among women who smoke. The risk of developing placental abruption increases by 25% in moderate smokers and 65% in heavy smokers. Your smoking may affect future pregnancies. Studies show you double your risk of placental abruption in a second pregnancy if you smoke during your first pregnancy.

Placenta previa occurs 25% more often in moderate smokers and 90% more often in heavy smokers. Cigarette smoking also increases the risk of miscarriage, premature rupture of membranes and fetal death or death of a baby soon after birth. Risk is directly related to the number of cigarettes a woman smokes each day. Risk can be even greater if you smoke more than a pack of cigarettes a day.

The best thing to do is quit smoking completely before and during pregnancy. If you can't quit totally, reduce the number of cigarettes you smoke to help reduce your risks.

Effects of Second-Hand and Third-Hand Smoke

Exposure to second-hand and third-hand smoke can be harmful for a mom-to-be and her baby. Second-hand smoke is smoke you breathe in when others around you are smoking. Third-hand smoke occurs when tobacco toxins stick to fabric, hair, skin and other surfaces, such as walls, carpets and floors, even after smoke has disappeared. It can be just as harmful as second-hand smoke. A clue to the presence of third-hand smoke is smell—if you can smell it, it's still there.

Exposure to either type of smoke increases a nonsmoker's risk of giving birth to a low-birthweight baby. Ask your partner, family members, friends and co-workers not to smoke around you while you're pregnant. Avoid situations that expose you to second-hand or third-hand smoke!

Alcohol

When you drink, so does your baby—the more you drink, the more your baby "drinks." Alcohol use by a pregnant woman carries considerable risk to her and her developing baby. The fetus is especially vulnerable to the effects of alcohol in early pregnancy.

Drinking during pregnancy has been associated with behavior problems in a child. The more alcohol a woman drinks, the more problems a child may experience. Drinking as little as two drinks a day has been associated with fetal-alcohol effects. Chronic use of alcohol during pregnancy can lead to fetal-alcohol syndrome (FAS); see the discussion below.

Your developing baby may be harmed by an alcohol level that has little apparent effect on you. A fetus cannot metabolize alcohol as quickly as an adult, so alcohol remains in its system much longer. Moderate use of alcohol has been linked to a greater risk of miscarriage. Studies show spina bifida is up to 60 times more common in babies exposed to alcohol before birth than in babies who were not exposed.

• •

Before pregnancy, Wendy drank socially, but she hadn't missed alcohol during her pregnancy. She felt that by abstaining from alcohol, she was doing something good for her baby. At a party, she was offered a glass of wine. The pregnancy was going well, and she hadn't had any problems; what would be the harm? She wasn't sure, so she decided to stay with fruit juice. At her next prenatal visit, she wanted to know how much alcohol she could drink safely. I supported Wendy in her decision not to drink at all during her pregnancy. I told her that research has not identified a "safe" amount of alcohol to consume during pregnancy. The more we learn, the more it appears that even a little alcohol might be harmful.

• •

The word is spreading about alcohol use in pregnancy, but one study found many pregnant women in North America ignore the advice. In that study, four times as many women said they drank alcohol during pregnancy than those who had been interviewed in an earlier study. Don't put your baby at risk! Pass up *all* alcohol during your pregnancy.

You may wonder about recipes that call for alcohol. It's OK to eat food that contains alcohol if it has been baked or simmered for *at least 1 hour.* Cooking for that length of time cooks out almost all of the alcohol content.

Some women wonder if nonalcoholic wine and beer are safe to drink during pregnancy. Even though they are labeled "no alcohol," these beverages contain *some* alcohol—about 0.5%. Because we don't know what alcohol-intake level is safe for the fetus, it's a good idea to avoid these beverages.

If you drink during pregnancy, it may affect sperm production in a male child born from that pregnancy. Researchers have noted an association between alcoholic intake of the mother and sperm concentration in her adult son.

Taking drugs with alcohol increases the risk of damage to the fetus. Drugs that cause the greatest concern include analgesics, antidepressants and anticonvulsants.

Some researchers believe heavy alcohol consumption by a baby's father before or at the time of conception may produce FAS in the baby. Alcohol consumption by the father has also been linked to intrauterine-growth restriction.

Be very careful about substances you use that may contain alcohol. Over-the-counter cough medicines and cold remedies often contain alcohol—as much as 25% of the preparation!

Fetal-Alcohol Syndrome and Fetal-Alcohol Exposure

Fetal-alcohol syndrome (FAS) is a collection of problems that affect children born to alcoholic women. Mild abnormalities have been associated with as little as two drinks a day (1 ounce of alcohol)—this is called *fetal-alcohol exposure (FAE).*

FAS occurs in 1 or 2 of every 1000 births. It is characterized by growth restriction before and after birth. Heart and limb defects and unusual facial characteristics, such as a short, upturned nose, a flat upper jawbone and "different" eyes, have also been seen in FAS children. These children may have behavioral problems, impaired speech and impaired gross-motor functions. FAS ranks with neural-tube defects and Down syndrome as a major cause of mental retardation in babies.

We advise women that any amount of alcohol is too much. It's best to avoid alcohol *completely* while you're pregnant!

Abuse of Other Substances

When we discuss *substance abuse*, we refer to use of drugs prohibited by law, but we also include use of legal medications, such as benzodiazepine or barbiturates. These substances may also have harmful effects during pregnancy, regardless of whether they are used for legitimate or illicit reasons.

Drug use can greatly affect your pregnancy. A woman who uses or abuses drugs may have more pregnancy complications because of her lifestyle. Women who use certain substances commonly display nutritional deficiencies; anemia and fetal-growth restriction are other risks. A pregnant woman who uses drugs may increase her risk of pre-eclampsia.

Marijuana

Marijuana contains tetrahydrocannabinol (THC), which crosses the placenta and enters the baby's system. Exposure can cause attention-deficit disorders, memory problems and impaired decision-making ability in children; these problems can appear in a child between 3 and 12 years of age.

Central-Nervous-System Drugs

When used during pregnancy, central-nervous-system stimulants, such as amphetamines, are associated with an increase in cardiovascular defects in babies. These babies frequently show signs of withdrawal, poor feeding, seizures and other problems.

Tranquilizing agents include benzodiazepines (Valium and Librium) and other agents; they have been associated with an increase in birth defects. Heavy use in pregnancy is also associated with infant withdrawal after birth.

Narcotics and Mind-Altering Drugs

Habitual use of morphine, Demerol, heroin and codeine can lead to physical dependence in the user. A pregnant woman who uses narcotics is subject to pre-eclampsia, preterm labor, fetal-growth problems and narcotic withdrawal in the baby following birth. The incidence of sudden-infant-death syndrome (SIDS) is *10 times higher* among babies born to mothers who used narcotics during pregnancy than babies whose mothers did not.

Intravenous drug use is frequently accompanied by health problems, such as AIDS, hepatitis and endocarditis. Any of these problems is extremely serious during pregnancy.

Hallucinogens, such as LSD, mescaline, hashish and peyote, are still used by many people. Phencyclidine (PCP, angel dust) falls into this group. PCP is believed to cause abnormal development in human babies, although this has not been definitively proved.

Cocaine and Crack

Cocaine use can definitely complicate a pregnancy. Often a user consumes the drug over a period of time, such as several days. During this time, the user may eat or drink very little, with serious consequences for a developing fetus.

Continued use of cocaine or its stronger form, crack, can affect maternal nutrition and temperature control, which can harm the fetus. Cocaine use has been linked with many pregnancy problems. A woman who uses cocaine during the first 13 weeks of pregnancy faces an increased risk of miscarriage. Cocaine can damage the developing baby as early as *3 days after* conception!

Infants born to mothers who use cocaine during pregnancy often have mental deficiencies. Sudden-infant-death syndrome (SIDS) is also more common among these babies. Many babies are stillborn.

· ·

One of the most difficult discussions I've had was with Sally. When she came to see me for her yearly exam and Pap smear, she was upset and discouraged. Adam, her 10-year-old pride and joy, was now in fifth grade. He was having trouble in school and had been diagnosed with attention-deficit disorder. Her pregnancy had seemed to go OK 10 years ago. She hadn't been able to talk about it then, but she said she had continued using cocaine through the first part of her pregnancy. She was now contemplating another pregnancy. Sally realized that although there was nothing she could do now to change her pregnancy with Adam, she would do things differently with this baby.

· ·

Your Medical History

To give you and your baby the best care possible, your healthcare provider will ask you for a lot of information at your first prenatal visit. You can help by gathering the information before you meet.

DES Use by Pregnant Woman's Mother

In the 1940s, '50s and '60s, a nonsteroidal synthetic estrogen called *diethyl-stilbestrol (DES)* was given to some women to prevent miscarriage. The compound was even included in some prenatal vitamins. Research proved later that DES caused problems in some of the female offspring of women who used it, including an increased risk of miscarriage and premature labor when the younger women became pregnant. A higher rate of ectopic pregnancy has been blamed on DES-related Fallopian-tube deformities and uterine deformities. DES can also affect uterine-muscle development, resulting in an abnormally shaped uterus.

Because DES was prescribed from the 1940s through the 1960s, most affected women have passed through their years of conception. However, as an older pregnant woman, it could be significant for you. Ask your mother if she took DES while she was pregnant with you. If you were exposed to DES through your mother's use of the medication, some researchers recommend prenatal counseling before pregnancy about the risks of miscarriage, premature delivery, ectopic pregnancy and other problems.

Preparing Your Medical History

Check family records and ask family members if anyone in the family has suffered from the problems listed on pages 64 and 65. Be sure your partner does the same with his family. This information may help your healthcare provider address potential problems.

I dislike having to go to my prenatal visits—it always takes so long. Do I really have to go to them?

Yes! Keeping your appointments for prenatal care is one of the most important things you can do to help guarantee a healthy baby.

Depression

Depression can occur at any time during a person's life. If you have a history of major depression, you're at increased risk of depression during pregnancy. In fact, between 3 and 5% of all women experience a major depression during pregnancy. It's estimated another 15% have some degree of depression.

If you're being treated for depression when you get pregnant, it's important to continue treatment. Treating depression is as important as treating any other problem. If you take antidepressants, *don't stop* unless advised to do so by your healthcare provider. Studies show up to 70% of women who stop taking antidepressants during pregnancy relapse into depression. Stopping your medication can raise stress hormones, which increases your risks of problems during pregnancy. The risks to you and your baby from depression may be greater than your risk of taking antidepressants. We know depression can be difficult to manage without using drug therapy.

There may be a very small increased risk of birth defects with some medicines used to treat depression when taken during the first trimester. It may help to switch to an antidepressant that is safer during pregnancy, including fluoxetine (Prozac), citalopram and escitalopram (Lexapro). Pregnancy may affect your body's ability to use lithium. If you take an SSRI, the dose may need to be increased during the third trimester to maintain your normal mood. Talk to your healthcare provider about your medication before pregnancy or as soon as you confirm your pregnancy.

There is continued concern about the safety of Paxil during pregnancy. Research suggests that using the drug in the first trimester of pregnancy may be tied to an increased risk of some problems in baby. However, do *not* stop taking your antidepressant medicine without first consulting your healthcare provider.

If you're feeling depressed, your level of vitamin D may be low. Talk about it with your healthcare provider. Other suggestions for dealing with depression include getting some exercise and being sure you get enough B vitamins, folic acid and omega-3 fatty acids. You can get omega-3 fatty acids by including walnuts, flaxseed, salmon and scallops in your meal plan. Taking about 3.5g of omega-3 fatty acids every day has been shown to help fight depression.

Additional therapies include massage and reflexology. Another option is light therapy, similar to the type of treatment given to those who suffer from "seasonal affective disorder."

Depression during Pregnancy

Depression *during* pregnancy does occur. Experts believe it's one of the most common medical problems seen in pregnant women. Studies show up to 25% of all moms-to-be experience some degree of depression, and nearly 10% will experience a major depression. If left untreated, 50% of women who are depressed during pregnancy will experience postpartum depression.

Treating depression during pregnancy is important for your health and baby's health. This is one of the many reasons healthcare providers make treating depression a priority.

Depression is actually more common *during* pregnancy than after giving birth. If you have a family history of depression, you may be at higher risk during pregnancy. If you don't have enough serotonin, researchers believe you may be at higher risk. If you've been struggling with infertility or miscarriage, you may also be more prone to depression.

If you're depressed, you may not take good care of yourself. Babies born to depressed women may be smaller or born prematurely. Some women use alcohol, drugs and cigarettes in an attempt to ease their depression. You may also have trouble bonding with your baby after birth.

Consider the following to measure your risks of being depressed. You may be at higher risk if:

- you experienced mood changes when you took oral contraceptives
- your mother was depressed during pregnancy
- you have a history of depression
- you feel sad or depressed longer than 1 week
- you're not getting enough sleep and rest
- you have bipolar disorder—pregnancy can trigger a relapse, especially if you stop taking your mood-stabilizing medications

Symptoms and Treatment

It may be hard to differentiate between some of the normal pregnancy changes and signs of depression. Many symptoms of depression are similar to those of pregnancy, including fatigue and sleeplessness. The difference is how intense the symptoms are and how long they last. Some common symptoms of depression include:

- overpowering sadness that lasts for days, without an obvious cause
- difficulty sleeping or waking up very early
- wanting to sleep all the time or great fatigue (this can be normal early in pregnancy but usually gets better after a few weeks)
- no appetite (as distinguished from nausea and vomiting)
- lack of concentration
- thoughts of harming yourself

We know women who are depressed are more likely to develop diabetes, and women who develop diabetes are more likely to be depressed. This is also true for pregnant women. If you have diabetes and untreated depression, then become pregnant, it can be serious if you don't get help. You may have a difficult time caring for yourself. This could lead to difficulties in controlling weight gain and sugar levels. Your risk of addictive-substance abuse, such as alcohol use and cigarette smoking, may increase. And you may not be able to meet the nutritional demands of your pregnancy.

Babies born to mothers with untreated depression can have many problems. They often cry a lot, have difficulty sleeping, are fussier and are difficult to soothe.

If you have symptoms and they don't get better in a few weeks or every day seems to be bad, seek help as soon as you recognize you might be depressed. Call your healthcare provider, or bring it up at your next prenatal visit. There are steps to take to help you feel better again. It's important to do it for yourself and your baby!

MEDICAL HISTORY CHART

If the problem applies to you, your partner or another family member, check off the box in the appropriate column.

Problem	You	Partner	Family
AIDS/HIV	☐	☐	☐
Alcohol abuse	☐	☐	☐
Allergies	☐	☐	☐
Anemia	☐	☐	☐
Cancer	☐	☐	☐
Cleft lip/palate	☐	☐	☐
Cystic fibrosis	☐	☐	☐
DES use by pregnant woman's mother	☐	☐	☐
Diabetes	☐	☐	☐
Down syndrome	☐	☐	☐
Drug abuse	☐	☐	☐
Epilepsy	☐	☐	☐
GBS infections	☐	☐	☐
Genital herpes	☐	☐	☐
Heart disease	☐	☐	☐

Problem	You	Partner	Family
Hemophilia	☐	☐	☐
Huntington's disease	☐	☐	☐
Hypertension (high blood pressure)	☐	☐	☐
Miscarriage	☐	☐	☐
Multiple pregnancies	☐	☐	☐
Muscular dystrophy	☐	☐	☐
Rubella (German measles)	☐	☐	☐
Sexually transmitted disease	☐	☐	☐
Sickle-cell disease	☐	☐	☐
Spina bifida	☐	☐	☐
Systemic lupus erythematosus	☐	☐	☐
Tay-Sachs disease	☐	☐	☐
Thyroid disease	☐	☐	☐
Urinary-tract infections	☐	☐	☐

Chapter 5

Pregnancy Encounters of the Usual Kind

At the beginning of any pregnancy, you won't know all the questions and concerns you may have. As your pregnancy progresses, many of the issues we cover here may become important to you. In this chapter, we'll look at some of the common interests a couple expecting a baby may have.

Your Due Date

A due date is important in pregnancy because it helps your healthcare provider determine when to perform certain tests or procedures. It also helps estimate baby's growth and may indicate whether you are overdue or in premature labor.

Most women don't know the *exact* date their baby was conceived, but they usually know the day their last menstrual period began. (*Last menstrual period* may be abbreviated *LMP.*) Because ovulation occurs about the middle of your cycle, or about 2 weeks before the beginning of the next period, a healthcare provider uses the first day of the last period and adds 2 weeks as an estimate of when conception occurred. By doing this, he or she can set a due date.

You can also calculate when your baby is due another way. Begin with the date of the first day of your last menstrual period; add 7 days and count back 3 months. This gives you the *approximate* date of delivery. For example, if your last period began on January 20, your estimated due date is October 27.

Gestational age (menstrual age) is yet another way to date a pregnancy. If your healthcare provider says you're 12 weeks pregnant, he or she is referring to gestational age. Your last menstrual period began 12 weeks ago, but you actually conceived 10 weeks ago.

Fertilization age (ovulatory age) can also be used to date your pregnancy. It is 2 weeks shorter than gestational age and dates from the actual day of conception. This is the age of the fetus. In the case of *12 weeks pregnant*, the fetus is actually 10 weeks old.

Your healthcare provider may also refer to your pregnancy by *trimesters*. Trimesters divide pregnancy into three stages, each about 13 weeks long. This division helps organize stages of development.

> **Time-Saving, Energy-Saving Tip**
>
> Do you like marinated meat but forget to put it in the marinade until it's too late? Try this—cut up raw meat for cooking. Place it in a large plastic freezer bag. Add marinade to the meat, seal the bag and put it in the freezer. When you pull the meat out of the freezer, it marinates while it thaws!

Childbirth-Education Classes

Childbirth-education classes can help you and your partner prepare for the birth of your baby. If a couple is prepared for labor and delivery, the experience is usually more relaxed, even enjoyable. Childbirth-education classes for couples in their 30s and 40s may be available in your area to meet your specific needs.

These classes are very popular. In fact, studies show that nearly 90% of all first-time expectant parents take some type of childbirth-education class.

How Classes Can Help You and Your Partner

Classes can help prepare you and your partner for labor and delivery. Studies have shown women who take childbirth-education classes need less medication, have fewer forceps or vacuum-extractor deliveries and feel more positive about the birth than women who do not take classes.

Classes cover many aspects of labor and delivery, including vaginal birth, Cesarean delivery, hospital procedures, ways to deal with the discomfort and pain of labor and delivery, various pain-relief methods and the postpartum or recovery period. Having this information available beforehand can make you feel more confident and prepared to cope with the birth experience.

What to Look for in a Childbirth-Education Class

Every class has a different style. There are many different questions to ask to help you evaluate whether a particular class is right for you. Each class should cover the following.

- What are the different childbirth methods?
- What is "natural childbirth"?
- What is a Cesarean delivery?

- What pain-relief methods are available?
- What you need to know (and practice) for the childbirth method you choose.
- Will you need an episiotomy?
- Will you need an enema?
- When is a fetal monitor necessary?
- What's going to happen when you reach the hospital?
- Is an epidural or some other type of anesthesia right for you?

In addition, consider the following before choosing a childbirth-education class for you and your partner or labor coach.

- Class was recommended by your healthcare provider.
- Class uses a philosophy shared by your healthcare provider and childbirth team.
- Class begins when you need it, in the seventh month of your pregnancy (earlier if you are having more than one baby).
- Class size is small, no more than 10 couples.
- Graduates are enthusiastic. (Locate people and ask about the class.)
- Class outline is informative and interesting.
- Class includes the time and opportunity to ask questions, practice techniques and talk to parents who have recently given birth.
- Class focuses on the specific needs of older pregnant couples.

Major Childbirth Philosophies

Couples often wonder if one type of childbirth method is better than another. Any method can be the right one for a couple, but it's best for partners to agree on the method. If the woman chooses a method that involves her partner greatly and the partner isn't willing or able to provide that level of involvement, it could lead to disappointment and anxiety.

There are three major childbirth-preparation methods/philosophies— Lamaze, Bradley and Grantly Dick-Read. Each philosophy offers its own techniques and methods. Other childbirth methods are also taught; see the discussion below.

Lamaze is the oldest technique of childbirth preparation. Through training, it conditions a mother to replace unproductive laboring efforts with effective ones. It emphasizes relaxation and breathing during labor and delivery. Partners are an important part of Lamaze classes.

Bradley classes teach the Bradley method of relaxation and inward focus. Teachers place strong emphasis on relaxation and deep abdominal breathing

• •

Lynne asked friends for suggestions for a pediatrician, and she and her partner, Ian, finally decided on one. They wanted to meet her before the baby was born. They weren't prepared for the experience. Lynne had been used to reading a magazine in the relative peace and quiet of my waiting room. The pediatrician's waiting room was very different. In one corner, a new mom was trying unsuccessfully to change a diaper. In another, two brothers fought over a book while their mom talked to another mom. Lynne and Ian were beginning to think they were in the wrong place when they were called to meet the pediatrician. They immediately felt at ease with Dr. Summers, who was busy but seemed competent and approachable. They were able to ask questions; when they left the office, they felt good about the choice they'd made. But they were sure it would take awhile to get used to the waiting room!

• •

to make labor more comfortable. Classes begin when pregnancy is confirmed and continue until after birth. Bradley class members have often decided they do not want to use any type of medication for labor-pain relief.

Grantly Dick-Read is a method that attempts to break the fear-tension-pain cycle of labor and delivery through education. These classes were the first to include fathers in the birth experience.

In addition to the three major childbirth methods described above, other methods are also practiced. Marie Mongan, a hypnotherapist, used the work of Dr. Grantly Dick-Read to develop *hypnobirthing*. She believes if you're not afraid, pain is reduced or eliminated, so anesthetics during labor are unnecessary.

Physical therapist Cathy Daub is the founder of *Birth Works Childbirth Education*. The goal of Birth Works is to help women have more trust and faith in their ability to give birth and to help build self-confidence. Classes are taught once a week for 10 weeks and may be taken any time during pregnancy. Some suggest you take them before you get pregnant or during your first trimester.

Birthing from Within was developed by Pam England, a midwife. She believes birth is a rite of passage, not a medical event. Classes center on self-discovery. Pain-coping measures are intended to be integrated into daily life, not just used for labor.

ICEA, *ALACE* and *CAPPA* are three associations that share a similar philosophy. They believe in helping women trust their bodies and gain the knowledge necessary for making informed decisions about childbirth. The International Childbirth Education Association (ICEA) most commonly certifies hospital and physician educators. The Association of Labor Assistants and Childbirth Educators (ALACE) and the Childbirth and Postpartum Professional Association (CAPPA) usually offer independent classes. Each of these groups teaches the stages of labor and coping techniques. Class series vary in length.

Choosing Your Class

At around 20 weeks of pregnancy, begin looking into classes offered in your area. You may have to sign up weeks before the class begins. You should start classes by the beginning of the third trimester (about 27 weeks). Plan to finish at least a few weeks before your due date.

Childbirth classes are offered in many settings. Most hospitals that deliver babies offer prenatal classes on-site. Labor-and-delivery nurses or midwives often teach the classes.

Classes are not only for first-time pregnant women. If you have a new partner, if it has been a few years since you've had a baby, if you have questions or if you would like a review of labor and delivery, consider taking classes. Classes may also be offered for women without a partner, such as a woman whose partner is away, as in the military, or for a single woman.

Ask your healthcare provider to recommend classes in your area. He or she knows what is available. Friends can also be good sources, or check *Childbirth Education* for your area on the Internet. Some insurance companies and HMOs offer partial or full reimbursement for fees.

Choosing Your Baby's Healthcare Provider

Choosing a healthcare provider for your baby is as important as choosing one for your pregnancy or the hospital where you will give birth. It's best to select someone and to visit this person before baby is born. Ask your pregnancy healthcare provider, your family practitioner, friends, co-workers and family members for names of people they know and trust. Or contact your local medical society and ask for a reference. Plan to visit this healthcare provider about 3 or 4 weeks before your due date. If the baby comes early, you'll be prepared.

The first visit is important, and your partner should attend with you. This is the ideal time for the two of you to discuss any concerns or questions about the care of your baby. The healthcare provider may offer helpful suggestions.

I need a healthcare provider for my expected baby. How do I find one?
It's helpful to decide on someone to care for baby before your baby is born. Ask for suggestions from friends, your pregnancy healthcare provider or family members. Call labor-and-delivery at the hospital where you will deliver, and ask the nurses to recommend someone.

At the meeting, you can discuss the healthcare provider's philosophy, learn his or her schedule and on-call policy, and clarify what you can anticipate from this person and the staff. When your baby is born, the healthcare provider will be notified so he or she can come to the hospital and check the baby. Selecting a person to care for baby before birth helps ensure baby will see the same healthcare provider for follow-up visits at the hospital and the office.

If you belong to an HMO, and there are a group of healthcare providers in pediatrics, arrange a meeting with one of them. If you have a conflict or don't see eye to eye with this person on important matters, you may be able to choose someone else. Ask your patient advocate for information and advice.

Questions to Ask a Pediatrician or Healthcare Provider
The questions below may help you create a useful dialogue with your pediatrician or healthcare provider. You may also have other questions to add to the list.

- What are your qualifications and training?
- Are you board certified? If not, will you be soon (are you "board eligible")?
- What hospital(s) are you affiliated with?
- Do you have privileges at the hospital where I will deliver?
- Will you do the newborn exam?
- If I have a boy, will you perform the circumcision (if we want to have it done)?
- What is your availability?
- Can an acutely ill child be seen the same day?
- How can we reach you in case of an emergency or after office hours?
- Who responds if you are not available?
- Do you return phone calls the same day?
- Are you interested in preventive, developmental and behavioral issues?
- How does the practice operate?
- Do you provide written instructions for well-baby and sick-baby care?
- What are your fees?

- Do your fees comply with our insurance?
- What is the nearest (to our home) emergency room or urgent-care center you would send us to?

Analyzing Your Visit

Some issues can be resolved only by analyzing your feelings after your visit. Below are some things you and your partner might want to discuss after your visit.

- Are the healthcare provider's philosophies and attitudes acceptable to us, such as use of antibiotics and other medications, child-rearing practices or related religious beliefs?
- Did the healthcare provider listen to us?
- Did he or she seem genuinely interested in our concerns?
- Do we feel comfortable with this person?
- Is the office comfortable, clean and bright?
- Did the office staff seem cordial, open and easy to talk to?

The Cost of Having a Baby

It costs a lot of money to have a baby, no matter where you live in the United States. Costs vary depending on how long you stay in the hospital, what type of anesthesia you have and whether you or your baby have complications.

At your first prenatal visit, ask about the fees for prenatal care, including delivery. Nearly every medical office employs someone who deals with insurance questions; he or she may know about things you haven't considered. Often this insurance person knows the answers to these questions or can help you get answers. Don't be embarrassed or afraid to ask questions about the financial side of your pregnancy. Every healthcare provider expects it.

You may also need to check with the hospital and your insurance company. When you communicate with an insurance company, have a list of questions ready. Write down the answers so you can refer to them later, especially if you need to discuss them with your healthcare provider.

Costs in Canada

The Canadian healthcare system is very different from the healthcare system in the United States. Canadians pay a healthcare premium on a monthly basis, and pregnancy costs vary depending on the province you live in. The healthcare provider who delivers your baby is paid by the government, not you.

Chapter 6

How Your Body Changes during Pregnancy

Pregnancy is a time of change. You will see yourself change in many ways—your abdomen will grow, your breasts will enlarge, your hands and feet may swell, among other changes. You may also see your role increase—from partner to partner/parent. If you're aware of many of the changes you may experience, you may feel more comfortable as they occur.

During the first trimester, you may notice little change in yourself, although your baby is growing and changing quite rapidly. You may not even realize you're pregnant until the middle or close to the end of this trimester. You gain little weight—probably no more than 5 pounds (2.25 kg) for the entire 13 weeks. Your abdomen grows a little; you may be able to feel your uterus about 3 inches (7.7 cm) below your bellybutton. You won't feel the fetus move during this time.

In the second trimester, others begin to notice you are pregnant. At the beginning of this period, you'll be able to feel your uterus about 3 inches below your bellybutton. By the end of the trimester, you'll feel your uterus about 3 inches above it. Average total pregnancy weight gain at the end of this trimester is 17 to 24 pounds (7.7 to 10.9 kg) including weight gained in the first trimester. During this time you will begin to feel your baby move.

The greatest change during the third trimester is growth of your baby. Your baby gains a great deal of weight during this time, although you may not. The average total weight gain for a normal-weight woman by delivery is between 25 and 35 pounds (11.4 to 15.9 kg).

Abdominal muscles are stretched and pushed apart as your baby grows. Muscles attached to the lower portion of your ribs may separate in the midline, called a *diastasis recti*. The condition isn't painful and doesn't harm the baby. Diastasis recti may still be present after the birth of your baby, but the separation won't be as noticeable. Exercising can strengthen the muscles, but a small bulge or gap may remain.

At my 20-week visit, my healthcare provider measured my abdomen. Why did she do this?

As you progress in your pregnancy, your healthcare provider needs a point of reference from which to measure the growth of your uterus. Some healthcare providers measure from the bellybutton. Some measure from the pubis symphysis, the place where pubic bones meet in the middle-lower part of your abdomen. Abdominal measurements can reveal a great deal. For example, a higher-than-expected measurement at 20 weeks may alert your healthcare provider to the possibility of twins or an incorrect due date. A lower than-expected measurement may mean your due date is wrong or some problem may be present. In either case, your healthcare provider may have you evaluated further by ultrasound.

Skin Changes

Most women experience skin changes during pregnancy. Some find their skin becomes less oily and softer. Others develop acne. Many skin changes are due to the hormones of pregnancy; skin often returns to normal after baby is born.

Many women believe their skin becomes more alive and glowing while they are pregnant. Although there is no medical fact to back this belief, many women do seem to "glow" during pregnancy.

Stretch Marks

Stretch marks, also called *striae distensae,* may occur more often in older women. These marks occur when the elastic fibers and collagen in deeper layers of your skin are pulled apart to make room for baby. When skin tears, collagen breaks down and shows through the top layer of skin as a pink, red or purple indented streak.

Nearly 9 out of 10 pregnant women develop stretch marks on their breasts, tummy, hips, buttocks and/or arms. They may appear any time during pregnancy. After birth, they may fade to the same color as the rest of your skin, but they won't go away completely.

To date, no one has found a reliable way of avoiding stretch marks. Women have tried many lotions, creams and other remedies, with little success. There

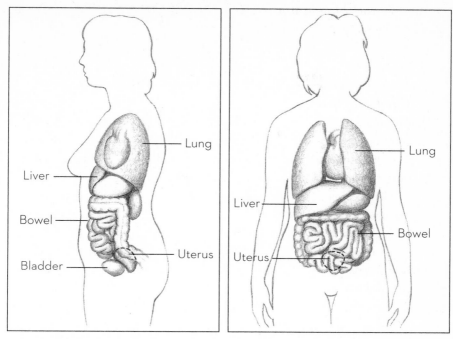

During the first trimester, you will notice few changes in your body.

is no harm in using lotion products, but they probably won't prevent you from getting stretch marks.

You can help yourself by gaining weight *slowly* and *steadily* during pregnancy. Any large increase in weight can cause stretch marks to appear more readily.

Drink lots of water, and eat healthy foods. Foods high in antioxidants provide nutrients needed to repair and to heal tissue. Eating enough protein and smaller amounts of "good" fats, such as flaxseed, flaxseed oil and fish oils, may also help you.

Stay out of the sun! Keep up with your exercise program.

Ask your healthcare provider about using creams with alpha-hydroxy acid, citric acid or lactic acid. Some of these creams and lotions improve the quality of the skin's elastic fibers.

Don't use steroid creams, such as hydrocortisone or topicort, to treat stretch marks during pregnancy without first checking with your healthcare provider. You absorb some of the steroid into your system, and it can pass to baby. And stretch creams really can't penetrate deeply enough to repair damage to your skin.

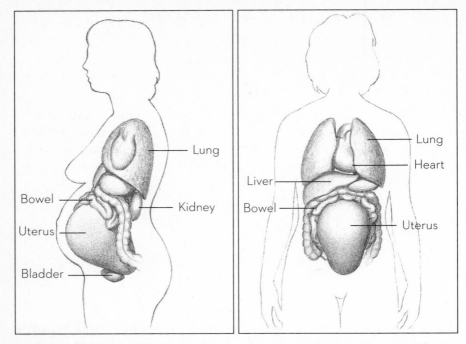

Your body undergoes fantastic changes later in pregnancy. Close to delivery, your uterus takes up a great deal of room and "rearranges" various organs.

Some additional treatments may help after baby is born. Retin-A or Renova, used in combination with glycolic acid, is fairly effective. Prescriptions are needed for Retin-A and Renova; you can get glycolic acid from your dermatologist. Cellex-C, with glycolic acid, also improves the appearance of stretch marks. The most effective treatment—but the most costly—is laser treatment. This is often done in combination with the medication methods described above. All of these treatments are done *after* pregnancy.

Surface Skin Changes

In some women, a vertical line appears along the midline of the abdomen, called the *linea nigra*. The linea nigra fades markedly after pregnancy but does not usually disappear completely.

Occasionally irregular brown patches appear on the face and neck of a pregnant woman, called *chloasma* or *mask of pregnancy*. We believe this change is caused by the hormonal changes of pregnancy. Usually dark patches disappear completely or get lighter after your baby is born. (Oral contraceptives may cause similar pigmentation changes.)

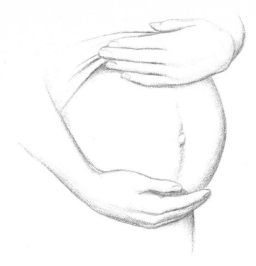

The *linea nigra* is a vertical line that appears along the abdominal midline in some pregnant women.

During pregnancy, you may develop small red elevations with branches extending outward on your skin. These changes are called *vascular spiders, telangiectasis* or *angiomas*. They usually occur on the face, neck, upper chest and arms. After pregnancy they fade, but they may not disappear completely.

The palms of your hands may turn red during pregnancy. The condition is called *palmar erythema* and is fairly common. Palmar erythema is probably caused by increased estrogen and has no other symptoms. It's fine to use lotions on your hands, but the redness may not disappear until after delivery. Vascular spiders and red palms often occur together.

Itchy Skin

Pregnant women often have dry, itchy skin. Moisturizers can help, but you can also help your skin by eating omega-3 fatty acids. They're good for you and baby. Olive oil, almonds and macadamia nuts contain omega-3 fatty acids, so eat these if you don't eat fish.

If you have sensitive skin and experience itchy hives, rub milk of magnesia on the affected area. Rubbing it into the skin helps reduce itching.

Pregnancy can cause moles to appear for the first time or cause existing moles to grow larger and darken. If a mole changes, have your healthcare provider check it.

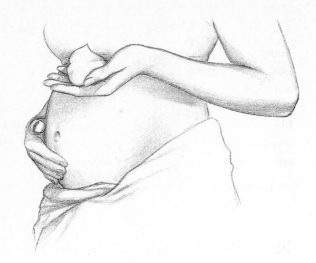

Cream and lotion can help soothe irritated skin, especially on the abdomen.

Pruritis gravidarum is an itching problem that occurs later in pregnancy. About 20% of all pregnant women suffer from it. The itching is harmless but can be annoying. As your uterus grows and fills your pelvis, abdominal skin and muscles stretch to accommodate it. Stretching the skin can cause itching.

Don't scratch—it can make itching worse. Use lotions to help reduce itching; you may use some cortisone creams occasionally. Discuss it with your healthcare provider.

Cholestasis of Pregnancy

A sudden attack of itching on the palms and soles may indicate cholestasis of pregnancy. Itching then spreads to the rest of the body. Cholestasis of pregnancy, also called *intrahepatic cholestasis of pregnancy* (ICP) or *prurigo gravidarum,* is a condition in which a woman has severe itching all over the body, but there's no rash. The condition is rare.

Intense itching all over begins in the third trimester. Usually it's much worse at night. Treatment includes anti-itch creams and UVB light treatments. Symptoms generally disappear a few days after baby's birth.

Plaques of Pregnancy (PUPP)

Some women have a severe, itchy rash of red bumps that begins on the tummy and spreads to the lower body, then to the arms and legs. This is called *plaques of pregnancy, toxemic rash, polymorphic eruption of pregnancy* or *pruritic urticaria pappules* (PUPP). With plaques of pregnancy, your healthcare provider may first rule out scabies.

Maintaining Body Temperature

Your baby relies on you to maintain correct body temperature. An elevated body temperature in a pregnant woman for an extended period may harm a developing fetus. For this reason, avoid hot tubs, saunas, steam rooms and spas. There is some controversy about the safety of using electric blankets/pads during pregnancy. Until we know more, stay warm other ways, such as with down comforters or extra blankets. Or snuggle with your partner. We advise not using an electric blanket or electric warming pad.

PUPP is the most common skin problem pregnant women experience. It may be caused by the skin stretching rapidly, resulting in bumps and inflammation. This condition usually appears in first pregnancies during the third trimester. It often affects women who gain a lot of weight or those who are expecting multiples.

Itching can be so severe that relief may be all you think about, especially at night, which may cause you to lose sleep. PUPP usually resolves within a week after delivery and doesn't usually come back with future pregnancies.

Many treatments have been recommended for relief; talk to your healthcare provider about them. If you can't find relief, ask for some recommendations for home remedies that have worked for other women. If all else fails, a prescription for oral antihistamines, topical steroids or cortisone cream may be needed.

Pemphigoid Gestationis (PG, Herpes Gestationis)

Pemphigoid gestationis (PG) usually begins with blisters around the belly-button. It may occur in the second or third trimester or immediately after birth. The problem begins with sudden onset of intensely itchy blisters on the tummy in about 50% of cases. For the other 50%, blisters can appear anywhere on the body. It often resolves during the last part of pregnancy. It can flare up at delivery or immediately after baby's birth, which happens more than 60% of the time.

The goal of treatment is to relieve itching and to limit blister formation. Oatmeal baths, mild creams and steroids are used. PG usually eases a few weeks after delivery and can recur in your next pregnancies and with oral-contraceptive use.

Dental Care

See your dentist at least once during pregnancy for a regular dental checkup. Tell your dentist you're pregnant. If you need dental work, postpone it until after your first trimester, if possible. You may not be able to wait if you have an infection; an untreated infection could be harmful to you and your baby.

If possible, avoid dental X-rays while you're pregnant. If you must have one, be sure your abdomen and pelvis are completely shielded by a lead apron. Remind the office staff you're pregnant when you check in.

You may develop small nodules on your gums that bleed when you brush your teeth or eat. This condition is called a *pyogenic granuloma* or *pregnancy tumor*. It usually clears up after pregnancy, but don't ignore it if it causes you problems.

Antibiotics or pain medicine may be necessary if you have dental work. If you need medication, consult your pregnancy healthcare provider before taking anything. Many antibiotics and pain medications are OK to take during pregnancy.

Be careful about anesthesia for dental work during pregnancy. Local anesthesia is OK. Avoid gas and general anesthesia when possible. If general anesthesia is necessary, make sure an experienced anesthesiologist who knows you're pregnant administers it.

Gum Disease

You need to take good care of your teeth and gums. Good dental care is important because hormonal changes in pregnancy may cause dental problems. During pregnancy, hormones can make gum problems worse. Increased blood volume can cause gums to swell and make them more prone to infection.

Gingivitis is the first stage of periodontal disease. It appears as swollen, bleeding, reddened gums. It's caused by bacteria growing down into the spaces between the gums and teeth. Experts believe these bacteria can enter the bloodstream, travel to other parts of the body and cause infections in you.

Regular flossing and brushing help prevent gingivitis. Brushing with a power toothbrush, especially one with a 2-minute timer, may clean teeth more thoroughly and may help toughen gums.

Pregnancy may cause sore, bleeding, swollen gums. Gums are more susceptible to irritation during pregnancy and may bleed more often when you brush your teeth. The condition usually clears up by itself after the baby is born. Talk to your dentist if the problem becomes uncomfortable.

Braces during Pregnancy?

It seems people of all ages are getting braces these days, even older women. We've been asked by women about braces for their teeth during pregnancy. They want to know if it's OK to continue wearing braces, and they want to know if they can have braces put on when they're pregnant.

If you wear braces and have morning sickness and vomiting, you'll need to take very good care of your teeth. Brushing is important to clean acid off teeth. When your braces are tightened, you may want to eat soft foods, but that's acceptable for a few days. You can take acetaminophen for any discomfort.

If you're scheduled to have your braces put on, then discover you're pregnant, don't panic. Contact your orthodontist, and tell him or her you're pregnant. Discuss any plans regarding braces with your pregnancy healthcare provider *and* your orthodontist *before* any action is taken!

Concern arises if you need dental X-rays; they may be an essential part of the treatment plan. However, with modern equipment and use of digital radiography, these risks can be reduced. In addition, you may need to have one or more teeth pulled. Tooth extraction by itself may not be dangerous, but the anesthesia necessary to pull a tooth may not be good for you or baby. Your treatment plan must be discussed and agreed upon by your pregnancy healthcare provider and your orthodontist before you begin.

Emotional Changes

It's normal to be emotional about many things during pregnancy. You may cry at the slightest thing, daydream, experience mood swings, feel energy lows and fatigue. These are all normal aspects of pregnancy.

The changes in the levels of estrogen and progesterone in your body during pregnancy can have a big effect on your moods. And at its highest levels, progesterone has a calming effect on the body and may cause forgetfulness and cloudy thinking.

You may feel attached to your developing baby immediately or not for a while. Some women begin to feel attached as soon as they know they are pregnant. For others, it occurs when they hear their baby's heartbeat, at around 12 or 13 weeks, or the first time they feel their baby move, between 16 and 20 weeks.

During the first trimester of pregnancy, hormone production increases to support your body's pregnancy needs. Some women are more sensitive to these changes, especially those who are sensitive to similar hormonal shifts before menstruation. If you become weepy or edgy around your menstrual period, you may experience similar emotions as your body adjusts to pregnancy. Let your partner and other family members know it's normal for a pregnant woman to experience mood swings.

Sometimes during pregnancy, a woman will feel depressed. It can be normal to feel this way for a short time. However, it becomes more serious if you don't come out of it. Be aware you may be experiencing depression if you cry and feel down for longer than 2 weeks, feel worthless or hopeless, or don't take pleasure in most things. See the discussion of depression and depression during pregnancy in Chapter 4.

You may feel more emotional in the third trimester. Mood swings may occur more frequently, and you may be more irritable. You may feel anxious about the upcoming labor and delivery. Try to relax and let go of your feelings. Talk to your partner about how you're feeling and what you are experiencing; ask for his help and understanding. This may be a good time to practice relaxation exercises.

In addition, during your third trimester, you may discover your nesting instinct—the overwhelming urge to clean and get organized. Experts believe this may be caused by an increase in oxytocin.

Feeling Your Baby Move

One of the greatest joys of pregnancy is feeling your baby move inside you. The first time a woman feels her baby move is different for every woman. It can also be different from one pregnancy to another.

Many women describe the first feelings of fetal movement as a gas bubble or fluttering in their abdomen. It may be something you notice for a few days before you realize what it is. Movements become more frequent and identifiable—that's how you'll know what you're feeling is baby moving. You'll feel the movement below your bellybutton.

Some women feel movement as early as 16 weeks, but if it's your first baby, it may be 19 or 20 weeks before you are sure you feel the baby move. At first you probably won't feel your baby move every day—that's normal. As your baby grows, movements become stronger and probably more regular.

Babies' Movements Are Different

The movement of every baby is different. One baby may move less than another. If your baby has been very active, then is very quiet for a long while, you may want to discuss it with your healthcare provider. He or she will determine if there is cause for concern.

• •

When Kerri came in for her 28-week visit, she was tired and concerned. She had been up all night because the baby was kicking her.
She wanted to know if this was OK. Was it a bad sign about the
baby? Could it be moving too much? I reassured her this wasn't bad
and told her I'd rather have a baby move a lot than not enough.

• •

Some women complain their baby is extremely active during the night, and
it keeps them awake. There really isn't much you can do about it, but you can
try changing your position in bed. Avoid exercising just before bed—it may
cause baby to move more.

Taking acetaminophen or relaxing in a warm (not hot) bath may help. Between 20 and 32 weeks of pregnancy, the fetus can move between 200 and 500
times a day, kicking, rolling and wiggling!

Occasionally you might feel pressure from your baby. For relief, rest on
your opposite side for a while. For example, if you feel pressure under your
right ribs, lie on your left side.

Women sometimes ask if some of the pressure they feel low in their pelvis
means the baby is falling out of the birth canal. Your baby can't "fall out." If
you experience this sensation, what you're probably feeling is the pressure of
baby as it moves lower in the birth canal. If this occurs, tell your healthcare
provider about it. A pelvic exam may be done to check how low the baby's
head is.

Monitoring Baby's Movements

A healthcare provider may ask a pregnant woman to monitor the baby's movements if she has had a difficult pregnancy, a previous stillbirth or a medical
condition, such as diabetes. Recording the movements at certain times each
day may provide the healthcare provider with additional information about
the baby's status.

Some Pregnancy Discomforts You May Experience

Along with the many joys of pregnancy, there are some discomforts. Most of
them are minor, although it may not seem that way at the time! At the beginning of pregnancy, you may have the urge to urinate frequently. If you have
to urinate, don't wait to go to the bathroom; it could lead to a urinary-tract
infection.

During pregnancy, your immune system works differently. Your immunity to infection is altered to keep your body from rejecting the fetus. This may make you more susceptible to illness, like the flu. It can also increase a woman's risk of serious illness, such as pneumonia and respiratory problems, if she doesn't take care of herself during pregnancy.

As you progress through pregnancy, you may have to deal with constipation. Toward the end of pregnancy, swollen hands and feet may be a problem along with more frequent heartburn. See the discussion of many of these common discomforts in Chapter 11. Below are various situations you might experience; let's look at some of them and see what you can do to relieve them.

Uterine Tightening

Your uterus tightens and contracts throughout pregnancy. (If you don't feel this, don't worry.) As your uterus grows, you may feel slight cramping or even pain in the lower abdominal area, on your sides; this is normal. However, if contractions are accompanied by bleeding from the vagina, *call your health-care provider immediately!*

Braxton-Hicks contractions during pregnancy are painless, nonrhythmical contractions you may feel when you place your hands on your abdomen. You may also feel them in the uterus itself. These contractions may begin early in pregnancy and continue at irregular intervals throughout pregnancy. They are *not* signs of true labor.

Some women experience tingling, numbness or pressure in the uterine area or abdomen. These feelings are associated with increased pressure as the baby moves lower in the birth canal. To help decrease pressure on pelvic nerves, veins and arteries, lie on your left side.

Round-Ligament Pain

Round ligaments lie on either side of the uterus. As your uterus gets bigger, these ligaments stretch, becoming longer and thicker. Quick movements can overstretch the ligaments, causing round-ligament pain. This is not harmful to you or your baby but can be uncomfortable.

Slow down; be careful about making quick movements. If you feel pain, lie down and rest. Most healthcare providers recommend acetaminophen if the pain bothers you. Tell your healthcare provider if it gets worse.

Urinary Discomfort

One of the first symptoms of early pregnancy is frequent urination. The problem continues off and on throughout pregnancy. You may have to go to the bathroom at night when you never did before. It usually lessens during the second trimester, then returns during the third trimester, when the growing baby puts pressure on the bladder.

Some women experience urinary-tract infections during pregnancy; they are also called *bladder infections, cystitis* and *UTIs.* If you have an infection, take the entire course of antibiotics prescribed for you. See also the discussion of urinary problems in Chapter 4.

You'll do yourself a favor by not "holding" your urine. Empty your bladder as soon as you feel the need. Drink plenty of fluids; unsweetened cranberry juice helps kill bacteria and may help you avoid infections. For some women, urinating after having intercourse is helpful.

Increased Vaginal Discharge

It's normal to notice an increase in vaginal discharge or vaginal secretion during pregnancy. The discharge, called *leukorrhea,* is usually white or yellow and fairly thick; it is not an infection. We believe the discharge is caused by the increased blood flow to the skin and muscles around the vagina.

The discharge that accompanies a vaginal infection is often foul smelling, has a greenish or yellowish color, and causes itching or irritation around or inside the vagina. If you have these symptoms, notify your healthcare provider. Treatment is often possible; many medicinal creams and ointments are safe to use during pregnancy.

Do *not* douche if you have a heavy vaginal discharge during pregnancy; in fact, we do not recommend douching for any reason during pregnancy. Most healthcare providers agree douching can be dangerous during pregnancy because it can cause an infection or bleeding, or even break your bag of waters (rupture your membranes). It can also cause more serious problems, such as an air embolus. An air embolus results when air gets into your circulation from the pressure of the douche. It is rare but can be a serious problem.

> ### Time-Saving, Energy-Saving Tip
> In early and late pregnancy, you may feel the need to urinate more frequently. If you need to use the bathroom when you're out and about, there's usually one very close. Grocery stores, drug stores, discount stores, department stores, malls, convenience stores—nearly all of them have restrooms that are open to the public. If you don't see one, ask the store manager where it is. Don't make yourself wait until you get home.

If you have an annoying discharge, wear a light pad if necessary. Avoid wearing panty hose and nylon underwear; choose underwear with a cotton lining.

Other Common Changes

Pregnancy hormones circulating through your body may trigger changes in your hair. You may notice less hair loss than usual. After your baby is born, the hair you retained during pregnancy usually falls out. If this happens to you, don't worry—you're not going bald!

The same hormones that encourage the growth of your hair also influence your nails. You may have problems keeping your nails filed to a practical length. Enjoy them!

Some women experience increased facial hair during pregnancy. Usually it's not a problem, but check with your healthcare provider if it worries you. Facial hair will probably disappear or decrease after pregnancy, so wait until after baby's birth before making any decisions about permanent hair removal.

Pregnancy hormones can elevate your body temperature slightly, which may lead to greater perspiration. If you perspire heavily, keep fluid levels up to avoid dehydration.

Breast Changes

Your breasts undergo many changes during pregnancy. After about 8 weeks, breasts normally start getting larger. You may notice they are lumpy or nodular. Tenderness, tingling and breast soreness early in pregnancy are common and normal.

The nipple area may change. Before pregnancy, the areola (the dark area surrounding the nipple) is usually pink, but it can turn brown or red-brown and may enlarge during pregnancy and lactation.

During the second trimester, a thin, yellow fluid called *colostrum* is formed; it is the precursor to breast milk. Sometimes it leaks from the breasts or can be expressed by squeezing the nipples. Leaking is normal. Leave your breasts alone; don't express the fluid. Wear breast pads inside your bra if leaking becomes embarrassing.

Some women have *inverted nipples,* which are flat or retract (invert) into the breast. Women with inverted nipples may find breastfeeding more difficult, but it is not impossible.

To determine if you have inverted nipples, place your thumb and index finger on the areola. Gently compress the base of the nipple; if it flattens or retracts into the breast, you have inverted nipples.

Plastic breast shields worn under your bra during the last few weeks of pregnancy create a slight pressure at the base of the nipple that helps draw out the nipple. Ask your healthcare provider for further information.

Lightening

A few weeks before labor begins or at the beginning of labor, the head of your baby begins to enter the birth canal, and your uterus seems to "drop" a bit. This is called *lightening*. Don't be concerned if it happens to you.

A benefit of lightening is it allows you more room to breathe. However, as your baby descends into the birth canal, you may notice more pressure in your pelvis, bladder and rectum, which may be uncomfortable.

Chapter 7

How Your Baby Grows and Develops

While baby is growing inside your uterus, it goes through the most incredible changes of its life. From a few small cells, it grows into a fully developed baby in about 9 months.

The first 13 weeks of pregnancy represent the most critical period of development for the baby. During this time, the fetus is most susceptible to effects from outside influences, such as medications you take or other substances you ingest or are exposed to.

By the end of the first half of your pregnancy—20 weeks—your baby has developed nearly all of its organs. During the last half of pregnancy, these organs mature, and baby grows and gains weight until it is ready to be born.

Your baby goes through an early period of development, called *embryonic development,* which lasts from fertilization through week 8. The *fetal development* period lasts from week 9 until baby is born.

Trimesters of Pregnancy

During the first 8 weeks of pregnancy, your baby is called an *embryo.* During the rest of your pregnancy, the developing baby is referred to as a *fetus.*

Your pregnancy is divided into three 13-week periods called *trimesters.* The first trimester is the one of greatest change for the developing baby. During this time, your baby grows from a collection of cells the size of the head of a pin to a fetus the size of a grapefruit. Organs begin to develop, and your baby begins to look like a baby.

At the beginning of the second trimester, your baby weighs less than an ounce (25g) and is only about 4 inches (11cm) long. By the beginning of the third trimester, it is almost 16 inches (40cm) long and weighs more than 2 pounds (1kg). At delivery, baby will weigh close to 7½ pounds (3.4kg) and be about 21½ inches (54cm) long.

The first trimester is the one of greatest change for the developing baby. Very few, if any, structures in the fetus are formed after 12 weeks of pregnancy. In fact, by the time you miss a period, 80% of baby's organ development has already occurred. This means your baby has formed all of its major organ systems by the end of the first trimester. However, these structures continue to grow and to mature until your baby is born.

When is it determined that I will have a girl or a boy?
At the time of fertilization. Sperm are either male or female—all eggs are female. If a male sperm (carrying a Y chromosome) fertilizes the egg, you will have a boy. If a female sperm (carrying an X chromosome) fertilizes the egg, you will have a girl.

If a baby is born before 38 weeks of pregnancy, he or she is called a *preterm baby*. An infant born between the 38 and 40 weeks of pregnancy is called a *term baby* or a *full-term infant*. A baby delivered after 42 weeks of pregnancy is called a *postterm baby*.

Normal Fetal Development

The Baby's Size

Sometimes women express concern about giving birth to a large baby. Many factors affect how big your baby will be. If you are in good health, have no medical problems, don't gain too much weight and take good care of yourself during pregnancy, you'll probably have an average-size baby. Although weight varies greatly from baby to baby, the average baby at term weighs 7 to 7½ pounds (3.2 to 3.4kg).

Some maternal factors do affect the size of a baby at birth, including hypertension and diabetes, which are more common in older pregnant women. Hypertension during pregnancy can cause intrauterine-growth restriction (IUGR), which results in smaller babies. Diabetes can cause blood-sugar problems. Blood-sugar levels are higher in those with gestational diabetes or mild diabetes that is not under control. Diabetes exposes the baby to higher sugar levels, resulting in a larger baby.

In cases of insulin-dependent diabetes, the result may be a smaller baby. Women with insulin-dependent diabetes may have circulation problems, which can result in IUGR and decreased blood flow to the baby.

The Fetal Environment

Your baby is growing and developing inside a complex system within your body. There are three major parts to this system, and each relies on the other to work together as a complete unit. Your baby's first home consists of the placenta, the umbilical cord and the amniotic sac. Together they provide nourishment, warmth and protection while your baby matures and prepares to live on its own outside your uterus.

The Placenta

The placenta is a soft, round or oval organ that grows with your baby. At 10 weeks, it weighs about ½ ounce (12g); by the time your baby is born, it weighs about 1½ pounds (680g).

When the early pregnancy implants in your uterus, the placenta grows and sends blood vessels into the uterine wall. These blood vessels carry nourishment and oxygen from your blood to baby for your baby's use. Baby's waste products pass back into your bloodstream through these vessels for disposal by your body.

We once believed the placenta acted as a barrier to all outside substances, but we now know this is not the case. In some instances, the placenta cannot keep your baby from being exposed to substances you are exposed to or you ingest. We know alcohol, most medications, other substances (such as nicotine) and many vitamins, minerals and herbs cross the placenta to your baby. This is one reason women should avoid some substances during pregnancy.

The placenta is important to your pregnancy and remains so until the birth of your baby. At that time, when your uterus begins to shrink after your baby is born, the placenta detaches from it and is delivered on its own.

The Umbilical Cord

The umbilical cord is the connection between your baby and the placenta. It is usually about 24 inches (60cm) long. The cord is gray or white, coiled or lumpy, and contains two arteries to carry baby's blood to the placenta, where it absorbs oxygen and nutrients. A vein in the umbilical cord carries blood and nutrients back to the baby.

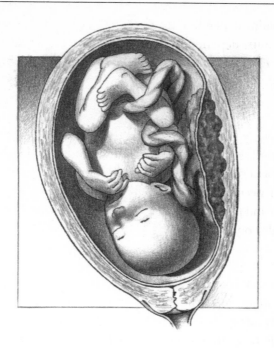

Rarely knots form in an umbilical cord. Experts believe knots form as the baby moves around early in pregnancy. A loop forms in the umbilical cord, and when the baby moves through the loop, a knot is completed. You can't do anything to prevent it.

You may have heard about saving blood from your baby's umbilical cord for future use or for donation for use by others. See the discussion in Appendix A. Talk with your healthcare provider about cord-blood banking if you're interested in learning more.

The Amniotic Sac

The amniotic sac is a bag inside your uterus that contains your baby and the amniotic fluid surrounding it. Early in pregnancy, amniotic fluid comes from the amniotic membrane covering the placenta and cord. Later in pregnancy, the fluid is mainly composed of fetal urine and fluid excreted by fetal lungs.

As your pregnancy progresses, the amount of amniotic fluid produced increases. This continues until close to the time of delivery, when it begins to decrease.

Amniotic fluid keeps the sac from collapsing and enables the baby to move around so muscles and joints can develop. Fluid regulates temperature and cushions the fetus from injury. It also helps a baby's lungs to mature, as fluid passes into and out of fetal lungs when the baby's chest moves in and out in a type of "breathing."

By 21 weeks, the fetal digestive system has developed enough to enable the fetus to swallow amniotic fluid. The fetus absorbs much of the water contained in the swallowed fluid.

Swallowing amniotic fluid may encourage development of the fetal digestive system. It may condition the digestive system to function after birth. By term, a baby may swallow large amounts of amniotic fluid—as much as 17 ounces (500ml) of amniotic fluid in a 24-hour period.

Amniotic fluid is an important gauge of fetal well-being. If you have amniocentesis, amniotic fluid is removed from your uterus for study. The amount of fluid can also be an indication of fetal health; ultrasound is used to evaluate the amount of fluid in the sac. Too much fluid may indicate a malformation in the spinal cord or digestive system. Too little may signal fetal bladder or kidney problems.

The Presence of Meconium

The term *meconium* refers to undigested debris from swallowed amniotic fluid in the fetal digestive system. Meconium is a greenish-black to light-brown substance your baby may pass from its bowels into amniotic fluid. This can happen before or at the time of delivery.

The presence of meconium in amniotic fluid may be caused by fetal stress, although not always. The baby can swallow meconium in the amniotic fluid just before birth or at the time of birth. If inhaled into the lungs, meconium may cause pneumonia or pneumonitis.

Meconium can be detected when your water breaks. Before then, the only way to know about it is by amniocentesis. If meconium is present at delivery, an attempt is made to remove it from the baby's mouth and throat with a small suction tube so the baby won't swallow it.

Can a Baby Hear Inside the Womb?

A baby *can* hear inside the womb. But "hearing" in a fetus is really a matter of feeling vibrations in the skull that are then transmitted to baby's inner ear. It may be similar to living near a busy airport.

The developing baby hears a constant murmur of noises. By the middle of the second trimester, your baby will begin hearing many sounds from you— your beating heart, lungs filling with air, swishing blood and digesting food. Baby hears your voice as it vibrates through your bones. Lower-pitched sounds are heard more clearly in utero than high-pitched ones.

There is evidence that by the third trimester the fetus responds to sounds it hears. Researchers have noted fetal heart rate increases in response to tones heard through the mother's abdomen.

Too much noise may be harmful to an unborn baby. A baby exposed in utero to noise levels between 85 and 95 decibels (common at rock concerts and dance clubs) is three times more likely to suffer from high-frequency hearing loss.

Newborns prefer their mother's voice to a stranger's, which suggests they recognize her voice. Babies also prefer their mother's native language, and they respond strongly to a recording of an intrauterine heartbeat.

Problems for a Developing Fetus

During the embryonic period (the first 8 weeks of baby's growth), the embryo is most susceptible to factors that can interfere with its development. Most birth defects originate during this period.

Some things that have a bad effect (teratogenic) at one point in pregnancy are safe at other times; rubella is one example. The most critical period is the first 13 weeks. If the fetus is infected with rubella during the first trimester, heart defects often occur. Infection later can be less serious for the fetus. The box on page 94 shows critical periods of fetal development.

Your Medication Use

Some medications you take could harm a developing fetus; others are safe at any time during pregnancy. Still others are safe for one part of pregnancy but not advised for another. It's best to avoid medications during pregnancy unless you discuss them with your healthcare provider *before* taking them. See the discussion of medication use during pregnancy that begins in Chapter 14.

> *Time-Saving, Energy-Saving Tip*
>
> Do you sometimes find you just don't have time to wash your hair, but you want it to feel fresher? If you have light-colored hair, an easy way to remove some oil and dirt is to put a little baby powder in your palms (start with a little; add more if you need it), and run hands through your hair. Start at the front, and fluff your hair as you go. Brush briskly to distribute powder through your hair and to remove oil and dirt. Style as usual.

Premature Birth

It's hard to believe, but today a baby born at only 25 weeks gestation may survive. Some of the greatest advances in medicine have been in the care of

Critical Periods of Fetal Development

Time Period	Fetal Development Affected
3 to $5\frac{1}{2}$ weeks	Central nervous system
$3\frac{1}{2}$ to $5\frac{1}{2}$ weeks	Heart
$3\frac{1}{2}$ to 7 weeks	Upper and lower limbs
$3\frac{1}{2}$ to $7\frac{1}{2}$ weeks	Eyes
$3\frac{1}{2}$ to $8\frac{1}{2}$ weeks	Ears
$5\frac{1}{2}$ to 8 weeks	Teeth
$5\frac{1}{2}$ to $8\frac{1}{2}$ weeks	Palate
$6\frac{1}{2}$ to 9 weeks	External genitalia
20 to 36 weeks	Brain and lungs

premature babies. Because of advances in technology, fewer than 10 deaths per 1000 are reported in premature births.

However, babies born extremely early are usually in the hospital a long time and often have serious problems. See the complete discussion of premature labor and birth in Chapter 18 and see Appendix C, which deals with premature babies.

Intrauterine-Growth Restriction (IUGR)

Intrauterine-growth restriction (IUGR) indicates a fetus is small for its gestational age. Weight is below the tenth percentile (in the lowest 10%) for the baby's gestational age. This means 9 out of 10 babies of normal growth are larger.

When gestational age is appropriate—meaning dates are correct and the pregnancy is as far along as expected—and weight falls below the tenth percentile, it's a cause for concern. Growth-restricted fetuses have a higher rate of problems than infants in the normal-weight range.

Diagnosing IUGR can be difficult. Your doctor measures you at each visit to see how your uterus and baby are growing. A problem is usually found by measuring the uterus over a period of time and finding no change. If you measured 10¾ inches (27cm) at 27 weeks gestation and at 31 weeks you measure only 11 inches (28cm), your doctor might become concerned about IUGR and may order tests.

Diagnosing this problem is one important reason to keep all your prenatal appointments. You may not like being measured and weighed at every appointment, but it helps your doctor see if your pregnancy is growing and baby is getting bigger.

IUGR can be diagnosed or confirmed by ultrasound. Ultrasound may also be used to assure baby is healthy and no malformations exist that must be taken care of at birth.

When IUGR is diagnosed, avoid doing anything that could make it worse. Bed rest is another treatment. See the discussion of bed rest in Chapter 17. Resting on your side enables the baby to receive the best blood flow, and better blood flow is the best chance it has to improve growth. If maternal disease causes IUGR, treatment involves improving the mother's health.

An infant with IUGR is at risk of dying before delivery. Avoiding this may involve delivering the baby before it is full term. Infants with IUGR may not tolerate labor; a Cesarean delivery is more likely because of fetal stress. The baby may be safer outside the uterus than inside of it.

• •

Becky said she weighed 9 pounds at birth, and all her brothers and sisters were also big. She was worried her baby would be so big she'd need a Cesarean delivery. I reassured her that her pregnancy growth had been normal and told her it was difficult to estimate the size of the baby. She laughed and relaxed a little when I told her if 100 healthcare providers tried to guess the weight of her baby, the guesses would range from 6 to 8 pounds. When she delivered the baby, it weighed 8 pounds, and Becky did fine.

• •

Causes of IUGR

What causes IUGR? Many conditions can increase the chance of intrauterine-growth restriction or a small fetus. Research shows a woman who has delivered a growth-restricted infant may be more likely to do so again in subsequent pregnancies.

Lifestyle choices can cause IUGR. Smoking can inhibit a baby's growth. The more cigarettes smoked, the smaller the baby. Alcohol and drug use can

How Often Birth Defects Actually Occur

Birth defects aren't as common as you might think. Below is a chart showing how often they occur in North America.

Cleft lip/cleft palate	1 in 730 births
Clubfoot	1 in 1000 births
Congenital heart defects	1 in 125 births
Dislocated hips	1 in 400 births
Down syndrome	1 in 900 births
Neural-tube defects	1 in 1600 births
Pyloric stenosis	1 in 250 births
Sickle-cell disease	1 in 400 births of Black/ African-American babies

also restrict growth. Anything that causes baby to receive less nutrition can be a factor.

A woman who doesn't gain enough weight may have a growth-restricted baby. Research indicates when you eat fewer than 1500 calories a day for an extended time, IUGR may result, so practice good nutrition and eat a healthful diet during pregnancy. Don't restrict normal pregnancy weight gain.

Pre-eclampsia and high blood pressure (hypertension) can have a marked effect on fetal growth. Cytomegalovirus, rubella, kidney disease and other infections may also restrict fetal growth. Maternal anemia may be a cause.

Women who live at high altitudes are more likely to have babies who weigh less. Carrying more than one baby may also be causes of a smaller-than-normal baby.

Other reasons for a small baby, unrelated to IUGR, include the fact that a woman who is small might have a small baby. In addition, an overdue pregnancy can lead to an undernourished, smaller baby. A malformed or abnormal fetus may also be smaller, especially when chromosomal abnormalities are present.

Ways to Deal with IUGR

The greatest risk associated with IUGR is stillbirth (the baby dies before delivery). Delivery of the baby before full term may be required to avoid this serious problem. The following advice may help you avoid giving birth to a low-birthweight baby.

- Gain enough weight during pregnancy. This may mean changing your body image and your eating habits.
- Quit smoking before pregnancy, and avoid second-hand and third-hand smoke.
- Get prenatal care as soon as you find out you're pregnant. Keep all your prenatal appointments.
- Follow your healthcare provider's suggestions and instructions during your pregnancy.
- If you're considering fertility treatment, understand the risks as well as the benefits of ART and multiple births (multiple births often deliver early or prematurely).
- Ask your healthcare provider about screening for lower-genital-tract infections early in pregnancy.
- Wait at least 18 months between delivery of one baby and conception of the next.

Hydrocephalus

Hydrocephalus causes an enlargement of the fetus's head. It occurs in about 1 in 2000 babies and is responsible for about 12% of all severe fetal malformations found at birth.

The organization and development of the baby's brain and central nervous system begin early. Cerebral spinal fluid circulates around the brain and spinal cord; fluid must be able to flow without restriction. If openings are blocked and flow is restricted, it can cause hydrocephalus (sometimes called *water on the brain*). Fluid accumulates, and the baby's head becomes enlarged.

Hydrocephalus is only a symptom, and it can have several causes. Once hydrocephalus is diagnosed, a cause is sought; these include spina bifida, meningomyelocele and omphalocele. Sometimes intrauterine therapy—therapy performed while the fetus is still in the uterus—is possible. See the discussion in the following section.

Prenatal Treatment of the Fetus

In this discussion, "prenatal treatment" refers to treatment of the baby, not treatment of a pregnant woman. Treatment of a fetus in utero has proved to be a valuable tool in saving the lives of some babies.

Cordocentesis

The earliest form of in-utero treatment involved blood transfusions to fetuses with a life-threatening form of anemia. We now have more refined blood-transfusion techniques. Cordocentesis is a transfusion procedure by which blood is introduced directly into the fetal bloodstream through the umbilical cord.

The greatest use of medication in utero is to hasten development of fetal lungs. If you're at high risk for a preterm birth, your healthcare provider may recommend this treatment to ensure that your baby's lungs are adequately developed before birth. If a baby is born before its lungs are mature, it can develop respiratory-distress syndrome.

If your healthcare provider believes you are at risk of delivering your baby before 34 weeks gestation, he or she may prescribe corticosteroid injections. This medication passes from your bloodstream into the fetus's bloodstream, reducing the risk of infant death or the risk of complications, such as breathing problems. It appears to be safe for both mother and fetus.

A less common problem that may be treated before birth with medication is a heart-rhythm disturbance. Medication is usually given to the mother to treat her baby. In some cases, healthcare providers deliver medication directly to the fetus via cordocentesis.

Other problems cordocentesis is used for include inherited inborn errors of body chemistry. Treatment with medication given to the mother has been very successful.

Fetal Surgery

Fetal surgery can treat various problems while a baby is still growing inside the mother. Open surgery or closed-uterus surgery may be performed.

Most surgeries, whether open or closed-uterus, are not performed until at least 28 weeks of pregnancy. Surgeries treat a variety of problems, including urinary-tract blockages, tumors and fluid in the lungs.

With *open surgery*, the surgeon makes a Cesareanlike incision in the mother's abdomen, partially removes the fetus, performs surgery, then returns the fetus to the uterus. Open surgery carries risks for mother and baby. One problem with open surgery is it may stimulate uterine contractions, which can lead to premature birth. The surgery exposes the mother to all the risks of surgery, including anesthesia problems and infections. After open surgery, the mother must have a Cesarean delivery when it is time to deliver the baby.

Closed-uterus procedures are more common than open surgeries. With this surgery, miniature cameras guide a needle-thin fiberoptic instrument into the fetus's body while the fetus remains inside the uterus. The most successful closed-uterus surgeries are associated with the opening of urinary-tract blockages.

Chapter 8

Tests for You and Your Baby

Tests for you and your baby during pregnancy are an important part of prenatal care. From amniocentesis to weight checks, every test provides your healthcare provider with important information. He or she uses the information to plan the best course of treatment for you and your developing baby. Tests can also help reassure you that baby is doing well as it develops.

The first challenge of pregnancy may be figuring out if you really are pregnant! Before you invest in a home pregnancy test or go to your healthcare provider's office to have a pregnancy test, look for the following signs and symptoms of pregnancy:

- missed menstrual period
- nausea, with or without vomiting
- fatigue
- breast changes and breast tenderness
- metallic taste in your mouth
- frequent urination
- food aversions or food cravings
- new sensitivity or feelings in your pelvic area

At-Home Tests

Home Pregnancy Tests

Your healthcare provider may ask you to take a home pregnancy test when you miss a period to help determine if you're pregnant. These tests are so accurate that your healthcare provider may rely on them as an initial screening for pregnancy. Sometimes a woman misses a period because of stress, excessive physical exertion or dieting, not pregnancy. If the test is positive, make your first prenatal appointment.

Home pregnancy kits were first introduced in 1976; in 1999 the average price was between $15 and $20. Tests in 2012 average between $6 to $10. Some even cost as little as $1—and they're accurate. A study compared pregnancy tests from dollar stores with tests used in doctors' offices and clinics. It found the dollar-store tests were as sensitive as more expensive tests.

Tests detect the presence of *human chorionic gonadotropin* (HCG), a hormone of early pregnancy. Pregnancy tests can show positive results even before you miss a menstrual period. Most tests are positive 7 to 10 days after you conceive! However, most healthcare providers recommend you wait until you miss your period before taking a test to save you money and emotional energy.

Some at-home pregnancy tests can pick up lower levels of HCG than others. Some are more sensitive. For women who want to test early, these products may be good choices.

The best time to take a home pregnancy test is the *first day after* your missed period or any time thereafter. If you take the test too early, you may get a result that says you aren't pregnant when you really are! This happens for about 50% of the women who take the test *very early*.

Gender-Prediction Test Kits

You may have seen gender tests advertised that use your blood or a urine sample to determine baby's sex. They are often offered on the Internet. But experts agree tests available may not offer accurate results.

One over-the-counter test claims it can predict your baby's sex as early as 10 weeks of pregnancy. Called the *IntelliGender's Gender Prediction Test,* it uses a urine test to provide immediate results that indicate baby's gender based on a color match. Green indicates boy, and orange indicates girl. However, before you rush off to buy the test, you should realize test results are actually only about 80% accurate. They only indicate the *possibility* of determining whether baby is a girl or a boy.

To do the test, you use your first morning urine. You need to avoid sexual relations for at least 48 hours before taking the test, and you can't be taking any hormones, such as progesterone.

The *Pink or Blue* test is another at-home test developed to determine baby's gender by examining DNA of the mom-to-be. Research has shown fetal DNA can be found in a mother's bloodstream. A woman sends a small sample of her blood to the lab, and results of the test (boy or girl) are sent to the parents-to-be. The makers of the product claim the test is 95% accurate and can predict a baby's sex as early as 6 weeks after conception (8 weeks of pregnancy).

Some medical authorities are concerned some couples may consider ending a pregnancy because of baby's sex based on the result of these tests. If you have questions or concerns, discuss them with your healthcare provider.

Tests You May Have

Tests at Your First Prenatal Visit

Your healthcare provider will probably order a battery of tests during your first or second visit. These may include the following:

- a complete blood count (CBC) to check iron stores and to check for infections
- urinalysis and urine culture
- a test for syphilis
- cervical cultures, as indicated
- rubella titers, for immunity against rubella
- blood type
- Rh-factor
- a test for hepatitis-B antibodies
- alpha-fetoprotein
- Pap smear

The results of these tests give your healthcare provider information he or she needs to provide the best care for you. For example, if testing shows you have never had rubella (German measles) and you never received the rubella vaccine, you know you need to avoid exposure during this pregnancy and to receive the vaccine before your next pregnancy.

Later in pregnancy, your healthcare provider may repeat some tests or order new tests. For example, 28 weeks of pregnancy is the best time to pick up blood-sugar problems.

Quantitative HCG Test

A special type of pregnancy test, called a *quantitative HCG test,* is a blood test done in the first trimester. Your healthcare provider may order it if there is concern about miscarriage or ectopic pregnancy. The test measures the hormone HCG (human chorionic gonadotropin), which your body produces early in pregnancy in rapidly increasing amounts. Two or more tests done a few days apart identify the change in the amount of the hormone. You may also have an ultrasound.

Routine Tests

At every prenatal visit, your healthcare provider will weigh you and check your blood pressure. Simple as they are, these two tests provide a great deal of information. Not gaining enough weight, or gaining too much, can indicate problems.

High blood pressure can be significant during pregnancy, especially as you near your due date. By taking your blood pressure throughout pregnancy, your healthcare provider establishes what is normal for you. Changes in blood pressure readings alert him or her to potential problems.

As your baby grows, your healthcare provider measures you to check to see how much your uterus has grown since your last visit. He or she also listens to the fetal heartbeat.

Third-Trimester Tests

If you're like most women, your pregnancy progresses normally and you're in good health in your third trimester. At each prenatal visit, growth of the uterus is measured. Your healthcare provider also checks your weight and blood pressure and may perform a urinalysis. Checking your blood pressure and urine are important during the last trimester to help detect *pre-eclampsia,* a condition more common in first-time pregnancies and in older pregnant women. See the discussion of pre-eclampsia in Chapter 17.

In this last trimester, you may have an internal examination to see whether your cervix has begun to thin and dilate, to evaluate the size of your pelvis and to see if your baby is in the head-down position. You will usually have this examination in the last few weeks of pregnancy. However, it can't predict when you will go into labor.

Other tests may be ordered if your baby is postterm (overdue), your pregnancy is considered high risk or your physician believes your baby might have a problem. Possible tests include a nonstress test (NST), contraction stress test (CST), ultrasound and a biophysical profile (BPP). These tests help determine the well-being of mother and baby, or the kind of problem you or your baby may be experiencing.

> ### Time-Saving, Energy-Saving Tip
> Cleaning up the kitchen can be tiring, especially during pregnancy. To avoid unnecessary boil overs when cooking, try this neat trick. Place a toothpick between the pan and the lid to let steam escape so nothing boils over. Or place a wooden spoon across the top of an open pan. No messes to clean up!

Specialized Tests You May Have

Ultrasound

An *ultrasound* exam may be one of the most exciting tests you have during pregnancy! You and your partner can actually see your growing baby. The test is a valuable tool for your healthcare provider because it enables him or her to check for many details of fetal development. (*Ultrasound, sonogram* and *sonography* refer to the same test.)

Most healthcare providers routinely perform ultrasound exams on their pregnant patients. Some healthcare providers perform ultrasounds only when there is a problem.

Ultrasound exams pose no threat to you or your baby. The possibility of adverse effects has been studied many times without any evidence of problems.

Ultrasound gives a 2-dimensional picture of the developing embryo or fetus (see page 107 for information on 3-dimensional ultrasounds). It involves use of high-frequency sound waves made by applying an alternating current to a device called a *transducer*. The transducer sends and receives sound waves.

> **When can I have an ultrasound to find out if I'm having a girl or a boy?**
> Usually by 18 weeks, ultrasound can reliably determine if you're carrying a boy or a girl.

As you lie on your back, the transducer moves over gel that has been spread on your abdomen. The transducer picks up echoes of sound waves as they bounce off the baby, then a computer translates them into a picture, similar to radar used by airplanes or ships to create a picture of the terrain under a night sky or on the ocean floor.

Before the test, you may be asked to drink 32 ounces (1 quart; almost 1 liter) of water. The water makes it easier for the technician to see your uterus. The bladder lies in front of the uterus; when your bladder is full, the uterus is pushed up and out of the pelvic area and is more visible on the ultrasound.

For information on tests you may have during labor and delivery, see Chapter 18.

When your bladder is empty, your uterus lies farther down in the pelvis and is harder to see.

An ultrasound can help confirm or determine your due date, determine if there is one baby or multiples and determine if major physical characteristics of the fetus are normal. You can have an ultrasound any time during pregnancy.

Whether you have an ultrasound during your pregnancy depends on several factors, including problems such as bleeding, previous problem pregnancies and your insurance coverage. If your pregnancy is high risk, you may have several ultrasound exams.

A healthcare provider may order an ultrasound to learn vital information about a fetus's brain, spine, face, major organs, limbs or sex. An ultrasound can show where the placenta is, so it is used with other tests, such as amniocentesis. The test can also provide information on fetal growth, the condition of the umbilical cord and the amount of amniotic fluid in the uterus.

Healthcare providers perform an ultrasound for many reasons. Some of the more common reasons include the following:

- to identify an early pregnancy
- to show the size and growth rate of the embryo or fetus
- to measure the fetal head, abdomen or femur to determine the duration of pregnancy
- to identify some fetuses with Down syndrome
- to identify fetal abnormalities, such as hydrocephalus
- to identify the location, size and maturity of the placenta
- to identify placental abnormalities
- to detect an IUD
- to differentiate between miscarriage, ectopic pregnancy and normal pregnancy

If you are at least 18 weeks pregnant when you have an ultrasound, you may be able to determine the sex of your baby, but don't count on it. It isn't always possible to tell the sex if the baby has its legs crossed or is in a breech presentation.

Ultrasound at around 20 weeks may be done to determine if the placenta has attached normally and is healthy. If you have an ultrasound exam in the third trimester, your healthcare provider is looking for particular information. Performed later in pregnancy, this test can accomplish many things:

- evaluate the baby's size and growth
- determine the cause of vaginal bleeding
- determine the cause of vaginal or abdominal pain

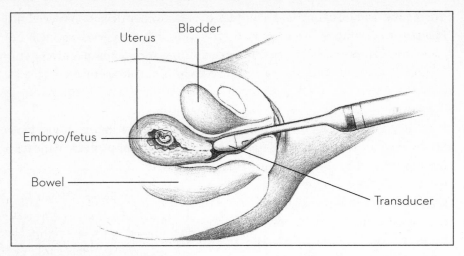

Vaginal probe ultrasound.

- detect some fetal malformations
- monitor a high-risk pregnancy
- measure the amount of amniotic fluid
- determine which delivery method to use
- determine maturity of the placenta

Breathing movements, body movements and muscle tone can be checked. If the baby is too big, it may need to be delivered by Cesarean delivery. If the baby is very small, other decisions can be made.

The cost of an ultrasound varies. An average cost is about $150 but can range from $200 to $500. With many insurance plans, ultrasound is an extra—not part of the normal fee for prenatal care. Ask about cost and coverage *before* having an ultrasound. Some insurance plans require preapproval for the test.

You may be able to get a CD or DVD of your ultrasound; ask about it when your test is scheduled to find out what you need to bring. An ultrasound may also include black-and-white photos you can keep. You can usually take your partner with you to the exam, so arrange to have the ultrasound when he can join you. You may want others to come, such as your mother or older children. Ask if that is possible when you schedule your ultrasound.

Vaginal Ultrasound

A *vaginal probe ultrasound* or *transvaginal sonography* may be helpful in evaluating problems early in pregnancy, such as possible miscarriage or ectopic pregnancy. The instrument (probe transducer or other device) is placed just inside the opening of the vagina; it does not touch the cervix and will not cause bleeding or miscarriage. This type of ultrasound sometimes gives better information earlier in pregnancy than an abdominal ultrasound.

3-Dimensional Ultrasound

Pictures are so clear with a *3-dimensional ultrasound* the image almost looks like a photograph. This ultrasound provides detailed, clear pictures of the fetus in the womb. For the pregnant woman, the test is almost the same as a regular ultrasound. The difference is that computer software translates the picture into a 3-D image. This advanced ultrasound is used when the healthcare provider suspects abnormalities and wants to take a closer look.

> ### Time-Saving, Energy-Saving Tip
>
> With the addition of a new baby, you may need additional hanging space in a closet. Short of adding on a new room, what can you do? One quick solution is to raise the existing closet rod 12 to 24 inches, then hang another rod about 2 to 3 feet below it. Presto—you've doubled your closet space!

Amniocentesis

Amniocentesis is a test done on fetal cells and is often offered to women over 35 or women whose screening-tests results are abnormal. Most women who have amniocentesis are being screened for chromosomal defects, such as Down syndrome, Turner's syndrome or neural-tube defects (spina bifida). The test can pick up some specific gene defects, including cystic fibrosis and sickle-cell disease. Other problems the test can identify include:

- skeletal diseases, such as osteogenesis imperfecta
- fetal infections, such as herpes or rubella
- central-nervous-system disease, such as anencephaly
- blood diseases, such as erythroblastosis fetalis
- chemical problems or deficiencies, such as cystinuria or maple-syrup-urine disease
- fetal sex, if sex-specific problems, such as hemophilia or Duchenne muscular dystrophy, must be identified

Amniocentesis may be performed to determine if the baby of an Rh-negative woman is having problems. It may also be done to determine fetal lung maturity before delivery.

It may be a good idea to have amniocentesis if your healthcare provider suggests it, even if you would not end your pregnancy should results indicate a problem. If a problem is detected, you and your family can prepare for it.

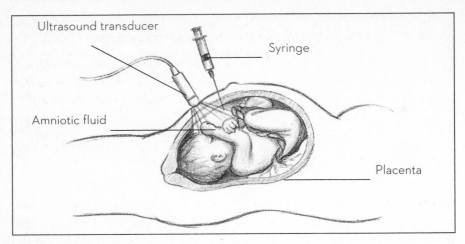

Amniocentesis near the end of pregnancy can determine if a baby's lungs are mature.

You can gather information about the problem so you and your family are informed about what lies ahead.

The test may also indicate the need for additional tests to determine if the fetus might have other problems. If any are found, steps can be taken to ensure the delivery goes smoothly and any necessary procedures are done as soon after the birth as possible.

Not every pregnant woman needs amniocentesis. It is often performed on women who fit any of the following criteria:

- they will deliver after their 35th birthday
- they have had a previous baby with a birth defect
- they have a family history of birth defects
- they have a birth defect themselves
- their partner has a birth defect

Ultrasound is used to locate a pocket of fluid where the fetus and placenta are out of the way. Skin over the mother's abdomen is cleaned and numbed with a local anesthetic. A needle is passed through the abdomen into the uterus, and fluid is withdrawn with a syringe. About 1 ounce (30g) of amniotic fluid is needed to perform the tests. The test can identify about 40 fetal abnormalities.

Bleeding from the fetus to the mother can occur during amniocentesis, which can be a problem because fetal and maternal blood are separate and

Amniocentesis in a Multiple Pregnancy

In a multiple pregnancy, genetic testing can be a complicated procedure. For example, in most multiple pregnancies, each baby lies in its own sac. Abdominal punctures are required to withdraw fluid from each sac, which can increase the risk of complications. In the case of one sac shared by the two babies, only one puncture is necessary.

may be different types. This is a particular risk to an Rh-negative mother carrying an Rh-positive baby (see the discussion in Chapter 17) and may cause isoimmunization. An Rh-negative woman should receive RhoGAM at the time of amniocentesis to prevent isoimmunization.

Over 95% of women who have amniocentesis learn their baby does *not* have the disorder the test was done for. Fetal loss from amniocentesis complications is estimated to be less than 3%. Discuss the risks with your healthcare provider before the test. Only someone with experience, such as a physician at a medical center, should perform the test.

A disadvantage of amniocentesis is the time at which it is performed. Amniocentesis is usually performed for prenatal evaluation at around 16 weeks of pregnancy, making termination of a pregnancy (if that is what the woman chooses) more difficult. Some healthcare providers perform the test at around 11 or 12 weeks. However, not everyone agrees this early use is beneficial.

Alpha-Fetoprotein Testing

The *alpha-fetoprotein (AFP)* test is a blood test done on the mother-to-be. As your baby grows inside you, it produces alpha-fetoprotein in its liver. Some alpha-fetoprotein crosses fetal membranes and enters your circulation. It's possible to measure AFP by drawing your blood; too much or too little alpha-fetoprotein in your blood can be a sign of fetal problems.

Measurement of the amount of alpha-fetoprotein in your blood can help your healthcare provider predict problems in your baby, such as spina bifida or Down syndrome. However, AFP detects only about 25% of Down syndrome cases. If Down syndrome may be indicated, additional detailed diagnostic tests will probably be ordered.

The AFP test is not done on all pregnant women, although it is required in some states. It is not used routinely in Canada. AFP is often used with other tests as part of a multiple-marker test—a triple-screen test or a quad-screen test; see the discussions below. If the test isn't offered to you, ask about it. There is relatively little risk, and it tells your doctor how your fetus is growing and developing.

The AFP test is usually performed between 16 and 18 weeks of pregnancy. Timing is important and must be correlated to the gestational age of your pregnancy and to your weight. One important use of the test is to help a woman decide whether to have amniocentesis.

If AFP detects a possible problem, more definitive testing may be ordered. An elevated alpha-fetoprotein level can indicate problems with the fetus, such as spina bifida or anencephaly. An association has been found between a low level of alpha-fetoprotein and Down syndrome. AFP can detect the following:

- neural-tube defects
- severe kidney or liver disease
- esophageal or intestinal blockage
- Down syndrome
- urinary obstruction
- osteogenesis imperfecta (fragility of the baby's bones)

If your alpha-fetoprotein level is abnormal, your doctor may choose to do a higher-level ultrasound, amniocentesis or CVS to look for suspected problems. This ultrasound may also help determine how far along in pregnancy you are.

One problem with the AFP test is a high number of false-positive results; that is, the results say there is a problem when there isn't one. If 1000 women take the AFP test, 40 test results come back as "abnormal." Of those 40, only one or two women actually have a problem.

If you have an AFP test and your test result is abnormal, don't panic. You'll take another test and have an ultrasound. Results from these second tests should give you a clearer answer. Be sure you understand what "false-positive" and "false-negative" test results mean. Ask your healthcare provider to explain what each result can mean to you.

Multiple-Marker Tests

Tests that go beyond alpha-fetoprotein testing are available to help your healthcare provider determine if your child might have Down syndrome and to rule out other problems in your pregnancy. They are called *multiple-marker* tests and include the triple-screen test and the quad-screen test.

The Triple-Screen Test

The *triple-screen* test helps identify problems using three blood components—alpha-fetoprotein, human chorionic gonadotropin (HCG) and a form of estrogen produced by the placenta called *unconjugated estriol.*

Abnormal levels of these three blood chemicals can indicate Down syndrome. For older mothers, the detection rate is higher than 60%, with a false-positive rate of nearly 25%. Abnormal results of a triple-screen test are usually double-checked with ultrasound and amniocentesis.

The Quad-Screen Test

The *quad-screen* test is similar to the triple-screen but adds a fourth measurement—the blood level of *inhibin-A,* a chemical produced by the ovaries and the placenta. This fourth measurement raises the sensitivity of the standard triple-screen test by 20% in determining if a fetus has Down syndrome. The quad-screen test identifies almost 80% of fetuses with Down syndrome. It has a false-positive rate of 5%.

Chorionic Villus Sampling (CVS)

Chorionic villus sampling (CVS) analyzes chorionic villus cells, which eventually become the placenta. The test detects genetic abnormalities; sampling is done early in pregnancy. The advantage of CVS is that a healthcare provider can diagnose a problem earlier in pregnancy.

The test can be done at 9 to 11 weeks instead of 16 to 18 weeks, as with amniocentesis. Some women choose CVS so they can make a decision about their pregnancy earlier. If a woman decides to terminate a pregnancy, the procedure may carry fewer risks when performed earlier in pregnancy.

To perform the test, an instrument is placed through the cervix or through the abdomen to remove a small piece of tissue from the placenta. If your doctor recommends CVS, ask about its risks. The test should be performed only by someone experienced with the technique. The risk of miscarriage is small—between 1 and 2%—and the test is considered as safe as amniocentesis. If you have CVS and are Rh-negative, you should receive RhoGAM after the procedure.

A special listening machine, called a *doppler,* magnifies the sound of the baby's heartbeat so it can be heard. It's usually possible to hear the baby's heartbeat around your 12-week visit.

Fetoscopy

Because of advances in fiber optics, we are able to look at a fetus or placenta as early as 10 weeks into its development. Ultrasound cannot provide the same degree of detail. *Fetoscopy* enables the healthcare provider to look through a fetoscope to detect even subtle abnormalities and problems.

The healthcare provider makes a small incision in the mother's abdomen and places a small scope through the abdomen and uterus. The healthcare provider uses the fetoscope to examine the fetus and placenta.

The test is specialized and is not done very often. It is usually recommended if you have given birth to a child with a birth defect that cannot be detected by any other test. If your healthcare provider suggests fetoscopy to you, discuss it with him or her. The risk of miscarriage is 3 to 4%. Only someone experienced at it should do the procedure.

Fetal Fibronectin (fFN)

It can be difficult to determine if a woman is at risk of delivering a preterm baby. Many symptoms of preterm labor mimic various discomforts of pregnancy. However, a test is available that can help doctors make this determination.

Fetal fibronectin (fFN) is a protein found in the amniotic sac and fetal membranes. After 22 weeks of pregnancy, fFN is not normally present until around week 38.

When present in cervical-vaginal secretions of a pregnant woman after 22 weeks (before week 38), it indicates increased risk for preterm delivery. If absent, risk of premature labor is low, and the woman probably won't deliver within the next 2 weeks. fFN can rule out early delivery with 99% accuracy.

The test is performed like a Pap smear. A swab of vaginal secretions is taken from the top of the vagina, behind the cervix. It is sent to the lab, and results are available within 24 hours.

Percutaneous Umbilical Blood Sampling (PUBS)

Percutaneous umbilical blood sampling (PUBS), also called *cordocentesis,* is a test done on the fetus while it is still inside the uterus. The test has improved the diagnosis and treatment of Rh-incompatibility and other blood disorders. Results can be available within a few days, but it carries a slightly higher risk of miscarriage than amniocentesis does.

Guided by ultrasound, a fine needle is inserted through the mother's abdomen into a tiny vein in the umbilical cord of the fetus. A small sample of the baby's blood is removed for analysis. Blood disorders, infections and Rh-incompatibility are detectable with PUBS.

If the fetus is found to be Rh-positive and its mother is Rh-negative, health-care providers have time to give it a blood transfusion, if necessary. This procedure can help prevent life-threatening anemia that can develop if the mother is isoimmunized (she has antibodies that attack her baby's blood). (See the discussion of Rh-compatibility in Chapter 17.) If you are Rh-negative, you should receive RhoGAM after this procedure.

Tests for Blood-Sugar Levels

Many doctors test every pregnant woman for diabetes, usually around the end of the second trimester. Testing is particularly important if you have a family history of diabetes. Blood tests used to diagnose diabetes are a fasting blood-sugar and glucose-tolerance test (GTT).

For a *fasting blood-sugar test,* you eat your normal meal the evening before the test. In the morning, before eating anything, you go to the lab and have a blood test done. A normal result indicates diabetes is unlikely. An abnormal result (a high level of sugar in the blood) needs further study.

Further study involves the *glucose-tolerance test (GTT).* You must fast after dinner the night before this test. In the morning at the lab, you are given a solution with a measured amount of sugar in it to drink. It is similar to a bottle of soda pop but doesn't taste as good. After you drink the solution, blood is drawn at predetermined intervals, usually at 30 minutes, 1 hour and 2 hours and sometimes even 3 hours. Drawing the blood at intervals gives an indication of how your body handles sugar. If you need treatment, your healthcare provider can devise a plan for you.

Nuchal Translucency Screening

Nuchal translucency screening is a test to help healthcare providers and pregnant women find out if a fetus has Down syndrome. Results are available in the first trimester.

A detailed ultrasound allows the doctor to measure the space behind baby's neck. When combined with blood tests, the results of these *two* tests (ultrasound and blood test) can be used to predict a woman's risk of having a baby with Down syndrome.

Because results are available early, a couple may make earlier decisions regarding the pregnancy, if they choose to do so. When this test is done between 10 and 16 weeks of pregnancy, it accurately detects Down syndrome more than 95% of the time. In fact, it is the single-most powerful screening tool for Down syndrome. One study showed that doing this test in women with a higher risk of having a baby with Down syndrome increased the rate of detection of Down syndrome from 60 to 80%.

Fetal MRI

Ultrasound is the standard test used to diagnose birth defects and other fetal anomalies. It is usually the first test used, but there are some limitations to ultrasound evaluation. If a pregnancy involves an obese mother-to-be, decreased fluid around the baby (oligohydramnios) or an abnormal fetal position, ultrasound may not reveal problems. In addition, its optimal use is in midpregnancy, so earlier or later use of the test may not be as helpful.

Another test in use has fewer limitations—fetal MRI. Fetal MRI (magnetic resonance imaging) provides excellent tissue contrast and is not limited by maternal obesity or fetal position. This test is most helpful when findings from ultrasound are unclear or cannot be seen clearly.

Unlike X-ray and CT scans, MRI does not use ionizing radiation. Several studies have demonstrated the safety of MRI on human embryos and fetuses. To be cautious, MRI is still not advised during the first trimester. The test is used to identify conjoined twins, a diaphragmatic hernia, oligohydramnios, various large tumors, diagnosing fetuses with brain abnormalities and masses in the neck.

It's important to note ultrasound is more widely available and less expensive than MRI. Ultrasound is still the first choice for diagnosing fetal problems. However, MRI can be helpful in special situations, as mentioned above.

Instant Risk Assessment (IRA)

A screening test for Down syndrome, called *IRA* (Instant Risk Assessment), offers women faster results at an earlier stage in pregnancy and has a 91% accuracy rate. IRA has two parts, a blood test and an ultrasound. Women receive a collection kit from a provider or hospital.

The mother-to-be pricks her finger and marks a card in the kit with her blood, which is sent to an IRA lab for analysis. It is tested for levels of HCG (human chorionic gonadotropin) and a substance called *pregnancy-associated plasma protein A*. Both are produced by the placenta and help maintain the uterine lining, but elevated levels have been associated with Down syndrome.

The second part of the test, the ultrasound, is a nuchal translucency exam, in which an ultrasound measures the space on the back of the baby's neck.

The more space in this area, the higher the chance that baby has Down syndrome. Your doctor can schedule the ultrasound.

Cystic Fibrosis Screening Tests

Cystic fibrosis (CF) is a genetic disorder that causes digestive and breathing problems. It causes the body to produce sticky mucus that builds up in the lungs, pancreas and other organs, which can lead to respiratory and digestive problems. Those with the disorder are usually diagnosed early in life.

We are now able to determine whether there is a risk of having a baby with CF. You and your partner can be tested before pregnancy to determine if either of you are carriers. A test can also be done in the first and/or second trimester of pregnancy to see if the baby has cystic fibrosis.

For your baby to have cystic fibrosis, *both* parents must be carriers. If only one parent is a carrier, the baby will not have CF. A carrier does *not* have CF. You could be a carrier even if no one in your family has CF. You could also be a carrier if you already have children and they do not have CF. Your chance of carrying the gene for cystic fibrosis increases if someone in your family has CF or is a known carrier.

Screening for cystic fibrosis is often part of genetic counseling. One test available is called *Cystic Fibrosis (CF) Complete Test.* It can identify more than 1000 mutations of the CF gene. A panel that screens for 23 CF mutations is the recommended test.

If you and your partner are Caucasian, the American College of Obstetricians and Gynecologist (ACOG) recommends CF screening. Cystic fibrosis is the most common birth defect in this group. Screening is also recommended for those at higher risk for CF, such as Ashkenazi Jews. The screening test uses a blood sample or a saliva sample.

If both you and your partner carry the CF gene, your baby has a 25% chance of having cystic fibrosis. Your developing baby can be tested for CF during your pregnancy with chorionic villus sampling around week 10 or 11 of pregnancy. Amniocentesis may also be used to test the baby.

Some CF gene mutations cannot be detected by the current test; you could be told you don't carry the gene when in fact you do. The test cannot detect all CF mutations because researchers don't know all of them at this time. However, unknown CF gene mutations are rare.

If you believe cystic fibrosis is a serious concern or if you have a family history of the disease, talk to your healthcare provider. Testing is a personal decision you and your partner must make.

Many couples choose not to have the test because it would not change what they would do during the pregnancy. In addition, they do not want to expose the mother-to-be or the developing fetus to the risks of CVS or amniocentesis. However, testing is recommended so care can be provided to baby immediately after birth if he or she has CF.

Jewish Genetic Disorders

A group of medical conditions considered genetic disorders occur more commonly among Ashkenazi Jews, who are of eastern European descent. About 95% of the Jewish population in North America is of Ashkenazi heritage. Some of the diseases found in this group also affect Sephardi Jews and non-Jews; however, the conditions are more common among Ashkenazi Jews— sometimes 20 to 100 times more common.

Much research has been done to determine why these disorders occur more frequently in the Ashkenazi Jewish population. Researchers believe two processes are at work—the founder effect and genetic drift.

With the *founder effect*, genes that cause certain problems just happened to occur among the founders of the Ashkenazi Jews. They emigrated to eastern Europe around 70 A.D. Before they left Palestine, these disorders were probably as common among all other groups in the area. When the Ashkenazi Jews settled together in Europe, they carried these genes.

Because Ashkenazi Jews do not often marry outside their faith or community, the genes were not spread among other communities. This is called *genetic drift*. The presence of the genes was not decreased by introducing genes from outside the community, so many of the problems remained within this group.

Some diseases and conditions occur within other Jewish groups, such as Sephardi Jews. Sephardi Jews are of Spanish or Portuguese descent, and particular disorders occur within this group, probably for the same reasons they occur among Ashkenazi Jews.

Various conditions are considered "Jewish genetic disorders." However, we know people of other ethnic backgrounds can inherit some of these diseases. Some diseases and conditions are not usually found outside the various Jewish populations and are rare in the general population. These disorders include:

- Tay-Sachs disease
- Bloom syndrome
- factor-XI deficiency
- familial dysautonomia (Riley-Day syndrome)
- Fanconi anemia (Group C)

- Gaucher disease
- glucose-6 phosphate dehydrogenase deficiency (G6PD)
- glycogen storage disease, type III
- mucolipidosis IV
- Niemann-Pick disease (Type A)
- nonclassical adrenal hyperplasia
- nonsyndromic hearing loss
- torsion dystonia

Screening tests are available for some of the diseases listed above. One test targets 11 genetic diseases and is designed for couples in which one or both members are of Ashkenazi or Sephardi Jewish descent. Many diseases can be identified before pregnancy or in early pregnancy. Discuss testing with your healthcare provider if you're interested.

Pap Smear

Often on your first prenatal visit, you will have a Pap smear if it's been a year or more since your last test. If you've had a normal Pap smear in the last few months, you won't need another one.

A Pap smear is done to look for abnormal cells, called *precancerous, dysplastic* or *cancerous* cells, in the cervical area. The goal of a Pap smear is to discover problems early so they can be dealt with more easily. If you have an abnormal Pap smear, it usually identifies the presence of an infection, a precancerous condition or some other condition.

Prenatal Genetic Tests for Specific Problems

Prenatal genetic tests are being used to test for specific problems. Some of the conditions they test for are discussed here. Familial Mediterranean fever is a disease found in people of Armenian, Arabic, Turkish and Sephardic Jewish background. Prenatal testing helps identify carriers of the recessive gene so diagnosis can be made quickly in a newborn to avoid a potentially fatal medical problem. Canavan's disease is most commonly found in people of Ashkenazi Jewish background. Canavan's disease screening can be combined with Tay-Sachs screening to determine if a fetus is affected. Congenital deafness is a condition caused by the connexin-26 gene. If a couple has a family history of inherited deafness, this test may identify the problem before birth. When identified before birth, measures can be taken to manage the problem immediately.

Women who deliver vaginally may see a change in abnormal Pap smears. One study showed that 60% of a group of women who were diagnosed with high-grade squamous intra-epithelial lesions in the cervix before giving birth had normal Pap smears after their babies were born. Researchers believe dilatation of the cervix during labor may slough off the precancerous cells or the baby may scrape them off as it moves down the birth canal.

If your Pap smear reveals any signs of an infection, it is treated immediately. If the first test reveals a precancerous condition, called *dysplasia,* the next step is usually a *colposcopy.* In a colposcopy, a microscope is used to examine your cervix to look for abnormal areas. If any are found, a sample of the tissue is removed, a procedure called a *biopsy.* Usually your healthcare provider won't perform a biopsy until after your pregnancy. An abnormal Pap smear during pregnancy is a special situation and must be handled carefully.

Home Uterine Monitoring

Some women are monitored during pregnancy with *home uterine monitoring.* This monitor records a pregnant woman's contractions while she is at home, then transmits the information by telephone to her healthcare provider. It is used to identify women at risk of premature labor.

Kick Counts

As baby gets bigger, kicks get stronger. Toward the end of pregnancy, you may be asked to record how often you feel baby move. This test is done at home and is called a *kick count.* It provides reassurance about baby's well-being; this information is similar to that learned by a nonstress test.

Your healthcare provider may use one of two common methods. The first is to count how many times the baby moves in an hour. The other is to note how long it takes for baby to move 10 times. Usually you can choose when you want to do the test. After eating a meal is a good time because baby is often more active then.

Pelvic Exam

Your healthcare provider will usually perform a pelvic examination at the first or second prenatal visit and again in late pregnancy. In early pregnancy, it helps evaluate the size of the uterus and determine how far along you are in pregnancy. In late pregnancy, it reveals many things:

- the presentation of the baby—whether the baby is head first or breech
- the dilatation of the cervix—how much the cervix has opened (if at all)
- effacement—how much the cervix has thinned

- station—how low the baby is in your birth canal
- shape and size of your birth canal or pelvic bones

After a pelvic exam late in pregnancy, your healthcare provider may tell you some numbers, such as "2 and 50%." This means your cervix has dilated 2 centimeters and is 50% thinned out.

Information collected during the exam is helpful if you go to the hospital thinking you're in labor. At the hospital, you'll be checked again. Knowing the measurements from your last pelvic exam can help medical personnel determine if you are in labor.

A pelvic exam does not tell your healthcare provider *when* you'll go into labor. Labor can start at any time, regardless of the condition of your cervix.

Tests for the Woman Expecting Multiples

We know the chance of a multiple birth increases as a woman gets older. If you are carrying more than one baby, the number of tests you receive, and when you receive them, will be different. Some researchers recommend if you are at least 32 years old and your healthcare provider determines you're carrying more than one baby, you should have chromosome testing, such as amniocentesis or chorionic villus sampling. Research indicates there is a slightly higher chance of an abnormality when a woman is carrying two or more babies.

Kay did most of the talking at her prenatal visits. I mainly listened to this bubbly, excited first-time mom-to-be. I don't think her husband, Bob, said a word. They both came for her 18-week visit, when we were doing an ultrasound. Kay had been a little unsure about her last period, and her uterus seemed larger than expected, so we hoped her ultrasound would help us determine if we had the right due date. The ultrasound told us a lot—her due date was right, but she was carrying twins! Kay was in shock; all she could do was gasp. Bob was ecstatic—he whooped with joy. They left with Kay shaking her head and Bob grinning from ear to ear. At her next visit, Kay and I talked about twins and twin pregnancies.

In many cases, screening tests are the first indication a woman is carrying more than one baby. Sometimes these tests give an "abnormal" result. An abnormal test result does not necessarily indicate the babies have a problem; it

> Ultrasound at the mall can be hazardous to you and baby because untrained technicians doing the test on you may not use equipment correctly.

alerts the healthcare provider to perform follow-up tests.

Often with a multiple pregnancy, blood tests are repeated around week 28 to check for gestational diabetes. Tests can also reveal if the mother-to-be is anemic, which is more common in women carrying multiples.

You may have more tests if other problems develop. If there's an indication of preterm labor or pre-eclampsia, you may have amniocentesis to check lung maturity in the babies. Premature lung disease is a serious complication for multiples who are delivered too early.

Tests to Avoid during Pregnancy

There is no known safe amount of radiation from X-ray tests for a developing fetus. X-ray exposure may harm the baby. Don't have any X-rays during pregnancy unless it's an emergency. The medical need for an X-ray must always be weighed against its risk to your pregnancy. Discuss the procedure with your pregnancy healthcare provider before *any* X-ray is taken during pregnancy. This warning also applies to dental X-rays.

Computerized tomographic scans, also called *CT scans* or *CAT scans,* are a specialized X-ray. The test involves the use of X-ray with computer analysis. Many researchers believe the amount of radiation received from a CT scan is far lower than from a regular X-ray. However, it is probably wise to avoid even this amount of exposure, if possible.

If you're over 35, you may have had a baseline mammogram, or breast X-ray, which is usually repeated every 2 years after the age of 40. If you had a mammogram before pregnancy, you're ahead of the game. If not, don't have one until after baby is born. Unless you have a good reason for undergoing the test, such as a breast lump, don't expose your developing baby to this type of radiation.

With radiation exams, risk to the fetus appears to be the greatest between 8 and 15 weeks of gestation (between the fetal age of 6 weeks and 13 weeks). Some physicians believe the only safe amount of radiation exposure for a fetus is *no* exposure.

Magnetic resonance imaging (MRI) is a widely used diagnostic tool. No harmful effects have been reported from its use in pregnancy, but pregnant women are advised to avoid MRI during the first trimester of pregnancy.

Chapter 9

More Than One Baby!

A multiple pregnancy almost always surprises expectant parents. However, because of today's advanced testing techniques, especially ultrasound, most parents know about it early enough to prepare for their new arrivals.

The rate of multiple births has increased greatly in recent years. Since 1980, the rate of twin births has increased 70%, and statistics show that over 3% of all births in the United States are multiple births. If you're expecting more than one baby, you're not alone!

Women having babies later in life accounts for nearly 35% of all multiple births. Age 30 seems to be the magic age beyond which the number of multiple births increases. Over 70% of all multiple births are to women over age 30. In the United States, the highest number of multiple births occurs in women over 40; the next highest group is women between the ages of 30 and 39.

When talking about pregnancies of more than one baby, in most cases we refer to *twins*. The chance of a twin pregnancy is more likely than pregnancy with triplets, quadruplets or quintuplets (or even more!). However, we are experiencing more triplet and higher-order births. A triplet birth is not very common; it happens about once in every 7000 deliveries. (Dr. Curtis has been fortunate to deliver two sets of triplets in his medical career.) Quadruplets are born once in every 725,000 births; quintuplets once in every 47 million births!

How a Multiple Pregnancy Occurs

A multiple pregnancy occurs when a single egg divides after fertilization or when more than one egg is fertilized. It also happens with fertility treatments, when more than one fertilized egg is placed in the uterus.

Twins from one egg occur about once in every 250 births around the world. Twins from two eggs occur in 1 out of every 100 births in white women and 1 out of 79 births in black women. In certain areas in Africa, twins occur once in every 20 births! Hispanic women also have a higher incidence of twins.

The occurrence of twins in Asian populations is less common—about 1 in every 150 births.

No matter how it occurs, being pregnant with two or more babies can affect you in many ways. Your pregnancy will be different, and the type of adjustments you may need to make may be more extensive. These changes and adjustments may be necessary for your health and the health of your babies. Work closely with your doctor and other healthcare professionals to help ensure your pregnancy is healthy and safe.

Why Multiple Births Occur

The increase in multiple births among older women has been attributed to higher levels of gonadotropin, the hormone that stimulates the ovaries to develop and to release eggs. As you age, the level of gonadotropin increases, and you're more likely to produce two eggs during one menstrual cycle. Most twin births in older women are fraternal twins—babies born from two different eggs.

Twin fetuses usually result (over 65% of the time) from the fertilization of two separate eggs; each baby has his or her own placenta and amniotic sac. These are called *dizygotic* (two zygotes) *twins* or *fraternal twins*. With fraternal twins, you can have a boy and a girl.

About 35% of the time, twins come from a single egg that divides into two similar structures. Each has the potential of developing into a separate individual. These are known as *monozygotic* (one zygote) *twins* or *identical twins*.

Either or both processes may be involved when more than two fetuses are formed. What we mean by that is triplets may result from fertilization of one, two or three eggs, or quadruplets may result from fertilization of one, two, three or four eggs.

The incidence of twin births can run in families, on the *mother's* side. One study showed that if a woman is a twin, her chance of giving birth to twins is about 1 in 58. If a woman is the daughter of a twin, she also has a higher chance of having twins. Another study reported that 1 out of 24 (4%) twins' mothers was also a twin, but only 1 out of 60 (1.7%, about the national average) of the fathers was a twin.

Multiple births are also more common with in-vitro fertilization. This may be due to the frequent use of fertility drugs to increase the chance of pregnancy or the introduction of several fertilized eggs into the uterus in hopes that at least one will implant. Pregnancy with twins as a result of a fertility treatment most often results in fraternal twins. In some cases of higher-number fetuses, a pregnancy can result in fraternal *and* identical twins, when more than one egg is fertilized (dizygotic twins) and, in addition, one or more of the eggs divides (monozygotic twins).

The percentage of male fetuses decreases slightly as the number of fetuses in a pregnancy increases. In other words, as the number of babies a woman carries increases, her chances of having more girls also increases.

Your chance of having triplets is 1 in 7000. One patient came to the office for her visit wearing a memorable T-shirt:

Not one
Not two
But three . . .
and no drugs.

(The "no drugs" meaning "no fertility drugs.")

Special Issues for Identical Twins

With monozygotic (identical) twins, division of the fertilized egg occurs between the first few days and about day 8. If division of the egg occurs after 8 days, the result can be twins that are connected, called *conjoined twins*. (Conjoined twins used to be called *Siamese twins*.) These babies may share important internal organs, such as the heart, lungs or liver. Fortunately this is a rare occurrence.

Identical twins may face some risks. There is a 15% chance they will develop a serious problem called *twin-to-twin transfusion syndrome*. There is one placenta, and the babies' blood vessels share the placenta. The problem arises when one baby gets too much blood flow and the other too little. See the discussion that begins on page 126.

With monozygotic twins, there is a chance several different types of diseases may occur in both twins during their lifetimes. This is less likely to happen with dizygotic twins.

Due to health concerns, it may be important later in life for your children to know whether they were monozygotic or dizygotic. Before delivery, tell your doctor you would like to have the placenta(s) examined (with a pathology exam) so you will know whether your babies were monozygotic or dizygotic. It may be valuable information in the future. Even if there are two placentas, research shows it doesn't mean twins are dizygotic; nearly 35% of all monozygotic twins have two placentas.

If you have already given birth to a set of fraternal twins, your chance of having another set of twins quadruples! Other reasons for multiple fetuses include some women having more children, being very tall or obese, recently discontinuing oral contraception or taking large doses of folic acid. Studies have shown the twin birth rate for women who took folic acid can be as high as double the rate of women who did not take large doses of folic acid.

Having more children (or pregnancies) can also result in more than one baby. This is true in all populations and may be related to the mother's age and female hormone changes.

Discovering a Multiple Pregnancy

Diagnosis of twins was more difficult before ultrasound was available. However, most multiple pregnancies are discovered well before delivery. Today, it's uncommon to discover twin pregnancies just by hearing two heartbeats. Many people believe when only one heartbeat is heard, there could be no possibility of twins. This may not be the case. Two rapid heartbeats may have a similar or almost identical rate. That could make it difficult to determine that there are two babies.

Measuring and examining your abdomen during pregnancy is important. A healthcare provider usually finds out a woman is carrying more than one baby because she has a larger-than-expected uterus. Usually a twin pregnancy is noted during the second trimester because you are too big and growth seems too fast for a single pregnancy. Other signs include more severe nausea and/or vomiting, and hearing more than one fetal heartbeat.

Ultrasound examination is the best way to diagnose a multiple pregnancy.

Increased Risks Associated
with a Multiple Pregnancy

If a woman is pregnant with more than one baby, her risk of problems during pregnancy increases. You can minimize your risks, and possibly avoid them, with good prenatal care and careful attention to your health. Possible pregnancy problems include the following:

- increased risk of miscarriage
- fetal death
- fetal malformations
- low birthweight or growth restriction
- pre-eclampsia
- problems with the placenta, including placental abruption and placenta previa
- maternal anemia
- maternal bleeding or hemorrhage
- problems with the umbilical cords, including entwinement or tangling of the babies' umbilical cords
- hydramnios or polyhydramnios
- labor complicated by abnormal fetal presentation, such as breech or transverse presentation
- premature labor
- difficult delivery and Cesarean delivery

Birth defects are more common with identical twins than fraternal twins. The incidence of minor malformations in a multiple pregnancy is twice as high as it is in a singleton pregnancy, and major malformations are also more common.

One of the biggest problems with multiple pregnancies is premature delivery. As the number of fetuses increases, the length of gestation and the birthweight of each baby decreases, although this is not true in every case.

The average length of pregnancy for twins is about 37 weeks. For triplets it is about 35 weeks. For every week the babies remain in the uterus, their birthweights increase along with the maturity of organs and systems.

It's important to continue your pregnancy as long as possible, which may best be accomplished by bed rest. You may not be able to carry on with regular activities during your entire pregnancy. If your healthcare provider recommends bed rest, follow his or her advice.

Weight gain is important with a multiple pregnancy. You will probably be advised to gain more than the normal 25 to 35 pounds, depending on the number of fetuses you are carrying. With twins, if you were normal weight before pregnancy, you may be advised to gain 40 to 54 pounds (18 to 24.5 kg). For overweight women, a weight gain between 31 and 50 pounds (14 to 22.7 kg) may be recommended. A weight gain between 25 and 42 (11.3 to 19 kg)pounds may be recommended for obese women. If you're expecting triplets, your weight gain will probably be between 50 and 60 pounds (22.7 to 27.2 kg) if you are normal weight before pregnancy.

Pay strict attention to your eating plan; eat wisely and nutritiously for all of you. Extra rest is essential. Most pregnant women need at least 2 hours of extra rest each day.

When you're pregnant with more than one baby, you will probably be monitored more closely. You may have more frequent checkups and more tests.

Beginning around 20 weeks of pregnancy, you will probably visit your healthcare provider every other week until week 30. Then you may be seen once a week until delivery. You may have ultrasound more frequently to monitor babies' growth. Your blood pressure is watched closely because of preeclampsia, which is twice as common in multiple pregnancies.

Follow your doctor's instructions closely. Every day and every week you're able to keep the babies inside you are days or weeks you won't have to visit them in an intensive-care nursery while they grow, develop and finish maturing.

Twin-to-Twin Transfusion Syndrome (TTTS)

Twin-to-twin transfusion syndrome (TTTS), also called *chronic intertwin transfusion syndrome,* occurs only in identical twins who share the same placenta. The condition can range from mild to severe and can occur at any point during pregnancy, even at birth.

TTTS cannot be prevented; it's not a genetic disorder nor a hereditary condition. We believe it occurs in 5 to 10% of all identical-twin pregnancies. These problems do not occur in twins who each have a placenta.

In TTTS, twins also share some of the same blood circulation. This allows the transfusion of blood from one twin to the other. One twin becomes small and anemic. Its body responds by partially shutting down blood supply to many of its organs, especially the kidneys, which results in reduced urine output and a small volume of amniotic fluid.

The other twin grows large, overloaded with blood. It produces excessive amounts of urine so it is surrounded by a large volume of amniotic fluid. Its

When a Multiple Pregnancy Isn't a Multiple Pregnancy

Some women are told early in pregnancy they are carrying twins, only to discover later they are carrying only one baby. Early ultrasound exams reveal two babies; later ultrasounds of the same woman show one baby disappeared, but the other baby is OK. We believe one of the pregnancies dies and is absorbed by the mother's body. This is one reason many healthcare providers prefer not to predict a twin birth before 10 weeks of pregnancy.

blood becomes thick and difficult to pump through its body; this can result in heart failure, generalized soft-tissue swelling and death.

Twins are often very different in size. There can also be a large difference in their weights. TTTS is a progressive disorder, so early treatment may help prevent complications.

Symptoms of TTTS

There are symptoms of the syndrome your healthcare provider looks for. If your abdomen enlarges quite rapidly over a 2- to 3-week period, it may be caused by the buildup of amniotic fluid in the recipient twin. The result can be premature labor and/or premature rupture of membranes. If one twin is small for its gestational age or one is big for its gestational age, it may indicate TTTS. In addition, your healthcare provider may suspect TTTS if any of the following is seen during an ultrasound:

- large difference in the size of fetuses of the same gender
- difference in size between the two amniotic sacs
- difference in size of the umbilical cords
- one placenta
- evidence of fluid buildup in the skin of either fetus
- indications of congestive heart failure in the recipient twin

An additional problem may develop in either twin. With this condition, fluid accumulates in some part of the fetus, such as in the scalp, abdomen, lungs or heart.

Diagnosing and Treating TTTS

Report any of the following to your healthcare provider, especially if you know you're expecting twins:

- rapid growth of your uterus
- abdominal pain, tightness or contractions
- sudden increase in body weight
- swelling in the hands and legs in early pregnancy

The syndrome may also be detected with ultrasound examination of the uterus. It's important to find out whether twins share the same placenta. It's preferable to learn this in the first trimester because in the second trimester it can be harder to discover whether they share a placenta.

If the syndrome is mild or undetected on ultrasound, the appearance of the babies at birth may identify it. A complete blood cell count done after birth will show anemia in one twin and excess red blood cells (polycythemia) in the other.

If diagnosed, the Twin to Twin Transfusion Syndrome Foundation recommends weekly ultrasounds after 16 weeks until the end of the pregnancy to monitor the condition. They recommend this be done even if the warning signs of TTTS have decreased.

The most common treatment for TTTS is amnioreduction, in which large volumes of amniotic fluid are drained from the sac of the larger twin. A needle is placed through the mother's abdomen, and fluid is drained. The procedure is repeated, as necessary.

In another procedure, a hole punched between the two amniotic sacs can help equalize the fluid between the sacs. However, neither of these procedures stops the twin-to-twin transfusion.

Some cases of TTTS do not respond to amnioreduction. A small-scope laser procedure may be done to seal off some or all of the blood vessels the twins share. Usually only one procedure is necessary during the pregnancy. Survival rates are also about 60% with this procedure. This treatment is most successful if done before 26 weeks of pregnancy.

With laser treatment, a detailed ultrasound exam is done first to help locate the abnormal connection. Then a thin fiber-optic scope is placed through the mother's abdomen, through the wall of the uterus and into the amniotic cavity of the larger twin. By looking directly at the placenta, blood connections can be found and sealed with a laser beam. This separates the circulation of the fetuses and ends twin-to-twin transfusion. However, this requires doing the procedure while the babies are still in the womb and may cause complications.

The most conservative treatment is to watch and wait. The pregnancy is followed closely with frequent ultrasound exams, with the choice of delivering the twins by Cesarean delivery if medically necessary.

Newborns with twin-to-twin transfusion syndrome may be critically ill at birth and require treatment in a neonatal intensive care unit (NICU). The smaller twin is treated for anemia, and the larger twin is treated for excess red blood cells and jaundice.

Take Care of Yourself

Taking care of yourself when you are expecting more than one baby is the best way to take care of your developing babies. An important thing to remember with a multiple pregnancy is to take things more slowly from the beginning of your pregnancy until delivery.

A multiple pregnancy is more stressful for your body than a singleton pregnancy, and your needs increase in many areas. You may need bed rest in your second trimester, even hospitalization, if you experience complications. With some multiple pregnancies, planned hospitalization at 28 to 30 weeks may be recommended. Bed rest at home or in the hospital can help prevent or stop premature labor. It gives the babies the best chance to grow because bed rest increases blood flow to the uterus.

Coping with Discomfort

When you're expecting more than one baby, your discomfort may be more pronounced; you may experience more problems, or problems may last longer. When you're carrying twins, you get "big" earlier, and you are larger than with a singleton pregnancy. This can cause you more discomfort, such as difficulty breathing, back pain, hemorrhoids, varicose veins, pelvic pressure and pelvic pain. Treatment is often the same for you as for a woman with a singleton pregnancy.

It may be harder to lose your pregnancy weight after having twins, so stick to the weight-gain goal your healthcare provider gives you during your pregnancy. Carrying two or more babies causes greater hormonal and physiological changes in your body, which may cause you to hold onto the weight you gain during pregnancy for a longer period.

Exercising with a Multiple Pregnancy

As a general rule, women carrying more than one baby should *not* exercise during pregnancy because of problems with premature delivery. Walking and swimming may be permissible for you, but check with your healthcare provider first.

If you do get the OK to exercise, don't do anything strenuous—stop immediately if you feel overexerted! As much as you want to stay in shape, you may have to forgo all exercise until after your babies are safely delivered.

Your Nutrition with a Multiple Pregnancy

If you're expecting more than one baby, your nutrition and weight gain are extremely important during pregnancy. Food is your best source for nutrients, but keep taking your prenatal vitamin every day. The vitamins and iron in prenatal vitamins are necessary to your well-being and the well-being of your babies.

Iron supplementation may be essential. If you're anemic at the time of delivery, a low blood count could have a negative effect on all of you. Your chance of needing a blood transfusion could be higher.

If you don't gain weight early in pregnancy, you have a greater chance of developing pre-eclampsia. Your babies may also be tiny. Don't be alarmed when your healthcare provider discusses the amount of weight he or she wants you to gain. Studies show if you gain the targeted amount of weight with a multiple pregnancy, your babies are often healthier. In addition, gaining half of your weight by week 20 can be beneficial for your babies, especially if they are born early.

How can you gain the amount of weight you need to gain? Just adding extra calories won't benefit you or your growing babies, so avoid junk food because it's full of empty calories.

Get your calories from specific sources. Make your calories count—eat nutritious foods. In addition, eat an extra serving of a dairy product and an extra serving of a protein each day. These will provide you with the extra calcium, protein and iron you require to meet the needs of your growing babies. Discuss the situation with your doctor; he or she may suggest you see a nutritionist.

Delivering More Than One Baby

Multiple fetuses are often delivered early. How babies are delivered often depends on how they are lying in the uterus. All possible combinations of fetal

positions can occur. Possible complications include abnormal presentation of one or more of the babies, prolapse of the umbilical cord (the umbilical cord comes out ahead of the babies), placental abruption, fetal stress or bleeding after delivery.

Because there is higher risk, precautions are taken before delivery and during labor. These include the need for an I.V., the presence of an anesthesiologist, the ability to perform an emergency Cesarean delivery and the availability and possible presence of pediatricians or other medical personnel to take care of the babies.

With twins, all possible combinations of fetal positions can occur. Both babies may come head first (vertex). They may come *breech*, meaning bottom or feet first. They may be lying sideways or *oblique*, meaning at an angle that is neither breech nor vertex. Or they may come in any combination of the above.

I'm carrying twins. Will I need a Cesarean delivery?
Not necessarily. Delivery of twins has more complications than delivering one baby, but many twins can be delivered vaginally. Discuss it with your healthcare provider.

When both twins are head first, a vaginal delivery may be attempted and may be accomplished safely. It may be possible for one baby to deliver vaginally. However, the second one could require a Cesarean delivery if it turns, the cord comes out ahead of the baby or the baby is stressed following delivery of the first fetus. Some doctors believe delivery of two or more babies is more safely accomplished with a Cesarean delivery.

After delivery of two or more babies, medical personnel pay close attention to maternal bleeding because of the rapid change in the size of the uterus. With more than one baby, it is greatly overdistended. Medication, usually oxytocin (Pitocin), is given by I.V. to contract the uterus to stop bleeding so the mother doesn't lose too much blood. A heavy blood loss could produce anemia and make a blood transfusion or long-term treatment with iron supplementation necessary.

Other Considerations

Working during Pregnancy

Often a physician advises a woman expecting twins to stop working at least 8 weeks before her due date. Ideally, you should stop working at 28 weeks with a twin pregnancy—24 weeks if your job requires standing or other physical exertion. Your healthcare provider may recommend full or partial bed rest. These are only general suggestions and will not apply in every case.

Childbirth-Education Classes

It's a great idea to take childbirth-education classes for any pregnancy. If you're expecting twins, triplets or more, schedule your classes to begin at least 3 *months* before your due date. If you have time, a brief course in Cesarean birth might also be worthwhile if you can find one in your area.

Breastfeeding More Than One Baby

One of the greatest challenges for parents of multiples is deciding how to feed them. If you have more than one baby, you should be able to breastfeed them. You may find it a little more challenging, but many mothers have done it. You may have to be creative in your approach, but with time, you'll probably work it out quite well.

Breastfeeding your babies, even if it's only for one or two feedings a day, gives them the protection from infection that breast milk provides. Research has shown that even the smallest dose of breast milk gives babies an advantage over babies only fed formula.

If babies are early, and you can't nurse them, begin pumping! Pump from day one, and store your breast milk for the time babies are able to receive it.

In addition, pumping tells the body to produce breast milk—pump and the milk will come. It just takes some time.

There is no *one way* to feed a baby. You may find your baby does well with breast *and* bottlefeeding. Bottlefeeding doesn't always mean you feed your baby formula. You can also bottlefeed expressed breast milk. Supplementing with formula allows your partner and others to help you feed the babies. You can breastfeed one while someone else bottlefeeds the other. Or you can nurse each one for a time, then finish the feeding with formula. In either case, someone else can help you feed the babies.

Extra Help after Babies Are Born

Even the most efficient woman discovers that having more than one baby can be exhausting. Extra help can make a tremendous difference in everyone's life. Your time of greatest need is immediately after your babies are born. Ask for help from family, neighbors and friends for the first 4 to 6 weeks after you bring your babies home. You might also consider hiring someone to come in to help, such as a nurse, postpartum doula or other healthcare professional.

Postpartum Doulas

In addition to doulas who help during pregnancy, labor and delivery, there are also *postpartum doulas.* These women help ease the transition into parenthood for any parent, not just those of multiples. A postpartum doula will help a new mother and her family learn to enjoy and to care for the new baby through education and hands-on experience.

A postpartum doula provides emotional and breastfeeding support and ensures a new mother is fed, well hydrated and comfortable. She may go with mom and baby to pediatrician appointments. A postpartum doula may also take care of grocery shopping, preparing meals and other household tasks. She may even help tend older children.

Services provided by a postpartum doula are most often used in the first 2 to 4 weeks after babies are born, but support can last anywhere from one or two visits to visits for 3 months or longer. Some doulas work all day; others work 3- to 5-hour shifts during the

> ### Time-Saving, Energy-Saving Tip
> Before your babies' births, consider hiring someone to come in for the first few weeks or months to help you out. Caring for more than one baby is exhausting, and you'll need time and help to discover efficient ways to care for your babies and yourself. Having someone available at night can be especially convenient. If you cannot afford help, ask a relative who is able to come for an extended visit to help you get back on your feet.

day or after-school shifts until dad gets home. Some doulas work evenings, and some work overnight.

If you think you may want a postpartum doula to help you with the babies, make arrangements a few months before your due date. Even though you don't know exactly when babies will arrive (unless you're having a scheduled Cesarean delivery), contract with a postpartum doula in advance to be sure of her availability. Costs range between $15 and $30 an hour for this service, depending on a postpartum doula's additional training and experience.

Chapter 10

How Age Affects Your Pregnancy

Most women over age 35 have problem-free, healthy pregnancies and deliver healthy babies. However, age does affect pregnancy. If you experience any of the situations covered in this chapter, be sure to discuss it with your healthcare provider.

Many women want to know why pregnancy in a woman who is in her 30s or 40s is considered "higher risk." After age 35, risks of medical problems, such as high blood pressure, and risks for baby, such as Down syndrome, increase each year. Medical professionals originally chose the age of 35 as the dividing line between normal risk and high risk because of risks associated with the amniocentesis test.

The age of 35 is no longer as meaningful because amniocentesis is much safer now. The estimated risk of a miscarriage after amniocentesis is less than 3%. Perhaps more important, 75% of all babies born with Down syndrome (the most common reason for a woman to have the test) are born to women *under* 35.

A healthcare provider may treat an older woman with more caution. More office visits, more testing, genetic counseling and screening for problems associated with pregnancy in an older woman may be recommended.

Labor and delivery options may be more limited; you might be discouraged from using a birthing center because your age puts you at greater risk. However, good prenatal care can significantly reduce obstetrical complications associated with age. Most women into their 40s can have healthy pregnancies and deliver healthy babies.

Older pregnant women are often well informed about pregnancy. They are typically interested in what's happening to them and their developing babies, and they are willing to ask questions. They want to be part of the decision-making process in their healthcare. They usually seek prenatal care early and often prepare for pregnancy before getting pregnant. For these reasons, many experts believe risk does not increase greatly just because a woman is older. Other factors also influence a woman's health risks during pregnancy. Still, pregnancy in your 30s and 40s slightly increases the risk of some problems.

Some Pregnancy Problems in Older Women

Problems healthcare providers see more often in older pregnant women include gestational diabetes, high blood pressure, placental problems, more miscarriages, more Cesarean births and a slightly higher risk of giving birth to a baby with genetic or chromosomal abnormalities.

Beginning in their late 30s, women are more likely to develop medical conditions associated with reproductive organs, such as uterine fibroids and muscle tumors, which may cause pain or vaginal bleeding as pregnancy progresses. After 40, a woman may feel the physical strains of pregnancy more. She may be more bothered by hemorrhoids, incontinence, varicose veins, vascular problems, muscle aches and pains, back pain and a harder, longer labor.

Two serious pregnancy risks increase for women in their 40s—miscarriage and birth of a child with Down syndrome. Miscarriage ends about 40% of pregnancies in women who get pregnant after age 40.

The national average for Cesarean deliveries is over 30%, and the rate rises with age. The Cesarean-delivery rate for pregnant women between 40 and 54 years old is nearly double the rate for women younger than 20.

The risk of a pregnancy ending in stillbirth (the baby is dead upon delivery) has fallen for women of all ages in recent years. For a mother older than 35, the risk is about 7 in 1000. The risk of some birth defects does *not* increase for older mothers.

Genetic Counseling

If you are older than 35, your healthcare provider may recommend genetic counseling for you and your partner. Healthcare professionals interpret information gathered from interviews, tests and health histories, then share the results with you both.

Genetic counseling seldom provides exact information. Counselors describe information in terms of percentages and odds. No one will tell you what to do; they provide you with information and support so you can make your own decisions.

Counseling can help you and your partner understand your current situation, its diagnosis and prognosis. It can help you in family planning and provide support to you and your family. Counselors can help you explore options for the present and future.

Genetic counseling is a complicated process and requires input from several different professionals. These professionals can include a medical geneticist, genetic counselor, social worker, psychologist or psychiatrist, laboratory specialists, clergy, parent groups and others.

Ask your genetic counselor any questions you have about the information you are given. This person can help you understand and use the resources available and help you understand what is involved in making important decisions.

> **Time-Saving, Energy-Saving Tip**
>
> As we age, it's important to take care of our skin. Being an older pregnant woman means this task may be even more important to you. Try the following tips for healthy skin. Wear lots of sunscreen—a moisturizer with sunscreen is a good choice even if you do wear makeup. A facial can help with puffiness, or put slices of cold cucumbers on your closed eyelids to reduce swelling. If you wear makeup, remove it every night before bed, even if you're exhausted. Then wash your face and apply moisturizer.

As information is gathered, it may be necessary to share it with other members of your family. If a gene abnormality is identified, your sister, for example, will probably want to know about it before she starts her own family.

In the past, genetic counseling was offered only to older women or after the birth of a child with a defect. With increased awareness and advances in technology, today we can provide couples with information before conception. The three major areas we focus on are reproductive history, family history and consanguinity (partners are related).

When to Seek Genetic Counseling

Genetic counseling is advised in a number of situations:

- either partner has a family history of birth defects, mental retardation, chromosome abnormality or neurological disorders
- either partner has a family history of neural-tube defects (such as spina bifida)
- the couple has previously given birth to a child with a chromosomal abnormality
- either partner has a chromosomal abnormality
- the woman is a carrier of a sex-chromosome disorder
- the woman will be 35 or older at the time of birth

- the woman has had three or more miscarriages
- the woman has been exposed to teratogens (environmental factors harmful to the fetus)
- with consanguinity (couple is related)
- either partner is in a high-risk ethnic group

Your Reproductive and Family Medical History

When a genetic counselor asks questions about your *reproductive history,* he or she seeks information on any type of pregnancy loss, miscarriage, stillbirth or perinatal death (death of the baby at the end of pregnancy or after birth). Other important information can include fertility problems, the type and duration of contraception, and environmental exposures.

Your *family history* can be important in determining a high-risk situation. Information essential to your genetic counselor includes the following:

- a description of the health status of you, your partner and siblings
- cause of death of any relatives
- age at death of these relatives
- any birth defects in relatives

Your family history helps identify abnormalities that occurred in relatives and helps predict the likelihood of these defects occurring in your child.

Ethnic background can be an important aspect of family history. For example, if both partners are of Ashkenazi Jewish descent, there is an increased risk of giving birth to a baby with Tay-Sachs disease. Some people of African and Mediterranean descent are at an increased risk for having a baby with sickle-cell disease.

If you are unsure of all the information a family history requires, ask your parents and other family members for help. By working together, you will be able to provide the data necessary for the most thorough evaluation.

I'm 37; do I need genetic counseling?
The answer to this question depends on many factors. Discuss all your options with your healthcare provider.

Consanguinity

Consanguinity (being related by birth to your partner, such as a cousin) can create problems. A related couple may have a high risk of having a child with a genetic birth defect, especially if there is a family history of genetic defects. (First cousins have 1/16 of their genes in common.) If you're related to your partner, tell your genetic-counseling team.

Prenatal Testing

Prenatal testing does not guarantee the birth of a normal baby; it only provides information about malformations or disorders that can be specifically tested for. Some birth defects can't be found or are difficult to find before a baby is born, such as phenylketonuria, cleft lip and cleft palate. Other problems, such as chromosome abnormalities, may be identified by various tests, including amniocentesis, ultrasound, chorionic villus sampling and fetoscopy.

Testing for a fetal abnormality allows for termination of a pregnancy, if that is desired. Sometimes a prenatal diagnosis may call for prenatal surgery in utero (in the uterus) to correct various conditions, such as kidney blockage or omphalocele (congenital hernia of the navel).

Results learned from prenatal testing can be used to make special arrangements for care of the baby after birth, if necessary. Results may also influence which method of delivery is chosen.

Counseling and support of a couple or family can help prepare them for what lies ahead after baby's birth. Support can include social services, mental-health counseling (psychiatrist, psychologist, social worker) and spiritual guidance.

For some couples, counseling is the beginning of the grieving process over the loss of the "perfect baby." Counseling can help a couple begin to deal with the possible death of the fetus or baby, or the challenges associated with a child with special needs.

Counseling after Baby's Birth

When a couple gives birth to a child with a birth defect or a genetic disorder, genetic testing of the couple may be recommended after the birth, especially if they desire more children. Testing may alert the couple to problems that could arise in subsequent pregnancies.

Most infants with problems are identified at birth or shortly afterward. Babies born with problems are usually grouped in one of three categories:

- babies with obvious malformations at the time of birth
- babies who are "sick" or have a difficult time immediately after birth
- babies who appear normal at birth but develop abnormalities later

An accurate diagnosis is important. Helpful sources of information include family history, laboratory results, physical exam, pregnancy history (including medications, complications and environmental exposures), growth and development history during the pregnancy and after the birth, and photographs of the baby.

This information can provide guidance about what lies ahead and various treatments that might be available. Genetic counseling after a baby is born with a birth defect is most helpful in answering the question, "What are the chances of it happening again?"

If the risk of recurrence of a problem is low, some families choose to have more children. If the risk is high or if prenatal diagnosis is not available, a couple may decide not to have children.

In some cases, a couple may opt for donor insemination, if that might prevent a problem. Donor insemination uses donor sperm to achieve pregnancy. The partner's sperm is not used if he has a chromosomal disorder or is a carrier of a chromosomal disorder. Or a couple may choose donation of eggs if the woman has a genetic problem.

Understanding Basic Genetics

Human cells contain 46 chromosomes each (*diploid number*); each sperm and each egg contain 23 chromosomes (*haploid number*). *Chromosomes* are composed of DNA and proteins that contain genes. Each cell contains 23 pairs of chromosomes—one chromosome of each pair is inherited from each parent.

Of the 23 pairs, 22 are *autosomes* (nonsex chromosomes) and one pair is the sex chromosomes, X and Y. In a normal woman, the sex chromosomes are represented by two X (XX) chromosomes, and in the normal man by X and Y (XY) chromosomes.

Chromosome analysis usually involves blood cells. Chromosomes are viewed through a microscope, then photographed and enlarged. They are then arranged in pairs, called a *karyotype;* a karyotype is used to identify abnormalities in the number of chromosomes.

Healthcare providers can examine individual chromosomes for abnormalities. We have learned that too much or too little chromosome material can cause an abnormality.

Incidence of Genetic Disease

The hoped-for and anticipated outcome for every pregnancy is a normal, healthy baby. It is expected and taken for granted. However, that is not always the case. We believe nearly half of all first-trimester miscarriages are caused by some type of chromosomal abnormality. About 1% of all babies born have a chromosomal abnormality; 4 to 7% of perinatal deaths (death after birth) are attributed to chromosomal problems.

Among newborns, 3 to 5% are born with a major birth defect, such as a heart defect; many of these birth defects have a genetic component. In the United States, this represents as many as 225,000 children each year.

Mental retardation is another area of concern. It is estimated that genetic problems cause 70% of mental retardation. Genetic counseling may offer an indication that this might occur.

Chromosomal Abnormalities

Chromosomal abnormalities can occur in any cell, and they can occur as an *abnormal chromosome number* or as an *abnormality in the structure* of the chromosome itself. With Down syndrome, an individual has 47 chromosomes instead of the normal 46. With Turner's syndrome, the individual has 45 chromosomes.

A loss, a gain or a repositioning of chromosome material identifies a structural abnormality. Terms used to describe these various conditions include *additions, duplications, deletions, inversions* and *translocations.*

A couple of possible causes of chromosomal abnormalities are advanced parental age and radiation exposure of mother, father or fetus, which can affect gene regulation. *Advanced parental age* usually refers to the mother's age, but some research has also implicated the father's age. Age is a factor for the mother because we believe females are born with all the eggs they will ever have. Women are exposed to radiation and other teratogens in the environment throughout their lives. These exposures have an additive effect—the more teratogens a woman is exposed to, the greater the chance of damaging her eggs.

Radiation exposure, such as X-rays, can damage genetic material and affect gene function and regulation. Genes control development of the fetus, its organs and growth. Three of the most common examples of chromosomal abnormalities are discussed below.

Down syndrome is the most common chromosomal abnormality; it occurs in about 1 in 800 births. An extra chromosome causes this syndrome. Those born with Down syndrome can live fairly long lives and may be moderately to severely mentally retarded. About half have congenital heart disease; particular physical abnormalities are common to the syndrome.

Trisomy 18 (Edwards' syndrome) is a severe chromosome abnormality occurring in approximately 1 in 6000 births. An abnormal chromosome 18 causes the syndrome. Babies with trisomy 18 have multiple abnormalities of major organs.

Trisomy 13 (Patau's syndrome) occurs about once in 5000 births. An extra chromosome 13 causes the syndrome. Babies born with trisomy 13 may have multiple abnormalities.

Sex-Chromosome Abnormalities

Abnormalities of sex chromosomes are relatively common—1 in every 500 births. It is believed this type of abnormality causes about 25% of all miscarriages. We discuss three of these syndromes below.

Turner's syndrome occurs about once in every 10,000 female births. It is the most common chromosome abnormality identified in miscarriages. Instead of having two X chromosomes, a baby girl born with Turner's syndrome has only one X chromosome, called *45X*. A mature girl with Turner's syndrome is short, sexually underdeveloped, with a webbed neck, very small ovaries and often heart and kidney problems. The condition may not be identified until she reaches puberty.

Klinefelter's syndrome is found in approximately 1 in every 1000 males. The most common characteristic is very tall stature when the boy reaches maturity. These boys are born with an extra sex chromosome, thus the *47XXY* label. A boy is underdeveloped sexually and has small testes.

Fragile-X syndrome (also called *X-linked*) is one of the most common causes of mental retardation in males. Major physical characteristics include large ears, large hands and language-development delays.

Congenital Infections

Rubella was one of the first maternal infections researchers identified as the cause of fetal malformations. Other infections that can cause malformations include cytomegalovirus (CMV), toxoplasmosis, herpes simplex, parvovirus 19 and syphilis.

Congenital infections can cause problems in a baby. These range from major birth defects, such as heart defects, to newborn infection at birth.

Velocardiofacial Syndrome (VCFS)

Velocardiofacial syndrome (VCFS) is a genetic condition that may be hereditary. It is known by many names, including *Shprintzen syndrome, craniofacial syndrome* and *conotruncal anomaly face syndrome.* VCFS is one of the most common syndromes in humans, second only to Down syndrome in frequency.

Health Risks of Older Pregnant Women by Age

Risk	30–34	35–39	40+
Uterine bleeding	8%	9%	9%
Diabetes	35%	48%	65%
Heart disease	7%	8%	9%
Hypertension	34%	38%	47%

VCFS is characterized by various medical problems. The immune system, endocrine system and neurological system may be involved. Symptoms do not all occur 100% of the time. Most people with VCFS exhibit a small number of problems; many problems are relatively minor.

The exact cause of velocardiofacial syndrome is unknown; however, investigators have identified a chromosomal defect in people with VCFS. Most children who have been diagnosed with this syndrome are missing a small part of chromosome 22.

It is estimated that VCFS is inherited in only 10 to 15% of cases. Most of the time neither parent has the syndrome nor carries the defective gene. The occurrence of congenital heart disease is most often the leading factor in diagnosis.

Down Syndrome

Nearly every pregnant woman receives information on Down syndrome. When you're older, you may be offered various tests to determine whether your fetus is affected by the condition.

Down syndrome was given its name by British physician J. Langdon Down in the 19th century. He found babies born with the syndrome have an extra chromosome 21. Symptoms of the condition are present to some degree in all babies born with the syndrome. These symptoms include mental retardation, a sloping forehead, short, broad hands with a single palm crease, a flat nose or absent nose bridge, low-set ears and a dwarfed physique.

Through medical research, we know that some women are at higher risk of giving birth to a child with Down syndrome. Women with increased risk include older women, those who have previously given birth to a child with Down syndrome and those who have Down syndrome themselves.

The statistical risk of delivering a baby with Down syndrome increases with age. However, there are some positive aspects to these statistics. If you're 45, you have a 97% chance of *not* having a baby with Down syndrome. If you're 49, you have a 92% chance of delivering a child *without* Down syndrome.

Your risk of delivering a child with Down syndrome, depending on your age, is shown below:

- at age 25, the risk is 1 in 1300 births
- at 30, 1 in 965 births
- at 35, 1 in 365 births
- at 40, 1 in 109 births
- at 45, 1 in 32 births
- at 49, 1 in 12 births

Tests to help detect Down syndrome include amniocentesis, chorionic villus sampling, alpha-fetoprotein test, quad-screen test, triple-screen test, instant risk assessment, nuchal translucency screening and ultrasound. Discuss them with your healthcare provider for further information.

Diagnosing Down Syndrome before Birth

Many tests can help diagnose Down syndrome in a developing fetus. They're not offered to every woman; they are usually offered only to women at high risk, those 35 and older carrying one baby and those over 32 carrying multiple fetuses. However, the American College of Obstetricians and Gynecologists (ACOG) now recommends that *all* pregnant women be offered Down syndrome testing. Their recommendation is based on the fact that the majority of babies born with Down syndrome are born to younger women. Some women at higher risk choose not to take the tests because they wouldn't terminate their pregnancy even if the child had Down syndrome.

If you are concerned about Down syndrome, have one or more of the tests listed below. You might have the test if you and your partner (and the rest of the family) want to be mentally and emotionally prepared for this special child. You might want the test if you would consider terminating your pregnancy.

Many families say they would welcome any child into their lives, no matter what his or her condition. If this is your attitude, enjoy your pregnancy and don't worry about it.

Down Syndrome Children Are Special

People want to know if there are any positive aspects of giving birth to a child with Down syndrome. The answer is, "Yes!"

A few years ago, I delivered a Down syndrome child for Anne, a patient in her early 40s. We did an amniocentesis early in the pregnancy and knew to expect Down syndrome. A year later, she reported to me the joy and love this special child had brought the entire family. Anne told me, "I don't know what our family would have been like without the blessing of this very special child. We cherish her."

As a society, we have come to realize children born with Down syndrome bring a special, valuable quality of life into our world. Down children are well known for the love and the joy they bring to their families and friends. They remind us of the pleasure in accomplishing simple tasks when they learn new skills. They embody the concept of unconditional love, and we can often learn how to cope and to grow as we interact with them.

Rearing a child with Down syndrome can be challenging, but many who have faced this challenge are positive about the impact these special children have in their lives. If you have a child with Down syndrome, you may work harder for every small advancement in your child's life, but your rewards will be great. You may experience frustration and feelings of helplessness at times, but every parent has these feelings at some time.

Often we only hear about the negative side of raising a child with Down syndrome. We hear about the worst-case scenario and never hear about the other side of the issue. All women carrying a child with Down syndrome need to know the following facts.

The average IQ for a child with Down syndrome is between 60 and 70. Most are in the low, mildly retarded range. Some children with Down syndrome have normal IQs. IQ scores for those with Down syndrome have risen steadily in the last 100 years. Less than 5% of those with Down syndrome are severely to profoundly retarded.

The reading levels of Down syndrome children who are in special-education programs in public schools range from kindergarten to twelfth grade. The average is about third grade.

Nearly 90% of those with Down syndrome are employable as adults. Most adults with Down syndrome are capable of living independently or in group homes. A person with Down syndrome who survives infancy has a life expectancy of 55 years or more.

Many families are on waiting lists to adopt a child with Down syndrome. A child with Down syndrome usually makes a positive impact on a family.

It's Your Decision

If you're carrying a child with Down syndrome, you and your partner have many things to consider. Many couples welcome the birth of this special child into their families. Others elect to terminate the pregnancy.

Whatever decision you make, it must be *your* decision. Do not allow yourself or your partner to be pressured into making any decision without your full understanding of the situation. Seek information. Talk to parents of children with Down syndrome. Make your decision based on the feelings you and your partner share. There are positive and negative aspects to consider, as there are with any child. Whatever decision you make may be difficult; involve your healthcare team and your partner in the process.

Chapter 11

Coping with Common Pregnancy Discomforts

In this chapter, we look at ways to cope with some of the more common discomforts of pregnancy. Being pregnant causes changes in your body; some of them are uncomfortable. Being aware of what they are before you experience them (if you do) may help relieve anxiety.

Back Pain and Backaches

If you experience back pain during pregnancy, you're not alone. Between 50 and 80% of all women have back and hip pain at some time during pregnancy. Pain usually occurs during the third trimester as your tummy grows larger. However, pain may begin early in pregnancy and last until well after delivery (up to 5 or 6 months).

It's more common to have mild backache than severe problems. You may experience backache after walking, bending, lifting, standing or excessive exercise. Some women need to be careful getting out of bed or getting up from a sitting position. Be careful to lift correctly.

The hormone relaxin may be part of the problem. It's responsible for relaxing joints that allow your pelvis to expand to deliver your baby. However, when joints relax, it can lead to pain in the lower back and legs. Other factors include your weight gain (another good reason to control your weight), larger breasts and your bigger tummy, which can cause a shift in posture.

A change in joint mobility may cause discomfort in the lower back, especially during the last part of pregnancy. All your joints are looser. Check with your healthcare provider if back pain is a persistent problem for you.

I have back pain every day. Is this normal?

This is a common symptom in many normal pregnancies. Many women
use heat or ice packs, massage and acetaminophen for relief.

Lower-back pain is common during pregnancy, but occasionally it indicates
a serious problem, such as a kidney stone. If pain is constant or severe, contact
your healthcare provider.

What can you do to prevent or lessen your pain? Try some or all of the following tips as early in pregnancy as possible. They'll pay off for you later in
pregnancy.

• Watch your weight gain; avoid gaining too much weight or gaining
  weight too fast.
• Stay active; continue exercising during pregnancy. Exercise to strengthen
  stomach, arm and thigh muscles.
• Swimming, walking and nonimpact aerobics may be beneficial.
• Do your Kegel exercises (see page 208).
• Practice good posture.
• Lift correctly—place feet shoulder-width apart, under your buttocks.
  Bend at the knees; lift with arms and legs, not your back!
• Get up and move around often. Don't stand or sit in the same place for a
  long time.
• Stretch muscles to keep them limber.
• Be sure your mattress provides good support.
• Lie on your side when you sleep. Sleep on your left side with a pillow be-
  tween your knees to align legs. Many pillows on the market are designed
  specifically for this purpose.
• Get out of bed slowly, swinging your legs to the floor and pushing up
  with your arms. Don't twist.
• Take a warm (*not* hot) bath.
• Get a prenatal massage.
• Get off your feet and lie down for 30 minutes on your side.
• Use heat on the painful area.
• Ask your healthcare provider about wearing a lower-back brace or preg-
  nancy support garment.

Treat backache with heat, rest and analgesics, such as acetaminophen.
When you have lower-back pain, use an ice pack for up to 30 minutes three

Use extra pillows to support your abdomen or your legs as your pregnancy progresses.

or four times a day. If pain lasts, switch to a heating pad, sticking with the same regimen.

Fatigue in Pregnancy

During the first stages of your pregnancy, you may find one of the main things on your mind is getting enough rest. Fatigue is one of the first signs of pregnancy. Do yourself a favor by taking it easy and resting when possible. Don't worry—fatigue is normal, especially in early pregnancy. Your body uses a lot of energy as your baby grows.

Don't lie on your back or stomach when you sleep or rest; learn to sleep on your side early in pregnancy. After week 16, lie only on your side. As your uterus grows, it presses on important blood vessels that run down the back of your abdomen. Lying on your back decreases circulation to your baby and to the lower parts of your body. You may notice it's harder to breathe when you lie on your back.

When you're resting or sleeping, elevate your feet to keep blood moving throughout your body, especially your legs. Rest your top leg on a pillow. Pregnancy pillows that support the entire body can offer great relief.

Drink lots of fluids. Watch your diet; avoid sugar because it can make fatigue worse. If you can't sleep enough at night to make you feel rested, nap during the day. If you can't nap, sit down and relax—listen to music or read if that helps. When you relax, lie on your side to help ease any swelling or discomfort in your legs. Use extra pillows to support your abdomen or your legs as your pregnancy progresses.

Dealing with Stress

Pregnancy is stressful! Studies show pregnancy ranks #12 in a list of life's most stressful events. Normal stress probably won't hurt you or your pregnancy, but major stress may increase your risk of premature birth. Learning to manage stress can go a long way in making your life more manageable—when you're pregnant and when you're not!

During pregnancy, stress can be caused by many things. Hormone changes can cause you to react in ways that aren't normal for you, which can be stressful. Your body is changing, which stresses many women. You may have worked very hard to get and/or to maintain your figure. Now that you're pregnant, there's not much you can do about it.

You can't always eliminate stress, but you can learn to cope with it. The following suggestions may help you deal with everyday stressful situations.

- Get enough sleep each night. Lack of sleep can make you feel stressed.
- Rest and relax during the day. Read or listen to music during a quiet period. Slow down your daily activities.
- When you feel anxious or upset, practice deep breathing and relaxation exercises you learn in childbirth-education classes.
- Talk about it instead of acting out when you have problems. Be specific and listen to what others tell you in response. Work together toward practical solutions.
- Take time out. When stress gets to be too much for you, go into another room and stretch, practice breathing exercises or listen to soothing music.
- When you feel stressed, stop and take a few slow, deep breaths to help turn off the stressed part of your nervous system.
- Set realistic priorities. Manage your time with priorities in mind. Use a daily calendar. Learn to say, "No."
- Exercise can help you work off stress. Take a walk or visit the gym. Put on an exercise video for pregnant women. Do something active and physical (but not too physical) to relieve stress. Ask your partner to join you.
- Turn your thoughts to good things; it actually sends a chemical message to your brain that flows through your entire body and helps you relax.
- Eat nutritiously. Having enough calories available through the day will help avoid "lows."
- Decide to be more positive. Smiling instead of frowning can help ease stress.
- Do something you enjoy, and do it for you.

- If smells are important to you, include them in your life. Burn scented candles, or buy fragrant flowers to help you relax.
- Seek help. You may need outside help to make it through a difficult time or to change behavior patterns. If necessary, ask your healthcare provider for a referral.
- Don't go it alone. Share concerns with your partner, or find a group of pregnant women you can talk with.

Pregnancy can also make your partner feel stressed. Encourage him to try some of these stress-relieving activities if he's also feeling the stress of pregnancy.

Constipation

Bowel habits often change during pregnancy. Constipation is common and often accompanied by irregular bowel habits and hemorrhoids. These problems are usually the result of a slowdown in the movement of food through the gastrointestinal system and the ingestion of iron as supplements or in prenatal vitamins.

Two situations add to the problem of constipation in pregnancy. One is increased hormones—your body produces progesterone, which relaxes the smooth muscles of the intestinal wall and stomach, resulting in a slowdown of digestion. Second, your blood volume increases; you may not be drinking enough fluid to keep up with the increase, which can cause dehydration in you.

To help relieve the problem, increase your fluid intake. Eat foods that contain a lot of water, such as frozen juice treats, watermelon or a slush made with fresh lemon juice and water. In addition, foods with lots of fiber hold onto water longer, which helps soften your stools. For example, eating lentils or bran cereal can help increase fiber intake.

Exercise may be beneficial; try to exercise three or four times a week. It helps shift body position, which may stimulate your bowels and increase muscle contractions that help move food through your intestines.

Many healthcare providers suggest prune or apple juice or a mild laxative, such as milk of magnesia, Metamucil or Colace. However, avoid excessive use of *any* preparation that contains magnesium. High-fiber foods, such as bran and prunes, may help relieve constipation.

Don't use laxatives, other than those mentioned above, without consulting your healthcare provider. Try not to strain when you have a bowel movement; straining can lead to hemorrhoids. If constipation is a continuing problem, discuss it at your next office visit.

Headaches

Some pregnant women experience headaches during pregnancy. Increased hormone levels and increased blood volume can contribute to headaches. Headaches may also be caused by blood-sugar-level changes, changing hormones, dehydration or lack of sleep.

You may experience more *tension headaches* during pregnancy; they can be caused by many things, including stress, fatigue, heat, noise, thirst, hunger, loud music and bright lights. Some foods can trigger a headache, including peanuts, chocolate, cheese and some meats. Congested sinuses may also increase headaches. Tension headaches may decrease in the second and third trimesters of pregnancy as your body (and mind) adjust to your pregnancy.

Cluster headaches come in groups, last about an hour each time and can continue for weeks or months. Acetaminophen is OK to use for these types of headaches.

You may hesitate to take medication for headaches during pregnancy. Try any of the following medicine-free techniques for headache relief.

- Use deep-breathing exercises and relaxation techniques.
- Drink plenty of fluids so you don't become dehydrated.
- Close your eyes and rest in a quiet place.

- Eat regularly.
- Avoid foods or substances that can cause headaches.
- Apply an ice pack to the back of your head.
- Get enough sleep.
- Exercise to help relieve headaches.
- Massage your neck and shoulders to help relax tight muscles.
- Put a warm washcloth over your nose and eyes to relieve a sinus headache.
- Put a cold pack on the base of your neck.
- Massage your head/neck/shoulder area, or ask your partner to do it for you.

If your headache doesn't go away using these techniques, you may take regular or extra-strength acetaminophen. If this doesn't help, call your healthcare provider.

Migraine Headaches

Migraine headaches are often an inherited disorder. Nearly one in five pregnant women has a migraine at some point during pregnancy. A migraine can last for a few hours up to 3 days. Some women suffer more during pregnancy because of their changing hormone levels. Be aware that a headache or migraine that doesn't go away in late pregnancy could signal pre-eclampsia.

A migraine headache is characterized by severe, throbbing pain and is aggravated by physical activity, such as walking. Nausea, vomiting or diarrhea often accompany a migraine headache.

Some women who regularly experience migraines do not suffer from them during pregnancy; others have worse migraine headaches, especially in the first trimester. For some, the second and third trimesters are migraine-free.

You can attempt to deal with migraine headaches without medicine. Lie in a darkened room with a cold compress on your forehead. Try various relaxation methods, such as listening to relaxation tapes, doing deep-breathing exercises or practicing meditation/yoga exercises. Avoid things that might trigger a migraine, including aged cheese, cured meat, chocolate, caffeine, cigarette or cigar smoke, bright lights, stress or disruptions in sleeping or eating patterns.

Ginger may help with migraines. Studies show a pinch of powdered ginger in water may be as effective as prescription medicine. When you first feel symptoms of a migraine, mix ⅓ teaspoon of powdered ginger in a cup of water. Drink this mixture three or four times a day for 3 days for relief.

If the above measures don't help, talk with your healthcare provider; he or she will prescribe the safest medication available. Do *not* take any medication,

Other conditions can cause nausea and vomiting in early pregnancy besides morning sickness, including pancreatitis, gastroenteritis, appendicitis and pyelonephritis as well as some metabolic disorders. If you don't have morning sickness in early pregnancy then experience nausea and vomiting later in your pregnancy, it's not morning sickness.

other than acetaminophen, for a migraine headache without discussing it first with your healthcare provider.

Heartburn and Indigestion

Heartburn? Indigestion? Which one is it?

Some people who suffer from heartburn say they are suffering from indigestion. However, indigestion isn't the same thing as heartburn. Although they have similar triggers and treatment may be the same in many instances, they are different.

Indigestion is a condition and refers to an inability to digest food or difficulty digesting food. It includes a vague feeling of discomfort and pain in the upper abdomen and chest, a feeling of fullness and bloating, and may be accompanied by belching and nausea.

Several things can trigger indigestion, including overeating, eating a particular food, drinking alcohol or carbonated beverages, eating too fast or too much, eating fatty or spicy foods, drinking too much caffeine, smoking or eating too much high-fiber foods. Studies show that anxiety and depression can worsen symptoms. Other causes include a duodenal ulcer or gastric ulcer and use of antibiotics, aspirin and/or NSAIDs.

If you have indigestion, you can take steps to relieve it. Eat foods that agree with you; avoid spicy foods. Eat small meals frequently. If you need antacids after meals, use them but don't overmedicate yourself.

One of the most frequent discomforts of pregnancy, especially among older pregnant women, is heartburn. *Heartburn* is a burning discomfort related to the lower end of the esophagus and is felt behind the lower part of the sternum; it may be a symptom of indigestion. It occurs when your digestive tract relaxes and stomach acid creeps back into the esophagus.

Heartburn may begin early in pregnancy and often becomes more severe as pregnancy progresses. Women often want to know the difference between heartburn and indigestion.

Two main causes of heartburn during pregnancy are a reflux (backing up) of stomach acids into the esophagus and the hormonal changes of pregnancy. During pregnancy, your body produces hormones that relax involuntary muscles; one such muscle normally prevents stomach acids from backing up into the esophagus. Because the muscle isn't doing its usual job, you experience heartburn. You may notice heartburn during the third trimester especially, when the expanding uterus crowds the stomach and intestines. This can cause some stomach contents to back up into the esophagus.

Antacids may provide considerable relief. Follow your healthcare provider's instructions and/or package directions relating to pregnancy. Don't overdo it and take too much in an effort to find relief. You can use some antacids, such as Amphojel, Gelusil, milk of magnesia and Maalox, without too much concern. However, avoid excessive use of any product that contains sodium or magnesium. Sodium can contribute to water retention. Excessive use of magnesium antacids has been linked to magnesium poisoning. In addition to taking antacids, try the following suggestions.

- Eat smaller meals more frequently.
- Avoid overeating.
- Use less fat when cooking.
- Avoid carbonated beverages.
- Don't eat foods you know give you heartburn, such as rich or spicy foods.
- Avoid eating before bedtime.
- When lying down, elevate your head and shoulders.
- Wear loose clothing.
- Stay upright after meals, especially in late pregnancy.
- Chew gum for 30 minutes after meals and when heartburn strikes. Chewing gum increases saliva production, which counteracts stomach acids.
- Suck on hard candy to promote saliva production.
- Get some exercise, but don't eat for the 2 hours before you begin. Use smooth moves to avoid pushing acids into your esophagus.
- Reduce stress in your life.

Another way to help relieve heartburn is to mix the juice of ½ lemon and a pinch of salt in 8 ounces of water, and drink it before meals. After meals, 1 teaspoon of honey may help ease discomfort.

Two popular over-the-counter medications are Pepcid AC (for acid control) and Tagamet HB (for heartburn relief). However, we advise women *not* to use these products during pregnancy unless there is clear indication they are needed. Don't take these or any other medication without first discussing the situation with your healthcare provider.

> Gina was having a hard time with heartburn. She loved to eat Italian food, Mexican food and spicy foods, but she paid for it. With a few modifications, she found she could eat the things she liked and not suffer from heartburn afterward. She ate earlier in the evening, at least 2 hours before going to bed. She ate smaller amounts, and she always carried antacids, such as Tums or Mylanta. She started to call her antacids "my after-dinner mints"!

GERD

GERD (gastroesophageal reflux disease) or *acid-reflux disease* may be mistaken for heartburn during pregnancy. It is very common but often overlooked.

How can you tell the difference? With GERD, stomach acid flows back up into the esophagus. The three most common symptoms of acid-reflux disease include heartburn, sour or bitter taste, and difficulty swallowing. Other symptoms may include persistent cough, hoarseness, upset stomach and chest pain.

Be careful with the foods you eat. Eating too much food that is spicy, highly acidic or high in fat may aggravate acid reflux.

Only your healthcare provider can determine if you have GERD, so talk to him or her at a prenatal appointment if you have concerns. He or she may prescribe medication that is safe to use during pregnancy. If you're now taking prescription or over-the-counter medication to treat your problem, check with your healthcare provider before continuing its use.

Hemorrhoids

Hemorrhoids can be an uncomfortable problem during pregnancy. *Hemorrhoids* are dilated blood vessels (varicose veins) of the rectum that can itch, bleed and hurt. They appear around the area of the anus or inside the anus. They are caused by decreased blood flow in the area around the uterus and pelvis because of the weight of the uterus, causing circulation blockage. Older women are especially vulnerable to developing hemorrhoids; they may have some dilated blood vessels around the rectum even before pregnancy.

Some women have the problem only during pregnancy, when body tissue changes, with some loss of elasticity. Pressure from your enlarging uterus blocks blood flow in the pelvic area. These changes encourage hemorrhoid formation.

Pregnant women most often develop hemorrhoids during the second and third trimesters. Hemorrhoids may worsen toward the end of pregnancy. They may also get worse with each succeeding pregnancy.

Eat lots of fiber, and drink lots of fluid. Stool softeners and bulk fiber products may also help. Fiber tablets, wafers or fiber products you can add to any food or drink without adding texture may also be beneficial. If you have hemorrhoids, try any or all of the following suggestions for relief.

- Rest at least 1 hour every day with your feet and hips elevated.
- Take warm baths for relief.
- Suppository medications, available without a prescription, may help.
- Stool softeners can prevent hard stools from forming; hard stools can aggravate delicate tissues.
- At work, try to arrange a time every day to take off your shoes and put up your feet.
- Apply ice packs, cold compresses or cotton balls soaked in witch hazel to the affected area.
- Don't sit or stand for long periods.
- Over-the-counter products that contain hydrocortisone may help relieve itching and swelling. Ask your doctor about them.
- If you experience pain, acetaminophen may help relieve it.

After pregnancy, hemorrhoids usually improve, but they may not go away completely. Continue to use the treatment methods discussed above when pregnancy is over.

Time-Saving, Energy-Saving Tip

When you have a backache, swelling or other pregnancy discomforts, an ice pack may offer relief. If you don't have any commercial ice packs at home, make your own! Fill a heavy-duty zipper freezer bag with 1 part rubbing alcohol to 3 parts water. Add some food coloring (blue or green are good choices) so you won't mistake it for something else. Freeze, then use it when you need it. You can make many different sizes—as many as there are sizes of freezer bags. This enables you to cover a small or a large area.

Discuss the situation with your healthcare provider if hemorrhoids become a major problem. In rare cases, the problem is relieved with surgery after pregnancy.

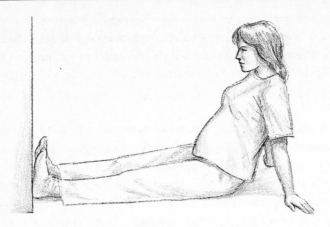

Stretching your legs can help relieve leg cramps. Sit on the floor, and place your feet flat against the wall. Pull toes away from the wall, keeping heels on the floor. Repeat six to eight times when you experience leg cramps.

Leg Cramps

Leg cramps, also called *charley horses,* can be bothersome during pregnancy, especially if you experience them at night. Cramps are characterized by a sharp, grabbing pain in the calf. A cramp is a spasm in two sets of muscles that forces your foot to point involuntarily.

The best way to relieve a leg cramp is to stretch muscles. Flex or bend your foot to stretch leg muscles in the opposite direction. You can do this by standing up or by gently pressing the knee down with one hand while you gently pull the upper part of the foot toward you with your other hand. Stretching exercises before you go to bed at night may help. Don't point your toes or stretch your legs before getting out of bed. The following suggestions may help relieve or prevent leg cramps.

- Wear maternity support hose during the day.
- Take warm (not hot) baths.
- Do stretching exercises.
- Have your partner massage your legs.
- Take acetaminophen for pain.
- Rest on your left side.
- Use a heating pad set on low for up to 15 minutes (no longer) on the cramp.
- Avoid standing for long periods of time.
- Don't wear tight or restrictive clothing.

One study showed women who eat high amounts of saturated fat—the kind found in cheese and red meat—in the year before they got pregnant had a higher risk of suffering severe morning sickness during pregnancy.

Some medical experts believe leg cramps occur more frequently if there is an imbalance of calcium and phosphorous in the body. Don't consume more calcium than you need—1200mg is the recommended daily dose during pregnancy. That's about 4 cups of milk. (See also the chart on page 188 for the calcium content of some foods.) Soft drinks, snack foods and processed foods are high in phosphates; you may need to cut down on them or eliminate them from your diet. Drinking lots of water may help prevent leg cramps.

If you want to try a folk remedy, mix together 2 teaspoons of apple-cider vinegar and 1 teaspoon of honey in a glass of warm water. Drink it before bed.

Morning Sickness

An early symptom of pregnancy for many women is nausea, sometimes accompanied by vomiting, often called *morning sickness.* About 50% of all pregnant women experience nausea and vomiting, about 25% of pregnant women have nausea only and 25% experience no symptoms. The condition may affect you, especially if you suffer from motion sickness or migraines before pregnancy.

Morning sickness usually occurs around week 6 and lasts until week 12 or 13, when it usually starts to subside. Sometimes it can last throughout pregnancy.

The problem may be worse in the morning. Whether it occurs in the morning or later in the day, morning sickness often starts early and improves throughout the day as you become active.

Morning sickness is more common in women carrying multiples. Heartburn and reflux can also impact morning sickness, making nausea and vomiting worse.

There is some good news about morning sickness—women with nausea and vomiting in pregnancy have a lower incidence of miscarriage. The sicker you are, the lower the chance you will miscarry.

Be aware that morning sickness can affect your pregnancy weight gain. For many women, weight gain may not begin until the beginning of the second trimester, when nausea and vomiting often pass.

Try the following suggestions to deal with the nausea and vomiting related to morning sickness.

- Eat small portions of nutritious food throughout the day instead of three large meals.
- Eat a snack, such as dry crackers or rice cakes, *before* you get out of bed in the morning. Or ask your partner to make some dry toast for you.
- Avoid heavy, fatty foods.
- Keep up your fluid intake—fluids may be easier to handle than solids and will help you avoid dehydration.
- Alternate wet foods with dry foods. Eat only dry foods at one meal, then wet foods and liquids at the next.
- Try fresh ginger—it's a natural remedy for nausea. Grate it onto vegetables and other foods. Or make a tea with it.
- Avoid things that trigger your nausea, such as odors, movement or noise.
- Suck on a fresh-cut lemon when you feel nauseated.
- Get enough rest.
- Avoid getting sweaty or overheated, which can contribute to nausea.
- Apply pressure to pressure points on your wrists. (See the illustration and instructions on page 161.)
- Wear a *ReliefBand*. See the box below.

There is no completely successful treatment for pregnancy nausea and vomiting. Research has found that quite a few women find relief by taking vitamin B_6 supplements. It's good therapy to try because it's readily available and inexpensive. Ask your healthcare provider about taking PremesisRx, a once-a-day tablet. If vitamin B_6 alone doesn't work, he or she might want to add doxylamine, an antihistamine.

You can also ask about taking over-the-counter antinausea medication, such as Emetrol. In addition, ask your healthcare provider about using a

A *ReliefBand* may help relieve morning sickness. It's worn like a wrist watch on the inside of your wrist. It stimulates nerves in the wrist with gentle electric signals; this stimulation is believed to interfere with messages between the brain and stomach that cause nausea. It has various stimulation levels to allow you to adjust signals for maximum control for individual comfort. It can be used when nausea begins, or you can wear it before you feel ill. It doesn't interfere with eating or drinking. It's water resistant and shock resistant, so you can wear it just about any time!

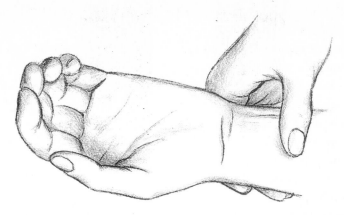

To help relieve nausea, find the pressure point three fingers above your wrist fold. Press on the point on each wrist at the same time—you'll probably need help doing this. Hold for 1 minute; repeat 3 times.

different prenatal vitamin that might be easier on your stomach. You might ask about taking a regular multivitamin—not a prenatal vitamin—or a folic-acid supplement during the first trimester.

Acupressure, acupuncture and massage may also prove helpful when dealing with nausea and vomiting. Acupressure wristbands, worn for motion and seasickness, and other devices help some women feel better.

This is an extremely important period in the development of your baby. Don't expose your unborn baby to herbs, over-the-counter treatments or any other "remedies" for nausea that are not known to be safe during pregnancy.

If your morning sickness is wearing you down, call your doctor's office. Ask about different ways to deal with morning sickness. Reassurances that this situation is normal and your baby is OK can be comforting.

Hyperemisis Gravidarum

Nausea does not usually cause enough trouble to require medical attention. However, a condition called *hyperemesis gravidarum* (severe nausea and vomiting) causes a great deal of vomiting, which results in loss of nutrients and fluid. Only 1 to 2% of all pregnant women experience hyperemesis gravidarum.

If you experience severe vomiting and can't eat or drink, you may be suffering from hyperemesis gravidarum. If you're unable to keep down 80 ounces of fluid in 24 hours, if you lose more than 2 pounds a week or 5% of your prepregnancy weight, or if you vomit blood or bile, contact your doctor immediately!

You may need to be treated in the hospital if you become dehydrated and lose weight. You will receive fluids and electrolytes intravenously and can usually resume liquids and eating solid food after a couple of days. Hypnosis is another treatment that can be successful.

An interesting note: Studies show if you experience hyperemesis gravidarum, your chance of having a daughter increases by more than 75%. Experts believe the cause is an overabundance of female hormones produced by the fetus and mother-to-be in the first trimester.

Normal Swelling in Pregnancy

During the last part of pregnancy, your ankles and feet may swell; some women also observe swelling in their hands and fingers. Swelling often begins around week 24. Nearly all pregnant women suffer from swollen fingers, ankles and feet.

Swelling occurs because your body produces as much as 50% more blood and fluids to meet your baby's needs. Some of this extra fluid leaks into your body tissues. When your enlarging uterus pushes on pelvic veins, blood flow in the lower part of your body is partially blocked. This pushes fluid into your legs and feet, causing swelling.

The best way to deal with the swelling is to improve your circulation through exercise and position changes. When possible, walk short distances. Do ankle circles while standing in line or sitting in a chair. Flexing your feet and ankles during the day helps keep blood circulating. When sitting, press your toes down as if you were pushing on the gas pedal of your car to accomplish the same thing.

To deal with normal swelling in legs and feet, wear sneakers, flats or shoes with low heels (no higher than 1½ inches) that fit comfortably. Choose the right kind of shoe for you. An ideal shoe has a 1-inch heel, good arch support, a roomy, box-shaped toe and adjustable straps or laces.

Prenatal massage may help with swelling. Eat foods high in potassium; a potassium deficiency may allow your cells to fill with water, increasing swelling. You can also try standing on your tiptoes—it helps pump blood back to the heart.

If swelling becomes extreme, especially during the last trimester, consult your health-

Time-Saving, Energy-Saving Tip
If your hands swell so much you can't wear rings, put your rings on a pretty chain and wear them around your neck or wrist.

care provider; it could be a sign of problems. Lie on your left side as frequently as possible. Don't stand for long periods.

Sciatic-Nerve and Sacroiliac-Joint Pain

Many women experience an occasional excruciating pain in their buttocks and down the back or side of their legs as pregnancy progresses. It is called *sciatic-nerve pain* or *sciatica*. The sciatic nerve is located behind the uterus, in the pelvic area, and runs down into the leg. We believe pain is caused when the enlarging uterus puts pressure on the nerve.

The best treatment is to lie on your opposite side to help relieve pressure on the nerve. Sitting on a tennis ball on a hard surface may also help. If you have to stand for any length of time, rest the toes of one foot on some object that is 3 to 4 inches off the ground, such as a thick book (the phone book or a dictionary works great!) to relieve pressure on the sciatic nerve.

Some people may mistakenly refer to sciatic-nerve pain as *sacroiliac pain*. However, sciatica pain and sacroiliac pain are not the same thing. Sciatica is a sharp, searing pain. *Sacroiliac joint pain (SJP)* is joint related and feels like a sharp jolt of pain on either side of the back or hips. It may extend down your legs. Warm baths (not hot) and acetaminophen may help.

Sleep Problems

Are you having trouble sleeping? Nearly 80% of all pregnant women have trouble sleeping at some time during pregnancy. Some reasons include hormone changes, altered respiration and the increased size of the abdomen. A short nap during the day may pep you up and help make up for sleep lost during the night.

Many moms-to-be wake up five or more times a night, which can cause fatigue during the day. Baby's movements, leg cramps and shortness of breath may also keep you up during the night later in pregnancy. You need to get enough rest during the night, especially late in pregnancy. Research shows women who slept fewer than 6 hours at night were four times more likely to have a Cesarean delivery.

Varicose Veins

Varicose veins, also called *varicosities* or *varices,* are large, distended veins deep under the skin. They are caused by problems with the one-way circulatory

Tips for Getting a Good Night's Sleep

- Go to bed and wake up at the same times each day.
- Don't drink too much fluid at night. Decrease fluid intake after 6pm.
- Avoid caffeine after late afternoon.
- Get regular exercise.
- Sleep in a cool bedroom; 70F (21.1C) is the maximum temperature for comfortable sleeping.
- If you experience heartburn at night, sleep propped up.

valves inside veins. Valves become clogged with blood then grow larger, which keeps blood from flowing through the vein as it should.

They occur to some degree in most pregnant women; however, varicose veins develop more often in older women. There seems to be an inherited predisposition to varicose veins that can become more severe during pregnancy. If your mother had varicose veins, you are more likely to develop them.

Varicose veins usually occur in the legs but can also be found in the birth canal or vulva. Hemorrhoids are varicose veins. Pressure from the uterus and the change in blood flow during pregnancy can make varices worse. Varicose veins in the legs, birth canal, vulva or rectum (hemorrhoids) can cause pain and discomfort.

Symptoms vary; for some women varicose veins are only a blemish or purple-blue spot on the legs, causing little or no discomfort except in the evening. For other women, varices are bulging veins that require elevation at the end of the day or other measures. They can cause itching and aching in the affected area.

You may also experience *spider veins*. They are small groups of dilated blood vessels near the skin surface. You see them most commonly on face and legs.

Varicose veins may get worse during pregnancy. Increasing weight (from the growing baby, uterus and placenta), tight clothing that constricts at the waist or legs, and standing a great deal can worsen varicose veins. If you continue to have problems with varicose veins after pregnancy, you may need surgery.

The most effective way to prevent varicose veins is to improve circulation in your legs, especially through exercise and changes in position. Exercising regularly helps improve blood flow through the veins. Walk when possible, and do ankle circles while sitting and standing. Even sitting and rocking in a rocking chair can help—rocking contracts and relaxes leg muscles, which moves blood from your feet to your heart.

When you lie down, lie on your left side to improve blood flow. Elevate your hips and legs. Keep your total pregnancy weight gain within normal range—between 25 and 35 pounds for a normal-weight woman.

Drinking citrus juice or eating citrus fruit may help with varicose veins. The vitamin C helps keep capillary and vein walls strong. Eating spinach, broccoli and asparagus may help lessen the severity of varicose veins. These foods are high in vitamin K, which helps activate a protein that impedes the mechanism that can lead to vein distortion.

If you get varicose veins during pregnancy, ask your healthcare provider about wearing medical support hose to reduce swelling and ease leg pains. Many types of maternity support hose or graduated-compression stockings are available. Maternity support hose help many women, but they can be very difficult to get on. The following tricks can help.

Put on your support hose before you get out of bed in the morning—your legs may tend to swell as soon as you get up. (You may need to change your habits and bathe before you go to bed.) Turn the stockings inside out before you put them on. Starting at the toe, unroll the stockings up your leg.

Choose clothes that don't restrict circulation at the knee or groin. Wear loose panties to help prevent vulvar varicosities (varicose veins in the vulva area) from causing discomfort.

Spend as little time as possible on your feet. Wear flat shoes. Don't cross your legs at the knee, and don't stand for long periods. If you must stand, bounce gently on the balls of your feet every few minutes.

Vision Changes

Some women notice changes in their vision during pregnancy. If you experience vision changes or problems during pregnancy, talk to your healthcare provider. If you notice your contact lenses don't seem to fit as well, your corneas may be swollen from fluid retention. Unless perfect vision is necessary for your work, wait to get a new prescription. Your eyes should return to normal after pregnancy.

Chapter 12

Nutrition and Weight Management

The fetus growing inside you has many nutritional needs—needs *you* must fulfill through the foods you eat. A pregnant woman who eats a healthful diet during pregnancy is much more likely to give birth to a healthy baby. Eating well reduces the risk of complications and limits some pregnancy side effects.

You can meet most nutritional needs by eating a well-balanced, varied diet. The *quality* of your calories is extremely important—if a food grows in the ground or on trees, it's better for you nutritionally than if it comes from a can or a box.

You may have heard the adage "a pregnant woman is eating for two." Many women take this to mean they can eat twice as much. Not true! The saying really means you must be concerned about getting the best nutrition for yourself *and* for your growing baby. You need to eat twice as smart!

Some women have the false idea they can eat all they want during pregnancy. Don't fall into this trap. Don't gain more weight than your healthcare provider recommends during your pregnancy—it can make you uncomfortable and it may be harder to lose the extra pounds after baby is born.

Your Caloric Needs in Pregnancy

If your weight is normal before pregnancy, your caloric intake should average about 2200 calories a day during the first trimester of pregnancy. You need to add up to 300 calories to that number during the remainder of your pregnancy, depending on your prepregnancy weight. (See the discussion of weight management during pregnancy that begins on page 191.)

Extra calories are the foundation of tissue growth in you and your baby. Your baby uses the energy from your calories to create and to store protein, fat and carbohydrates, and to provide energy for its body processes to function. You use the extra calories to support the changes your body goes through during pregnancy. Your uterus increases in size many times, your breasts increase in size and your blood volume increases by 50%, among other changes.

Calories aren't interchangeable. You can't eat whatever you want and expect to get the best nutrition for you and your baby; eating right takes care and attention. Where the calories come from is as important as the number you consume. You need to eat foods high in vitamins and minerals, especially iron, calcium, magnesium, folic acid and zinc. Fiber and fluids are also essential because pregnancy can cause constipation problems. Eating a wide variety of foods each day can supply you with the nutrients you need. Choose from dairy products, protein foods, fruits and vegetables, and breads and cereals. Avoid junk food, a lot of processed foods and foods loaded with empty calories.

During pregnancy, eat 6 to 7 ounces of protein every day to cover the growth of the embryo/fetus, placenta, uterus and breasts. There is no recommended dietary allowance (RDA) for daily carbohydrate intake during pregnancy. Most experts believe carbohydrates should make up about 60% of the total number of calories in your diet. If you're eating 2200 calories a day, you would consume about 1320 carbohydrate calories.

You probably don't need to worry about inadequate fat intake; in the North American diet, fat intake is usually excessive. There is no recommended daily amount for fat intake during pregnancy. Don't avoid all fats, but use them sparingly. Measure how much you use of each, and read labels.

Food-Group Recommendations

Be good to yourself and your baby. Eat the recommended number of servings from each food group every day. If you're carrying multiples, add one more serving each of dairy products and protein each day. Discuss your nutrition plan with your healthcare provider or a registered dietitian.

Dairy Products

Dairy products contain calcium, which is important for you and your growing baby. You need to consumer 1200mg of calcium each day. The calcium content of many packaged

If you're watching your calorie intake, you might choose low-fat foods to help you cut back on calories. They can be a good choice, but they won't help you if you still eat too many calories. Many people believe the kind of food they eat matters more than the amount they eat. In many cases, they eat more calories of a low-fat food than they would if they ate a higher-fat food! Don't get caught in this trap.

foods is listed on the nutrition label. Foods you might choose from this group, and their serving sizes, include the following:

- ¾ cup cottage cheese
- 2 ounces processed cheese (such as American cheese)
- 1 ounce hard cheese (such as Parmesan or Romano)
- 1 cup pudding or custard
- 1 8-ounce glass of milk
- 1½ ounces natural cheese (such as cheddar)
- 1 cup yogurt

If you want to limit the fat content of dairy products, choose skim milk, low-fat yogurt and low-fat cheese instead of whole milk and ice cream. The calcium content is unaffected in low-fat dairy products. Refer to the box on page 188 for other common foods with calcium.

•••

Lupe began having food cravings early in her pregnancy. Her craving for ice cream could have been a problem. She knew if she ate it as often as she wanted to, her weight would be out of control. She found that by using self-control and substituting low-fat frozen yogurt for higher-calorie ice cream, she was able to have a treat once in a while and still manage her weight.

•••

Protein

Amino acids in protein are critical to the growth and repair of the embryo/fetus, placenta, uterus and breasts. The recommended amount of protein in pregnancy is 6 to 7 ounces a day, about twice the amount normally recommended. Foods you might choose from this group, and their serving sizes, include the following:

- 2 tablespoons peanut butter
- ½ cup cooked dried beans
- 2 to 3 ounces cooked meat
- 1 egg

Poultry, fish, lean cuts of red meat, dry beans, eggs, nuts and seeds are all good protein sources. If you need to watch your calorie intake, skinless chicken and fish are better choices than beef or pork. If you choose fish, keep your total weekly intake to a maximum of 12 ounces.

Fruits and Vegetables

Fruits and vegetables will be a very important part of your pregnancy eating plan. Fruit is good for you, and it tastes good. It's an excellent source of many important vitamins and minerals, so enjoy many types of fruit. Because they change with the seasons, fruits and vegetables are a great way to add variety to your menu. Some fruits and vegetables are good sources of iron, folic acid, calcium and fiber; check a nutritional guide for particular information about vegetables. (Your produce grocer may be able to answer your questions.)

Time-Saving, Energy-Saving Tip

One way to add low-calorie salads and extra fiber to your eating plan is to keep ready-to-use salad greens handy in the refrigerator. Wash and dry your salad fixings, then layer them in large, plastic zipper-lock bags or plastic containers. Place paper towels between layers, press air out and seal. Greens stay fresh for much longer.

Fruits you might choose, and their serving sizes, include the following:

- ¾ cup grapes
- ½ cup fruit juice
- 1 medium banana, orange or apple
- ¼ cup dried fruit
- ½ cup canned or cooked fruit

Include one or two servings each day of a fruit rich in vitamin C, such as orange juice or orange slices. Fresh fruits are also a good source of fiber, which can help relieve constipation.

Vegetables you might choose from this group, and their serving sizes, include the following:

- ¾ cup vegetable juice
- ½ cup broccoli, carrots or other vegetable, cooked or raw
- 1 medium baked potato or sweet potato
- 1 cup raw, leafy vegetables (greens)

Eat a variety of vegetables for good nutritional balance in your diet. Eat at least one leafy green or deep-yellow vegetable a day for extra iron, fiber, vitamin C and folic acid. Avoid all types of sprouts during pregnancy. Research tells us sprouts may cause salmonella infections in people with altered immune systems.

Grain Products

Foods from this group are nearly interchangeable, so it shouldn't be hard to get all the carbohydrates you need. If you don't like pasta, choose rice. If cereal isn't appealing, choose bread. Foods you might choose from this group, and their serving sizes, include the following:

- 1 large tortilla, corn or flour
- ½ cup cooked pasta, cereal or rice
- ½ small bagel
- 1 slice bread
- 1 medium roll

Fats and Sweets

Be careful with fats and sweets, unless you are underweight and need to add a few pounds. Although sugar adds flavor to food, it has little nutritional value. Use it sparingly.

Watch your intake of butter, margarine, oils, salad dressing, nuts, chocolate and sweets. Foods in this group are often high in calories but low in nutritional value. Use them sparingly. Foods from this group, and their serving sizes, include the following:

- 1 tablespoon sugar or honey
- 1 tablespoon olive oil or other type of oil
- 1 pat margarine or butter
- 1 tablespoon jelly or jam
- 1 tablespoon prepared salad dressing

Sweets and junk food are full of empty calories. Replace these treats with nourishing choices, such as a piece of fruit or a slice of whole-wheat bread. You'll satisfy your hunger and your nutritional needs at the same time.

Understanding Serving Portions

You may believe it will be difficult for you to eat all the portions you need for the health of your growing baby. However, many people overeat because they

don't understand what a "portion" or "serving" really is.

Supersizing in fast-food restaurants and huge meal portions at other restaurants have skewed our idea of what a normal portion size really is. For example, a blueberry muffin is now about 500 calories. Twenty-five years ago, it was about

200 calories. Look for the following serving sizes when you eat—they're what a "normal" portion size is:

- 1 cup of vegetables—the size of a lightbulb
- 1 serving of juice—a champagne flute
- 1 pancake—the size of a CD
- 1 teaspoon of peanut butter—the end of your thumb
- 3 ounces of fish—an eyeglass case
- 3 ounces of meat—a deck of playing cards
- 1 small potato—a 3 x 5 index card

Read labels for portion sizes; a common mistake is to read the calorie/nutrient information on a label and not take into account the *number of servings* each package contains. Even a very small package may contain two or more servings, doubling or tripling the calories if you eat the whole thing.

••

Terry had a habit of going out for fast food every day for lunch before she got pregnant. But during her pregnancy, she was very tired by midday and needed to rest. She discovered if she brought a sack lunch to work, she could eat a healthful meal, then lie down on a couch in the staff lounge for 45 minutes. She got some rest and enjoyed her afternoon work a lot more.

••

To learn the *correct* serving size for each of the food groups, check out the USDA's website, www.cnpp.usda.gov; it lists actual serving portions. For example, a large bagel may be *four* to *five* grain servings! If you don't have access to a computer, ask your healthcare provider for some guidelines or nutrition handouts.

Other Food Facts

Junk Food

You may have to forgo most junk food while you're pregnant. Junk food is high-calorie, high-fat food that contains little nutrition for you or your baby. It's probably fine to eat some now and then, but don't make it a regular part of your diet.

Avoid chips, sodas, cookies, pie, chocolate, candy, cake and ice cream. Instead, select foods that are high in fiber and low in sugar and fat, such as fruits and vegetables, legumes, dairy products and whole-grain crackers and breads.

Food Cravings

Cravings for particular foods during pregnancy are normal. (Sometimes the chosen foods appear a little strange to other people!) Cravings can be both good and bad. If you crave foods that are nutritious and healthful, go ahead and eat them in moderate amounts. If you crave foods high in sugar and fat, loaded with empty calories, be careful about eating them. Sometimes you can get rid of a craving by eating fresh fruits and vegetables.

We don't know why women sometimes crave unusual foods or food combinations during pregnancy. Hormonal and emotional changes that occur during pregnancy may have something to do with it.

Pica—Nonfood Cravings

Some women experience *pica* during pregnancy. They crave nonfood items, such as dirt, clay, laundry starch, chalk, ice, paint chips and other things. We don't know why pregnant women develop these cravings. Some experts believe it may be caused by an iron deficiency. Others think pica may be the body's attempt to get vitamins or minerals not being supplied in the food the woman eats. Still others speculate that pica cravings may be caused by an underlying physical or mental illness.

Pica cravings may be harmful to your baby and you. Eating nonfood items could interfere with nutrient absorption of healthy foods and result in a deficiency.

If you have pica cravings, don't panic. Call your healthcare provider immediately. He or she will develop a plan with you to help deal with these cravings.

Food Aversions

On the opposite side of cravings is food aversion. Some foods you usually love or foods you have eaten without problems before pregnancy may now make you sick to your stomach. This is common. The hormones of pregnancy have a significant impact on the gastrointestinal tract, which can affect your reaction to certain foods.

During pregnancy and lactation, the level of cholesterol in your blood rises naturally because of hormone changes. It probably won't make sense to have your cholesterol tested while you're pregnant or nursing.

What Foods Do Pregnant Women Crave?

One study of pregnant women found they craved the following foods:
- Chocolate (33% of the time they craved foods)
- Other desserts, such as ice cream (20% of the time)
- Citrus (19% of the time)

If you have food aversions, try to substitute foods to get the nutrients you need. For example, drink calcium-fortified juice if you can't drink milk. Meat making you ill? Try eggs, beans or nuts.

Caffeine

You may be more sensitive to caffeine during pregnancy. For many years, the Food and Drug Administration (FDA) has recommended pregnant women avoid caffeine. It isn't good for you or baby.

Caffeine is a component of many beverages and foods, including coffee, tea, cola drinks and chocolate. Some medications, such as cough medicines and headache preparations, contain a lot of caffeine. Read labels on foods, beverages and over-the-counter medications to determine caffeine content. Eliminate as much caffeine from your diet as possible. Experts recommend a pregnant woman not consume more than 200mg of caffeine in any one day.

As a central-nervous-system stimulant, caffeine can affect calcium metabolism in both you and your baby. Drinking as little as two 8-ounce cups of coffee a day may increase your risk of early miscarriage. Pregnant women who drink 800mg of caffeine a day are at risk of delivering a baby with decreased birthweight and a smaller head size. Half that amount of caffeine in a pregnant woman (400mg) may affect a baby's developing respiratory system. One study showed exposure before birth may also be linked to sudden infant death syndrome (SIDS).

Cut down on caffeine, or eliminate it from your diet. Caffeine crosses the placenta to the baby—if you're jittery, your unborn baby may suffer from the same effects. And caffeine passes into breast milk, which can cause irritability and sleeplessness if you breastfeed baby.

Read labels on the products you buy. Caffeine is found in many beverages and foods, including coffee, tea, various soft drinks and chocolate. It may even be added to some foods you eat. The list below details the amounts of caffeine from various sources:
- coffee, 5 ounces—from 60 to 140mg and higher
- tea, 5 ounces—from 30 to 65mg

- baking chocolate, 1 ounce—25mg
- 1½ ounce chocolate bar—10 to 30mg
- cocoa, 8 ounces—5mg
- soft drinks, 12 ounces—from 35 to 55mg
- pain-relief tablets, standard dose—40mg
- allergy and cold remedies, standard dose—25mg

Herbal Use in Pregnancy

If you normally use herbs and botanicals in the forms of teas, tinctures, pills or powders to treat various medical and health problems, stop! We advise you *not* to treat yourself with an herbal remedy during pregnancy *without checking first with your doctor!*

You may believe an herbal remedy is safe, but it could be dangerous during pregnancy. For example, if you're constipated, you may decide to use senna as a laxative. However, senna stimulates uterine muscles and may cause a miscarriage. Or you may use St. John's wort before pregnancy. Avoid it now—St. John's wort can interfere with various medications, including some pain-relief medicine and antidepressants. In addition, avoid dong quai, pennyroyal, rosemary (used for digestive problems, not cooking), juniper, thuja, blue cohosh and senna during pregnancy.

Play it safe—be extremely careful with any substance your doctor has not specifically recommended for you. Always check with him or her first before you take anything!

Herbal Teas

Some types of herbal tea are good for you and may help relieve certain pregnancy discomforts, which may make herbal tea a good alternative to coffee or regular tea. The herbal teas listed below are delicious and safe to use during pregnancy:

- chamomile   helps digestion
- dandelion   helps reduce water retention and soothe an
                            upset stomach
- ginger root   helps ease nausea and nasal congestion
- nettle leaf   rich in iron, calcium and other vitamins and minerals
                            that are good for a pregnant woman
- peppermint   relieves gas pain and calms stomach acids; use alone
                            or mix with chamomile
- red raspberry   helps relieve nausea and stabilize hormones

You can safely drink red-raspberry-leaf tea during pregnancy; it may make labor a little shorter. But don't drink it until after the first trimester.

Don't drink green tea before conceiving and/or during pregnancy. Studies show it can interfere with your body's absorption of folic acid. Other herbal teas are not safe to use during pregnancy because they could harm your developing baby. Herbs and teas to *avoid* during pregnancy include blue or black cohosh, pennyroyal leaf, yarrow, goldenseal, feverfew, psyllium seed, mugwort, comfrey, coltsfoot, juniper, rue, tansy, cottonroot bark, large amounts of sage, senna, cascara sagrada, buckthorn, male fern, slippery elm and squaw vine.

I often use herbal and natural medications—up to six different ones a day. These substances are safe during pregnancy, aren't they?
Treat herbs as you would prescription or over-the-counter medications. Ask before you take them! Herbs can be useful, but they can also be harmful when taken during pregnancy.

Sweetener Use during Pregnancy

Many women use sugar and/or artificial sweeteners before pregnancy. Are they safe during pregnancy?

Caloric sweeteners include processed and unprocessed sugars, such as granulated sugar, brown sugar and corn syrup. Unprocessed sugars include honey, agave nectar and raw sugar. Caloric content ranges from 16 to 22 calories per teaspoon. If you use caloric sweeteners, you're adding empty calories to your meal plan.

Artificial (noncaloric) sweeteners help a woman cut calories. Some common artificial sweeteners include aspartame, acesulfame K, sucralose, stevia and saccharin. Can a pregnant woman use artificial sweeteners?

Aspartame is used in many foods and beverages to help reduce calories and is sold under the brand names Nutrasweet and Equal. It's a combination of two amino acids—phenylalanine and aspartic acid. If you suffer from phenylketonuria, you can't use aspartame. You must follow a low-phenylalanine diet or your baby may be adversely affected.

Sucralose, sold under the brand name Splenda, is made from sugar and is found in a variety of products. It passes through the body without being metabolized. Your body doesn't recognize it as a sugar or a carbohydrate, which makes it low calorie.

Stevia is a product made from the leaves of the stevia plant. It is sold under the brand names PureVia and Truvia. Ask your healthcare provider for information about using it during pregnancy.

Saccharin is an artificial sweetener used in many foods and beverages. Although it is not used as much today as it was in the past, it still appears in many foods, beverages and other substances. Saccharin is also added to many foods and beverages.

Research has determined artificial sweeteners are probably safe to use in small amounts during pregnancy. However, if you can avoid them, it's best *not* to use them during pregnancy. Eliminate any substance you don't really need from the foods you eat and the beverages you drink. Do it for the good of your baby.

Late-Night Snacks

Late-night nutritious snacks are beneficial for some women, especially if they must eat many small meals a day. However, many women should not snack at night because they don't need the extra calories. For others, food in the stomach late at night can cause heartburn or indigestion.

Eating Out

It's OK to eat out at restaurants; just be careful about what you eat. Avoid raw or undercooked meats or raw seafood, such as sushi. Avoid foods that may not agree with you.

At a restaurant, your best choices may be cooked chicken or fish, fresh vegetables and salads, but be careful with calorie-loaded salad dressings if you're concerned about excessive weight gain. Avoid spicy foods or foods that contain a lot of sodium. Chinese food often contains large amounts of monosodium glutamate (MSG, a sodium-containing product). You may retain water after eating these foods.

Some Food Precautions

Salmonella

Salmonella poisoning is caused by bacteria. Problems range from mild gastric distress to a severe, sometimes fatal, food poisoning. This situation can be serious for a pregnant woman and her developing baby if it prevents a woman from getting enough fluid or eating nutritiously. Almost 1400 salmonella strains have been identified.

We know cracked raw eggs may be contaminated with salmonella organisms. These organisms are found in uncracked eggs as well if a hen's ovaries are contaminated. Salmonella bacteria can be found in raw chicken and other raw poultry.

Bacteria are destroyed in cooking, but it's prudent to take additional precautions against salmonella poisoning. You can help avoid salmonella if you practice the following.

- Clean counters, utensils, dishes and pans with a disinfecting agent. Wash your hands after preparing any poultry or products made with raw eggs. You could pick up salmonella from these surfaces on your hands and transfer it to your mouth or another surface.
- Cook all poultry thoroughly.
- Avoid foods made with raw eggs, including salad dressings (Caesar salad), hollandaise sauce, eggnog, homemade ice cream made with eggs or any other food made with raw or undercooked eggs.
- Don't eat cookie dough or cake batter.
- Boil eggs 7 minutes for hard-cooked eggs.
- Poach eggs for 5 minutes.
- Fry eggs for 3 minutes on *each* side.
- Avoid sunny-side up eggs (those not turned during frying). Cook the entire egg thoroughly, not just part of it.

Listeriosis

Every year about 1500 cases of listeriosis, a form of food poisoning, are reported in the United States. About 500 of these cases occur in pregnant women, who are more susceptible to infection. Pregnant women are 20 times more likely to get listeriosis than other healthy adults.

Babies born to moms who had listeriosis are at higher risk of developing severe complications. Researchers believe there might be a link between listeriosis and miscarriage and stillbirth. Newborns can have infections similar to group-B strep. Treatment is with antibiotics, such as ampicillin.

To prevent listeriosis, avoid unpasteurized milk and any foods made from unpasteurized milk. You also need to be careful of other products that aren't pasteurized, such as some cheeses. Avoid unpasteurized soft cheeses such as Camembert, Brie, feta, Gorgonzola, bleu cheese and Roquefort. *If they have been made with pasteurized milk,* these soft cheeses are OK to eat during pregnancy. Read labels very carefully.

Be careful buying fruit juice at a farmers' market or a farm stand. It may not be pasteurized. Unpasteurized fresh juice can contain bacteria, viruses and parasites.

Undercooked poultry, red meat, seafood and hot dogs can also contain listeriosis. Cook all meat and seafood thoroughly before eating. Be careful about cross contamination of foods. If you place raw meat or poultry, raw seafood or uncooked hot dogs on a counter or other surface during preparation, thoroughly wash the surface with soap and hot water or a disinfectant *before* you place any other food on the same surface.

Phenylketonuria

Phenylketonuria (PKU) is a condition in which the body is unable to use phenylalanine properly, and it accumulates in body fluids. The accumulation can lead to mental retardation and other nervous-system disorders in you or your developing baby. If you suffer from phenylketonuria, follow a diet low in phenylalanine. Avoid the artificial sweetener aspartame.

Facts about Fish

Eating fish is healthful, particularly during pregnancy. Fish contains omega-3 fatty acids; this substance may help prevent pregnancy-induced hypertension and pre-eclampsia, which are both greater risks for older pregnant women.

Women who eat a variety of fish during pregnancy have longer pregnancies and give birth to babies with higher birth weights, according to some studies. This is important because the longer a baby stays in the uterus, the better its chances are of being strong and healthy at delivery.

Many fish are safe to eat, and you should include them in your diet. Most fish is low in fat and high in vitamin B, iron, zinc, selenium and copper. Many fish choices are an excellent healthful addition to your diet, and you can eat them as often as you like. See the box on page 180 for a list of good fish choices.

Omega-3 Fatty Acids

Some researchers believe eating fatty fish or ingesting omega-3 fatty acids in another form (such as fish-oil capsules) may enhance your baby's intellectual development. Studies show fish oil is important to fetal brain development. One study of pregnant women showed that when a pregnant woman eats fish oil, it reaches the brain of the developing fetus.

Omega-3 fatty acids are good for your skin. They keep it lubricated and help reduce any skin inflammation.

Include omega-3 fatty acids in your eating plan. Anchovies, herring, mullet, mackerel (not King mackerel), salmon, sardines and trout are some fish with a lot of omega-3 fatty acids. Fish-oil capsules may be another option for increasing omega-3 fatty-acid intake. If you buy fish-oil capsules, choose the *filtered* type because they don't contain pollutants. Don't exceed 2.4g of omega-3 fatty acids a day. Be aware that fish-oil capsules may upset your stomach. To solve this problem, freeze them or take them with meals or at bedtime.

Some Cautions about Fish

Some fish are contaminated with a dangerous substance as the result of pollution. People who eat these fish are at risk of methyl-mercury poisoning. *Mercury* is a naturally occurring substance as well as a pollution byproduct. Mercury becomes a problem when it is released into the air as a pollutant. It settles into the oceans and from there winds up in some types of fish.

The FDA has determined that a certain level of methyl mercury in fish is dangerous for humans. We know methyl mercury can pass from mother to fetus across the placenta. Research has shown that 60,000 children born each year are at risk of developing neurological problems linked to the consumption of seafood by the mothers-to-be. Because of rapid brain development, a fetus may be more vulnerable to methyl-mercury poisoning.

The Food and Drug Administration (FDA) and Environmental Protection Agency (EPA) recommend pregnant women not eat swordfish, shark, king mackerel or tilefish. A woman should limit her fish and shellfish intake to *no more than 12 ounces a week.* Twelve ounces is two average servings. The FDA suggests choosing a variety of fish and shellfish that are lower in mercury. The amount of mercury in fish varies widely.

There is controversy about eating tuna during pregnancy. Studies indicate pregnant women and those trying to conceive should not eat tuna (fresh or frozen) more than once a month. Canned tuna may be a little safer, but don't eat more than one 6-ounce can a week. Talk to your doctor about it at a prenatal appointment if this is a favorite food for you.

When choosing fish, you may want to double-check tilapia. Farm-raised tilapia is one of the most highly consumed fish in America; however, it has

Good Fish and Shellfish Choices

Below is a list of fish you can eat as often as you like during pregnancy, as long as *you don't exceed 12 ounces of fish in any one week.*

bass	catfish	cod	croaker
flounder	freshwater perch	haddock	herring
mackerel	marlin	ocean perch	
orange roughy	Pacific halibut	pollack	red snapper
salmon	scrod	sole	

You may eat the following shellfish if you thoroughly cook them. *Again, don't exceed 12 ounces of fish in any one week.*

clams	oysters
crab	scallops
lobster	shrimp

very low levels of omega-3 fatty acids and very high levels of unhealthy omega-6 fatty acids.

Some freshwater fish may also be risky to eat, such as walleye and pike. To be on the safe side, consult local or state authorities for any advisories on eating freshwater fish in your area.

Other environmental pollutants can appear in fish. Dioxin and PCBs (polychlorinated biphenyls) are found in some fish, such as bluefish or lake trout; avoid them. Parasites, bacteria, viruses and toxins can also contaminate fish. Eating infected fish can make you sick, sometimes severely so. Sushi and ceviche are fish dishes that could contain viruses or parasites. Raw shellfish, if contaminated, could cause hepatitis A, cholera or gastroenteritis. Avoid *all* raw fish during pregnancy! If you're craving raw fish, such as sushi, eat a California roll (no raw fish) or shrimp tempura. Dishes made with *cooked* eel and rolls with *steamed* crab and veggies are acceptable.

Other fish to avoid during pregnancy include some found in warm tropical waters, especially Florida, the Caribbean and Hawaii. Avoid the following "local" fish from those areas—amberjack, barracuda, bluefish, grouper, mahi mahi, snapper and fresh tuna.

If you're unsure about whether you should eat a particular fish or if you want further information, contact the Food and Drug Administration.

Drink Plenty of Fluids

You need to drink water during pregnancy—lots of it! Water enables your body to process nutrients, develop new cells, sustain blood volume and regulate body temperature—all very important during pregnancy. Your blood volume increases during pregnancy; drinking extra fluids helps you keep up with this change. You may feel better during pregnancy if you drink more liquid than you normally do.

When you don't drink water, you can become dehydrated. If you're dehydrated, you can become fatigued more easily. Being dehydrated may reduce the amount of nutrients baby receives from you. Your blood thickens, making it harder to pass nutrients to baby. Dehydration may also increase your risk of high blood pressure and pre-eclampsia, and it may cause contractions.

Water is important in regulating body temperature. In fact, for each degree above 98.6F (37C), you need to drink an extra pint of water (or other fluid) each day to help bring down a fever.

Our bodies contain 10 to 12 gallons (38 to 45l) of water. Studies show that for every 15 calories your body burns, you need about 1 tablespoon (15ml) of water. If you burn 2000 calories a day, you need to drink well over 2 quarts (1.9l) of water! As calorie needs increase during pregnancy, so does your need for water.

New guidelines suggest 100 ounces (3l) of fluid a day should be consumed during pregnancy. Water should account for at least 50 ounces (1.5l) of your fluid intake. Water in food can make up another 20 ounces (600ml). The other 30+ ounces (90+ml) should come from milk, juice and other beverages. Sip water and other fluids throughout the day. Some women drink water, one glass at a time, throughout the day. (Decrease your intake later in the day so you don't have to go to the bathroom all night long.)

Many women wonder if they have to drink water—can they drink other beverages besides water? Water is the best source of fluid, but you can drink other fluids to help meet your needs. Don't substitute foods that contain a lot of water for drinking water. You won't be as hydrated unless you actually *drink* water. And keep the consumption of caffeinated beverages low. Tea, coffee and cola may contain sodium and caffeine, which act as diuretics. They essentially *increase* your water needs.

Drinking water may ease some of the common problems women experience during pregnancy. Headaches, uterine cramping and bladder infections may be less of a problem for you when you drink lots of water.

To determine if you're drinking enough fluid, check your urine. When it's light yellow to clear, you're getting enough water. Dark yellow urine is a sign you need to increase your fluid intake. And don't wait until you get thirsty to drink something. By the time you get thirsty, you've already lost at least 1% of your body's fluids.

When you exercise, drink a cup of water before you begin your workout. Then drink ½ cup to 1 cup of water every 20 minutes while you are exercising to help prevent dehydration.

Your Drinking Water

Water supplies in the United States are some of the least-contaminated in the world. Most of our country has high-quality drinking water. Most experts agree tap water in the United States is safe to drink. Often tap water contains minerals that have been removed from bottled water.

Drinking water contaminated with chemical byproducts from chlorine may not be safe for you to drink. One study showed an increased rate of problems when women drank water with chlorinated byproducts.

Chlorine is often added to drinking water to disinfect it. When added to water that contains organic matter, such as from farms or lawns, it can form unhealthy compounds (for pregnant women), such as chloroform. Check with your local water company if you're concerned.

Do *not* rely on bottled water as safer than tap water. One study showed nearly 35% of over 100 brands of bottled water were contaminated with chemicals or bacteria. However, tap water must meet certain minimum standards if it is supplied by a municipal water company, so you know it's safe to drink. In addition, some bottled water contains sugar, caffeine or herbs.

Your Fiber Intake

Fiber is important in your diet. The average American doesn't consume enough fiber, which is important for your good health.

Just about everyone needs to eat more fiber. Experts suggest total fiber intake for women of childbearing age be 15g for every 1000 calories you eat. That means if you're eating a meal plan that is 2300 calories/day, you need about 33g of fiber every day! Most people take in only about 15g a day. In addition to helping you with constipation—a problem many women face during pregnancy—fiber may help reduce your risks of diabetes, heart disease, some cancers and obesity.

Fiber is not absorbed in your digestive tract. That's one reason it helps with constipation; it helps move food through your body as you digest it. There are two types of fiber—soluble and insoluble. Soluble fiber will dissolve in water; insoluble won't. Both sources are good for you.

Many foods are good sources of soluble or insoluble fiber. Good sources of soluble fiber include apples, berries, flaxseeds, nuts, oat bran, oranges and strawberries. Soluble fiber slows digestion, which helps you feel full longer. It also helps stabilize blood sugar, important during pregnancy, and helps inhibit the body's absorption of cholesterol and fat.

Good sources of insoluble fiber include brown rice, carrots, cucumbers and whole wheat. As long as you drink enough fluid, insoluble fiber can help you deal with constipation.

Don't go whole hog and start eating tons of fiber. You may need to increase your intake gradually. This can help you avoid bloating and flatulence (gas). Fiber will attract water, so you need to drink lots of fluid if you add fiber to your diet.

Below is a list of fiber sources you might include in your meal plan. It may be better to get a little too much (you can cut back if you feel bloated or have a lot of gas) than not enough.

- brown rice, cooked 1 cup—3.5g fiber
- whole-wheat bread, 2 slices—3.8g fiber
- black beans, ½ cup—7.5g fiber
- almonds, 1 ounce—3.5g fiber
- pear, 1 large—6.5g fiber
- blueberries or blackberries, 1 cup—3.5g fiber
- carrots, cooked, ½ cup—3.5g fiber
- peas, cooked, ½ cup—4.5g fiber
- potato, baked with skin, 1 medium—3g fiber

Be sure to read labels on food cans and packages to help you keep track of your fiber intake. A label will include the amount of *dietary fiber* so you can keep track of your daily intake.

Salt, Sodium and Pregnancy

Sodium is a chemical that helps maintain the proper amount of fluid in your body. (Table salt, a compound comprised of sodium and chloride, is about half sodium.) During pregnancy, sodium can also affect your baby's system.

Using too much or too little of it can cause problems. You need some sodium; you just don't need a lot.

You need sodium during pregnancy to help deal with your increased blood volume. Aim for between 1500 and 2300mg a day. Consuming too much sodium may cause fluid retention, swelling and high blood pressure.

You can't avoid something unless you know where to find it. With sodium, that can be tricky. It's in the salt shaker and in salty-tasting foods, such as pretzels, chips, salted nuts, dill pickles, soup and meats. It's frequently used as a preservative in foods that don't taste salty, such as canned and processed products, fast foods, cereals, desserts, carbonated beverages and sports drinks— even some medications. Read nutrition labels. You can also buy pamphlets or books that list the sodium content of common foods and fast foods.

The Challenge of Being Vegetarian during Pregnancy

Some women choose to eat a meatless diet because of personal or religious preferences. Other women find that during pregnancy, the sight of meat makes them feel ill. Many pregnant women want to know if eating a *vegetarian* diet—a food plan without meat—is safe. Following a vegetarian diet while you're pregnant can be safe and healthful if you pay close attention to the foods and combinations of foods you eat.

Most women who eliminate meat from their diets eat a more nutrient-rich variety of foods than those who eat meat. These women may make an extra effort to include more fruits and vegetables in their food plans when they eliminate meat products.

If you choose a vegetarian eating plan, be sure you eat enough calories to fuel your pregnancy. During pregnancy, you need to consume between 2200 and 2700 calories a day, depending on your prepregnancy weight. (See page 193 for a chart about weight gain during pregnancy.) In addition to eating enough calories, you must eat the *right* kind of calories. Choose fresh foods that provide a variety of vitamins and minerals. Avoid too many fat calories because you may gain extra weight. Eat enough different sources of protein to provide energy for the fetus and for you. Discuss your daily diet with your healthcare provider at your first prenatal visit. He or she may want you to see a nutritionist if you have any pregnancy risk factors.

It's important to get the vitamins and minerals you need. If you eat a wide variety of whole grains, dried beans and peas, dried fruit and wheat germ,

Omega-3 fatty acids are found in animal foods, including grass-fed beef and eggs from hens fed special diets. If you're a vegetarian or you don't like fish, add tofu, canola oil, flaxseed, soybeans, walnuts and wheat germ to your food plan because these foods contain linolenic oil, which is a type of omega-3 fatty acid.

you should be able to meet your body's demands for iron, zinc and other trace minerals.

If you're not eating meat because it makes you ill, ask your healthcare provider for a referral to a nutritionist. You may need help developing a good eating plan. If you're a vegetarian by choice and have been for a while, you may know how to get many of the nutrients you need.

There are different vegetarian nutrition plans, each with unique characteristics. If you are a *lacto* vegetarian, your diet includes milk and milk products. If you are an *ovo-lacto* vegetarian, your eating plan includes milk products and eggs. A *vegan* diet includes only foods of plant origin, such as nuts, seeds, vegetables, fruits, grains and legumes. A *macrobiotic* diet limits foods to whole grains, beans, vegetables and moderate amounts of fish and fruits. A *fruitarian* diet is the most restrictive; it allows only fruits, nuts, olive oil and honey.

Macrobiotic and fruitarian diets are too restrictive for pregnant women. They do not guarantee the optimal intake of the vitamins, minerals, protein and calories you need for proper fetal development. Other vegetarian diets can provide complete nutrition for you and your growing baby; vegan diets, lacto diets or ovo-lacto diets can work if you eat a wide variety of foods in the right quantities.

As a vegetarian, your goal is to consume enough calories to maintain and to gain weight during pregnancy. You don't want your body to use protein for energy because you need it for your growth and your baby's growth.

Minerals are also a concern. By eating a wide variety of whole grains, legumes, dried fruit, beans and wheat germ, you should be able to get enough iron, zinc and other trace minerals. If you don't drink milk or include milk products in your diet, you must find other sources of vitamins D, B_2, B_{12} and calcium. See the discussion of vitamins and minerals in the section that follows.

Vitamin and Mineral Needs during Pregnancy

Vitamins and minerals are important for good nutrition. Eating a nutritious, varied diet helps ensure you get most of the vitamins and minerals you need. Your healthcare provider may suggest you take a prenatal vitamin every day. Vegetarians may need to pay special attention to getting enough of some vitamins and minerals.

Iron Supplementation

Iron is one of the most important elements for your body; women need more iron than men do because of menstruation. However, most women do not get enough iron in their diet. Research shows that between the ages of 20 and 50, American women consume only about two-thirds of the Recommended Dietary Allowance (RDA) of 15mg of iron a day. The average woman's diet seldom contains enough iron to meet the increased demands of pregnancy.

Your iron needs are higher during pregnancy because your blood volume increases by as much as 50% to support the oxygen needs of your baby and the placenta. In the third trimester, your need for iron increases even more. Your baby draws on your stores to create its own stores for the first few months of its life.

You will also need adequate iron reserves to draw on during and after baby's birth. The uterus's oxygen requirements increase with labor contractions, and you will lose some blood during a normal delivery.

If you have an iron deficiency, you feel tired, have trouble concentrating, get sick easily or suffer from headaches, dizziness or indigestion. An easy way to check for iron deficiency is to examine the inside of your bottom eyelid— it should be dark pink. Or look at your nail beds; if you're getting enough iron, they will be pink.

A healthy woman absorbs only 10 to 15% of the iron she consumes. To ensure you have enough iron in your diet, eat a variety of iron-rich foods, such as chicken, lean red meat, dried fruits, organ meats, such as liver, heart and kidneys, egg yolks, spinach, kale and tofu.

Your body stores iron efficiently, so you don't need to eat these foods every day. However, you do need to eat them on a regular basis. Eat vitamin-C foods and iron-rich foods together because the body absorbs iron more easily when consumed with vitamin C. (A spinach salad with orange sections is a nutritious example.)

Prenatal vitamins contain about 60mg of iron. You may not need extra iron if you eat a healthful diet and take your prenatal vitamins every day. Discuss it with your healthcare provider.

The iron you ingest can cause constipation. Work with your healthcare provider to minimize this side effect while making sure you get enough iron.

Vegetarians and others who eat very little meat are at greater risk of iron deficiency during pregnancy. If you're a vegetarian, pay close attention to this aspect of your diet. Fish, poultry and tofu are all excellent iron sources. Most legumes and peas also contain significant amounts of the mineral. Many breakfast foods and breads are now iron fortified.

Dried fruit and dark leafy vegetables are good sources of iron. Cook in cast-iron pans because traces of iron will attach to whatever you're cooking. Don't drink tea or coffee with meals because tannins present in those beverages inhibit iron absorption by 75%. If you are a lacto or ovo-lacto vegetarian, don't drink milk with foods that are iron rich; calcium reduces iron absorption.

Getting Enough Calcium

Calcium is important in the diet of every woman, especially women in their 30s and 40s. During pregnancy, your needs increase because your developing baby requires calcium to build strong bones and teeth, and you need calcium to keep your bones healthy. The daily requirement for a nonpregnant woman is between 800 and 1000mg of calcium. During pregnancy, your needs increase to 1200mg or more a day. Discuss it with your healthcare provider.

Dairy products are excellent sources of calcium and vitamin D, which is necessary for calcium absorption. It may be difficult for you to get enough calcium without eating dairy foods. Most prenatal vitamins contain only a small amount of the calcium you need. If your calcium intake is inadequate, your baby may draw needed calcium from your bones, which increases your risk of developing osteoporosis later in life.

If you are lactose intolerant and unable to drink milk, a condition that is more frequent among older women, you may be able to eat hard cheeses and yogurt. Lactose-reduced or lactose-free dairy products are also available. You may be able to use Lactaid, a preparation that helps your body deal more efficiently with lactic acid. Discuss the situation with your healthcare provider.

You may also choose nondairy sources of calcium; calcium is found in legumes, spinach, some fish, nuts and other foods. Some foods are now fortified with calcium. Read nutrition labels. The chart on page 188 lists some common calcium-containing foods.

Foods with Calcium

Food	Serving Size	Amount of Calcium
Almonds	¼ cup	95 mg
Beans, dried, cooked	1 cup	90 mg
Bok choy	½ cup	79 mg
Collards	½ cup	179 mg
Milk, 2%	8 ounces	300 mg
Orange juice, calcium-fortified	6 ounces	300 mg
Sardines	3 ounces	324 mg
Spinach, cooked	½ cup	140 mg
Tofu processed with calcium sulfate	4 ounces	434 mg
Trout	4 ounces	250 mg
Waffle	1 medium	180 mg
Yogurt, fruit	8 ounces	345 mg
Yogurt, plain	8 ounces	400 mg

If you need to watch your calories and avoid unnecessary fats, choose your calcium sources wisely. Select low-fat products and those with reduced-fat content. Skim milk and low-fat, fat-free and part-skim cheeses are better choices than whole milk and regular cheese.

Some foods interfere with your body's absorption of calcium. Be very careful about consuming salt, protein, tea, coffee and unleavened bread with a calcium-containing food.

Many women grow tired of drinking milk or eating cheese or yogurt to meet their calcium needs during pregnancy. Below are some suggestions for adding calcium to your diet.

- Make fruit shakes with milk and fresh fruit.
- Drink calcium-fortified orange juice.
- Add nonfat milk powder to recipes.
- Cook brown rice or oatmeal in low-fat or nonfat milk instead of water.
- Drink calcium-fortified skim milk.

- Make soups and sauces with undiluted evaporated nonfat milk instead of cream.
- Eat calcium-fortified breads.

If you and your healthcare provider decide calcium supplements are necessary, you will probably take calcium carbonate combined with magnesium, which aids calcium absorption. Avoid supplements derived from animal bones, dolomite or oyster shells because they may contain lead.

Folic Acid

Vitamin B$_9$ is beneficial to all pregnant women. The synthetic form of this B vitamin is *folic acid*. *Folate* is the form found in food. Folic-acid deficiency can result in a type of anemia called *megaloblastic anemia*. Additional folic acid may be necessary for situations in which pregnancy requirements are unusually high, such as a pregnancy with twins or triplets, alcoholism or Crohn's disease.

Prenatal vitamins contain 0.8 to 1mg of folic acid, sufficient for a woman with a normal pregnancy. Most women do not need extra folic acid during pregnancy.

A neural-tube defect called *spina bifida* afflicts nearly 4000 babies born in the United States every year. It develops in the first few weeks of pregnancy, when the fetus is highly susceptible to some substances or the lack of them. Research has proved nearly 75% of all cases of spina bifida can be prevented if the mother takes 0.4mg of folic acid a day, beginning 3 or 4 months *before* pregnancy. Folic acid for this purpose is required only through the first 13 weeks of pregnancy.

If a woman gives birth to a baby with spina bifida, she may need extra folic acid in subsequent pregnancies to reduce her chances of having another baby with the same problem. Some researchers, in hopes of significantly decreasing the chances of this serious problem, recommend *all* women of childbearing age take 0.4mg of folic acid a day.

Folate is found in a variety of foods. Many cereals and bread products are fortified with folic acid. Although it is sometimes difficult to get enough folic acid through food intake alone, a varied diet can help you reach this goal. Common foods that contain folate include asparagus, avocados, bananas,

> Eating a breakfast of 1 cup of fortified cereal, with milk, and a glass of orange juice supplies about half of your daily requirement of folic acid.

black beans, broccoli, egg yolks, green beans, lentils, liver, citrus fruit, peas, plantains, spinach, strawberries, wheat germ and yogurt.

A word of warning—give up green tea before conceiving and during pregnancy. Studies show it can interfere with your body's absorption of folic acid.

Getting enough folic acid is usually not a problem for vegetarians. Folate is found in many fruits, legumes and vegetables (especially dark leafy ones).

Vitamin A

Vitamin A is essential to human reproduction. Vitamin-A deficiency in North America is rare; most women have adequate stores of the vitamin in the liver.

What concerns healthcare providers is the *excessive use* of vitamin A before conception and during early pregnancy. (This concern extends only to the retinol forms of vitamin A, often derived from fish oils. The beta-carotene form, usually derived from plants, is believed to be safe.) Studies indicate that elevated levels of the retinol form of vitamin A during pregnancy may cause birth defects.

The RDA of vitamin A is 2700 international units (IU) a day for a woman of childbearing age (5000IU is a maximum dosage). The requirement is the same whether a woman is pregnant or not. Most women get the vitamin A they need during pregnancy from the foods they eat. Supplementation during pregnancy is not recommended. Be cautious about taking *any* substances you have not discussed with your healthcare provider. This includes vitamin A.

Vitamin B

The *B vitamins*—B_6, B_{12} and folic acid (B_9)—influence fetal nerve development and red-blood-cell formation. If your vitamin-B_{12} level is low, you could develop anemia. Milk, eggs, tempeh and miso provide vitamins B_6 and B_{12}. Other good sources of B_6 include bananas, potatoes, collard greens, avocados and brown rice. (See page 189 for folic-acid information.)

Vitamin E

Vitamin E is important during pregnancy because it helps metabolize polyunsaturated fats and contributes to building muscles and red blood cells. Vitamin E appears in adequate quantities in meats, but if you don't eat meat, it can be harder to get from the rest of your diet. If you're a vegetarian or not eating meat, pay particular attention to getting enough vitamin E to meet the minimum requirements.

Unbleached, cold-pressed vegetable oils (such as olive oil), wheat germ, spinach and dried fruits are all good sources of vitamin E. Ask your healthcare provider if your prenatal vitamin contains 100% of the RDA for vitamin E.

Zinc

Zinc stabilizes the genetic code in cells and ensures normal tissue growth in the fetus. It may help prevent miscarriage and premature delivery and can help regulate blood sugar in you and your baby.

Some thin women can increase their chances of giving birth to bigger, healthier babies by taking zinc supplements during pregnancy. In one study, babies born to thin women who took zinc during pregnancy were an average 4.5 ounces (128g) heavier, and head circumference was 0.16 inch (0.4cm) larger. Zinc also plays a critical role in immune functions.

Zinc is found in many foods, including seafood, meat, nuts and milk. Prenatal vitamins include 15 to 25mg of zinc, an adequate amount for most women.

If you're a vegetarian, you're more likely to have a zinc deficiency, so pay close attention to getting enough zinc every day. Lima beans, whole-grain products, nuts, dried beans, dried peas, wheat germ and dark leafy vegetables are all good sources of this mineral.

Fluoride

Benefits of fluoride supplementation during pregnancy is controversial. Some researchers believe fluoride supplements result in improved teeth in your child, but not everyone agrees. Fluoride supplementation in pregnancy has not been found to be harmful to baby. Some prenatal vitamins contain fluoride.

Weight Management

Every woman needs to gain a certain amount of weight during pregnancy. Proper weight gain helps ensure you and your baby are healthy at the time of delivery.

The recommended weight gain during pregnancy for a normal-weight woman is 25 to 35 pounds (11.25 to 15.75kg). If you're underweight at the start of pregnancy, expect to gain between 28 and 40 pounds (12.5 to 18kg). If you're overweight before pregnancy, you probably should not gain as much as other women during pregnancy. Acceptable weight gain for you is between 15 and 25 pounds (6.75 to 11.25kg). If you're obese, the recommendation is a gain of between 11 and 20 pounds (5 to 9kg) for an entire pregnancy. Rec-ommendations vary, so discuss the matter with your healthcare provider. Eat nutritious, well-balanced meals during your pregnancy. Do *not* diet now!

Many healthcare providers suggest a weight gain of ⅔ of a pound (10 ounces; 283g) a week until 20 weeks as an average for a normal-weight woman, then 1 pound (0.45kg) a week until the end of your pregnancy. This is only an average; actual suggestions vary according to the individual.

It isn't unusual not to gain weight or even to lose a little weight early in pregnancy. Your healthcare provider will keep track of changes in your weight.

Watch your weight, but don't be obsessive about it. If you're in good shape, with an appropriate amount of body fat when you get pregnant and you ex-ercise regularly and eat healthfully, you shouldn't have a problem with exces-sive weight gain.

Increasing Your Caloric Intake

During pregnancy, you need to increase your calorie consumption; the aver-age recommended increase is about 300 calories a day. Some women need more calories; some women need fewer. If you're underweight when you begin pregnancy, you will probably have to eat more than 300 extra calories each day. If you're overweight, you may have less need for extra calories. See the discussions below.

The key to good nutrition and weight management is to eat a balanced diet throughout your pregnancy. Eat the foods you need to help your baby grow and develop. Choose wisely. For example, if you're overweight, avoid high-calorie peanut butter and other nuts as a protein source; choose water-packed chicken or low-fat cheeses instead. If you're underweight, high-calorie ice cream and milk shakes are acceptable dairy sources.

Be Prepared to Gain Weight

Getting on the scale and seeing your weight increase is hard for some women, especially those who watch their weight closely. You must acknowledge at the beginning of pregnancy that it's OK to gain weight—it's for the health of your baby. You can control your weight gain by eating carefully and nutritiously, but you must gain enough weight to meet the needs of your pregnancy. Your healthcare provider knows this; that's why your weight is checked at every prenatal visit.

In the past, women were allowed to gain a very small amount of weight during pregnancy, sometimes as little as 12 to 15 pounds (5.5 to 6.75kg) for an entire pregnancy! Through research and advances in technology, we have

General Weight-Gain Guidelines for Pregnancy

Weight before Pregnancy	Recommended Gain (pounds)
Underweight	28 to 40 (12.6 to 18kg)
Normal weight	25 to 35 (11.25 to 15.75kg)
Overweight	15 to 25 (6.75 to 11.25kg)
Obese	11 to 20 (5 to 9kg)
Morbidly obese	Your healthcare provider will determine weight gain

Another way to figure how much weight you should gain during pregnancy is to look at your BMI (body mass index). BMI guidelines for weight gain during pregnancy include the following:
- BMI of less than 18.5—gain between 28 and 40 pounds (12.6 to 18kg)
- BMI of 18.5 to 25—gain between 25 and 35 pounds (11.25 to 15.75kg)
- BMI of 26 to 29—gain between 15 and 25 pounds (6.75 to 11.25kg)
- BMI of 30 or more—gain between 11 and 20 pounds (5 to 9kg)
- BMI of 40 and over—healthcare provider will determine weight gain

Ask your healthcare provider to help you figure your BMI if you don't know how to do it.

learned these restrictive weight gains were not in the best interests of mother or baby.

When You're Underweight

If you're underweight when you begin pregnancy, you face special challenges. Studies show 20% of all pregnant women fail to gain the amount of weight their healthcare provider recommends. You may need to gain between 28 and 40 pounds (12.5 to 18kg) during your pregnancy. Gaining weight will supply your baby the nutrients it needs to grow and to develop.

Weight loss during the first trimester is not uncommon if you have morning sickness. If you're underweight when you become pregnant and lose weight because of morning sickness or other problems, talk to your healthcare provider.

If you don't gain enough weight during pregnancy, you're at higher risk of preterm delivery, some birth defects, low birthweight or having a baby with

heart or lung problems. Being underweight may also contribute to various pregnancy problems, including pre-eclampsia, gestational diabetes and intrauterine-growth restriction.

You may find if you're underweight you need to gain extra weight during pregnancy. Below are some tips to help you reach that goal.

- Don't drink diet sodas or eat low-calorie foods.
- Choose nutritious foods to help you gain weight, such as cheeses, dried fruits, nuts, avocados, whole milk and ice cream.
- Eat foods with a higher calorie content.
- Try to add nutritious, calorie-rich snacks to your daily menu.
- Avoid junk food with lots of empty calories.
- You may need to exercise *less* if you burn too many calories in these activities.
- Eating small, frequent meals may help improve digestion and absorption of nutrients.

If you're underweight, make a good nutrition plan at the beginning of pregnancy. Ask your doctor about seeing a dietician to help you.

Eating Disorders

About 7 million women in the United States have an eating disorder; eating disorders are becoming more recognized in pregnant women. Experts believe that as many as 1% of all pregnant women suffer from some degree of eating disorder. The two primary eating disorders are anorexia nervosa and bulimia nervosa. Other eating disorders include restricting calories or food, and weight obsession, but those afflicted with them don't meet the anorexia or bulimia criteria.

Distribution of Pregnancy Weight

7 to 10 pounds	Maternal stores (fat, protein and other nutrients)
4 pounds	Increased fluid volume
2 pounds	Breast enlargement
2 pounds	Uterus
7 ½ pounds	Baby
2 pounds	Amniotic fluid
1 ½ pounds	Placenta

Women with *anorexia* usually weigh less than 85% of what is normal for their age and height. They are often extremely fearful of becoming fat, have an unrealistic body image, purge with laxatives or by vomiting, and binge. *Bulimia* is characterized by repeated binging and purging; a woman may feel a lack of control over the situation. A bulimic binges and purges at least twice a week for a period of 3 months or more.

It's often difficult for any woman to see her body gain the weight that is normal with a pregnancy. It may be even harder for a woman with an eating disorder to see the pounds add up. It may take a lot of hard work and effort to accept these extra pounds, but you must try to do it for your good health and the good health of your baby.

Eating disorders may worsen during pregnancy. However, some women find their eating disorder gets better during pregnancy. For some, pregnancy is the first time they can let go of their obsessions about their bodies.

If you believe you have an eating disorder, try to deal with it *before* you get pregnant. An eating disorder affects you *and* your baby! Problems associated with an eating disorder during pregnancy include the following:

- a weight gain that is too low
- a low-birthweight baby
- miscarriage and an increased chance of fetal death
- intrauterine-growth restriction (IUGR)
- baby in a breech presentation (because it may be born too early)
- high blood pressure in the mother-to-be
- depression during and after pregnancy
- birth defects

- electrolyte problems in the mother-to-be
- decreased plasma volume
- low 5-minute Apgar scores after baby's birth (see Chapter 19)

Your body is designed to provide your baby with the nutrition it needs, even if it has to take it from your body stores. For example, if your calcium intake is low, your baby will take the needed calcium from your bones. This could lead to osteoporosis for you later in life.

More frequent prenatal visits and monitoring during pregnancy are often recommended for a woman with an eating disorder. Researchers believe eating disorders may disrupt the way nutrients are delivered to the fetus, which could result in slower fetal growth or IUGR. Your healthcare provider will want to keep close tabs on how your baby is growing. Antidepressants may also be used to help treat the problem. An eating disorder may increase your risk of postpartum depression.

Talk to your healthcare provider about your problem as soon as possible. It's serious and can adversely affect both you and your baby.

Where Does the Weight Go?

A weight gain of 25 to 35 pounds (11.25 to 15.75kg) may sound like a lot when the baby only weighs about 7 pounds (3.15kg); however, weight is distributed between you and your baby. Weight gained normally during pregnancy is distributed as shown in the box on the previous page.

Special Cautions for Overweight Women

If you're overweight when you get pregnant, you're not alone. Statistics show up to 38% of all pregnant women fall into this category. Over 72 million Americans are considered obese, and 12 million are considered morbidly obese.

The National Academy of Sciences Institute of Medicine has added a new category to pregnancy weight-gain guidelines. The category is for obese women, and the recommendation is a weight gain of between 11 and 20 pounds (5 to 9kg) for an entire pregnancy. Some experts also cite morbid obesity as a subcategory of obesity; experts suggest weight gain should be determined on an individual basis for women in this category.

You are considered *overweight* if your body mass index (BMI) is between 25 and 29; over 30, you are considered *obese*. If you have a BMI of 40 or over, you are considered *morbidly obese*.

Being overweight brings special challenges. Pregnancy can be harder on you and your baby, and it can contribute to a variety of problems. You may have more problems with backaches, varicose veins and fatigue. Baby's shoulders may be too broad to fit through the birth canal (shoulder dystocia). In addition, your baby may be overdue. Morbid obesity brings additional risks.

A prenatal meeting with an anesthesiologist may be recommended because obese pregnant women have a higher risk for anesthesia complications. In addition, studies show overweight/obese women often have a slower progression of labor from 4 to 10cm dilatation compared with normal-weight women.

Research shows over 65% of all overweight women gain *more weight* than their healthcare provider recommends during pregnancy. Gaining too much weight may increase your chances of a Cesarean delivery. It can make carrying your baby more uncomfortable, and delivery may be more difficult. Studies also show it's harder to lose any weight you gain during pregnancy after baby is born.

Babies are at risk if a mom-to-be is overweight or obese. Various birth defects have been attributed to overweight/obesity. Cleft palate and cleft lip are more common in children born to obese women. Overweight/obese women have lower levels of prolactin, which can result in a decreased milk supply.

Women who are overweight may need to see their healthcare provider more often during pregnancy. Ultrasound may be needed to pinpoint a due date because it's harder to determine the size and position of a baby; abdominal fat layers make manual examination difficult. You may be screened for gestational diabetes. Other diagnostic tests may also be necessary during pregnancy. Diagnostic tests may also be done on your baby as your delivery date approaches.

Take Care of Yourself

Try to gain your total-pregnancy weight *slowly*. Weigh yourself weekly, and watch your food intake. Eat nutritious, healthful foods, and eliminate those with empty calories. A visit with a nutritionist may help you develop a healthful food plan.

Do *not* diet during pregnancy. To get the nutrients you need, choose nonfat or low-fat products, meats, grain products, fruits and vegetables. Many supply a variety of nutrients. Take your prenatal vitamin every day throughout your entire pregnancy.

Talk to your healthcare provider about making exercise part of your daily routine. Discuss swimming and walking, which are good exercises for *any* pregnant woman.

Eat regular meals—5 to 6 *small* meals a day is a good goal. This helps maintain blood-sugar levels and helps with nutrient absorption. Your total calorie intake should be between 1800 and 2400 calories a day. Keeping a daily food diary helps you track of how much you're eating and when you're eating. It can help you identify where to make changes, if necessary.

When You're Eating for More Than Two

When you're expecting two or more babies, you face an even greater nutritional challenge. Taking your prenatal vitamin every day provides some assurance you're getting the nutrients you need, but the best sources of nutrients and calories for you and your developing babies are the foods you eat. Proper food choices can provide you with adequate protein, calories and calcium.

When you're expecting more than one baby, nutrition and weight gain are important. If you don't gain weight early in pregnancy, you may be at risk for developing pre-eclampsia. Your babies are more likely to be significantly smaller at birth than others.

Target Weight Gain with Multiples

Weight gain is important with a multiple pregnancy. You will probably be advised to gain more than the normal 25 to 35 pounds (11.25 to 15.75kg), depending on the number of fetuses you're carrying. With twins, if you were normal weight before pregnancy, you may be advised to gain 40 to 54 pounds (18 to 24.5kg). If you're expecting triplets, your weight gain will probably be between 50 and 60 pounds (22.7 and 27kg).

If you are overweight and expecting twins, a weight gain between 31 and 50 pounds (14 to 22.7kg) may be recommended. A weight gain between 25 and 42 pounds (11.25 and 19kg) may be recommended for obese women pregnant with twins.

Usually women who gain the targeted amount of weight during pregnancy lose it after delivery. One study showed women who gained the suggested amount of weight during a twin pregnancy were close to their prepregnant weight 2 years after delivery. You don't have to carry the extra weight forever, so don't worry about it now.

When you consider the average size of the babies (about 7½ pounds each, 3.4kg) and the weight of the placentas (1½ pounds, 0.68kg for each), plus the weight of the additional amniotic fluid, you can see where some of the extra weight gain goes. Don't be alarmed when your healthcare provider discusses this target weight gain with you, even if it seems like a lot.

Research shows higher weight gains (within targeted ranges) are associated with better fetal growth. Better fetal growth means healthier babies.

Chapter 13

Exercise during and after Pregnancy

Experts agree exercise during pregnancy is safe and beneficial for most pregnant women, if it is done properly. Exercise can be even more beneficial for women who are pregnant in their late 30s and early 40s. It can help you feel more energetic and help you deal more effectively with the demands of pregnancy, career and family.

Today, most pregnant women are advised to exercise moderately for 30 minutes *every* day. More than 60% of all pregnant women do some sort of exercise. The aim of exercise during pregnancy is to stay fit.

Exercise during pregnancy is good for you. Research shows if *you* exercise during pregnancy, *your baby* may have a healthier start in life. Exercising may also help reduce your chances of having gestational diabetes and pregnancy-induced hypertension. And it's believed exercise may increase growth of the placenta while reducing stress and blood pressure in you.

Discuss exercising during pregnancy with your healthcare provider at your first prenatal visit. If you decide later to start exercising or to change your current exercise program, be sure to talk with him or her before you begin or make any changes.

Some women should *not* exercise during pregnancy. If you experience any of the following, do not exercise until you have discussed it with your healthcare provider:

- a history of incompetent cervix, preterm labor or repeated miscarriages
- high blood pressure early in pregnancy
- multiple fetuses (twins, triplets, more)
- diagnosed heart disease
- pre-eclampsia
- vaginal bleeding

In the past, exercise was not always approved for a pregnant woman. Healthcare providers were concerned about the redirection of blood flow from the fetus during exercise. We now know that although this occurs to a small degree, it isn't harmful.

Any exercise that involves joint movement forces water in the tissues back into the blood and helps pump blood back to the heart. If your ankles or legs swell, exercise can help with the problem. Stationary bicycling is excellent for relieving these symptoms.

What are the best types of exercise for me to do during pregnancy?
Choose something you can do regularly throughout your pregnancy, no matter what the weather is like. Low-impact activities—walking, swimming, riding a stationary bicycle—are good choices.

If You Exercise Regularly

Women who love to exercise are willing to juggle hectic schedules to fit it into their daily routine. They believe exercise is necessary to help them feel fit, control their weight and look their best. They don't want to give up exercising or its benefits because of pregnancy.

If you exercise on a regular basis before pregnancy, you may need to modify your exercise goals and take things a little easier during pregnancy. The goal of exercising at this time is overall good health. Exercise makes you feel better physically, and it can give you an emotional boost—but don't overdo it.

There are benefits to continuing a moderate exercise program during your pregnancy. The discussion below identifies some of them.

Some healthcare providers believe women who exercise during pregnancy enjoy a shorter recovery time after birth. Because exercise keeps you fit, you may bounce back more quickly.

You may have to change or modify your exercise program during pregnancy because of changes in your body. Your center of gravity shifts, so you need to adjust your exercise for that. As your abdomen grows larger, you may not be able to do some activities very comfortably, and you may have to eliminate others.

During pregnancy, your heart rate is higher; you don't have to exercise as vigorously to reach your target-heart-rate range. Be careful not to put too much stress on your cardiovascular system. If your heart rate is too high, slow down but don't stop completely. Continue exercising at a moderate rate. If your heart rate is too low and you don't feel winded, you may pick up the pace a bit, but again, don't overdo it. Check your pulse rate frequently to make sure you aren't overexerting.

> Joan was concerned because it was hard to find time to exercise regularly. I told her to try exercising at her desk at work, doing ankle and leg exercises. This helped her keep her legs toned and also helped her with leg cramps and swelling.

Women who jog or run regularly often want to continue this activity during pregnancy. If you're used to jogging and have been involved in regular jogging before pregnancy, you can continue in moderation during pregnancy after getting your doctor's OK. Listen to your body when it tells you to slow down—don't get overheated, stop if you feel tired and drink lots of water.

The Exercise Payoff

Exercise during pregnancy can help you feel more in control of your body and relieve some of the common aches and pains of pregnancy. Exercise improves circulation and helps you adjust to carrying the extra weight you gain during pregnancy. Regular, moderate exercise can also help?

- relieve backache
- prevent constipation and varicose veins
- strengthen muscles needed for delivery
- make you feel better about yourself
- ease labor and delivery
- leave you in better shape after delivery
- control weight gain

Other exercise benefits include an increase in energy, nausea control, improvement in sleep, feeling better overall and having an easier time losing weight after pregnancy. Exercise also increases the release of growth hormone, which may help protect you from illness.

Try water aerobics to help relieve back and pelvic pain. Once a week may really help. Doing low-impact aerobics for at least 2 hours a week may help reduce your risk of preterm birth. Ten minutes of yoga or Pilates increases your blood flow and stretches your muscles.

If You've Never Exercised Before

Some women don't like to exercise or don't exercise on a regular basis. When many of these women discover they're pregnant, they begin to think about the benefits of exercise; they want to know whether it's safe to begin an exercise program during pregnancy. If you've never exercised before, you *must* discuss it with your healthcare provider before you begin.

It's possible to start exercising now; however, begin gradually. Your age may affect your ability to exercise. If you've never exercised, you may find it a little more difficult to begin because of less flexibility and tighter muscles.

Jasmine never liked regular exercise, but she found being pregnant gave her the incentive and motivation to engage in a health-club program specifically designed for pregnant women. It helped her feel more in control of her health while she was pregnant, and she felt she was doing something positive for her body. After she delivered her baby, she continued exercising. She really missed it if she didn't.

If your pregnancy is uncomplicated, you should be able to exercise as long as you're comfortable doing so. The key is not to do too much, too fast. Don't be afraid exercising might do something to hurt your developing baby; most moderate exercise is safe.

If exercise is approved for you, start with a *moderate* exercise program. Walking is an excellent choice. Riding a stationary bike can be enjoyable. Swimming and other water exercises are also good for a beginner; the water provides your body with a lot of support. Prenatal yoga or pregnancy Pilates classes may be a good choice during your first trimester.

Exercise Risks

Exercise during pregnancy isn't without some risks, including increased body temperature, decreased blood flow to the uterus and possible injury to you.

Your age is probably not an important factor, however. Most experts recommend you reduce your exercise to 70 to 80% of your prepregnancy level. If you have problems with bleeding, premature labor or cramping or have had problems in previous pregnancies, you may have to modify or eliminate exercise, as advised by your healthcare provider.

We know the increased hormone levels of pregnancy soften connective tissues, which may make your joints more susceptible to injury. Avoid full sit-ups, double leg raises and straight-leg toe touches.

It was once believed exercise could cause preterm labor because of a temporary increase in uterine activity following exercise. However, studies prove this isn't a problem in a normal pregnancy. The fetal heart rate increases somewhat during and immediately after exercise, but it stays within the normal fetal range of 120 to 160 beats a minute. A moderate exercise program should not cause any problems for you or your baby.

Effects of Exercise on Your Body

You may notice some changes in how your body responds to exercise during pregnancy. Your growing abdomen can put a strain on your respiratory system; you may feel out of breath sooner than usual. Don't work out to the point you can't talk or have trouble breathing. At that point, you're working too strenuously; cut back on your workout.

You may need to alter the way you work out. For example, breaking workouts up into smaller increments may help you fit them into your day. Four 10-minute walks may be easier to accomplish than one 40-minute walk.

Avoid becoming overheated during your workout. Work out in a well-ventilated room, and drink lots of water while you exercise. Drink water before, during and after exercising; dehydration may cause contractions.

If you're doing free weights, sit down when you can. In your third trimester, don't lift more than 15 pounds of weight. Instead, increase the number of reps.

Avoid the following sports activities during your pregnancy:

- scuba diving
- water skiing
- surfing
- horseback riding
- downhill skiing
- cross-country skiing
- riding on a snowmobile
- any contact sport

Beneficial Exercises during Pregnancy

Keep in mind a few general precautions about exercising during pregnancy that apply to most pregnant women. Your healthcare provider may want to discuss additional precautions that apply specifically to you.

If you participate in a competitive sport, such as tennis, you may be able to continue, but expect to change the level at which you play. Don't get carried away or overwork yourself. The goal is not to win the game but to maintain fitness and have a good time! You may want to pick a less-strenuous sport to participate in during pregnancy. Some are listed below; most are considered acceptable for women of any age in a normal, low-risk pregnancy:

- walking
- swimming
- low-impact aerobics designed specifically for pregnant women
- water aerobics
- stationary bicycling
- regular cycling (if you're experienced)
- jogging (if you jogged regularly before pregnancy)
- tennis (played moderately)
- yoga or Pilates (don't lie on your back after 16 weeks of pregnancy)

Swimming and Water Exercises

Some women say that while they're pregnant, the only time they really feel comfortable is in the water. Being in the water can have a calming effect, and it can help reduce swelling.

Because water supports you, you will feel much lighter, and you won't have to worry about keeping your balance. Water also supports the weight of the fetus, relieving some stress in your lower back. That enables you to adopt a more relaxed posture and to enjoy a greater range of motion while in the water.

Being in the water reduces the effect of gravity, and this in turn reduces pressure on your joints—a great temporary relief for some women. In addition, exercising in the water makes it significantly easier for your heart to pump blood. That's a real benefit, especially if you have hypertension.

A balance ball may be a good purchase. Exercising on a big exercise ball is easier on your back while it strengthens core muscles. Some women use them during labor to help relieve pain!

You can get a good workout in the water. Water exerts 12 times the resistance of air on limbs—you'll expend more energy moving through water than you would walking on a street.

Your baby is well protected inside your body in the water. There are actually three barriers to provide protection—the amniotic membrane that surrounds the baby, the cervix and the vagina. Don't be concerned about water getting to the baby. However, if your bag of waters has broken, do not exercise in the water.

Pregnancy Aerobics, Yoga and Pilates Classes

Classes designed for pregnant women can be a good exercise choice. They concentrate on your unique needs, such as strengthening abdominal muscles and improving posture. When choosing a class, be sure the instructor has proper training and the class meets guidelines developed by the American College of Obstetricians and Gynecologists (ACOG).

If there are no classes available in your area, exercise DVDs for pregnant women may be available online, at your local library or video store. They are a good alternative to aerobics classes.

Exercise Guidelines for Pregnancy

Consult your healthcare provider *before* you begin any exercise program. Follow the tips below to keep you healthy and in good shape.

- Try to exercise every day for at least 20 to 30 minutes.
- Start your exercise routine with a 5-minute warm-up, and end with a 5-minute cool-down period.

Water Exercise Guidelines

Consider the following suggestions if you want to work out in water or swim as part of your exercise regimen.

- Be sure pool water is warm enough but not hot. The ideal temperature of the water should be between 80 and 84F (26.5 and 29C). Avoid hot tubs and spas because water is too hot for baby.
- Drink plenty of fluids before you begin exercising and during exercise. Dehydration can occur even in a pool.
- Eat easily digested foods 30 minutes to 1 hour before you work out; choose fruit or a whole-wheat product.
- To help you keep your footing when you exercise in the pool, wear aquatic shoes, tennis shoes or jogging shoes in the water. Be sure the shoe has a good tread so you don't slip.

> If you feel lethargic, *don't* skip a workout! Instead, decrease how hard you exercise or for how long.

- Wear comfortable clothes that offer support, such as a support bra and good athletic shoes.
- Drink plenty of water before, during and after exercise.
- Don't exercise strenuously for more than 15 to 20 minutes.
- Check your pulse rate frequently.
- Be careful exercising in hot, humid weather—work out early in the morning and drink lots of water.
- After 16 weeks of pregnancy, avoid exercises that require you to lie on your back.
- Keep your body temperature below 100.4F (38C).
- Exercise during the coolest part of the day.
- Stop immediately and consult your physician if you experience any problems.

Be aware of problems that might develop while you exercise. If you notice any unusual occurrences, report them to your healthcare provider immediately. These include:

- pain
- bleeding
- dizziness
- extreme shortness of breath
- palpitations
- faintness
- abnormally rapid heart rate
- back pain
- pubic pain
- difficulty walking
- breathlessness that doesn't go away
- chest pain
- loss of fetal movement

Nutritional Needs during Exercise

You know that your nutritional needs increase during pregnancy. If you exercise, you'll probably burn more calories and may have to adjust your meal plan. Be sure you eat enough calories to ensure a balanced diet. You may need to eat more than a pregnant woman who is not exercising at your level.

Discuss with your healthcare provider how much more you should eat. Make sure any additional calories are nutritious and supply your body with the protein, calcium and carbohydrates you need—not sugar and fat.

Prenatal Exercises to Do at Home or at Work

Sometimes you may find it difficult to exercise at a health club or somewhere else outside your home. You can do the exercises in this section at home or at work. Try all of them, and incorporate those you like into your regular schedule.

Weight Lift with Cans

Next time you're putting away groceries, build up arm muscles by doing a little weight lifting with each can (milk jugs and water bottles also work well). As you put a can away, flex your arm a couple of times to work arm muscles. Alternate arms for a balanced workout.

Work Out in Line

When you're standing in line at the grocery store, post office or anywhere else, do some creative exercises. Rise up and down on your toes to work your calves. Spread your feet apart slightly, and do subtle knee lunges to give quadriceps a workout. Clench and relax buttocks muscles. Do some Kegel exercises (see the following page) to strengthen vaginal muscles. Contract stomach muscles. These exercises help you develop and strengthen some of the muscles you'll use during labor and delivery.

Standing Stretches

If you're forced to stand in one place for a long time, step forward slightly with one foot. Place all your weight on that foot for a few minutes. If you're still waiting, do the same exercise for the other foot. Alternate the leg you begin with each time.

It's probably a good idea to wear some type of support for your abdomen when exercising.

Reaching-Stretching

You probably have to reach for things at home or at the office. When you do, make it an exercise in controlled breathing. Before you stretch, inhale, rise up on your toes and bring both arms up at the same time. When you're finished, drop back on your heels, and exhale while slowly returning your arms to your sides.

Sitting Quietly

Anytime you're sitting quietly—at home, at the office, in your car, on a bus or a train—do this breathing exercise to strengthen abdominal muscles. Breathe deeply and contract stomach muscles; hold for a couple of seconds, then exhale slowly. Do this whenever you get the chance.

Bending to Relieve Backache

While standing at the kitchen counter or a counter at work, bend your knees and lean forward from your hips. Hold the position for a few minutes. This exercise is an excellent way to relieve back stress.

Rising from a Chair

Some women find it difficult to get out of a chair gracefully during pregnancy. This exercise helps you maintain your grace and is also beneficial. Use leg muscles to lower yourself into and raise yourself out of a chair. Slide to the front edge of the seat, then push up with your legs to get out of the chair. Use your arms for balance.

Kegel Exercises

Kegel exercises strengthen pelvic muscles. Practicing helps you relax your muscles for delivery. While sitting, contract the lowest muscles of your pelvis as tightly as you can. Tighten muscles higher in the pelvis in stages until you reach the muscles at the top. Count to 10 slowly as you move up the pelvis. Hold briefly, then release slowly in stages, counting to 10 again. Repeat two or three times a day.

You can also do the Kegel exercises by tightening the pelvic muscles first, then tightening the anal muscle. Hold for a few seconds, then release slowly,

Stretch at least a couple of times a week. Stretching may lower stress levels and help calm you.

in reverse order. To see if you're doing the exercise correctly, briefly stop the flow of urine while you are urinating—the muscles you use to do this are the same muscles you use in the Kegel exercises.

Your Pregnancy Workout

Practice the exercises in the previous section and add the following ones to your routine. You may have to set aside extra time to do these exercises. If you combine them with some form of aerobic exercise, such as walking, swimming or bicycling, you'll get a thorough workout.

Arm Reaches
Relieves upper backache and tension in shoulders, neck and back

Sit on the floor in a comfortable position. Inhale as you raise your right arm over your head. Reach as high as you can while stretching from the waist. Bend your elbow and pull your arm back down to your side as you exhale. Repeat for your left side. Do 4 or 5 times.

Pelvic Curl
Strengthens abdominal muscles, and relieves back stress

Crouch on your hands and knees, with your back relaxed. Do not arch your back. Inhale and relax. As you exhale, pull your buttocks under and forward until you feel your back straighten at the waist and your abdomen tighten. Hold for a count of 5, then exhale and relax. Do this exercise 4 or 5 times whenever you can.

Tailor's Seat
Develops pelvic-floor strength

Sit on the floor, bring feet close to your body and cross your ankles. Apply gentle pressure to your knees or the inside of your thighs. Hold for a count of 10, relax and repeat. Do this exercise 4 or 5 times.

Tailor Press

Develops pelvic-floor and quadricep strength

Sit on the floor and bring the soles of your feet together as close to your body as you can comfortably. Place hands under your knees, and gently press down with your knees while resisting the pressure with your hands. Count to 5, then relax. Increase number of presses until you can do 10 presses twice a day.

Shoulder Circles

Relieves upper backache and tension in shoulders, neck and back

Inhale while slowly moving your left shoulder forward and upward, to form the top half of a circle. Slowly move the shoulder to the back then down to complete the circle as you exhale. Repeat with right shoulder. Do 4 or 5 times for each shoulder.

Wall Push-Away

Develops upper-back, chest and arm strength, and relieves lower-leg tension

Stand a couple of feet away from a wall, with your hands in front of your shoulders. Place hands on the wall and lean forward. Bend your elbows as your body leans into the wall. Keep heels flat on the floor. Slowly push away from wall and straighten. Do 10 to 20 times.

Hip and Back Stretch

Reduces back tension, and increases blood flow to the feet

Place your left hand on the back of a chair or on a wall. Lift your right knee to the side of your tummy, and put your right hand under your right thigh. Round your back and bring your head and pelvis forward. Hold position for a count of 4, straighten up, then lower leg. Repeat with left leg. Do 2 or 3 times.

Side Leg Lifts

Tones and strengthens hip, buttock and thigh muscles

Lie on your left side, with your body in alignment. Support your head with your left hand, and place your right hand on the floor in front of you for balance. Inhale and relax. While exhaling, slowly raise your right leg as high as you can without bending your knee or your body. Keep foot flexed. Inhale and slowly lower your leg. Repeat on right side. Do 10 times on each side.

Your After-Pregnancy Workout

After your baby is born, continue the exercises you did during pregnancy. Add some of the following exercises to help you focus on specific areas, especially abdominal muscles. Do these exercises when your healthcare provider gives you permission. Start slowly and gradually work harder. If you had a Cesarean delivery, ask your healthcare provider which exercises to avoid until you get his or her OK.

Back Bridge

Strengthens back, legs and buttocks

Lie flat on your back on the floor, with knees bent and feet flat. Inhale, then slowly lift buttocks and back in a straight line. Hold for 4 seconds. Exhale and lower your back to the floor so your upper back touches the floor, then your waist touches, then your pelvis touches last. Do 4 or 5 times.

The Crunch

Strengthens abdominal muscles

Lie flat on your back on the floor, with knees bent and feet flat. Put your hands on your abdomen. Suck in your abdomen, pulling your navel toward your spine. Hold 4 seconds and release. When you are able to do 8 repetitions, lift your head toward your chest. Hold for 4 seconds, then lower head and hold for 4 seconds. Work up to 10 repetitions.

Leg and Pelvic-Floor Strengthener

Strengthens legs and pelvic floor

Lie on your back with your arms out at your sides. Cross your right ankle over your left ankle; squeeze legs together. Hold 5 seconds and release. Repeat for other ankle. Do 5 times on each side.

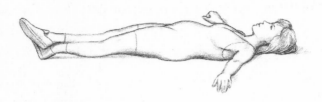

Back Stretch

Strengthens buttocks, back muscles and leg muscles

Kneel on hands and knees, with wrists directly beneath shoulders and knees directly beneath hips. Keep your back straight. Contract abdominals, then extend your left leg behind you at hip height. At same time, extend your right arm at shoulder height. Hold 5 seconds and return to kneeling position. Repeat on other side. Start with 5 exercises on each side, and gradually work up to 8.

Chair Squat

Strengthens hips, thighs and buttock muscles

Lightly grasp the back of a chair or a counter for balance. Stand with feet shoulder-width apart. Keep body weight over heels and torso erect. Bend knees and lower torso in squatting position. Don't round your back. Hold squatting position for 5 seconds, then straighten to starting position. Start with 5 repetitions and work up to 10.

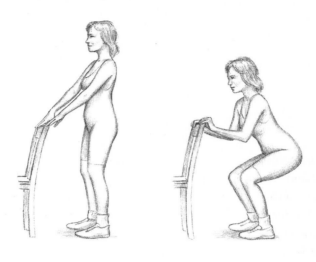

Leg Raises

Good for abdominal muscles

Lie flat on your back with legs straight. Slowly lift both legs from the hip at the same time, using abdominal muscles. Hold for 5 seconds. Slowly lower both legs together to the floor. Start with 2 repetitions and work up to 6.

Time-Saving, Energy-Saving Tip

One exercise you can do during pregnancy may also help during labor. Breath training decreases the amount of energy you need to breathe, and it improves the function of your respiratory muscles. These are the muscles you will use during labor and delivery. Practice these three exercises now for benefits in the near future.

- *Purse your lips.* Breathe in through your nose, and exhale through pursed lips. Making a little whistling sound is OK. Breathe in for 4 seconds, and breathe out for 6 seconds.
- *Diaphragm breathing.* Using your diaphragm muscle to breathe is beneficial. Lie on your back in a comfortable position. Place your hand on your abdomen while breathing. If you breathe using your diaphragm muscles, your hand will move up when you inhale and down when you exhale. If it doesn't, try using different muscles until you can do it correctly.
- *Bend forward to breathe.* If you bend slightly forward, you'll find it's easier to breathe. If you feel pressure as your baby gets bigger, try this technique. It may offer some relief.

Chapter 14

Your Current Medical Condition and Medications

The older you get, the more likely you are to develop various medical conditions—some serious, most not so serious. Medications used to treat those conditions may affect your baby during your pregnancy. We discuss some of those conditions and their treatments in this chapter.

You should be careful with *every* medication you take during pregnancy. Many people believe if they can buy something without a prescription, it must be safe to use. Or they believe they can use any amount of vitamins, minerals or herbal substances without hesitation.

Beware of this type of thinking! Many substances you use *can* affect your growing baby. Some effects can be serious. Other effects may be subtle and cause minor birth defects. The effects of others may not be evident for years.

Researchers once believed the placenta acted as a barrier to any agent the mother was exposed to. We now know that isn't the case. We have discovered *most* drugs can cross the placenta and could affect the fetus.

Medication Effects on Fetal Development

Some medications can affect fetal development; they are called *teratogens*. The study of abnormal fetal development caused by teratogens is called *teratology*. When a birth defect occurs, we want to know why it happened. This can be frustrating because in many instances we are unable to determine a cause.

The first 13 weeks of development (the first trimester) are the most critical time for a fetus exposed to teratogens. If an embryo is exposed during the first 2 weeks of development, the pregnancy might end in miscarriage. The most critical period of fetal development during the first trimester is between weeks 2 and 8.

The FDA is updating labels on prescription medication to include a *fetal-risk summary*. This will provide an indication of the possible drug effects on a developing baby. It is also updating labels to include information on the amount of a medication that may be present in breast milk. Included will be information on milk production and ways to reduce exposure for an infant.

Although the first trimester is very important, your baby's systems continue to grow and to develop throughout your pregnancy. Exposure to some substances can harm a baby even after the first trimester.

Talk to Your Healthcare Provider about Medications You Use

The best time to discuss current health concerns is before you become pregnant, but this isn't always possible. If you discover you're pregnant and are concerned about the medications you use, talk to your healthcare provider about it as soon as possible.

At your first prenatal visit, discuss all prescription and over-the-counter medicines, herbs, vitamins and minerals you take on a regular basis. You may have to stop taking a particular substance or adjust the dosage.

Never stop taking any medication you use for a chronic health problem without first consulting your healthcare provider! Some medication cannot and should not be stopped during pregnancy.

Medication Safety Guidelines

You're an important part of your healthcare team, especially during pregnancy. You have to make many decisions about how you will take care of your body during this important time. The suggestions below can help you decide what substances you can use before and during pregnancy.

- Don't use any unnecessary drugs while trying to conceive.
- Avoid all medications during the first trimester, if possible. If you must take a medication, consult your healthcare provider.
- Talk to your healthcare provider openly and honestly about medications you use. If you have a problem you normally treat with over-the-counter drugs, ask how to treat it during pregnancy.
- If you must use a prescription medication, ask your healthcare provider to prescribe it in its least potent strength.

You may be wondering about taking some medications you may have normally taken before pregnancy. See the chart on the opposite page that ad-

Medication Classification for Pregnancy

Medications a pregnant woman might use have been categorized by the Food and Drug Administration (FDA) to indicate the risk to the fetus if a mother-to-be takes them. If you have questions about any medications you take, ask your healthcare provider which category it fits into.

Category A—Adequate, well-controlled studies in pregnant women have not shown any risk to the fetus. Few medications have been tested to this level. A prenatal vitamin is considered a Category-A medication.

Category B—Animal studies indicate risk to a fetus is probably low, but human studies have not been done. Examples include some antibiotics, such as cefaclor.

Category C—There have been no adequate, well-controlled studies in animals or humans, but it is believed the medication is safe to use during pregnancy. An example is codeine.

Category D—Studies using animals have shown a harmful effect on the fetus, or studies have not been done in humans or animals. There is evidence of risk to the fetus, but it is believed benefits outweigh the risks. One example is phenobarbital.

Category X—There is evidence the medication causes birth defects. Risks outweigh any potential benefits for women. Accutane is a Category X-medication.

dresses different categories of medications. The medications listed on page 222 are considered *category-C medications* and are believed to be safe to use during pregnancy.

Prescription Medication Use during Pregnancy

Some prescription medications are more common than others; the discussion below includes common substances many women must take during pregnancy. *Please note: This information does not take the place of talking with your healthcare provider.*

Allergy Medication

If you use allergy medication, don't assume it's safe to take during pregnancy. Some types of allergy medication may not be advised, such as avoiding Sudafed during the first trimester. Many are combinations of several medicines you should be careful about using during pregnancy. Ask your doctor about your medicine, whether prescription or nonprescription, including nasal sprays.

Medications that are OK to use during pregnancy include antihistamines and decongestants. Claritin and Zyrtec are believed to be safe during pregnancy. Ask your doctor which brands are safest for you to use if your allergy problems interfere with your normal lifestyle. Under your doctor's supervision, you can continue taking allergy shots, but don't start them during pregnancy.

My healthcare provider has prescribed some medications that I take regularly. I'm not sure if I can take them during pregnancy. Should I stop taking them now or wait to talk about it at my first prenatal visit next week?

Call your healthcare provider's office and talk to the nurse. Some medications, such as thyroid medicine, are very important during pregnancy. Stopping them could cause problems.

Antidepressants

If you're being treated for depression when you become pregnant, it's important to continue treatment. Treating depression during pregnancy is as important as treating any other problem.

If you take antidepressants, don't stop unless advised to do so by your healthcare provider. There is a higher risk in abruptly stopping antidepressants. In addition, studies show that up to 70% of women who take antidepressants during pregnancy relapse into depression if they stop their medication.

Depression can be difficult to manage without using drug therapy. Medication you take is probably necessary for your good health and the good health of your baby. Left untreated, depression can contribute to premature birth, IUGR, low birthweight, stillbirth and low Apgar scores in baby after birth.

Stopping your medication can raise your stress hormones, which increases your risks of complications and problems. The risks to you and your baby may be greater than your risk of taking antidepressants.

There may be a very small increased risk of birth defects with some medications taken during the first trimester. You may benefit by switching to an antidepressant that has been shown to be relatively safe during pregnancy, including fluoxetine (Prozac), citalopram and escitalopram (Lexapro). Pregnancy may affect your body's ability to metabolize lithium. Talk to your healthcare provider as soon as you confirm your pregnancy.

If you take an SSRI, your dose may need to be increased during the third trimester to maintain your normal mood. There may be a small increased risk of persistent pulmonary hypertension in babies born to women who take SSRI antidepressants after 20 weeks of pregnancy.

There is continued concern about the safety of Paxil during pregnancy. Research suggests exposure to the drug in the first trimester of pregnancy may be associated with an increased risk of heart birth defects. If you're pregnant, do *not* stop taking your antidepressant medication without first consulting your healthcare provider.

Hormone-Replacement Therapy (HRT)

Today, the average age of menopause is 51. At menopause, you stop ovulating (necessary for conception) and stop having periods. The change is usually gradual, occurring over years, but it may be sudden. If you still have menstrual periods, you can probably still get pregnant.

In the past, women didn't start taking hormones (*hormone-replacement therapy* or *HRT*) until their periods stopped and they were certain of menopause. Today, more women start HRT at younger ages.

If you become pregnant while taking HRT, tell your healthcare provider immediately. There are minor risks associated with pregnancy if you have been taking female hormones.

Incontinence Medications

Incontinence may be more of a problem for women over 35. Do you take medicine to treat an overactive bladder?

The problem of overactive bladder occurs when the brain tells nerves in the bladder there's a need to urinate even if the bladder isn't full. Symptoms include going to the bathroom more than 12 times a day, getting up two or more times at night and a sudden, immediate need to go. You may also leak urine.

Medicines to treat the problem work by relaxing muscles. Some commonly prescribed medications include Ditropan, Detrol LA, Sanctura and Enablex. If you take any of these medications, you need to talk to your healthcare provider before pregnancy or as soon as you find out you're pregnant. He or she can advise you about continued use of your medicine during pregnancy.

Thyroid Medication

You need to continue taking thyroid medication throughout pregnancy. *Thyroid hormone* is made in the thyroid gland, which is found in the neck. It affects your entire body and is important to your metabolism. Thyroid hormone can affect your ability to get pregnant.

Thyroxin (medication for a low-thyroid or hypothyroid condition) can be taken safely during pregnancy. Propylthiouracil (medication for a high-thyroid or hyperthyroid condition) passes to the baby; you will probably be given the lowest amount possible during pregnancy.

Skin-Care Medications

Accutane (isotretinoin) is a common acne treatment. Do *not* take it if you are pregnant! A woman taking Accutane during the first trimester of pregnancy is at greater risk of miscarriage and birth defects in baby.

Retin-A (tretinoin) is a medication used to relieve minor wrinkling in the facial area. We don't know its effects on the fetus, so it's probably best to avoid Retin-A during pregnancy.

Occasionally steroid cream is prescribed for a skin condition. Before using it during pregnancy, discuss it with your healthcare provider. You may be able to use a safer preparation.

Tetracycline, an antibiotic, is often prescribed for skin problems. During pregnancy, avoid all tetracycline! Use of the drug during pregnancy can cause discoloration of your baby's permanent teeth later in life (one of the reasons tetracyclines should not be prescribed for children under age 8).

Other Prescription Medications

Some medications, such as Valium, Librium and Tranxene, are safe to use during pregnancy but should be prescribed *only* if absolutely necessary. As with any substance, don't take anything without consulting your healthcare provider.

If you have a headache bad enough to be considered a migraine, call your healthcare provider before you take anything for it. Before pregnancy, you may have been taking Imitrex for migraines; it is given by injection or in pill form. Avoid it during pregnancy; we do not know yet whether it is safe.

Common medications used for blood clots or phlebitis, called *anticoagulants,* are heparin and Coumadin. Heparin doesn't cross the placenta, so it is

Before you take a medication for a common malady, such as a headache or indigestion, try a nonmedication approach. For example, you might treat a headache with a cold compress or by resting in a dark room. Prevent indigestion by avoiding foods that trigger it, eating smaller meals and eating slowly.

safe to use during pregnancy. It's administered by injection or I.V. Don't use Coumadin during pregnancy because it may cause significant problems in the fetus or newborn.

Many asthma medications are OK to use during pregnancy. Inhalers, such as Proventil, are safe. For an asthma attack, your healthcare provider may prescribe prednisone; it is approved for use during pregnancy. Primatene Mist is not recommended.

Medicines to treat anemia can be important during pregnancy and are safe to use. These medications contain iron, which may cause side effects such as constipation, nausea or upset stomach.

Pregnancy is not the time to use *any* type of diet pill. Avoid prescription diet pills during pregnancy because they have not been proved safe. If you're taking diet pills when you find out you're pregnant, stop taking them immediately!

Nonprescription Medications

Many people, not just pregnant women, hold the false belief that medications they can buy without a prescription (over-the-counter medicine) are harmless. Nothing could be further from the truth. Carelessness with over-the-counter preparations could harm you and your developing baby.

Use caution when you take any over-the-counter (OTC) medication during pregnancy. Many OTCs contain aspirin, caffeine, alcohol or phenacetin, all of which should be avoided during pregnancy. For example, some OTC antidiarrheal medications contain aspirin. Cough syrups may contain as much as 25% alcohol (that's 50 proof!).

Use medications that contain ibuprofen with care; brand-name ibuprofen medications include Advil, Motrin and Rufen. Avoid Aleve (naprosyn) and Orudis (ketoprofen) until we know more about their safety during pregnancy. Read package labels, and talk with your healthcare provider or pharmacist before taking anything.

Category-C Medications

Medical experts believe category-C medications are safe to use during pregnancy. If you use any of these medications, check with your healthcare provider about continuing to use them. He or she will determine whether you should use the medication during pregnancy. Some Category-C medications you may use include acetaminophen, antacids, benzoyl peroxide, beta-adrenergic antagonists, cephalosporins, chlorpromazine, clindamycin, codeine (short term), corticosteroids, cotrimoxazole, cough lozenges, cromolyn, dextromethorphan, dimenhydrinate, diphenhydramine, doxylamine plus pyridoxine, erythromycin, fluoxetine, haloperidol, hydralazine, ipratropium, methyldopa, nitrofurantoin, penicillin, propylthiouracil. rantidine and tricyclic antidepressants.

Avoid cold remedies that contain iodine. It can cause serious thyroid problems in baby. If you regularly take Airborne to prevent colds when you aren't pregnant, it may be a good idea to skip it during pregnancy. It hasn't been tested on pregnant women. Be careful with antacids—they can interfere with iron absorption.

You may become constipated at some point during pregnancy and need a laxative. If you find a laxative is necessary for more than 2 or 3 days, contact your healthcare provider. He or she may advise you to make dietary changes to help with the problem.

Some medications for diarrhea are safe during pregnancy. Imodium is OK to use, but most healthcare providers recommend avoiding the pink bismuth-type preparations during pregnancy. If you have bloody diarrhea or diarrhea that lasts longer than a few days, contact your healthcare provider.

Don't overuse any product during pregnancy. You can get too much of a good thing. Your healthcare provider will not be angry or upset if you call the office with a question about a medication. It's much easier to answer a question and solve a potential problem about a medication *before* you take it.

Vitamin and Mineral Supplements

Be cautious about taking vitamin and mineral supplements during pregnancy. Often people don't think of vitamins and minerals as harmful, but they can

Safe Over-the-Counter Medications

Some OTC medications considered fairly safe to use while you're pregnant include:
- acetaminophen (Tylenol)
- antacids (Amphojel, Gelusil, Maalox, milk of magnesia)
- throat lozenges (Sucrets)
- decongestants (chlorpheniramine, Sudafed)
- antidiarrheal preparations (Kaopectate)
- anti-itch preparations (Benadryl)
- some cough medicines (Robitussin)
- hemorrhoid preparations (Anusol, Preparation H)

be, especially to your developing baby. Use only those vitamins and minerals your healthcare provider recommends you use or prescribes for you.

Many vitamin supplements and "megavitamins" sold in health-food stores contain very high amounts of minerals, vitamins and other substances. Even some foods contain extra vitamins and minerals. Some of these supplements could adversely affect your developing baby.

Avoid any vitamins or minerals other than your prenatal vitamin and iron and/or folic-acid supplements unless prescribed by your healthcare provider specifically for you. Read labels on various foods you eat. Don't self-medicate with other vitamins or minerals—you don't need them, and they can be dangerous if taken in excessive amounts.

Prenatal vitamins contain the recommended daily amounts of vitamins and minerals you need during pregnancy. They are prescribed to ensure your health and your baby's health.

Prenatal Vitamins

At your first prenatal visit, your healthcare provider will probably give you a prescription for prenatal vitamins. It's very important for you to take these vitamins for your *entire* pregnancy.

Each vitamin contains many essential ingredients for the development of your baby and your continued good health, which is why we want you to take them every day until your baby is born. A typical prenatal vitamin contains the following:

- calcium to build baby's teeth and bones and to help strengthen yours
- copper to help prevent anemia and to aid in bone formation
- folic acid to reduce the risk of neural-tube defects and to aid red blood cell production
- iodine to help control metabolism
- iron to prevent anemia and to help baby's blood development
- vitamins A, B_1 and E for general health
- vitamins B_2, B_3, B_6 for metabolism
- vitamin B_{12} to promote formation of blood
- vitamin C to aid in your body's absorption of iron
- vitamin D to strengthen baby's bones and teeth, and to help your body use phosphorus and calcium
- zinc to help balance fluids in your body and to aid nerve and muscle function

It's important to know *how* to take your medicine to get the greatest benefits. Read the label before you take it. Should you take it with food? Before food? After food? No food? A certain number of hours before or after food? When you get up? Before you go to bed? Should you drink extra liquids, avoid milk products or take it in some other special way? Knowing when you should and shouldn't mix a medication with a food or beverage can increase the benefits of the medicine. Some combinations can be dangerous. *Always* read directions for taking a medication. If you have questions, discuss them with your pharmacist or healthcare provider.

Sometimes, late in pregnancy, a woman stops taking her prenatal vitamins; she gets tired of taking them or she decides they aren't necessary. Studies show nearly half of all pregnant women who are prescribed prenatal vitamins don't take them regularly. The vitamins and iron in prenatal vitamins are essential to the well-being of your baby, so take your prenatal vitamins every day until your baby is born.

Immunizations and Vaccinations during Pregnancy

Immunizations and vaccinations protect you from diseases. A vaccine is given to provide you with protection against infection and is usually given by injection or taken orally. Each dose of a vaccine contains a very small amount of a weakened form of the disease. When you receive a vaccine, your immune system forms antibodies to fight the disease in the future. In most cases, this is enough to keep you from getting a disease. However, in some cases, it doesn't prevent the disease entirely but greatly reduces severity of the symptoms.

Vaccines come in three forms—live virus, killed (dead) virus and toxoids (chemically altered proteins from bacteria that are harmless). Most vaccines are made from killed viruses; it's impossible to get the disease after receiving this type of vaccine. With a live-virus vaccine, the virus is so weakened that if your immune system is normal, you probably won't get sick from it.

Many women of childbearing age in the United States and Canada have been immunized against measles, mumps, rubella, tetanus and diphtheria. A blood test for measles is necessary to determine immunity. The diagnosis of rubella is difficult without a blood test. Physician-diagnosed mumps or a mumps vaccination is necessary evidence of immunity.

Risk of Exposure

During pregnancy, try to decrease your chance of exposure to disease and illness. Avoid visiting areas known to have diseases. Avoid people (usually children) with known illnesses. It's impossible to avoid all exposure. If you have been exposed, or if exposure is unavoidable, the risk of the disease must be balanced against the potential harmful effects of vaccination.

Can I get a flu shot while I'm pregnant?
Yes, you can. In fact, most healthcare providers recommend a pregnant woman receive a flu shot while she's pregnant.

A vaccine must be evaluated in terms of its effectiveness and potential for complicating pregnancy. There is little information available on harmful effects on the developing fetus from vaccines. However, we know live-measles vaccine should *never* be given to a pregnant woman.

Vaccinations to Protect You during Pregnancy

The only immunizing agents recommended for use during pregnancy are the Tdap vaccine and the flu vaccine. The Tdap vaccine (tetanus, diphtheria and pertussis) can help you avoid whooping cough. Be sure to get a Tdap booster if it's been 10 years or more since your last one. In addition, if you work in the garden, with your hands in dirt, you need a booster.

Get a flu shot during pregnancy. If you get the flu during pregnancy, you have a greater chance of complications, such as pneumonia. Experts recommend *all* women who will be pregnant during flu season get a flu shot. A flu shot can protect you against three strains of influenza. Flu shots can be given safely during all three trimesters. Talk to your healthcare provider about it.

Other Vaccines during Pregnancy

As many as 35% of all pregnant women are at risk of contracting measles, mumps or rubella because they haven't been vaccinated or they have been vaccinated but their immunity has weakened. However, vaccination for measles, mumps and rubella (MMR) should be administered *only* when you are practicing birth control. You must continue to use contraception for at least 4 weeks after receiving this immunization.

A pregnant woman should receive primary vaccination against *polio* only if her risk of exposure to the disease is high. Only inactivated polio vaccine should be used.

If your healthcare provider believes you may be at risk for contracting *hepatitis B*, it's safe to take the vaccine during pregnancy. Talk with your healthcare provider if you have concerns.

If you have lung problems, asthma or heart problems, you may want to talk to your healthcare provider about the *pneumococcal vaccine* to protect you against bacteria that can cause pneumonia, meningitis and ear infections. A plus to taking this vaccine: One study showed antibodies you make after taking the vaccine pass to your baby and can protect him or her from ear infections for up to 6 months!

Cancer during Pregnancy

Pregnancy is a happy time for most women. Occasionally, however, serious problems can occur. Cancer during pregnancy is one serious complication that occurs rarely.

This discussion is included not to scare you but to provide you with information. It may not be a pleasant subject to discuss, especially at this time. However, every woman should have this information at hand. Because many women today wait until they are older to have babies, and cancer strikes more older women, it's good to have information available so you can discuss the situation with your healthcare provider if you are concerned about it.

Cancer occurs in about one in every 1000 pregnancies. Pregnancy may make it more difficult to diagnose the problem. Tremendous changes affect your body during pregnancy. Some researchers believe cancers influenced by increased hormones may increase in frequency during pregnancy. Increased blood flow may add to the spread of cancer to other parts of the body. Body changes during pregnancy can make it difficult to find or to diagnose an early cancer.

When cancer occurs during pregnancy, it can be very stressful for you and your partner. The healthcare provider must consider how to treat the cancer, but he or she is also concerned about the developing baby. How these issues are handled depends on when cancer is discovered. You, your partner and your healthcare provider must consider many issues before deciding on a course of treatment.

- Must the pregnancy be terminated?
- Can the malignancy affect the developing baby?
- Can therapy be delayed until after the baby is developed or delivered?
- How do medications, chemotherapy or radiation used to treat the cancer affect the fetus?

Cancer during pregnancy must be treated on an individual basis. Anti-cancer drugs stop cell division to help fight the cancer. If taken during the first part of pregnancy, they can affect cell division of the embryo.

Before a woman is treated, a procedure using letrozole and gonadotropin may be used. A woman's ovaries are stimulated to produce the maximum number of eggs. Eggs are then harvested before chemotherapy or radiation begins.

If you're now pregnant and have had cancer in the past, tell your healthcare provider as soon as you find out you're pregnant. He or she may need to make decisions about individualized care for you during pregnancy.

Breast Cancer

Breast cancer is the type of cancer discovered most often during pregnancy. It is uncommon in women younger than 35. Unfortunately, it may be harder to find breast cancer during pregnancy because of changes in the breasts, including tenderness, increased size and even lumpiness. About 2% of all women who have breast cancer are pregnant when it is diagnosed.

Breast cancer *can* be treated during pregnancy. Treatment varies, depending on the woman; surgery, chemotherapy, radiation or all three may be required. A physician will determine a course of treatment based on a woman's particular needs.

Some studies indicate that pregnancy is safe in women with a history of breast cancer if the cancer has been successfully treated. Other studies indicate chemotherapy for breast cancer during pregnancy may also be safe.

A form of breast cancer you should be aware of is *inflammatory breast cancer* (IBC). Although rare, it can occur during and after pregnancy and may be mistaken for mastitis, which is inflammation of the breast. Symptoms of inflammatory breast cancer include swelling or pain in the breast, redness, nipple discharge and/or swollen lymph nodes above the collarbone or under the arm. You may feel a lump, although one is not always present.

If you experience any of these symptoms, *do not panic!* Nearly all of the time it will be a breast infection related to breastfeeding. However, if you're concerned, contact your healthcare provider. A biopsy is used to diagnose the problem.

· ·

Quan-Li was a busy executive who never had time for breakfast. She might grab a diet cola and a bag of chips for lunch, and she often ate dinner out with clients. Her plan was to continue this regimen and take a prenatal vitamin during her pregnancy. We had a frank discussion about why her plan wouldn't work. I explained how her baby relied on her for its nourishment. I advised her that she couldn't eat that way for the entire pregnancy; she'd feel terrible and might not be able to continue working. With some help, Quan-Li made a commitment to follow a healthful eating plan and to take her prenatal vitamins every night after dinner.

· ·

Gynecologic and Other Types of Cancers

Various cancers of the female organs, including the cervix, the uterus, the vagina, the ovaries, the bladder and the Fallopian tubes, have been reported during pregnancy. Let us reassure you—these cancers are *very* rare during pregnancy, no matter what your age.

Cervical cancer occurs only once in about 10,000 pregnancies. However, about 1% of the women who have cancer of the cervix are pregnant when the cancer is diagnosed. Cancer of the cervix is extremely curable, especially when discovered early. That's one reason your Pap smear is important before and during pregnancy.

Bone tumors are rare during pregnancy. However, two types of noncancerous bone tumors can affect pregnancy and delivery. These tumors, *endochondromas* and *benign exostosis,* can involve the pelvis; tumors may interfere with labor. The possibility of having a Cesarean delivery is more likely with these tumors.

Other types of cancer, such as Hodgkin's disease, leukemia or melanoma, are very serious complications of pregnancy. Cancers of the blood occur in one of every 6000 pregnancies. If you are diagnosed with *any* form of cancer, you and your healthcare provider will discuss ways to treat it.

Cancer Treatments

Treating cancer during pregnancy can be difficult because of the effects various substances and procedures have on mother and fetus. Treatment can cause a variety of problems; a pregnant woman may also experience side effects.

Discuss any questions about cancer treatment during pregnancy with your healthcare provider. He or she can give you the best answers and help reassure you.

Connecting with other women and with couples who have experienced the same situation can be very helpful. One support group, *Hope for Two,* may be able to help you in many ways. Another group, *Pregnant with Cancer,* connects new cancer patients with survivors, which can provide you with a great deal of emotional and educational support. Their website is www.pregnantwith cancer.org.

Chapter 15

Pregnancy Can Affect Your Partner

Getting pregnant and having a baby involves both you and your partner. Although it's an exciting time for you, it may be a different experience for your baby's father—it may not be such an all-encompassing experience for him. A first-time pregnancy for you may or may not be a first pregnancy for your partner. However, it will be the first pregnancy he shares with you.

Sharing a pregnancy can teach you a lot about each other. You'll go through many changes and face new challenges together. Your partner may feel anxious about his ability to be a good father or to provide for you and the baby. Other challenges you both may face include making childcare decisions and choosing how each of you will allot your time and delegate responsibilities, such as who will do what chores.

While your body undergoes changes and you experience the wonder of a new life growing inside you, your partner will watch you change but can't really know what you're going through. Some men become jealous of the attention their pregnant partners receive. If you notice signs of jealousy, be understanding of your partner's feelings. Offer him support and love, and include him in your pregnancy as much as you can. Help him understand what you and the baby are going through.

Because your partner is less intimately involved with the pregnancy than you are, you may have to adjust your expectations of his enthusiasm and participation. You may need to encourage your partner to become more actively involved, such as by asking him to accompany you to prenatal visits.

Your partner can be a wonderful source of support. He can help prepare you for labor and delivery, and support you as you labor. He can share in the joy of the delivery of your baby. He can support you emotionally during pregnancy, which can be important to you both. Involve him as much as he is willing to be involved, and help him feel he's included in what's going on.

• •

Jim came with Bev for an ultrasound exam, and he couldn't wait to tell me he thought he had a new "medical breakthrough." He said he had been a little nervous about the pregnancy, afraid to touch Bev or her tummy. But one night, while they were lying in bed, he saw Bev's bellybutton move. He decided to feel it gently. He felt a foot or an arm, and when he pushed it, it pushed back! For the next 20 minutes, he continued the gentle pushing and feeling. This had become a regular evening activity that he looked forward to. He felt he was getting to know his baby's personality. Some nights it would want to "play" for 10 minutes, sometimes longer. Jim wanted to know if this was OK or harmful. I reassured him it was fine, and many couples bond with their baby in this way before it is born.

• •

Discuss *his* feelings about the pregnancy. He may have fears and uncertainties he hasn't voiced. Be open and direct with each other about your feelings—it can help both of you.

Some expectant fathers manifest physical problems during their partner's pregnancy. The condition is called *couvade,* a term taken from a Carib Indian tribe in which every expectant father engages in rituals that enable him to understand some of what his partner is experiencing. In our culture, an expectant father may experience headaches, irritability, weight gain, back and muscle aches, insomnia, fatigue and depression. Many of these symptoms are his body's way of signaling the tension level is high, and he must do something to relieve the stress.

To help relieve stress, a father can discuss his feelings and fears with other men, such as those who are taking the same childbirth-education classes. Exercise, reading and listening to music may also relieve stress; share our pregnancy books with him, especially *Your Pregnancy for the Father-to-Be.* When a man experiences headaches and shows other stress-related symptoms during his partner's pregnancy, it's time for the couple to start taking better care of each other so together they can take good care of their baby after it is born.

Your partner may feel increased anxiety as your pregnancy progresses. He may be concerned about your health, the health of the baby, sex with you,

For further information about pregnancy from a man's point of view, read our book *Your Pregnancy for the Father-to-Be.* It has a lot of information about pregnancy as your partner may experience it. You might consider giving it to your partner as a gift to celebrate your pregnancy.

labor and delivery, and his ability to be a good father. Share your own concerns with him; it may be enough to calm his anxieties. Understanding what your partner is feeling can help you adjust to his reactions to your pregnancy.

Your Partner Can Help You

Let your partner know there are things he can do for you during pregnancy. Tell him how important he is to you. Be specific about what you want so he can help you effectively. Some helpful things your partner can do are listed below.

- Keep stress to a minimum.
- Communicate about everything.
- Be patient and supportive.
- Promote good nutrition.
- Encourage exercise, and exercise with you.
- Help around the house when possible, and do the strenuous chores.
- Attend prenatal checkups when possible.
- Plan for the baby's arrival.
- Learn about the birth process.
- Read, study and prepare together.

Marta thought her pregnancy couldn't have come at a worse time. She had just been promoted, with more pay and greater responsibilities. She came to her first visit feeling unhappy and discouraged. She wanted a baby, but not right now. I told her that her reaction was not unusual; many of my patients have "accidents" or unplanned pregnancies. I encouraged her to look at the positive things about her pregnancy. She admitted that her husband was thrilled; he had assured her things would be fine. Later in the pregnancy, Marta expressed amazement about how she felt early on and about how well things were working out. I think she felt guilty about her earlier feelings and the time she lost feeling down about her pregnancy.

Ways to Reassure Your Partner

You can reassure your partner and help him grow more comfortable with your pregnancy and the idea of fatherhood. We have spoken with many pregnant couples, and they have passed on the following suggestions.

Reassure your partner about the impending birth. Let him know you're comfortable with whatever level of participation he is willing to give. Appreciate his help. He'll probably be more willing to offer his help if he knows it means something to you.

Listen when he talks. Encourage him to express his hopes, fears and expectations about the baby's birth and being a father. Be as supportive of him as you can be. Let him know you have faith in his abilities.

Talk about how you will divide responsibilities. List what you can do and what your partner can do. If possible, practice before baby's birth!

Help your partner learn about what it may be like living with a new baby. Together, take childbirth-education classes and other classes that are offered. Read our book *Your Baby's First Year Week by Week.* Tour the hospital, and discuss any questions and concerns you have.

Encourage your partner to be as involved with the baby as he can be. If he wants to take paternity leave from work, encourage it. Help him learn about diapering, feeding, bathing and living with a new baby.

Time-Saving, Energy-Saving Tip

An occasional mishap occurs in every home. Your kids (or you or your partner!) may accidentally spill a soft drink on your carpet. When this happens, try to take care of it while it's still wet. Dampen a paper towel, then blot the stain until it is dry. Mix 1 teaspoon mild hand-dishwashing liquid in 1 cup warm water; apply to the blotted stain. If you can still see remnants of the stain, apply a mixture of 2 tablespoons distilled white vinegar and 1 cup water. Blot with a clean paper towel.

Help Dad Bond with Baby

Bonding between parent and child is very important. It's easy for a mother to bond with her baby; they are linked in a number of physical ways. It's harder for a man to bond with baby, but you can help your partner do this. He can begin bonding with the baby before birth and continue after baby is born. Encourage your partner to do any of the following.

- Talk to the baby while it is in the uterus.
- Talk to the baby soon after birth. Babies bond to sound very quickly.
- Hold the baby close and make eye contact; a baby makes associations based on sight and smell.
- Feed the baby. It's easy if you bottlefeed. If you breastfeed, let dad give baby a bottle of expressed breast milk.
- Help with daily chores, such as changing diapers, holding the baby when it is restless, and bathing and dressing baby.
- Care for baby in ways that work for the both of them. Even if he doesn't do something the way you would, if it works for dad and baby, let them do it their way.

In my work, nearly all the phone calls I get are from women. When the answering service said they had Josh on the line, I thought they had the wrong healthcare provider. Josh explained that his wife, Anne, was a patient of mine, due in about 2 months. He was very upset. They had always been open and close during their marriage, but now he felt left out. They had lost some of the intimacy they had always shared. He confessed he wasn't sure what to do or how to get involved in the pregnancy. He feared Anne didn't need him, and they were drifting apart. I suggested Josh come with Anne on her next visit, and I'd help him "break the ice." At the visit, I brought up the topic of sex and intimacy during pregnancy. It turned out they both had some misconceptions. I told them this was normal. They might need to make some changes in their lovemaking, but they could still be intimate. Anne had felt Josh was a little aloof, but she didn't know what to do about it. It took some effort from both of them, but Josh confided in me at the delivery that things were much better. Anne really did need him after all.

Sex during Pregnancy

Most couples are concerned about sexual activity during pregnancy; however, men are more often concerned with this aspect of a relationship. It's an important topic, so discuss it with your healthcare provider. You will need to ask for individual advice and to rule out any complications. Most healthcare providers agree sex can be a part of a normal, low-risk pregnancy.

My husband and I are afraid that having intercourse might harm the baby. What can we do?
Take your partner with you to a prenatal visit, and ask your healthcare provider this question. Most couples can have normal sexual relations during pregnancy without risk. Some conditions are exceptions, such as an incompetent cervix.

Sex doesn't just mean sexual intercourse. There are many ways for couples to be sensual together, including giving each other a massage, bathing together and talking about sex. Whatever you do, be honest with your partner about how you're feeling—and keep a sense of humor!

Can Sex during Pregnancy Hurt the Baby?

Sexual activity doesn't harm a growing baby. Neither intercourse nor orgasm should be a problem if you have a low-risk pregnancy.

The baby is well protected by the amniotic sac and amniotic fluid. Uterine muscles are strong, and they also protect the baby. A thick mucus plug seals the cervix, which helps protect against infection. Discuss sexual activity with your healthcare provider, especially if your partner goes with you to your appointments. If he doesn't, assure him there should be no problems if your healthcare provider gives you the go-ahead.

Frequent sexual activity should not be harmful to a healthy pregnancy. Usually a couple can continue the level of sexual activity they are used to. If you are concerned, discuss it at an office visit.

How Pregnancy Affects You Sexually

Generally, women experience one of two sex-drive patterns during pregnancy. One is a lessening of desire in the first and third trimesters, with an increase

in the second trimester. The second is a gradual decrease in desire as pregnancy progresses.

During the first trimester, you may experience fatigue and nausea. During the third trimester, your weight gain, enlarging abdomen, tender breasts and other problems may make you less desirous of sex. This is normal. Tell your partner how you feel, and try to work out a solution that is satisfactory to both of you.

Pregnancy actually enhances the sex drive for some women. In some cases, a pregnant woman may experience orgasms or multiple orgasms for the first time. This is due to heightened hormonal activity and increased blood flow to the pelvic area.

Some women feel less attractive during pregnancy because of their size and body changes. Discuss your feelings with your partner. Tenderness and understanding can help you both.

You may find new positions for lovemaking are necessary as pregnancy progresses. Your abdomen may make some positions more uncomfortable than others. In addition, experts advise you not to lie flat on your back (for sex or anything else) after 16 weeks of pregnancy until baby's birth because the weight of the uterus restricts blood flow to the fetus. You might try lying on your side or use a position that puts you on top.

When to Avoid Sexual Activity

Some situations should alert you to abstain from sex during pregnancy. If you have a history of early labor, your healthcare provider may warn against intercourse and orgasm; orgasm causes mild uterine contractions. Chemicals in semen may also stimulate contractions, so it may not be advisable for a woman's partner to ejaculate inside her.

If you have a history of miscarriage, your healthcare provider may caution you against sex and orgasm. However, no data actually links the two. Avoid sexual activity if you have any of the following problems or conditions:

- placenta previa or a low-lying placenta
- incompetent cervix
- premature labor
- multiple fetuses
- ruptured bag of waters
- pain with intercourse
- unexplained vaginal bleeding or discharge
- inability to find a comfortable position
- an unhealed herpes lesion on either partner
- you believe labor has begun

Sexual Practices to Avoid

Avoid some sexual practices when you're pregnant. Don't insert any object into the vagina that could cause injury or infection. Blowing air into the vagina is dangerous because it can force a potentially fatal air bubble into a woman's bloodstream. (This can occur even if you are not pregnant.) Nipple stimulation releases oxytocin, which causes uterine contractions; you might want to discuss this practice with your healthcare provider.

Your Bed Rest Can Also Affect Your Partner

In some situations, a woman may be ordered to bed for part of her pregnancy. See the discussion of bed rest in Chapter 17. She may also have to abstain from sex. Bed rest can be unpleasant for the woman; however, it can also be difficult for her partner.

Partners of women with pregnancy complications carry a heavy load. In addition to worrying about their partners and the growing baby, they may also have to handle housework, cooking, childcare and care of their partners. It can be difficult for a man to handle his work and the added responsibilities at home. Resentment is common.

If you're advised that bed rest may help you, make sure you consider your partner's feelings. Let him know how valuable he is to you. Be supportive (this can be tough when you're the one in bed!), and try not to be overly demanding. Arrange for others to help out when possible.

Some Fears Men Express about Pregnancy

One survey revealed the following common fears among men approaching fatherhood:

- being able to participate in the birth
- doubts about their personal maturity
- dropping the baby
- having enough time for the baby
- in-laws and parents coming over too often
- losing the relationship they have with their partner after baby's birth
- losing their freedom
- providing adequately for the family
- the baby's crying
- whether they'll be good fathers

For all the inconveniences and disruptions in your life that bed confinement causes, the experience may strengthen your relationship. When he gives his time and attention to this demanding task, your partner is offering you his support and love. Let him know how much you appreciate it.

Domestic Violence

Domestic violence is an epidemic problem in the United States; every year almost 5 million women experience a serious assault by someone who says they love them. The term *domestic violence* refers to violence against adolescent and adult females within a family or intimate relationship. It can take the form of physical, sexual, emotional, economic or psychological abuse. Actions or threats of action are intended to frighten, intimidate, humiliate, wound or injure a person. Abuse affects all income levels and all ethnic groups.

Unfortunately, abuse does not usually stop during pregnancy. Research shows most women who experience violence during pregnancy may have experienced it before.

Research shows one in six women is abused during pregnancy. Domestic violence kills more pregnant women than any single medical complication of pregnancy. In fact, it accounts for 20% of all pregnancy-related deaths. Some studies indicate abuse may *begin* during pregnancy; still other studies show abuse can escalate during pregnancy. A startling fact to be aware of: Up to 60% of men who abuse their partners also abuse their children.

Abuse can be an obstacle to prenatal care. Some abused pregnant women do not seek prenatal care until later in pregnancy. They may miss more prenatal appointments. Women at risk may not gain enough weight, or they may suffer more injuries during pregnancy. Other risks include trauma to the mother, miscarriage, preterm delivery, vaginal bleeding, low-birthweight infants, fetal injury and a greater number of Cesarean deliveries.

If you're unsure if you are in an abusive relationship, ask yourself the following questions.

- Does my partner threaten me or throw things when he's angry?
- Does he make jokes at my expense and put me down?
- Has he physically hurt me in the past year?
- Has he forced me to perform a sexual act?
- Does he say it's my fault when he hits me?
- Does he promise me it won't happen again, but it does?
- Does he keep me away from family and friends?

If you answered "yes" to any of these questions, your relationship may be unhealthy, and it may be abusive.

Many victims of abuse blame themselves; *you are not to blame*. It isn't your fault, no matter what a boyfriend or spouse may say. If you're being abused, we encourage you to seek help immediately. Intervention can be lifesaving for you and your unborn child.

Talk to someone—a friend, relative, someone at your church and your healthcare provider are good resources. There are many domestic-violence programs, crisis hotlines, shelters and legal-aid services available to help you. Call the 24-hour National Domestic Violence Hotline at 800–799–7233 for help and advice.

Plan for your safety. This may include a "fast exit." A recommended safety plan includes the following.

- Pack a suitcase.
- Arrange for a safe place to stay, regardless of the time of day or night.
- Hide some cash.
- Know where to go for help if you are hurt.
- Keep needed items in a safe place, such as prescription medicines, health insurance cards, credit cards, checkbook, driver's license and medical records.
- Be prepared to call the police.

If you're hurt before you can leave permanently, go to the nearest emergency room. Tell personnel at the emergency room how you were hurt. Ask for a copy of your medical records, and give them to your own healthcare provider.

These steps may seem drastic, but remember: Domestic violence is a serious problem with serious consequences. Protect yourself and your unborn baby!

Many couples are concerned with the financial aspects of having a baby. Read the information that begins on page 243 dealing with making a will, checking life insurance and health insurance, and other financial considerations of being parents to help you plan for your baby.

Chapter 16

Will You Be a Single Mother?

Today, being a single mother isn't unusual. Nearly 40% of all babies in the United States are now born outside of marriage. Women of all ages have made the same decision you have, but most single mothers-to-be are in their 20s— the average age is 26½. Fewer than 15% of single mothers are divorced. Nearly 45% of single mothers consider themselves truly single. Eight percent of single moms have a same-sex partner.

Situations vary from woman to woman—the reason a woman chooses to have a child without a spouse is different for different women. Some women are deeply involved with the baby's father but have chosen not to marry. Some women are pregnant without their partner's support. Still other single women have chosen donor (artificial) insemination as a means of getting pregnant. No matter what the personal situation for each woman, single mothers share many concerns. We hope to cover many of these concerns in this chapter.

Families today are different than they were in the past. Many children don't have a complete set of parents or grandparents, even in the closest family units. In these situations, an older family friend can be just as loving as a grandparent. Encourage friends to take an active part in your child's life. Support groups for single parents can also be a valuable source of information and help. Ask your healthcare provider for the names of groups in your area.

As your pregnancy begins to show, people may ask why you chose to be a single mother. Answers to this question vary greatly. Marriage doesn't meet the needs of some women, but their desire to be mothers—to give birth and be a parent—is very strong.

In many situations—whether a mother is single, widowed or divorced—a child's overall environment is more important than the presence of a man in the household. Women head the majority of single-parent households in the

United States. Studies indicate if a woman has other supportive adults to depend on, a child can fare well in a home headed by a single woman.

It's Your Decision

People may ask you the most intimate questions during your pregnancy, especially if you are single. If you believe you need to answer their questions, decide early how detailed an explanation you want to provide.

Some people may think your choice is unwise and tell you you're crazy to have a baby alone. However, your true friends won't treat you this way. Once they understand your situation, they'll be supportive. If anyone gives you a hard time, change the subject. Don't discuss your reasons for having a baby with anyone unless you want to.

Even if you are "alone," you're not really alone. Seek support from family and friends. Mothers of young children can identify with your experiences—they have had similar ones recently. If you have friends or family members with young children, talk with them. You would probably share your concerns with these people if you were married. Try not to let your particular situation alter this.

Sometimes a single woman's family is against her decision to have a baby. If you're comfortable with your decision, ask family members to talk to you about the reasons they are uncomfortable with your pregnancy. You may not change their minds—you have no control over that. You *do* have control over your response. Learn to live with their disapproval or ignore it.

Some women choose not to marry their partners. If this is your situation, you may find people assume you and your partner are married, especially if you're pregnant and together. In most cases, it's nobody's business; however, do tell your healthcare provider about the situation.

Emotional upheavals aren't uncommon for many women during pregnancy. If coping with emotions is hard for you, talk with your healthcare provider. Office personnel will know about support groups, or they can direct you to a counselor if that's what you need.

> You may find yourself feeling separate and apart from family and friends. Make friends with other single moms for emotional and spiritual support. It will also provide you a support group for social interaction and exchanging child care and other tasks.

Many single moms find it easier to live and parent when they share expenses and daily activities with family or friends by living together.

Deciding Who Can Help You

Finding someone to count on for help during your pregnancy and after your baby arrives is a concern for many single pregnant women. One friend said she thought about whom she would call at 2am if her baby were crying uncontrollably. When she answered that question, she had the name of someone she believed she could count on in any type of emergency—during or after pregnancy!

Choose someone to be with you when you labor and deliver and someone who will be there to help afterward. The only part of labor and delivery that might require special planning because you're single is your plan to get to the hospital to deliver. One woman wanted her friend to drive but couldn't reach her when the time came. Her next option (all part of the plan) was to call a taxi, which got her to the hospital in plenty of time.

Finding a Labor Coach

Finding a labor coach probably won't be difficult. Not all women choose their partners for the job; you can ask a good friend or a relative. A woman who has given birth using the method you have chosen is an excellent choice. She understands your feelings and can identify closely with your experience.

If you can't think of someone, discuss it with your healthcare provider. He or she may suggest other single mothers who might volunteer to coach you during labor.

Professional labor coaches are available; they are called *doulas.* Contact Doulas of North America for information about trained doulas/labor coaches in your area.

Your Financial Situation

One of the most important aspects of your pregnancy and life with baby is your financial situation. Do you have insurance to cover baby? What about health insurance? Do you have a will and life insurance? These are things to address now or in the near future.

It's Time to Make Your Will

Are you like nearly 60% of all Americans—are you "will-less"? It's understandable; most people feel uncomfortable thinking about their own death and planning for it. But now is the time to rethink your procrastination if you don't have a will. You need to take care of it *before* your baby's birth. It's important to have a will for the sake of your child.

If you have already written a will, kudos to you. Now is the time to check it for any changes or additions you may want to make. You may want to make various changes, such as renaming or updating beneficiaries.

Name a Guardian

The most important aspect of a new or amended will is to name a guardian for your child. If something happens to you, who will care for him or her? Naming someone to care for your baby may be one of the most important things you can address at this time. Without a will that names a guardian, the courts decide who will care for your child.

There are a few things you must think about as you begin this process. Consider the following things as you consider whom you will choose for this important responsibility.

- Whom would you trust the most to care for your child?
- What is the age of this person?
- How good is his or her health?
- Is this person stable, financially and emotionally?
- Does he or she have a family, with children close to the same age? (This could be positive or negative.)
- Will your child grow up knowing this person?
- Does this person have the same values as you?
- Can this person handle the money you would leave for the care of your child?
- Whom could you choose if this person says "No" or couldn't care for your child in the future? (It's good to name at least two people in your will.)

Who Can Make Your Will?

Some people will tell you that you don't need an attorney to draw up your will if you don't have a lot of property or many assets. They believe the do-it-yourself will kits available in some stores or on various computer programs cover all the bases. Some are fairly thorough; however, if you're not an attorney, you may be saving money now, but it could cost your child later.

You want to make sure you dot all the *i*'s and cross all the *t*'s and you have jumped through all the legal hoops so your wishes will be followed. The only way you can guarantee that is to use an attorney to oversee writing your will.

The cost of hiring an attorney to draw up a will can run from a few hundred dollars to a thousand dollars or more. However, we believe it's worth it to give you the peace of mind that your wishes will be followed regarding who cares for your child and who inherits or handles your money and assets. In addition, you may want to have an attorney handle your will if you have a complicated life situation.

If you use a do-it-yourself will kit, you may want to ask an attorney to check it over for you when you're finished, to be sure you have covered everything. It may cost a little extra, but it could be well worth it if it saves your child problems in the future.

It's Time to Check Your Insurance

Now that you've made your will, it's time to arrange where some of the money will come from to care for your child. This is most often provided through a life-insurance policy. While you're examining your life insurance, also take a look at the other types of insurance you have. You need to examine your life insurance, health/medical insurance, disability insurance and homeowner's or renter's insurance. Look at the coverage you have now, and determine what type of coverage you'll need after baby's arrival. It's time to make any necessary changes!

When your employer provides insurance of any type, check with the human resources representative for specific information about insurance and its benefits. Don't overlook this important resource.

Life Insurance

If something happens to you, you want to be assured your child will be provided for and financially taken care of until he or she is an adult. It's important to have enough life insurance to cover raising your child through college. The U.S. government estimates it

> **Time-Saving, Energy-Saving Tip**
>
> If your kids string beads or if you have projects that have a lot of small parts, one easy way to keep them neat is to use an ice-cube tray to hold everything in easy-to-get-to compartments.

costs close to $300,000 to raise a child born today through the age of 18. Add to that the projected costs of college in 18 years. This is the amount of coverage you should have. You need enough coverage to ensure there will be enough money to care for your child.

Pull out any existing policies, and check the details. How much life-insurance coverage do you have? Do you have any coverage through your employer? How much is it? Most experts recommend 8 to 12 times a person's annual income to maintain a decent level of living for their children to grow up and to get through college.

Determine how much child-care expenses cost in your area for a year, and add the cost of any help you would need in your home. A sum 10 times that yearly amount would provide you with a cushion to help provide care for your child.

If you discover you need to increase your life-insurance coverage, the best advice we can give you is, "Shop around!" Various companies offer different rates for the same coverage. You can contact some agencies or check on the Internet; compare the cost of policies from several sources.

Disability Insurance—Do You Need It?

If you have an accident that requires you to take time off your job, disability insurance is good coverage to have. This insurance pays you a predetermined amount of money while you're disabled or unable to work. Most employers provide some disability insurance, but you should have enough insurance to cover between 65 and 75% of your income.

The drawbacks to disability insurance through an employer are that coverage stops when you leave the job and benefits are often fairly low. In addition, there is a difference, taxwise, between employer-sponsored policies and a policy you purchase on your own. If the company pays the premium, you'll pay taxes on any money you receive. If you pay the premium, income you receive is tax free.

If you decide to buy a policy, look for one guaranteed renewable that can't be canceled until you're 65. The best policies define "being disabled" as not being able to work at the job *you usually hold.* Some less-expensive policies pay you only if you cannot do *any* type of work. Avoid these cheaper policies. Also check out the waiting period—many policies provided by an employer have a 30- to 90-day waiting period. Premiums may be lower if you choose a longer waiting period before benefits begin.

Save for Emergencies and Other Important Needs

If your budget is stretched to its limits right now, how will you cope with an emergency? When something serious happens to you financially—loss of a job, unexpected financial costs, a major illness—will you be able to handle it?

Now is the time to make sure your family will have an emergency fund, if it's ever needed. You need an emergency fund to help you when you don't have money coming in, such as a layoff or if you quit your job. You need a minimum of at least 4 months of living expenses or $10,000 to $15,000, whichever is greater. That amount must cover many expenses, including mortgage or rent, utilities, food, transportation, loan payments, credit-card payments, child-care expenses—anything that needs to be paid to maintain your level of living.

If you do decide to establish an emergency fund, it's a good idea to be sure it is readily available. Put your money in a money-market fund or a higher-interest savings account so you'll have ready access to it.

Make the effort *now* to build this fund before baby's arrival. It could be very helpful if you can't return to work when you planned or if you incur additional expenses you had not planned for.

Saving for Your Child's Future

It's always a good idea to set money aside to use solely for your child so you have a fund to meet unexpected emergencies or to take care of various costs as the child grows up. One goal may be to pay for a college education; that is discussed below.

It's a good idea to start a savings account for baby's future. Add to it regularly; make it a part of your budget. As your child grows older, you can encourage him or her to add money to the account. This helps teach the child the value of saving and may help establish good savings habits. You don't have to save a lot of money every time you make a deposit. The key is to start early and be consistent—save a little every month or every paycheck.

Saving for College

It's a fact you'll soon realize—your baby will grow quickly. As unbelievable as it may seem now, it won't be long before he or she is old enough to go to college. In addition to the life-changing (for everyone) event of your offspring leaving home, you may be faced with the life-challenging experience of paying for it all!

It is estimated college expenses could reach $150,000 for a 4-year public university and over $350,000 for a private university by the time your child is ready for school. The earlier you start saving, the more time your money will have to grow. Saving something each month can add up to a significant amount of money in 18 years. The more you save each month, the greater the amount will be when your child needs it for college.

What can you do about it? The best solution we can offer is to start *right now* to save for your child's education. Talk to a financial advisor about how to do that.

The Cost of Child Care

Paying for child care can be a big-budget item in your household expenses. The cost of infant and toddler care (through age 3) is the highest—it can range from $200 to $400 (or more) a week, depending on the type of care you choose. If you have a nanny, the cost may run as high as $20,000 or more a year. For some families, child care can be 25% or more of the household budget.

Child-care costs don't drop dramatically as a child gets older—the average cost for a 4-year-old can be over $100 a week. In-home care costs can vary, depending on any placement fees and additional fees you negotiate based on extra tasks you want the caregiver to perform.

Public funding is available for some limited-income families. Title EE is a program paid for with federal funds. Call your local Department of Social Services for further information.

There are some other programs to help deal with child-care costs; they include a federal tax-credit program, the dependent-care-assistance program and earned-income tax credit. These programs are regulated by the federal government; contact the Internal Revenue Service for further information. Of all the children eligible to receive federal child-care assistance, only about 12% actually receive it because programs are not fully funded at this time.

In some situations, a child may have special-care needs. If your baby is born with a disability or a health problem and needs one-on-one attention, it may be harder to find good child care, and it may cost more for that care.

Will my healthcare provider, the office team or the nurses at the hospital treat me differently because I'm single?

No, they shouldn't. Today, many pregnant women are single, for one reason or another, so it isn't that unusual. Don't be afraid to ask questions or to ask for help.

Baby's Birth Certificate

You may be wondering how to fill out baby's birth certificate. You have options. You can fill in the father's name or leave it blank. If you don't want people to know the father's identity, you can leave it off the birth certificate. If baby's father is a donor, you can list the name as *unknown* or *confidential.*

You don't have to fill out a birth certificate before leaving the hospital. You may have a few months before this must be turned in. Consult an attorney in your area. However, you must realize you can't get a social-security number for your baby without providing a birth certificate.

You need to make a decision as to what last name baby will have. Yours? Dad's? In some states, if you are not married, the father must grant permission for you to use his last name. In some states, a man must sign a *parental acknowledgment* form before you can list him as the baby's father on the birth certificate.

Today, a father is required by law to pay child support, even if he is not involved in your child's life. Consult an attorney to check the laws in your state. If you put the baby's father's name on the birth certificate, it may make it easier to ask legally for child support. However, you need to understand this gives the father some legal rights.

Going Home from the Hospital

Going home from the hospital may seem overwhelming at first. You'll need lots of support when you come home with baby. You'll be fine if you plan ahead and enlist a little help. Consider asking family members, friends, co-workers and neighbors to help out. You'll probably need the most help the first month. Some chores and errands people can do include some alone time for you, laundry, cooking, cleaning and shopping.

A new baby is an incredible challenge in any situation. You may need more support from family and friends because you will have total responsibility for your new baby. If you feel you can't ask others for their time, consider hiring someone to stay with you at night for the first couple of weeks until you get on your feet.

Legal Questions

The decision to have a baby as a single woman has legal ramifications you may not have considered. The following questions have been posed by women who were single mothers. We provide them without answers because they're questions an attorney who specializes in family law should review. This information can help you clarify the kinds of questions you need to consider as a single mother. Use them as a basis for formulating questions about your own particular situation.

- A friend who had a baby by herself told me I'd better consider the legal aspects of this situation. What was she talking about?
- I've heard that in some states, if I'm unmarried, I have to get a special birth certificate. Is that true?
- I'm having my baby alone, and I'm concerned about who can make medical decisions for me and my baby. What can I do about this?
- I'm not married, but I am deeply involved with my baby's father. Can my partner make medical decisions for me if I have problems during labor or after the birth?
- If anything happens to me, can my partner make medical decisions for our baby after it is born?
- What are the legal rights of my baby's father if we are not married?
- Do my partner's parents have legal rights in regard to their grandchild (my child)?
- My baby's father and I went our separate ways before I knew I was pregnant. Do I have to tell him about the baby?
- I chose to have donor (artificial) insemination. If anything happens to me during my labor or delivery, who can make medical decisions for me? Who can make decisions for my baby?
- I got pregnant by donor insemination. What do I put on the birth certificate under "father's name"?
- Is there a way I can find out more about my sperm donor's family medical history?

- Will the sperm bank send me notices if medical problems appear in my sperm donor's family?
- As my child grows up, she may need some sort of medical help (such as a donor kidney) from a sibling. Will the sperm bank supply family information?
- I had donor insemination, and I'm concerned about the rights of the baby's father to be part of my child's life in the future. Should I be 'concerned?
- What type of arrangements must I make for my child in case of my death?
- Someone joked to me that my child could marry its sister or brother someday and wouldn't know it because I had donor insemination. Is this possible?
- What other things should I consider because of my unique situation?

Chapter 17

Pregnancy Problems
and Warning Signs

Some situations that occur during pregnancy may cause you concern. Some diagnoses, such as gestational diabetes and hypertension, are not unusual and cause little noticeable discomfort but are always serious. They must be treated for your health and baby's health.

If you feel uncomfortable or have questions about your condition, don't be afraid to ask for help. Call your healthcare provider to discuss your concerns. This book can help you formulate questions you may want to ask.

Although you may believe it's easier to get advice or information from family members or friends, *don't* rely on them for medical advice. Your healthcare provider has probably dealt with the same situation many times. The answers he or she gives you will be right for your particular pregnancy.

Pregnancy Warning Signs

If you experience any of the following signs or symptoms, call your healthcare provider immediately:
- vaginal bleeding
- severe swelling of the face or fingers
- severe abdominal pain
- loss of fluid from the vagina (usually a gushing of fluid but sometimes a trickle or a continual wetness)
- a big change in the movement of the baby or a lack of fetal movement
- high fever—more than 101.6F (38.7C)
- chills
- severe vomiting or an inability to keep food or liquids down

- blurred vision
- painful urination
- a headache that won't go away or a severe headache
- an injury or accident that hurts you or gives you concern about the well-being of your pregnancy, such as a fall or an automobile accident

Problems Some Women Experience

Bleeding during Pregnancy

Bleeding early in pregnancy doesn't always mean a problem; about one woman in five bleeds sometime in early pregnancy. Most of the time we can't say what causes bleeding, but we do know it is not always a problem. Tell your healthcare provider about any bleeding; he or she may want you to have an ultrasound.

Bleeding later in pregnancy raises concerns regarding premature labor, premature rupture of the membranes, placenta previa or placental abruption. If you bleed late in pregnancy, call your healthcare provider *immediately.* Your problem may not be serious, but your healthcare provider must evaluate it.

What are the most serious warning signs to watch for during my pregnancy?

Call your healthcare provider *immediately* if you experience bleeding heavier than a menstrual period, a gush of water from your vagina, severe pain or cramping.

Most women who experience bleeding during pregnancy want to know if they can take medicine or do something to stop the bleeding. Bed rest may help. You may be scheduled for an ultrasound, which may provide reassurance. Your healthcare provider will make treatment decisions based on your individual history. Follow his or her instructions.

Blood Clots

Some women develop blood clots, usually in their legs, during pregnancy. Conditions that refer to blood-clotting problems are also called *venous thrombosis, thromboembolic disease, thrombophlebitis* and *lower deep-vein thrombosis.* Clots may break loose, travel through the blood system and lodge elsewhere in the body, such as the lungs. Blood clots are an uncommon problem; however, they are a serious complication and can affect you and your baby.

Clots occur in pregnancy because of changes in blood circulation. The most likely cause of a blood clot in the legs is decreased blood flow, called *stasis*. Blood flow slows because of pressure from the uterus on blood vessels and changes in the blood and its clotting mechanisms.

A blood clot in the legs is not always a serious problem. Unlike deep-vein clots, clots in the superficial veins of the leg are treated with mild pain relievers, heat, elevation of the leg and support of the leg with an ace bandage or support stockings.

Deep-Vein Thrombosis

Clotting in the deep veins of the legs, called *deep-vein thrombosis, phlebitis* or *DVT* is serious. A blood clot that forms deep in the leg is more likely to break loose and travel to another part of the body, such as the lungs, heart or brain, where it can indirectly damage those tissues. Signs and symptoms of deep-vein thrombosis vary widely and can include the following:

- abrupt onset of symptoms
- paleness of the leg
- leg is cool to the touch
- a portion of the leg is tender, hot and swollen
- red streaks over the veins of the leg
- squeezing the calf or walking are very painful

In a pregnant woman, an ultrasound of the legs is the only test, other than a physical exam, to diagnose phlebitis. At other times, X-ray is used.

Deep-vein thrombosis is usually treated by hospitalization and administration of heparin, a blood thinner. While receiving heparin, a woman is required to stay in bed and apply heat to the elevated leg.

Heparin is safe to use during pregnancy. You inject yourself two or three times a day or receive heparin through a device called a *heparin pump* or through an intravenous drip attached to your arm.

Warfarin (Coumadin) cannot be given during pregnancy because it crosses the placenta and is unsafe for baby. After you deliver, you may be given warfarin for a few weeks, depending on the severity of the blood clot.

If you have had a blood clot with a previous pregnancy or at any other time, such as after surgery, share that information with your healthcare provider as soon as you know you're pregnant. You'll probably need heparin during this pregnancy.

Blood-Sugar Problems

Pregnancy affects your blood-sugar levels; *high blood sugar (hyperglycemia)* or *low blood sugar (hypoglycemia)* can make you feel dizzy or faint. Many healthcare providers routinely test pregnant women for blood-sugar imbalances during pregnancy. You can avoid or improve a blood-sugar problem caused by diet by eating balanced snacks and meals, by not skipping meals and by not going too long without eating.

Blood-Pressure Problems

It's normal for your blood pressure to change a bit during pregnancy. It often decreases slightly during the second trimester and increases toward the end of pregnancy. However, about 1 in 10 women experiences pregnancy-induced hypertension (PIH); pregnant women in their 30s and 40s have a higher incidence of PIH. Most women who develop high blood pressure during pregnancy don't have the problem when they aren't pregnant. See the discussion below.

Hypotension (low blood pressure) during pregnancy can cause dizziness. The problem usually occurs for two reasons. First, an enlarging uterus puts pressure on the *aorta* and *vena cava,* major vessels leading away from and into the heart. *Supine hypotension,* a related condition, occurs when you lie down; it is eased or prevented by not sleeping or lying on your back.

Second, rising rapidly from a sitting, kneeling or squatting position causes *postural hypotension.* Your blood pressure drops when you get up rapidly, as gravity pulls blood toward your feet and away from your brain, making you lightheaded. Postural hypotension happens more often as your pregnancy progresses and you get bigger. You can avoid postural hypotension by rising slowly from a sitting or lying-down position.

High blood pressure during pregnancy (PIH) is also called *gestational hypertension.* The problem usually disappears after baby is born. With PIH, the systolic pressure (the first number) increases to higher than 140ml of mercury or a rise of 30ml of mercury over your beginning blood pressure. A diastolic reading (the second number) of over 90 or a rise of 15ml of mercury also indicates a problem. An example is a woman whose blood pressure at the beginning of pregnancy is 100/60. Later in pregnancy, it is 130/95. This signals she may be developing high blood pressure or pre-eclampsia.

We have seen some articles in magazines and newspapers that incorrectly equate high blood pressure with pre-eclampsia. They are *not* the same problem. High blood pressure is one common sign of pre-eclampsia, but it must be accompanied by other serious symptoms for you to be diagnosed with pre-eclampsia. Follow your healthcare provider's advice about taking care of high blood pressure, but don't panic.

Your healthcare provider will be able to determine if your blood pressure is rising to a serious level by checking it at every prenatal appointment. That's one of the reasons it's so important to keep all your prenatal appointments.

PIH is treated with bed rest, increased fluid intake and avoidance of salt and sodium-heavy foods. Medications to lower blood pressure may be prescribed if diet changes don't work. Women who do not respond to these measures may be hospitalized.

Breast Lumps

Occasionally a woman develops lumps in her breasts during pregnancy. Because your breasts go through so many changes, it may be harder for you to discover a lump. Examine your breasts every 4 to 5 weeks throughout your pregnancy. The first day of the month is a good time to do it. Put it on your calendar!

If you discover a lump, tell your healthcare provider immediately. It's normal for breasts to change and to grow larger during pregnancy, but don't ignore a breast lump and hope it will go away. Lumps must be checked out.

After examination by your healthcare provider, you may undergo a mammogram or an ultrasound. If you have a mammogram, tell the technician you're pregnant so your abdomen can be shielded with a lead apron. Digital mammograms are available in some areas; they convert X-rays into electric signals similar to a digital camera. The images can be seen on a computer screen or printed on film. For a woman, it is the same as a regular mammogram. Ask your healthcare provider about them if you want more information.

A lump in the breast can usually be drained or aspirated. If not, a biopsy may need to be performed. With a biopsy, a sample of the tissue involved is taken. Depending on those findings, surgery or other treatment may be needed.

Ectopic Pregnancy

Ectopic pregnancy, sometimes called a *tubal pregnancy,* occurs about once in every 100 pregnancies when the fertilized egg implants outside the uterine cavity, usually in the Fallopian tube. One of the most common signs of ectopic pregnancy is pain. It isn't unusual to have mild pain early in pregnancy from a cyst on the ovary or from stretching of the uterus or ligaments. However, if pain is severe and causes you concern, call your healthcare provider.

You can't prevent an ectopic pregnancy. However, some factors increase its likelihood:

- pelvic infections, pelvic inflammatory disease (PID)
- previous ruptured appendix
- surgery on your Fallopian tubes (such as reversal of a tubal ligation or infertility surgery)
- use of an IUD for contraception
- previous ectopic pregnancy

Research shows chlamydia infection may be linked to ectopic pregnancy. One report showed 70% of the women studied who had an ectopic pregnancy also had chlamydia.

Diagnosis of an ectopic pregnancy can be difficult and may require some tests and some waiting. Tests include ultrasound, quantitative HCG and laparoscopy (a type of minor surgery). It may take days or a few weeks to make a definitive diagnosis.

Sometimes a healthcare provider orders a couple of quantitative HCG tests a few days apart. HCG is produced when you're pregnant; it increases rapidly early in pregnancy. A quantitative HCG tells how far along in pregnancy you are by assigning a number to your developmental stage. The numbers aren't exact, but they increase in a way that can help your healthcare provider decide if it is an abnormal pregnancy. The HCG test is not used in normal pregnancies but can be very helpful when there is concern about an ectopic pregnancy.

An ectopic pregnancy cannot be carried to full term. Surgery is almost always required to correct the problem, which results in loss of the pregnancy.

Falls

A fall is the most frequent cause of minor injury during pregnancy. Fortunately, a fall usually doesn't cause serious injury to mom or baby. Movement of the baby after a fall is reassuring. A possible problem after a fall may be indicated by any of the following:

- bleeding from the vagina
- a gush of fluid from the vagina, indicating rupture of membranes
- severe abdominal pain

If you fall, contact your healthcare provider; you may require attention. If you had a very bad fall, monitoring baby's heartbeat or having an ultrasound for further evaluation may be advised.

• •

It was a late-night call, and Rachael apologized for bothering me. She was 34 weeks pregnant and had fallen in her driveway while bringing in groceries. She had landed squarely on her bottom. She was OK but was concerned about the baby. The baby hadn't moved since the fall, and it scared her. She said she wasn't bleeding or leaking any fluid, but her uterus was tightening. She didn't know if it was contractions, but it was uncomfortable. I reassured her the baby was cushioned very well, better than she was, but it was still something to be concerned about. Even though it was late and cold outside, I asked her to go to the hospital to check things out. We all felt better after Rachael had a nonstress test—the baby was fine. The contractions stopped, and Rachael took some acetaminophen for her bumps and bruises. At her next visit, I told Rachael not to apologize for calls like that—it was the right thing to do.

• •

Fibroid Tumors

Fibroid tumors, also called *myomas* or *leiomyomas,* are growths that develop in the uterine wall or on the outside of the uterus; most are noncancerous (benign). If you have fibroids, the hormones of pregnancy can make fibroids grow larger. Complications include increased risks of having a Cesarean delivery, an abnormal position for baby, premature birth or hemorrhaging after baby's birth.

Fibroids may also slightly increase the chance of miscarriage and/or premature delivery, especially when growths are large. Placental abruption may occur more readily if the placenta embeds itself over a large fibroid. Fibroids have also been known to block the opening to the cervix. Discuss the situation with your healthcare provider if you're concerned.

Gestational Diabetes

Some women develop diabetes only during pregnancy; it is called *gestational diabetes.* Pregnant women over age 40 are more likely to develop gestational diabetes.

Gestational diabetes occurs when pregnancy hormones affect the way your body makes or uses insulin, a hormone that converts sugar in food into energy the body uses. If your body doesn't make enough insulin or if it doesn't use the insulin appropriately, the level of sugar in the blood rises to an unacceptable level. Several other factors can affect blood-sugar levels, including stress, the time of day (glucose values are often higher in the morning), the amount of exercise you do and the amount of carbohydrates in your diet.

Gestational diabetes affects about 10% of all pregnant women. If you have it with one pregnancy, there's a pretty high chance it will happen in future pregnancies. In addition, some women who develop gestational diabetes may develop type-2 diabetes within 10 years. Your best protection is to stay within the recommended weight-gain limits your healthcare provider gives you. Risk factors for developing gestational diabetes include:

- over 30 years old
- obesity
- family history of diabetes
- gestational diabetes in previous pregnancy
- previously gave birth to baby who weighed over 9½ pounds
- previously had a stillborn baby
- being Black/African-American, Latina/Hispanic, Asian, Native American or Pacific Islander
- poor prepregnancy diet

Good control of gestational diabetes is important. If left untreated, it can be serious for you and baby. You will both be exposed to a high concentration of sugar, which is not healthy for either of you. Symptoms of gestational diabetes include:

- blurred vision
- tingling or numbness in hands and/or feet
- excessive thirst
- frequent urination
- sores that heal slowly
- excess fatigue

Treatment of gestational diabetes centers on keeping your blood-glucose levels normal. Ways to deal with this include regular exercise and increased fluid intake. Diet is also essential in handling the problem; in fact, most women can control their gestational diabetes with diet and exercise alone. If gestational diabetes is controlled this way, you'll need to monitor yourself very closely to lower the risk of delivering an oversize infant.

Your healthcare provider will probably recommend a six-meal, 2000- to 2500-calorie-per-day eating plan. You may also be referred to a dietitian. Research shows women who receive dietary counseling, blood-sugar monitoring and insulin therapy (when needed) do better during pregnancy than women who receive routine care.

Eating a diet low in fat and high in fiber may help reduce your risk of getting gestational diabetes. A low intake of vitamin C may increase your risk.

For 10 to 15% of women with gestational diabetes, insulin is required to manage the problem. Insulin therapy is the first choice when medication is necessary. In some cases, oral medications, such as glyburide or Metformin, are used.

After baby's birth, nearly all women who experience the problem return to normal, and the problem disappears. However, gestational diabetes may not disappear immediately after delivery. It could take several weeks for it to go away. One or 2 months after pregnancy, your healthcare provider will probably do a special blood test to determine whether it is no longer a problem.

Incompetent Cervix

An *incompetent cervix* describes a condition in which a woman's cervix dilates (stretches) prematurely. It isn't painful, and usually the woman doesn't notice it. Membranes may rupture (her water breaks) without warning, and the baby is usually delivered prematurely. The problem is not usually diagnosed until after one or more deliveries of a premature infant without any pain before delivery. If it's your first pregnancy, you cannot know if you have an incompetent cervix.

Some researchers believe the condition occurs because of previous trauma to the cervix, such as a miscarriage or abortion. It may occur if surgery has been performed on the cervix.

Treatment is usually surgical. A weak cervix can be reinforced by sewing the cervix shut, called a *cerclage,* or sometimes called a *McDonald's suture.* At the end of the pregnancy, or when the woman goes into labor, the surgical stitch is removed and the baby is born normally.

Miscarriage and Stillbirth

Nearly every pregnant woman thinks about miscarriage at some time during pregnancy, but it occurs in only about 20% of all pregnancies. *Miscarriage* occurs when a pregnancy ends before the embryo or fetus can survive on its own outside the uterus, usually within the first 3 months. After 20 weeks, loss of a pregnancy is called a *stillbirth.* Many causes of miscarriage also apply to stillbirth, and in this discussion, we will use the term "miscarriage" to apply to both. We have also included a separate, brief discussion of stillbirth below.

Having a miscarriage is an emotional experience for any couple. It's normal for partners to blame themselves when a miscarriage occurs. However, it isn't your fault, so don't blame yourselves.

When a miscarriage occurs, the first questions women ask are "Did I cause it?" and "What could I have done to prevent it?" Most of the time we don't know why a miscarriage occurs; it can happen for many different reasons. The most common reason for early miscarriage is abnormal development of the embryo. Research indicates more than half of these miscarriages have chromosomal abnormalities.

Outside factors, such as radiation and some chemicals (drugs or medications), may cause a miscarriage. Maternal factors may also result in miscarriage. Several maternal factors have been identified:

- chromosomal problems
- hormonal problems
- anatomical problems with the uterus, including uterine scarring from surgery or a second-trimester abortion, and fibroids in the uterus
- chronic health conditions
- a high fever in early pregnancy
- autoimmune disorders
- unusual infections, such as listeriosis, toxoplasmosis and syphilis
- obesity, especially in women with a BMI higher than 35
- cigarette smoking
- drinking alcohol
- trauma from an accident or major surgery
- an incompetent cervix may be a cause of pregnancy loss after the first trimester

Caffeine use before and during pregnancy may increase the chance of miscarriage. Cut out as much caffeine as possible while you're trying to conceive and during early pregnancy. Once you're pregnant, don't take in more than 200mg in any one day.

In some cases, the uniting of the couple's sperm and egg results in a miscarriage. When the couple's genes unite at fertilization, the union can produce genetic abnormalities that cause a miscarriage.

Different medical descriptions of miscarriages actually describe different types of miscarriage. Medically speaking, there are six basic types.

A *threatened miscarriage* occurs when there is a bloody discharge from the vagina during the first half of pregnancy. Bleeding may last days or weeks. A woman may or may not experience cramping and pain. The pain may feel like a menstrual cramp or mild backache. Resting in bed is about all a woman can do.

An *inevitable miscarriage* occurs with rupture of membranes, dilatation of the cervix and passage of blood clots and tissue. Loss of the pregnancy is almost certain. The uterus usually contracts, expelling the embryo or products of conception.

With an *incomplete miscarriage,* the entire pregnancy may not be expelled. Only part of the pregnancy may be passed. Bleeding may be heavy and continues until the uterus is emptied.

A *missed miscarriage* can occur when an embryo that has died earlier is retained in the uterus. A woman may not bleed or have any other symptoms. The period between the failure of the pregnancy until the time the miscarriage is discovered is usually weeks.

Habitual miscarriage usually refers to three or more consecutive miscarriages. Another type of failed pregnancy can be classified under miscarriage. A *chemical pregnancy* occurs when an embryo forms and begins producing HCG, the hormone that makes a pregnancy test positive. However, the embryo dies very early, so there actually is no pregnancy.

The first warning sign of a miscarriage is bleeding from the vagina, followed by cramping. Call your healthcare provider immediately if you experience this! Unfortunately, in nearly all instances, there is little you or your healthcare provider can do to stop a miscarriage from happening. No surgical technique or medicine can stop a miscarriage.

Most experts recommend bed rest and decreased activity. Some recommend the hormone progesterone, but not all healthcare providers agree with its use. Ultrasound and blood tests may help your healthcare provider determine whether you are going to miscarry, but you may have to wait and see.

If you pass all of the pregnancy, bleeding stops and cramping goes away, you may be done with it. If everything is not expelled, you will require a dilatation and curettage (D&C), which is minor surgery to empty the uterus. A D&C is recommended so you won't bleed for a long period of time, risking anemia and infection.

If you're Rh-negative and have a miscarriage, you will receive RhoGAM. This applies *only* if you are Rh-negative.

Stillbirth

Stillbirth is the death of a fetus after 20 weeks of pregnancy. Various factors contribute to the occurrence of a stillbirth. Being older, having had more children and carrying more than one baby may be causes of some stillbirths. Nearly 50% of all unexplained stillbirths may be related to poor placental function, resulting in problems in the fetus.

Maternal obesity may also be a factor. If you are obese when you get pregnant, you have a higher risk of having a stillbirth.

Having a stillborn baby can be a traumatic experience for you, which can take time to recover from. You and your partner will probably have many questions and concerns. To help you find answers to your questions, discuss them with your healthcare provider. Ask if there is anything you can do to prepare for your next pregnancy, and ask what you might need to do during your next pregnancy to avoid another stillbirth.

Pre-Eclampsia

Pre-eclampsia, once called *toxemia of pregnancy,* can be a serious complication of pregnancy. Pre-eclampsia occurs *only* during pregnancy; left untreated, it poses a serious threat to you and your baby. Older women may be more likely to develop pre-eclampsia.

Most cases are mild and treatable. However, if pre-eclampsia worsens, it can quickly progress to a serious condition called *eclampsia,* which is accompanied by seizures or convulsions. A woman can also go into a coma.

We don't really know what causes pre-eclampsia. Some women are at greater risk of developing pre-eclampsia than others. Your chance of getting the problem increases if any of the following applies to you:

- age 35 or older
- family history of pre-eclampsia
- first pregnancy
- kidney disease
- lupus
- diabetes
- pregnancy with multiples
- overweight
- personal history of pre-eclampsia, combined with high blood pressure before pregnancy

A diet that is too low in protein may increase your risk of developing pre-eclampsia.

The best way to reduce the risk of developing pre-eclampsia or eclampsia is to keep all your prenatal appointments. Your healthcare provider will follow changes in your blood pressure throughout your pregnancy. With your help and cooperation, pre-eclampsia can usually be treated before it becomes serious.

Pre-eclampsia may develop after 20 weeks of pregnancy, though most cases occur after 30 weeks. Symptoms include hypertension, protein in the urine, a sudden weight gain, swelling and changes in muscle reflexes.

Certain signs indicate a worsening condition. Call your healthcare provider *immediately* if you have pre-eclampsia and develop any of these signs:

- pain under the ribs on the right side
- headache
- seeing spots or other vision changes

If your legs or feet are swollen, it does *not* mean you have pre-eclampsia. Most pregnant women experience some swelling, but a diagnosis of pre-eclampsia includes other symptoms, as described above.

For a mild case of pre-eclampsia, your healthcare provider will probably order bed rest until your blood pressure stabilizes. You will be advised to drink lots of water and to avoid salt and foods containing large amounts of sodium.

You will visit your healthcare provider more frequently. In some cases, you are given medication to lower your blood pressure. You may be given medication to protect against seizures.

If pre-eclampsia worsens, you may be admitted to the hospital for observation. Hospital staff measure your blood pressure several times a day and record your weight and the level of protein in your urine. They also monitor your developing baby, record fetal movements every day and perform a nonstress test.

If your blood pressure continues to rise and other symptoms worsen, the baby may need to be delivered to protect you from serious complications. Before delivery, you may receive magnesium sulfate intravenously to prevent convulsions during labor and baby's birth.

Premature Rupture of Membranes (PROM and PPROM)

When membranes rupture early in pregnancy, it is called *premature rupture of membranes (PROM)*. There are two categories of premature rupture. PROM refers to rupture of fetal membranes before the onset of labor and occurs in 8 to 12% of all pregnancies. PPROM is the *preterm-premature rupture of membranes* and refers to rupture of fetal membranes before 37 weeks of pregnancy. It occurs in 1% of all pregnancies.

The exact cause of PPROM is unknown. Black/African-American women appear to have a higher incidence of PPROM than white women. Smoking is strongly correlated with PPROM. Vitamin and mineral deficiencies have also been considered causes. Uterine bleeding is strongly tied to PPROM; infection also plays an important role in many cases. If you had PPROM with a previous pregnancy, you have a 35% chance it will occur again.

If ruptured membranes are not detected and treated within 24 hours, infection and other serious complications may occur. A test is available to diagnose whether membranes have ruptured prematurely; it is called *Amnisure*. It detects a protein found in amniotic fluid that isn't normally present in the vagina unless membranes have ruptured. It's a vaginal test but does not require use of a speculum or a vaginal exam. A sterile swab is inserted about 2 to 3 inches (5 to 7.5cm) into the vagina, and a sample is taken. Results are ready in about 10 minutes.

Rh-Disease and Sensitivity

It's important during pregnancy to know your blood type (O, A, B, AB) and your Rh-factor. The Rh-factor is a protein in your blood, determined by a genetic trait. Everyone has either Rh-positive blood or Rh-negative blood. If you have the Rh factor in your blood, you're Rh-positive—most people are Rh-positive. If you don't have the Rh-factor, you're Rh-negative.

Between 15 and 17% of the population in the United States is Rh-negative. Rh-negativity affects about 15% of the white population and 8% of the Black/African-American and Hispanic populations in the United States.

• •

When we did lab tests on Abbie, we discovered she was Rh-negative. Her mother was Rh-negative and had told Abbie stories about pregnancy problems she had 30 years before. Understandably, Abbie was nervous. I told her that years ago, it *was* a serious problem to be Rh-negative, but we have since solved the problem. We checked Abbie for Rh-antibodies, and she was negative for them. I told her we would check her again at 28 weeks and give her RhoGAM, a blood product, to help ensure she would not form antibodies during the last part of pregnancy. If the baby was Rh-positive, we would give her RhoGAM again after the birth. I reassured Abbie it wasn't anything to worry about and explained this is one reason we do all the blood tests we do.

• •

An Rh-negative woman who carries an Rh-positive child could face problems during pregnancy, which could result in a very sick baby. If you're Rh-positive, you don't have to worry about any of this. If you are Rh-negative, you *do* need to know about it.

Rh-disease occurs when there is an incompatibility between a mother's blood and her baby's blood. If you're Rh-negative, you can become sensitized (*isoimmunized*) if your growing baby is Rh-positive.

Antibodies are made when a mother has Rh-negative blood and the fetus has Rh-positive blood. Antibodies don't harm you, but if they cross the placenta, they can attack the blood cells of an Rh-positive baby. Antibodies can break down the baby's red blood cells, which results in anemia in the baby, which can be very serious.

You and your fetus do not share blood systems during pregnancy. However, in some situations, blood passes from baby to mother. This can happen with ectopic pregnancy, amniocentesis, chorionic villus sampling, cordocentesis, blood transfusion, bleeding during pregnancy, such as with placental abruption, or in an accident or injury, such as blunt-force trauma to the uterus in an auto accident.

With a first baby, if fetal blood enters the mother's bloodstream, the baby may be born before the woman's body can become sensitized. She probably won't produce enough antibodies to harm the baby. However, antibodies stay in the woman's circulation forever. In the next pregnancy, if these antibodies cross the placenta, they can attack the baby's red blood cells. Anemia can occur in the fetus because antibodies in the mom are already formed.

If you're Rh-negative, you'll be checked for antibodies at the beginning of pregnancy. If you have antibodies, you're already sensitized. If you're already sensitized, RhoGAM won't help.

If you don't have antibodies, you're unsensitized (this is good). You may be given RhoGAM to prevent you from becoming sensitized. RhoGAM is a product extracted from human blood. (If you have religious, ethical or personal reasons for not using blood or blood products, consult your healthcare provider or minister.) If your blood mixes with baby's blood, RhoGAM keeps you from becoming sensitized.

Your healthcare provider will probably suggest you receive RhoGAM around 28 weeks of pregnancy to prevent sensitization in the last part of pregnancy. You're more likely to be exposed to baby's blood during the last 3 months of pregnancy and at delivery. If you go beyond your due date, your healthcare provider may suggest another dose of RhoGAM.

RhoGAM is given within 72 hours after delivery if baby is Rh-positive. If your baby is Rh-negative, you don't need RhoGAM after delivery and you didn't need it during pregnancy.

After baby's birth, if blood tests show a larger than normal number of Rh-positive blood cells (from baby) have entered your bloodstream, you may be given RhoGAM. The RhoGAM treatment is necessary for every pregnancy.

Vasa Previa

Vasa previa is a condition in which blood vessels of the umbilical cord cross the interior opening of the cervix, lying close to it or covering it. It occurs once in about every 2000 to 3000 pregnancies.

When the cervix dilates or membranes rupture, unprotected vessels can tear. Or they can become squeezed together, which shuts off blood and oxygen to the baby. It can also occur when baby drops into position for delivery and presses on the vessels, which limits or shuts off blood supply to the baby. Danger may also occur when membranes rupture. Fetal vessels may rupture at the same time, causing loss of blood from the fetus.

Detecting the problem can be achieved with a 5-second color-ultrasound scan. The test shows vessels lying across the cervical opening and measures the speed of blood flow. Different rates of blood flow have distinct colors and reveal the location of the fetal blood vessels. However, this screening is not routine.

When a woman is diagnosed with vasa previa, she may be put on bed rest during the third trimester to help prevent labor. A Cesarean delivery is done after 35 weeks of pregnancy, with a success rate of over 95%.

Premature Labor and Premature Birth

Premature Labor

Sometimes a woman will begin labor before her baby is ready to be born. This is called *premature labor.* Your body begins the birth process before 37 completed weeks of pregnancy.

Your baby needs to remain inside your uterus until he or she is ready to be born. When a baby is born early, it can cause many problems for the baby.

The treatment most often prescribed for premature labor is bed rest, which means lying on your side in bed. Either side is OK, but the left side is best. Signs of premature labor include the following:

- cramps, with or without diarrhea
- feeling of baby pushing down
- contractions every 10 minutes or more frequently
- lower-back pain
- bleeding

Doctors advise bed rest because it works in many cases. However, bed rest means you may have to either stop or modify activities. See the discussion of bed rest that begins on page 274.

Some experts believe taking your prenatal vitamin every day may help reduce the risk of preterm birth by as much as 50%!

Bed rest was once the only treatment for premature labor; now we also have medications available. However, even if you take medication, you will probably be advised to rest in bed. Three types of medications relax the uterus and decrease contractions—magnesium sulfate, beta adrenergics and sedatives or narcotics. These drugs are taken orally or intravenously.

The goal in treating premature labor is to prevent baby from being born too early. Follow your healthcare provider's recommendations and advice regarding this important aspect of pregnancy.

Preterm or Premature Birth

When a baby is born too early, it is considered a preterm or premature birth. *Preterm birth* refers to a baby born prematurely; it is also called *premature birth*. Recent statistics show nearly 13% of all babies born in the United States are premature—that's over half a million babies a year. The rate of preterm births has increased by over 30% since 1980. Singleton preterm births have increased by nearly 15% since 1990. Nearly 25% of all preterm births are a result of pregnancy complications—a baby needs to be delivered early for its health and safety.

Preterm delivery of a baby can be dangerous because a baby's lungs and other systems may not be ready to function on their own. Your doctor may take steps to halt contractions if you go into labor too early. Most doctors start with bed rest and increased fluids to stop labor. Some medications, given orally, by injection or intravenously, also help stop labor.

Studies show it's dangerous for a baby to be born even a few weeks prematurely. A baby born between 34 and 37 weeks is called a *late preterm baby*. These infants are more likely to develop breathing difficulties and feeding problems and have trouble regulating body temperature. Risk of problems increases significantly for babies born between 34 and 37 weeks of pregnancy when compared to full-term infants. We once believed a baby's lungs are mature by 34 weeks, but we now know this is not true. These findings may impact elective Cesarean deliveries and induction of labor.

Although the cause of premature labor/delivery is unknown in most cases, we do know there is increased risk for the following reasons:

- a uterus with an abnormal shape
- a large uterus
- hydramnios
- an abnormal placenta
- premature rupture of the membranes
- incompetent cervix
- multiple fetuses
- abnormalities of the fetus
- fetal death
- retained IUD
- serious maternal illness
- incorrect estimate of gestational age
- giving birth at an older age
- singleton pregnancy from in-vitro fertilization
- short wait between pregnancies (less than 9 months)
- being a Black/African-American woman
- being under age 17 or over 35
- having an iron deficiency

Experts believe up to half of all premature births may be associated with infections. In addition, research shows that if it took you longer than 1 year to get pregnant, you may have a slightly higher chance of giving birth prematurely.

The Placenta

The *placenta* carries nourishment and oxygen from you to your developing baby and carries away baby's waste products. Various problems occasionally develop with the placenta, especially in older women; the most common include *placenta previa, placental abruption* and *retained placenta.*

Placenta Previa

When a woman has *placenta previa,* the placenta covers part or all of the cervix. The placenta may separate from the uterus as the cervix begins to dilate (open) during labor. This can cause heavy bleeding, which can be dangerous for mom and baby. Placenta previa affects about 1 in every 200 pregnant women in the last trimester of pregnancy.

Signs and symptoms of placenta previa vary, but the most characteristic symptom is painless bleeding. If you experience painless bleeding, your healthcare provider may order an ultrasound exam to determine the location of the placenta, if he or she is concerned about placenta previa. Your healthcare provider will not perform a pelvic exam because it may cause heavier bleeding. If you see another healthcare provider or when you go to the hospital, tell whomever you see that you have placenta previa and you should not have a pelvic exam.

If your healthcare provider determines you have placenta previa, you may have to curtail certain activities. Most recommend avoiding intercourse and not traveling in addition to avoiding pelvic exams.

With placenta previa, the baby is more likely to be in a breech position. To avoid bleeding, a Cesarean delivery is usually performed.

Placental Abruption

Placental abruption occurs when the placenta separates from the wall of the uterus before birth. Normally the placenta does not separate until after delivery of the baby. Separation of the placenta before birth can be dangerous for mother and baby.

Placental abruption occurs about once in every 80 deliveries. Its cause is unknown; however, certain conditions may make it more likely to occur, such as trauma to the mother from a fall or car accident, an umbilical cord that is too short, sudden change in the size of the uterus, as with the rupture of membranes, hypertension, a dietary deficiency in the mother or an abnormality of the uterus, such as a band of tissue in the uterus called a *uterine septum*.

Symptoms of placental abruption include the following signs, though not all may be present:
- heavy bleeding from the vagina
- uterine tenderness
- uterine contractions
- premature labor
- lower-back pain

Ultrasound may help diagnose placental abruption in some cases. If bleeding is severe, a woman may go into shock.

The most common treatment of placental abruption is delivery of the baby. However, the decision of when to deliver the baby varies, based on the problem's severity. Sometimes a Cesarean section is necessary, but each case is handled individually.

You may be able to help prevent placental abruption. A folic-acid deficiency may play a role in causing placental abruption, so you may be required to take extra folic acid during pregnancy. Maternal smoking and alcohol use may also increase the risk of placental abruption. If you smoke cigarettes or drink alcohol, stop both activities (it's also advisable for many other reasons). Cocaine use may also cause placental abruption.

Retained Placenta

Some women have problems delivering the placenta after their baby is born. The placenta usually separates from the implantation site on the uterus a few minutes after delivery. When the placenta does not deliver following baby's birth, we call it a *retained placenta*. Reasons for a retained placenta include a placenta attaching over a previous C-section scar or other incision scar on the uterus, attaching in a place that has been previously curetted, such as for a D&C or abortion, or attaching over an area of the uterus that was infected.

In some cases, the placenta doesn't separate because it's attached through the wall of the uterus. This can be very serious and cause heavy blood loss. In other cases, part of the placenta may deliver while part is retained. Your healthcare provider will check the placenta after delivery to be sure it has all been delivered.

The most significant problem with a retained placenta is bleeding after delivery, which can be severe. If the placenta cannot be delivered, your healthcare provider may attempt to remove the placenta by D&C. If the placenta is attached through the wall of the uterus, it may be necessary to remove the uterus by performing a hysterectomy; this is rare.

Emergency Surgery during Pregnancy

Emergencies occur, even during pregnancy. When you're pregnant, a medical emergency must be dealt with in ways that are best for you *and* your developing fetus. Sometimes surgical procedures are necessary. Some common reasons for surgery during pregnancy are gall-bladder removal, appendicitis, ovarian cysts, broken bones and dental emergencies.

Gallbladder Problems

Inflammation of the gallbladder, also called *cholecystitis,* occurs most often in women in their 30s and 40s. Treatment consists of pain medication and surgery. If you're pregnant, your healthcare provider will try to avoid surgery until after the baby is born, if possible. However, if pain is severe and does not improve with pain medication, surgery may be necessary. The ideal time to perform gallbladder surgery during pregnancy is the second trimester. The risk of miscarriage or premature delivery is lower.

The common surgical procedure for gallbladder removal requires general anesthesia and an incision, with a hospital stay of up to 2 or 3 days. If the surgeon uses laparoscopy, three or four small incisions are made, then the gallbladder is examined and removed. The hospital stay is about 1 day. In most cases, laparoscopy isn't recommended after 20 weeks of pregnancy.

Risks to the fetus from gallbladder surgery include premature labor, infection and risks associated with anesthesia. If you require surgery, you will be monitored closely to watch for and to prevent premature labor.

Appendicitis

The incidence of appendicitis is about 1 in every 2000 pregnancies. Diagnosis of appendicitis is more difficult during pregnancy because some of the symptoms, including nausea, vomiting and a high white-blood-cell count, are the same as those for a normal pregnancy or other problems. Pregnancy can also make diagnosis difficult because as the uterus grows larger, the appendix moves upward and outward, so pain and tenderness can be found in different locations than usual. (See the illustration below.) Diagnosis during pregnancy requires a physical exam, blood tests and ultrasound.

If you have appendicitis, you will require immediate surgery. It's major abdominal surgery and often requires a few days to recover in the hospital. Laparoscopy is used in some situations, but it may be more difficult to perform

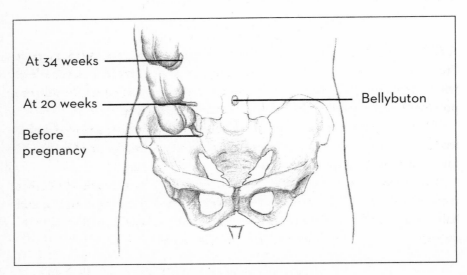

Location of appendix during pregnancy.

during pregnancy because of the enlarged uterus. Risks to the developing fetus with appendicitis include the risks associated with general anesthesia, infection and premature labor.

Ovarian Cysts

Ovarian cysts can be a serious complication during pregnancy. An *ovarian cyst* is a sac that develops in the ovary and consists of one or more fluid-containing chambers. It may have to be surgically removed because of pressure, twisting, bleeding or blockage of the birth canal. Ovarian cysts that develop in pregnancy are almost always benign.

These cysts can cause pain, bloating and abdominal swelling. Your healthcare provider will perform a physical exam and do an ultrasound to diagnose the problem. Treatment is usually pain medication and observation; surgery is usually avoided unless absolutely necessary.

If surgery is necessary, the cyst may be drained or removed. In some cases, the surgeon must remove the entire ovary. If surgery can be postponed, the safest time to do it is after the first trimester has ended.

Risks to the fetus vary, depending on when surgery is performed. In early pregnancy, loss of an ovary could mean loss of hormones necessary to support the pregnancy. Late in pregnancy, a cyst could block the birth canal, requiring a Cesarean delivery. Other risks include those associated with general anesthesia, infection and premature delivery.

Broken Bones

A fall or accident can break a bone, which may require X-rays and/or surgery. Treatment cannot be delayed until after pregnancy; the problem must be dealt with immediately. If you break a bone, insist your pregnancy healthcare provider be contacted before any test or treatment is done.

If X-rays are required, your pelvis and abdomen should be shielded with a lead apron. If the pelvis and abdomen cannot be shielded, the need for the X-ray must be weighed against the risks it poses to the fetus.

Anesthesia or pain medication may be necessary for a simple break that requires setting or pinning. Keep its use to a minimum. It is best for you and baby to avoid general anesthesia when possible. If general anesthesia is required, baby will be monitored closely during surgery.

Dental Emergencies

Some dental emergencies you might face during pregnancy include root canal, tooth extraction, a large cavity, an abscessed tooth or problems resulting from an accident or injury. It might be unwise to postpone treatment until after baby is born.

If you have a dental problem, contact your dentist and your pregnancy healthcare provider *before* doing anything. Your dentist and healthcare provider may find it helpful to talk before any final decisions are made.

Dental X-rays may be necessary. Be sure your abdomen is shielded with a lead apron before X-rays are taken. If possible, wait until after the end of the first trimester to have dental work done.

Avoid gas or general anesthesia for a dental procedure. Local anesthetics are fine, as are many antibiotics and pain medications. Be sure to consult your healthcare provider before taking any medications.

If you have a serious dental problem, such as an abscess, get it treated. Some problems, such as infection, that could result from not treating it are more serious than the normal risks associated with treatment.

Bed Rest

Bed rest is ordered for a woman to improve her chances of giving birth to a healthy baby. Today, one in five women spends at least 1 week in bed during pregnancy. If the condition is severe, hospitalization may be advised.

When a woman has to rest in bed, it can disrupt the normal routines of her family, especially when it lasts more than a short time. Adjusting to around-the-clock bed rest can be difficult.

A woman may be advised to rest in bed when certain conditions threaten the baby's or mother's health. These conditions include the following:

- a history of premature labor
- early rupture of the membranes
- pre-eclampsia
- high blood pressure
- multiple fetuses, especially triplets or more
- incompetent cervix
- premature labor
- risk of miscarriage
- intrauterine-growth restriction
- chronic heart condition
- diabetes, with complications

Resting in bed works two ways. First, lying down takes the pressure of the baby's weight off the cervix, which can help when a woman experiences premature labor. Second, resting on your side maximizes the blood flow to your uterus, which brings more oxygen and nutrients to the baby.

Bed rest can seriously disrupt your routine. You may not be able to work, and you may have to curtail other activities. Bed rest can be difficult when you have young children. Changing your routine can be stressful for people around you, including family members and co-workers. Ask your healthcare provider what you can do while you're on bed rest. Sometimes you aren't allowed to get out of bed except to eat, go to the bathroom and go to prenatal appointments. At other times, bed rest may be less restricted. You may be able to sit up or be a little more active for part of the day. You may have to take medication and limit your activities.

Time-Saving, Energy-Saving Tip

Saving plastic bread bags and plastic grocery bags can be handy but messy. A couple of ideas may help you organize these useful items. When you've finished with a roll of paper towels, push small plastic bags into the empty tube, and store it in your drawer or cupboard, ready to pull out a bag to use. If you purchase soda in 12-pack cartons, open the carton at the end, and save it when it's empty. Before you reseal the end of the carton, push plastic grocery bags into the carton. Reseal and pull bags through the hand opening at the top of the carton.

You may be advised to lie only on your left side to increase blood flow to the uterus. This position relieves pressure on the vena cava and increases blood flow to the uterus. You may be allowed to alternate between sides. However, you may *not* lie on your back. Lying on your back puts too much pressure from your uterus on the vena cava.

Staying in bed may be hard, but it's better to rest at home than in the hospital!

If You Have Children

Bed rest can be especially hard for a pregnant woman with young children at home. Try some of the following suggestions to help you make the experience more tolerable.

- Have someone come to your home to help during the day.
- If you can't find someone to come to your home, see if a friend or neighbor can take your children for all or part of the day.
- Keep books and toys nearby to help entertain your kids when they're with you.
- Ask your children to help. A child can put toys away or get something for you. Children love to feel important; asking them to help you can make them feel very grown-up.

- Do some quiet activities with your child; look at photo albums or read books together.

Keep a Positive Attitude

If you must rest in bed, try to stay positive! No matter how long you have to rest in bed—a few days or a few weeks—the goal is a healthy baby and a healthy mom. You may be upset or feel anxious. Keep in mind you're doing this for you and your baby. Give yourself (and your family, too!) a pat on the back.

Staying in bed isn't fun, especially if you haven't yet prepared for your baby's arrival. You may feel resentful. You may have to abstain from sex, which can add stress to an already difficult situation. You can make the experience more bearable if you plan for your time of confinement. The following suggestions may help you get through your time in bed.

- Spend the day in a room other than your bedroom. Use the living room or den sofa for daytime activities.
- Use foam mattress pads and extra pillows for comfort.
- Keep a telephone close at hand.
- If you work, ask your healthcare provider if you can read or work on projects at home.
- Keep reading material, the television remote control, your house or cell phone, your iPod or an MP3 player and other essentials nearby.
- Establish a daily routine. When you get up, change into daytime clothes. Shower or bathe every day. Comb your hair, and put on makeup if you usually wear it. Nap if you need it. Go to bed when you normally do.
- Keep food and drinks close at hand. Use a cooler to keep food and drinks cold. Use an insulated container for hot soup or coffee.
- For support, contact other women who have been on bed rest. The Internet can help you stay connected.

Chapter 18

Labor and Delivery

Labor and delivery is the process by which your baby is born. It may be different for a woman in her 30s or 40s than for a younger woman. Labor may be longer because the cervix may not dilate as easily as it does in a woman under 35. We also know that more older women need a Cesarean delivery.

Just as your uterus may not contract as readily during labor, it may not contract as quickly as it would for a younger woman *after* delivery. Postpartum bleeding may last longer and be heavier.

Your labor and delivery will be unique to you, no matter what your age. Every woman labors differently, and there is often a difference in the way a woman labors from one birth to another.

Choosing Where to Give Birth

It's important during the second trimester to consider where you want to give birth. In some situations, you may not have a choice. Or in your area, you may have several choices.

Whatever birthing setup you choose, the most significant considerations are the health of your baby and the welfare of you both. When you decide where to have your baby, be sure you have answers to the following questions, if possible.

- What facilities and staff are available?
- What is the availability of anesthesia? Is an anesthesiologist available 24 hours a day?
- How long does it take to respond and to perform a Cesarean delivery, if necessary? (This should be 30 minutes or less.)
- Is a pediatrician available 24 hours a day for an emergency or problems?
- Is the nursery staffed at all times?
- In the event of an emergency or a premature baby that needs to be transported to a high-risk nursery, how is it done? By ambulance? By helicopter? How close is the nearest high-risk nursery if not at this hospital?

These may seem like a lot of questions to ask, but answers can help put your mind at ease. When it's your baby and your health, it's good to know emergency measures can be employed in an efficient, timely manner when necessary.

There are various hospital setups available for labor and birth. With *LDRP (labor, delivery, recovery and postpartum)*, the room you are admitted to at the beginning of labor is the room you labor, deliver, recover and remain in for your hospital stay.

The concept of LDRP evolved because many women don't want to be moved from the labor area to a delivery area, then to another part of the hospital after delivery for recovery. The nursery is usually close to labor/delivery and the recovery area. This lets you see your baby as often as you like and have baby in your room for longer periods.

How will I know it's time to go to the hospital?

If you aren't sure, don't be afraid to call your healthcare provider or the hospital. General guidelines for going to the hospital include the following:

- You believe your water has broken.
- You are bleeding.
- You have contractions every 5 minutes, lasting 1 minute.

Another option is the *birthing room*; this generally refers to delivering your baby in the same room you labor in. Even if you use a birthing room, you may be moved to another area of the hospital for recovery and the remainder of your stay.

In many places, *labor-and-delivery suites* are available; you labor in one room, then move to a delivery room at the time of birth. Following this, you may go to a postpartum floor, which is an area in the hospital where you will spend the remainder of your hospital stay.

Most hospitals allow you to have your baby in your room as much as you want. This is called *rooming in* or *boarding in*. Some hospitals also have a cot, couch or chair that makes into a bed in your room so your partner can stay with you after delivery. Check the availability of various facilities in the hospitals in your area.

Packing for the Hospital

Packing for the hospital can be unnerving. You don't want to pack too early and have your suitcase staring at you. But you don't want to wait until the last minute, throw things together and take the chance of forgetting something important.

Pack about 3 weeks before your due date. Include things you'll need during labor for you and your labor coach and items you and baby will need after delivery, as well as for the hospital stay. See the discussions below.

Packing for Yourself

One advantage to packing early for your hospital trip is you'll have time to think about what you want to take with you. You will avoid "panic packing" and perhaps including items you don't need while forgetting ones you do. There are a lot of things to consider, but the list below should cover nearly all of what you might need:

- completed insurance or preregistration forms
- insurance card
- heavy socks to wear in the delivery room
- an item to use as a focal point
- 1 cotton nightgown or T-shirt for labor
- lip balm, lollipops or fruit drops to use during labor
- light diversion, such as books or magazines, to use during labor
- breath spray
- 1 or 2 nightgowns for after labor (bring a nursing gown if you're going to breastfeed)
- slippers with rubber soles
- 1 long robe for walking in the halls
- 2 nursing bras and pads
- 3 pairs of panties
- toiletries you use, including brush, comb, toothbrush, toothpaste, soap, shampoo, conditioner
- hair band or ponytail holder, if you have long hair
- loose-fitting clothes for going home
- sanitary pads, if the hospital doesn't supply them

You may also want to bring 1 or 2 pieces of fruit to eat after the delivery. Don't pack them too early!

Packing for Your Partner

It's a good idea to include some things in your hospital kit for your partner or labor coach to help you both during the birth:

- a watch with a second hand
- powder or cornstarch for massaging you during labor

- a paint roller or tennis ball for giving you a lower-back massage during labor
- iPod, tapes or CDs and a player, or a radio to play during labor
- camera
- list of telephone numbers and a long-distance calling card
- snacks

Packing for Baby

The hospital will probably supply most of what you need for baby, but you should have a few things:

- clothes for the trip home, including an undershirt, sleeper, outer clothes (a hat if it's cold outside)
- a couple of baby blankets
- diapers if your hospital doesn't supply them

Be sure you have an approved infant car seat in which to take your baby home. It's important to start your baby in a car seat the very first time in a car! Many hospitals will not let you take your baby home without one.

Before Labor Begins

Prepare for delivery in advance. Have your bag packed and ready. Have insurance papers filled out and available. At best, your prenatal classes will be over, and you will have visited the labor-and-delivery area of the hospital you have chosen. You will have made arrangements for your older children to be cared for by someone you trust. You will have everything at work organized so you can leave with a clear conscience. Doing these tasks will help put you in the best possible frame of mind for what lies ahead.

You may be impatient for your baby to be born. When the day finally comes, you'll experience new sensations as your body prepares to labor and to deliver your baby. Signs you may notice include the following:

- increase of Braxton-Hicks contractions (described below)
- feeling the baby drop lower into your pelvis
- weight loss or a break in weight gain
- increased pressure in the pelvis and rectum
- changes in vaginal discharge
- diarrhea

Braxton-Hicks contractions are painless, nonrhythmical contractions you may feel when you place your hand on your abdomen during pregnancy. They can begin early in pregnancy and usually continue until baby is born. They occur at irregular intervals and may increase in number and strength when your uterus is irritated.

The feeling of having your baby drop, also called *lightening,* means the baby's head has moved deeper into your pelvis. It is a natural part of the birthing process and can happen a few weeks or a few hours before labor begins or even during labor. Often a woman feels she has more room to breathe when baby descends into the pelvis, but this relief can be accompanied by more pelvic pressure and discomfort.

When Your Water Breaks

Your baby is surrounded by amniotic fluid in the uterus. As labor begins, the membranes that surround the baby and hold the fluid ("waters") may break, and fluid leaks from your vagina. You may feel a gush of fluid, followed by slow leaking, or you may just feel a slow leaking, without the gush of fluid. A sanitary pad helps absorb the fluid.

Not every woman's water breaks before she goes into labor. Often, membranes must be ruptured. Occasionally the bag of waters breaks before a baby is ready to be born. There are several ways a healthcare provider can confirm if your membranes have ruptured.

- By your description of what happened. For example, if you describe a large gush of fluid from your vagina.
- With nitrazine paper. Fluid is placed on the paper; if membranes have ruptured, the paper changes color.
- With a ferning test. Fluid is placed on a glass slide, allowed to dry, then examined under a microscope. A fernlike appearance indicates it is amniotic fluid.

If you believe your water has broken, call your healthcare provider immediately. You may be advised to go to the hospital.

If you're not near term, your healthcare provider may ask you to come to the office for an examination. You may not be ready to deliver your baby yet, and your healthcare provider will want to confirm your water has broken and to prevent any infection. Risk of infection increases when your water breaks.

True Labor or False Labor?

Considerations	True Labor	False Labor
Contractions	Regular	Irregular
Time between contractions	Come closer together	Do not get closer together
Contraction intensity	Increases	Doesn't change
Location of contractions	Entire abdomen	Various locations or back
Effect of anesthetic or pain relievers	Will not stop labor	Sedation may stop or alter frequency of contractions
Cervical change	Progressive cervical change	No cervical change

Going to the Hospital

Do you know when you should head for the hospital? You'll know it's time to go when contractions are 4 to 5 minutes apart for at least an hour. They will also be increasing in intensity and length, and they'll be coming closer together.

You may want to preregister at the hospital a few weeks before your due date. It will save time checking in when you're actually in labor, and it may help reduce your feelings of stress. Preregister with forms you receive from your healthcare provider's office or from the hospital. Fill out the forms early. If you wait until you're in labor, you may be in a hurry and concerned with other things.

Have your insurance card or insurance information with you—put it on top of the things you pack in your bag, along with your preregistration paperwork. Know your blood type and Rh-factor, your healthcare provider's name, your pediatrician's name and your due date.

Ask your healthcare provider how you should prepare to go to the hospital; he or she may have specific instructions for you. You might want to ask the following questions.

• When should I go to the hospital once I am in labor?
• Should I call you before I leave for the hospital?
• How can I reach you after regular office hours?
• Are there any particular instructions to follow during early labor?

Going to the hospital to have a baby can make anyone a little nervous, even an experienced mom. Make some plans before you go so you'll have less to worry about. Talk to your healthcare provider about what will happen during labor. Plan the route, and have your partner drive it a couple of times. Make alternative plans in case your partner can't be with you. Know how to get in touch with your partner 24 hours a day. Pack your bags.

After You're Admitted to the Hospital

After you're admitted to the hospital, you'll probably be settled into a labor room. You will be checked to see how much your cervix has dilated. A brief history of your pregnancy will be taken and vital signs noted, including blood pressure, pulse, temperature and your baby's heart rate. You may receive an enema or be started on an intravenous drip; blood will probably be drawn. You may have an epidural put in place, if you request one.

Your pubic hair may be shaved, although this isn't always necessary. Some women who choose not to have their pubic hair shaved later they say they experienced discomfort when their pubic hair became entangled in their underwear because of the normal vaginal discharge after the birth of their baby. It may be something to consider.

Intravenous Drip (I.V.)

Some women are concerned about having an intravenous drip (I.V.) started in their arm. An I.V. is necessary with an epidural anesthesia; however, if you have chosen not to have an epidural, an I.V. is not always required. Most physicians agree an I.V. is helpful if a woman needs medications or fluids during labor. It's also a good safety precaution for problems, such as bleeding; if a woman bleeds heavily before or during labor, medications or blood can be administered quickly. If you are concerned about having an I.V., discuss it with your healthcare provider at an office visit.

Enemas

Not every woman is required to have an enema to empty her bowels; usually you have a choice. There are benefits to having an enema in labor. It decreases

When a baby is born early—even by only a week or two—it may cause learning delays later in life.

the amount of fecal contamination during labor and at the time of delivery. It may also help you after delivery if you have an episiotomy because having a bowel movement very soon after delivery can be painful. Discuss any concerns you have about enemas at one of your prenatal appointments.

When Your Healthcare Provider Isn't Available

In some cases, when you get to the hospital, you may learn your healthcare provider is not available and someone else will deliver your baby. If your healthcare provider believes he or she might be out of town when your baby is born, ask to meet healthcare providers who "cover" when your healthcare provider is unavailable. Although your healthcare provider would like to be there for the birth of your baby, sometimes it isn't possible.

Will I Need an Episiotomy?

An *episiotomy* has been one of the most commonly performed procedures in obstetrics and has almost become routine in some places. In 2000, about 33% of women giving birth vaginally had an episiotomy. However, many experts believe it's being used less frequently now. Today, many healthcare providers let the tissue between the vagina and rectum tear naturally during childbirth.

An episiotomy is a controlled, straight, clean cut, made from the vagina toward the rectum during delivery. It's done to help avoid tearing as baby's head passes through the birth canal. An incision may be better than a tear or rip that could go in many directions. The cut may be made directly in the midline toward the rectum, or it may be a cut to the side. After delivery, layers are closed with absorbable sutures that don't require removal. An episiotomy heals better than a ragged tear.

Benefits of an episiotomy for a woman include a lower risk of trauma to the area from the tailbone to the pubic bone, less relaxation of pelvic organs with prolapse, less chance of stool and/or urine incontinence, and lower likelihood of sexual dysfunction. Benefits to baby may include more rapid delivery. However, there are disadvantages to an episiotomy. Research shows it may lead to a more difficult recovery, some sexual problems and increased risk of incontinence.

Discuss an episiotomy at a prenatal visit. Ask if it is routine or if it is done only when necessary. Some situations do not require an episiotomy, such as a small or premature baby. However, your healthcare provider may not be able to make this decision until delivery.

An episiotomy is not necessary for every woman. The more children a woman has, the less likely it is she will need one; it depends on the size of the baby. Factors leading to an episiotomy include the size of the mother's vaginal opening, the size of the baby's head and shoulders, the number of babies previously delivered and whether this delivery is a forceps or vacuum delivery.

Episiotomies are described according to the relative depth of the incision.
- 1st degree cuts only the skin.
- 2nd degree cuts the skin and underlying tissue, called *fascia*.
- 3rd degree cuts the skin, underlying tissue and rectal sphincter, the muscle that goes around the anus.
- 4th degree goes through the three layers described above and the rectal mucosa.

If you have an episiotomy, after baby's birth, epifoam may be prescribed to treat pain and itching. It comes in an applicator that provides a measured amount for each application. You may want to ask your healthcare provider about it. Other medications are also safe to use even if you breastfeed baby. Acetaminophen with codeine or other medications may be prescribed for pain.

Labor

Nearly every woman wants to know if labor will be painful. Every labor is different, in great part because of the level of pain you experience. Be aware that contractions *do* hurt. The only thing we can tell you, which is true for every labor, is that no two labors are alike, not even for the same woman. Because labor is different for every woman, no one can predict what your labor will be like before it begins.

Labor is defined as the dilatation (stretching and expanding) of your cervix. The cervix opens while your uterus, a muscle, contracts to push out your baby. It is believed both mom and baby release the hormone oxytocin, which triggers labor to begin.

Some women experience long, intense labors; others have short, relatively pain-free labors. We have found if a woman understands the labor process and what causes childbirth pain, she has a better chance of reducing it. When you hear about a *long labor,* most of the time is spent in early labor. During this time, you experience contractions that may start and stop or be weaker or farther apart than they will be in active labor. In *active labor,* the cervix dilates and contractions are stronger and more regular. The average length of *active* labor is between 6 and 12 hours.

When you are afraid of the pain you expect to experience during labor and delivery, you tense up. This can make pain worse.

Your uterus is a muscular sac shaped like an upside-down pear. This muscle tightens and relaxes during labor (contractions) to expel the baby. During labor, your bladder, rectum, spine and pubic bone receive strong pressure from the uterus as it tightens and hardens with each contraction. The weight of the baby's head as it moves down the birth canal also causes pressure.

Signs Labor May Begin Soon

You may bleed a little following a vaginal exam late in pregnancy or at the beginning of labor. Called a *bloody show,* it occurs as the cervix stretches and dilates. If it causes you concern or appears to be a large amount of blood, call your healthcare provider immediately.

Along with light bleeding, you may pass some mucus, sometimes called a *mucus plug.* Passing mucus doesn't always mean you'll have your baby soon or that labor is beginning.

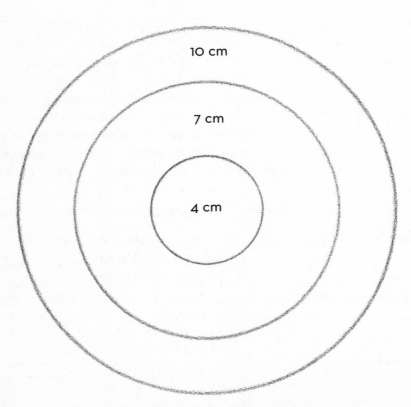

Dilation of the cervix from 4 to 10cm (shown actual size)

Stages of Labor

Labor is divided into three stages. Each stage feels distinctly different and has a specific purpose. The information below explains what you might expect during labor and delivery.

Stage 1—Early Phase	
What's happening	Cervix opens and thins out due to uterine contractions. Cervix dilates to about 2cm. This phase can last 1 to 10 hours.
Mother is experiencing	Membranes may rupture, accompanied by gush or trickle of amniotic fluid from vagina. Pinkish discharge may appear ("bloody show"). Mild contractions begin at 15- to 20-minute intervals; they last about 1 minute. Contractions become closer together and more regular.
What mother and labor coach can do	Food and drink may be restricted once labor begins. Mother may be able to stay at home for a while, if she is at term. Begin using relaxation and breathing techniques learned in childbirth class. If water has broken, if labor is preterm, if there is intense pain, if pain is constant or there is bright red blood, contact healthcare provider immediately!

Stage 1—Active Phase	
What's happening	Cervix dilates from about 2 to 10cm. Cervix continues to thin out. This phase can last 20 minutes to 2 hours.
Mother is experiencing	Contractions become more intense and closer together. Contractions are about 3 minutes apart and last about 45 seconds to 1 minute.
What mother and labor coach can do	Keep practicing relaxation and breathing techniques. An epidural can be administered during this phase.

Stage 1—Transition Phase

What's happening	Stage 1 begins to change to Stage 2. Cervix is dilated to 10cm. Cervix continues to thin out. This phase can last a few minutes to 2 hours.
Mother is experiencing	Contractions are 2 to 3 minutes apart and last about 1 minute. Mother may feel strong urge to push; she shouldn't push until cervix is completely dilated. Mother may be moved to delivery room if she is not in a birthing room.
What mother and labor coach can do	Relaxation and breathing techniques help counteract the mother's urge to push.

Stage 2

What's happening	Cervix is completely dilated. Baby continues to descend into the birth canal. As mother pushes, baby is delivered. Baby's nose and mouth are suctioned, and umbilical cord is clamped. This stage can last a few minutes to a few hours (pushing the baby can take a long time).
Mother is experiencing	Contractions occur at 2- to 5-minute intervals and last from 60 to 90 seconds. With an epidural, mother may find it harder to push. An episiotomy may be done to prevent vaginal tearing as baby is born.
What mother and labor coach can do	Mother will begin to push with each contraction after cervix dilates completely. Mother may be given analgesic or local anesthetic. Mother must listen to healthcare provider or nurse when baby is being delivered; he or she will tell mother when to push. As mother pushes, she may be able to watch baby being born, if mirror is available.

Stage 3	
What's happening	Placenta is delivered.
	Placenta is examined to make sure all of it has been delivered.
	Episiotomy is repaired.
	This stage can last a few minutes to an hour.
Mother is experiencing	Contractions may occur closer together but be less painful.
What mother and labor coach can do	Meet and hold the baby.
	Mother may need to push to expel the placenta.
	Mother may be able to hold baby while episiotomy is repaired.
	Nurse will rub or massage the uterus through the abdomen to help it contract and to control bleeding (during the next few days, the uterus will continue to contract to control bleeding).

Your Partner's Involvement

Well before your delivery date, talk with your partner about how you will stay in touch as your due date approaches. With cell phones, staying in touch is fairly easy. Arrange for a backup support person in case your partner cannot be with you or you need someone else to take you to the hospital.

Your partner can be a big help. He can help prepare you for labor and delivery and support you as you labor. He can share the joy of your baby's delivery. He can support you emotionally, which is important to you both.

Your partner may choose to be your labor coach. A labor coach can do a lot to help you through labor, including:

- time your contractions so you are aware of labor's progress
- encourage and reassure you during labor
- help create a mood in the labor room
- protect your privacy
- report symptoms or pain to the nurse or healthcare provider
- help you deal with physical discomfort

New Eating Guidelines for Labor and Delivery

In the past, women in labor have only been allowed sips of water or a few ice chips to relieve thirst. ACOG has issued updated guidelines. The reasons for the previous policy were concern about a woman vomiting and swallowing vomit into the lungs (aspiration) during labor and the risk of complications if anesthesia was required for a Cesarean delivery.

Updated recommendations indicate if you have a normal, uncomplicated labor, you may drink modest amounts of *clear liquids*, such as water, fruit juice without pulp, carbonated beverages, clear tea, black coffee and sports drinks. Avoid fluids that contain solid particles, such as soup.

Be sure to discuss eating and drinking during labor with your healthcare provider before labor begins. Follow his or her advice. The general recommendation is that if you're scheduled for a Cesarean delivery, you may drink clear liquids up to 2 hours before anesthesia is administered. You should refrain from eating solid food for 6 to 8 hours before surgery. If you have any risk factors, such as morbid obesity or diabetes, or if you may be at risk for a delivery involving forceps or a vacuum extractor, your fluid intake may be restricted.

Back Labor

Some women experience back labor; it occurs in about 30% of all deliveries. *Back labor* means most of the pain is concentrated in the back. The cause of back labor is a baby facing toward the mother's front. Each contraction forces the baby's head against the mother's lower spine, resulting in strong pain that does not completely disappear between contractions.

With back labor, delivery may take longer. The healthcare provider may have to rotate the baby's head so it comes out looking down at the ground rather than up at the sky.

Tests You May Have

Tests done on your baby during labor provide your healthcare provider with a great deal of information. These tests include the nonstress test, the contraction stress test, the biophysical profile, fetal blood sampling, external fetal monitoring and internal fetal monitoring.

Nonstress Test (NST)

A *nonstress* test (NST) is a simple, noninvasive procedure done at 32 weeks of pregnancy or later; it is performed in the healthcare provider's office or in the labor-and-delivery department at the hospital. This test measures how the fetal heart responds to the fetus's own movements and evaluates fetal well-being in late pregnancy. It is commonly used in overdue and high-risk preg-

Timing Contractions

It's important for your healthcare provider to know how often contractions occur and how long each one lasts. Knowing this, he or she can decide if it's time for you to go to the hospital. Contractions are timed to see how long a contraction lasts and how often contractions occur. Ask your health-care provider how to time your contractions. There are two ways to do it.

- Method 1—Start timing when the contraction starts, and time it until the next contraction starts. This is the most common method.
- Method 2—Start timing when the contraction ends, and note how long it is until the next contraction starts.

nancies. Information gained from a nonstress test gives reassurance your baby is doing OK.

While you're lying down, a monitor is attached to your abdomen. Every time you feel the baby move, you push a button to make a mark on the monitor paper. At the same time, the fetal monitor records the baby's heartbeat on the same paper.

Each time baby moves, the heart rate should accelerate by about 15 beats for about 15 seconds. When this occurs twice in a 20-minute period, the test is considered normal or *reactive.*

If the baby doesn't move or if the heart rate does not react to movement, the test is called *nonreactive.* This doesn't necessarily mean there is a problem—the baby may be sleeping. In more than 75% of nonreactive tests, the baby is healthy. When results are nonreactive, the test may be repeated in 24 hours or you may have additional tests, including a contraction stress test or a biophysical profile. See the discussion below.

Contraction Stress Test (CST)

If the nonstress test is nonreactive, you may need to have a *contraction stress test.* A contraction stress test (CST), also called a *stress test,* measures the response of the fetal heart to mild uterine contractions that mimic labor.

If you have had a problem pregnancy in the past or experienced medical problems during this pregnancy, your healthcare provider may order this test in the last few weeks of pregnancy. This test may be done every week, beginning around 32 weeks.

In some cases, the nonstress test may be ordered alone or both the nonstress test and the contraction stress test may be done. The contraction stress test is considered somewhat more accurate than the nonstress test.

This test is usually done in the hospital because it occasionally triggers labor. A monitor is placed on your abdomen to record the fetal heart rate. In some hospitals, nipple stimulation is used to make the woman's uterus contract. In other places, oxytocin is given intravenously in small amounts to make the uterus contract. Results indicate how well baby will tolerate contractions and labor.

A slowed heart rate after a contraction may be a sign of fetal stress. The baby may not be receiving enough oxygen or may be experiencing another difficulty. The healthcare provider may recommend delivery of the baby. In other cases, the test may be repeated the next day or a biophysical profile may be ordered. If the test shows no sign of a slowed fetal heart rate, the test result is reassuring.

Biophysical Profile (BPP)

A *biophysical profile* is a comprehensive test to help determine the fetus's health status. The test is commonly performed in high-risk situations, overdue pregnancies or pregnancies in which the baby doesn't move very much. It's useful in evaluating an infant with intrauterine-growth restriction. A biophysical profile measures five areas, which are identified and scored:

- fetal breathing movements
- gross body movements
- fetal tone
- reactive fetal heart rate
- amount of amniotic fluid

Ultrasound, external monitors and direct observation are all used to take the various measurements. Each area is given a score between 0 and 2; a total is obtained by adding the five scores together. The higher the score, the better the baby's condition.

A baby with a low score may need to be delivered immediately. Your healthcare provider will evaluate the scores, your health and your pregnancy before making any decisions. If the score is reassuring, the test may be repeated at intervals. Sometimes the test is repeated the following day.

Fetal Monitoring during Labor

In many hospitals, a baby's heartbeat is monitored throughout labor with *external fetal monitoring* and/or *internal fetal monitoring*. Fetal monitoring enables healthcare providers to detect problems early.

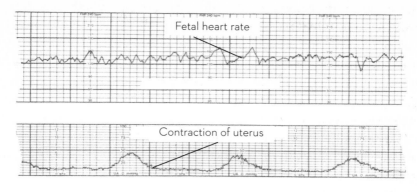

Fetal heart rate

Contraction of uterus

External fetal monitoring.

External fetal monitoring can be done before your membranes rupture. A belt with a recorder is strapped to your abdomen to pick up the baby's heartbeat. Internal fetal monitoring monitors the baby more precisely. An electrode is placed on the fetal scalp to measure the fetal heart rate.

Fetal blood sampling is another way to evaluate how well baby is tolerating the stress of labor. Before the test can be performed, your membranes must be ruptured and your cervix must be dilated at least 2cm. An instrument is passed into the vagina and through the dilated cervix to the top of the baby's head, where it makes a small nick in the baby's scalp. The baby's blood is collected in a small tube, and its pH (acidity) is checked.

Knowing the baby's pH level helps healthcare providers determine if baby is having trouble and is under stress. The test helps the healthcare provider decide whether labor can continue or if a Cesarean delivery is needed.

Evaluating Results of Fetal Monitoring

The American College of Obstetricians and Gynecologists (ACOG) recommends use of three categories to describe the results of fetal monitoring. *Category I* tracings are normal. *Category II* tracings are indeterminate; this means they aren't normal, but they aren't absolutely abnormal. They require evaluation, continued surveillance and re-evaluation. Eighty percent of all tracings fall into this category. *Category III* tracings are abnormal and require prompt evaluation.

Elements used to categorize results include fetal heart rate, variability, decelerations and reaction to contractions. Each case needs to be evaluated individually using fetal monitor tracings and other information regarding the pregnancy.

Evaluating Fetal Lung Maturity

The respiratory system is the last fetal system to mature. Premature infants commonly experience respiratory difficulties because their lungs are not mature. Knowing how mature baby's lungs are helps your healthcare provider make a decision about early delivery, if that must be considered.

If there are reasons the baby needs to be delivered early, fetal-lung-maturity tests can determine whether the baby will be able to breathe without assistance. Fluid for the tests is obtained by amniocentesis. Two tests used most often to evaluate a baby's lungs before birth are the *L-S ratio* and the *phosphatidyl glycerol (PG)* tests.

Coping with the Pain of Labor and Childbirth

Today, healthcare providers encourage frank discussions about the pain of labor and delivery. Childbirth is usually accompanied by pain, and pain varies among women, from very little to a lot. Research shows the *expectation* of pain can, in itself, evoke fear and anxiety. The best way to deal with pain is to become informed about it.

Many women believe they'll feel guilty after their baby is born if they ask for pain relief during labor. Sometimes they think the baby will be harmed by any medication they take. Some women believe they'll deprive themselves of the "complete birth experience." Others are concerned about cost and believe they can't afford an epidural if their insurance doesn't cover it.

> Pay attention to your breathing if you want to remain relaxed during labor.

You can learn about pain and pain relief through several channels. Childbirth-education classes are good sources of information. You can learn about pain-relief methods that don't require medication, such as breathing methods and relaxation techniques.

Talk to your healthcare provider about pain relief. Medication for pain relief is usually a personal choice, not a medical decision. If you choose to have anesthesia, some studies show it can speed up your labor because you're more relaxed.

Keep an open mind about ways to relieve pain during labor. You won't have any idea what your labor is going to be like and the pain you may experience until it begins. Your labor may be harder (or easier) than you expect. Listen to your body. Don't be a martyr; do what is necessary to get through labor and delivery. You may have a greater or lesser need for pain relief than you think. You can always change your mind if you need or want to.

Pain Relief without Medication

Some women don't want medication during labor to relieve pain. They prefer to use various techniques to deal with their pain. Breathing patterns and relaxation techniques are usually taught in childbirth-education classes.

Listening to instrumental music for at least 3 hours during early active labor may help you relax. Nondrug strategies for labor pain include continuous labor support, hydrotherapy, water immersion, hypnosis, continuous labor support and acupuncture.

For some women, *hydrotherapy* can help reduce pain. A warm (not hot) shower can relax and massage you. Hydrotherapy during labor has been shown to reduce the amount of stress hormones released in a woman's body. It has also been shown to decrease the frequency of contractions. *Water immersion* may also be suggested. It involves a warm bath during labor. It is most often used in early labor.

Hypnosis is sometimes called *hypnobirthing;* it may not be available everywhere. It can be effective for some women but may not be right for everyone. Visualization, relaxation and deep-breathing all work together in hypnotherapy to help you drop into a very deep state of relaxation so you may deal with your fear of pain. If you choose hypnotherapy to deal with pain, you'll have to prepare and practice for months before baby's birth.

Continuous labor support is often used by a nurse, midwife or doula, and includes touch, massage, application of cold or heat, and other ways to provide physical comfort. It also includes emotional support, which provides information to the mother and help with communication between the woman and those caring for her.

If you choose *acupuncture* for labor-pain relief, it may take some careful planning and the support of your acupuncturist. Its use requires an acupuncturist willing to be on call to come to the labor and delivery room.

....

Shelley was upset at her 32-week visit. Her husband's reserve unit had been activated, and he would be gone for at least 6 months. She was sure she would not be able to deliver without her husband as her labor coach. We talked about other possible coaches. Shelley didn't know that someone else could act as her coach. When she came in 2 weeks later, Shelley was happy to report her sister (who had delivered a year earlier) was thrilled and honored to help. They had even been to a prenatal class together to get ready.

....

Laboring Positions

Different laboring positions enable a woman and her partner (or labor coach) to work together during labor to find relief from labor pain. Most women in North America and Europe give birth on their backs in bed. However, some women try different positions to find relief from pain and to make the birth of their baby easier.

In the past, women often labored and gave birth in an upright position that kept the pelvis vertical, such as kneeling, squatting, sitting or standing up. Laboring in this position enables the abdominal wall to relax and allows the baby to descend more rapidly. Because contractions are stronger and more regular, labor is often shorter.

Today, many women ask to choose the birth position that is most comfortable for them. Freedom to choose the birth position can make a woman feel more confident about managing birth and labor. Studies show women who choose their own methods often feel more satisfied with the entire birth experience.

If this is important to you, discuss the matter with your healthcare provider. Ask about the facilities at the hospital you will use; some have special equipment, such as birthing chairs, squatting bars or birthing beds, to assist you. Positions you might consider for your labor are described below.

Some women use different laboring positions, such as the one shown above, to help them find pain relief. Discuss it with your doctor if you're interested in trying a different position for labor.

Walking and standing are good positions to use during early labor. Walking during labor keeps you upright, which may help dilate the cervix naturally. Walking may help you breathe more easily and relax more, although it won't necessarily make labor easier or reduce the chance of a Cesarean delivery. Standing in a warm shower may provide relief. When walking, be sure someone is with you to offer support (both physical and emotional).

Sitting can decrease the strength and frequency of contractions and can slow labor. Sitting to rest after walking or standing is acceptable; however, sitting can be uncomfortable during a contraction.

Crouching on hands and knees is a good way to relieve the pain of back labor. Kneeling against a support, such as a chair or your partner, stretches your back muscles. The effects of kneeling are similar to those of walking and standing.

Lie on your side when you can't stand, walk or kneel. If you receive pain medication, you will need to lie down. Lie on your left side, then turn on your right.

Lying on your back is the most common position used for labor, but it can decrease the strength and frequency of contractions, which can slow the process. It can also make your blood pressure drop and cause your baby's heart rate to drop. If you lie on your back, elevate the head of the bed and put a pillow under one hip so you are not flat on your back.

Massage for Relief

Massage is a wonderful, gentle way to help you feel better during labor. The touching and caressing of massage can help you relax. One study showed

If you're exhausted when you begin labor, you may be at a higher risk for a Cesarean delivery.

women who were massaged for 20 minutes every hour during active labor felt less anxiety and less pain.

Massage works great on many parts of a laboring woman's body. Massaging the head, neck, back and feet can offer a great deal of comfort and relaxation. The person doing the massage should pay close attention to the woman's responses to determine correct pressure.

With massage, the counterpressure helps reduce pain, and the interaction can help you feel closer to your partner. It lets you share the experience. Some women say using these methods brought them closer to their partners and made the birth experience a more joyful one.

Different types of massage affect a woman in various ways. You and your partner may want to practice the two types of massage described below before labor and for use during labor.

Effleurage

This light, gentle fingertip massage over the abdomen and upper thighs is used during early labor. Stroking is light but doesn't tickle, and fingertips never leave the skin.

Massage at any time in pregnancy and during labor and delivery can help a woman relax.

The labor coach should start with hands on either side of your navel. Hands move upward and outward, then come back down to the pubic area. Then hands move back up to the navel. Massage may extend down the thighs. It can also be done as a crosswise motion, around fetal-monitor belts. Fingers move across the abdomen from one side to the other between the belts.

Counterpressure Massage

Counterpressure massage is excellent for relieving the pain of back labor. The labor coach should place the heel of the hand or the flat part of the fist (a tennis ball can be used) against the tailbone. Apply firm pressure in a small, circular motion.

Analgesics and Anesthetics

Recent studies indicate more women are asking for pain relief during labor. There are many different types available. *Analgesia* is pain relief without total loss of sensation. *Anesthesia* is pain relief with partial or total loss of sensation.

Effective pain relief can be achieved with smaller doses of anesthetics, which can help reduce side effects and aftereffects. About 65% of all women who deliver at large hospitals ask for pain relief. In smaller hospitals, the number is under 50%.

Analgesia

Analgesia is injected into a muscle or vein to decrease the pain of labor, but you remain conscious. It provides pain relief but can make you drowsy, restless or nauseated. You may find concentrating difficult. Analgesia may slow baby's reflexes and breathing, so this medication is usually given during the early and middle parts of labor. Examples of analgesia are Demerol (meperidine hydrochloride) and morphine.

Anesthesia

There are three types of anesthesia—general anesthesia, local anesthesia and regional anesthesia. You are completely unconscious with *general anesthesia,* so it is used only for some Cesarean deliveries and emergency vaginal deliveries. Using a general anesthesia has certain disadvantages. Sometimes the mother vomits or aspirates vomited food or stomach acid into her lungs. The baby is also anesthetized and needs to be resuscitated after delivery. General anesthesia is not often used for childbirth. Its advantage is that it can be administered quickly in an emergency.

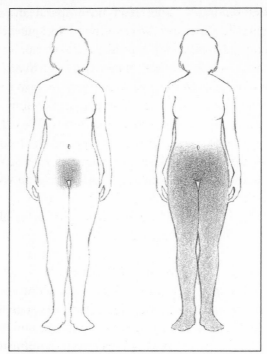

Local anesthesia.   Regional anesthesia.

Local anesthesia affects a small area and is useful for an episiotomy repair. It rarely affects the baby and usually has few lingering effects.

Regional anesthesia affects a larger body area and includes pudendal blocks, spinal blocks and epidural blocks. A *pudendal block* is an injection of medication into the pudendal nerve area in the vagina to relieve pain in the vaginal area, the perineum and the rectum. You remain conscious, and side effects are rare. Pudendal block is considered one of the safest forms of pain relief; however, it does not relieve uterine pain.

A *spinal block* involves medication injected into spinal fluid in the lower back, which numbs the lower part of the body. It works within seconds and is effective for up to 45 minutes; you remain conscious. This type of block is administered only once during labor, so it is often used just before delivery or for a Cesarean section. It works quickly and is an effective pain inhibitor. Up to 90% of all elective Cesarean deliveries are done with spinal anesthesia.

A spinal block may cause a woman's blood pressure to drop suddenly, which in turn can cause a decrease in the baby's heart rate. This type of anesthesia is not used if a woman is bleeding heavily or if the baby has an abnormal heartbeat. Another possible side effect from spinal anesthesia is severe headache if the needle punctures the covering of the spinal cord.

A walking spinal, also called *intrathecal anesthesia,* can be given to women who suffer extreme pain in the early stages of labor (dilated less than 5cm). This type of anesthesia won't affect your ability to push in the same way as a regular epidural will. See the discussion of epidurals below. A small amount of narcotic, such as Demerol, is injected through a thin needle into the spinal fluid, which eases the pain and causes few side effects. Because the dose is small, neither mother nor baby becomes overly drowsy. Sensory and motor functions remain intact, so the mother can walk around with help, sit in a chair or go to the bathroom.

One of the most commonly used pain-relief methods for labor and delivery is the *epidural block*. It is discussed below.

Epidural Block

An epidural block involves a tube inserted into a space outside your spinal column in the lower back. Medication is administered through the tube for pain relief; you remain conscious during delivery. The tube remains in place until after baby is born so pain-relief medication can be readministered; sometimes it is delivered continuously by pump. Many hospitals use patient-controlled epidurals—you press a button to receive more medication if you need it.

If you have an epidural, it can take up to 25 minutes before you experience pain relief. Most healthcare providers agree you can have an epidural anytime after active labor begins.

An epidural helps relieve painful uterine contractions, pain in the vagina and rectum as the baby passes through the birth canal, and the pain of an episiotomy. With an epidural, you should be able to feel enough pressure to push, but it does cause some loss of sensation in the lower part of the body. It may make it harder to push, so vacuum extraction or forceps may be necessary during delivery. If you have an epidural, you may spend longer pushing than if you have other pain relief. On the average, epidurals slow labor by 45 minutes.

Some medical conditions, such as scoliosis, previous back surgery, a serious infection when you begin labor or some blood-clotting problems, may prevent you from having an epidural. Talk to your healthcare provider at a prenatal visit if you have any of these conditions.

We've heard rumors that women who have tattoos on their lower backs can't have an epidural. However, no studies have shown this to be true. Discuss any concerns you have about anesthesia and your tattoos with your healthcare provider.

••

Martha was certain she wouldn't need an epidural. At one of her visits late in the pregnancy, she tried to make me promise I wouldn't make her have one. I explained that an epidural was an option, not a requirement, and no one would "make" her have one. I knew she thought I was trying to talk her into it, but I wasn't. Experience has taught me no matter how much a woman prepares, no one knows what labor will be like for her. I try to help a woman keep an open mind about the experience. Among her other requests, Martha didn't want an I.V., an enema and certainly not an episiotomy. Martha's labor turned out to be an adventure—a long one. At 3cm, she was screaming for relief. She got to 5cm and stayed there for quite a while. In the end, I had to do a Cesarean to deliver her 9-pound, 4-ounce healthy baby boy. I wasn't sure what her reaction was going to be after the birth. When I saw her the next day, Martha was in good spirits and very happy. She felt her expectations before delivery had been misdirected. She jokingly said to me, "The only thing on my list that didn't happen was an episiotomy."

••

An epidural block may cause a woman's blood pressure to drop suddenly, which can cause a decrease in the baby's heart rate. Epidurals are not used if a woman is bleeding heavily or if baby has an abnormal heartbeat. One other possible side effect is severe headache if the needle punctures the covering of the spinal cord. This is an unusual complication.

Some women have heard if they have epidural anesthesia during labor, they have a greater chance of having a Cesarean delivery. Research shows *no* connection between the use of epidurals and the rate of Cesarean sections. Nor is there evidence an epidural lengthens the first stage of labor (from the beginning of contractions to dilatation at 10cm). If it affects your ability to push during the second stage of labor, your healthcare provider can wait a little while and let the epidural wear off so you can push.

Baby's Birth Presentation

Most babies enter the birth canal head first, which is the best position for labor and delivery. However, some babies enter the birth canal in other positions.

A *breech presentation* means the baby is not in a head-down position; its legs or buttocks come into the birth canal first. If your baby is breech when it's time to deliver, your healthcare provider may try to turn the baby or you may need a Cesarean delivery.

One of the main causes of a breech presentation is prematurity of the baby. Near the end of the second trimester, the baby is commonly in the breech presentation. As you progress through the third trimester, the baby usually turns into the head-down presentation for birth.

For a long time, breech deliveries were performed vaginally. Then it was believed the safest delivery method was a Cesarean delivery; many healthcare providers still prefer to do a Cesarean for a breech presentation. However, some believe a woman can deliver a breech baby without difficulty if the situation is right.

Abnormal Birth Presentations

There are three different breech presentations and three other atypical presentations.

- Frank breech—Occurs when lower legs are flexed at the hips and extended at the knees. Feet are up by the face or head.
- Complete breech presentation—One or both knees are flexed (not extended).
- Incomplete breech presentation—A foot or knee enters the birth canal ahead of the rest of the baby.
- Face presentation—The baby's head is hyperextended so the face enters the birth canal first.
- Transverse lie—Baby is lying almost as if in a cradle in the pelvis. The head is on one side of the mother's abdomen, and the bottom is on the other side.
- Shoulder presentation—The baby's shoulder enters the birth canal first.

Can My Baby Be Turned?

Some healthcare providers try to turn a baby in the breech position. If your baby is in a breech position, your physician may attempt to change its position by using *external cephalic version (ECV)*.

With ECV, the healthcare provider places his or her hands on your abdomen. Using gentle movements, he or she manually tries to shift the baby into the head-down position. An ultrasound will usually be performed first to see the position of the baby and again during the procedure to guide the healthcare provider in changing baby's position.

A physician usually uses this method before labor begins or in the early stages of labor. It is successful in about half of the cases in which it is used. Not every healthcare provider is trained in the procedure.

When You're Overdue

You've been counting the days to your due date, but it's come and gone—and still no baby! You're not alone—nearly 10% of all babies are born more than 2 weeks late. Each year, healthcare providers induce labor for about 450,000 births. Labor is induced for a number of reasons, including overdue babies, chronic high blood pressure in the mother, pre-eclampsia, gestational diabetes, intrauterine-growth restriction and Rh-isoimmunization.

A pregnancy is considered overdue (postterm) *only* when it exceeds 42 weeks or 294 days from the first day of the last menstrual period. (A baby born at 41 weeks, 6 days is *not* considered overdue!)

Your healthcare provider will determine if baby is moving around in the womb and if the amount of amniotic fluid is healthy and normal. If the baby is healthy and active, you are usually monitored until labor begins on its own.

Tests may be done as reassurance that an overdue baby is fine and can remain in the womb. If signs of fetal stress are found, labor may be induced.

It's often hard to keep a positive attitude when you're overdue. But don't give up yet! Eat healthfully, and keep up your fluid intake. If you can do so without problems, get some mild exercise, like walking or swimming. You may feel better.

Rest and relax now because your baby will be here soon, and you'll be very busy. Use the time to get things ready for baby so you'll be all set when you both come home from the hospital.

Inducing Labor

There may come a point in your pregnancy when your healthcare provider decides to induce labor, which means labor is stimulated for the purpose of delivering your baby. It's a fairly common practice.

When your healthcare provider does a pelvic exam at this point in your pregnancy, it probably also includes an evaluation of how ready you are for an induction. Indications for induction of labor include the following:

• pregnancy 2 weeks past the due date
• indication baby isn't thriving in the uterus (from biophysical profile, non-stress or contraction stress tests)
• pre-eclampsia

Inducing labor increases the chances of having an emergency Cesarean delivery.

- signs the placenta is no longer functioning as well as it should
- acute or chronic illness that threatens the well-being of mother-to-be or baby
- pregnancy-induced hypertension
- premature rupture of membranes
- the bag of waters breaks but contractions do not begin in a reasonable amount of time
- chorioamnionitis (infection of the uterine membranes)

Your healthcare provider may use the *Bishop score* to evaluate you. It's a method of cervical scoring used to predict the success of inducing labor. Scoring includes dilatation, effacement, station, consistency and position of the cervix. A score is given for each, then they are added together to give a total score to help the healthcare provider decide whether to induce labor.

There are reasons *not* to induce labor, including a previous classical uterine incision (from a Cesarean delivery or other uterine surgery, such as fibroid removal), placenta previa, vasa previa, fetal malformation, such as hydrocephalus, umbilical-cord prolapse, an active genital herpes infection in the mother-to-be, invasive cervical cancer, multiple pregnancy and breech presentation. Your healthcare provider will keeps tabs on you and your baby so if induction is necessary, it can be done.

Vaginal Delivery of Your Baby

Most women have a vaginal birth. With a vaginal birth, your baby is delivered through the vaginal canal. With a Cesarean birth, baby is delivered through an incision in your lower abdominal area. See the discussion of Cesarean delivery that follows.

A vaginal birth begins with labor. There are three distinct stages of labor, as discussed on pages 287 to 289. In 10% of all vaginal births, the healthcare provider will use forceps or a vacuum extractor to help deliver your baby.

Forceps look like two metal hands. In a forceps delivery, the healthcare provider uses the instrument to help remove the baby from the birth canal. They are not used as often as they were in the past; today, physicians more often use a vacuum extractor.

A vacuum extractor is a plastic cup that fits on baby's head by suction. When you push during labor, your healthcare provider is able to pull gently and deliver the baby's head and body more easily.

Following delivery, you and baby are evaluated. During this time, you finally get to see and to hold your baby; you may even be able to feed him or her.

If you have an episiotomy, it will be repaired after the placenta is delivered. This can take up to 30 minutes.

You'll probably stay in the hospital from 24 to 48 hours after delivery, if you have no complications. If you do have complications, you and your healthcare provider will decide what is best for you and your baby.

Cesarean Delivery

When you have a *Cesarean delivery* (also called a *C-section*), your baby is delivered through an incision made in your abdominal wall and uterus. Research has shown women in their 30s and 40s have higher rates of Cesarean deliveries. The Cesarean-delivery rate for mothers between 40 and 54 years old is more than double the rate for women younger than age 20. Some of this increase can be attributed to the increased rate of multiple births. Cesarean deliveries may also be done when there is a problem during labor.

An *emergency Cesarean delivery* is one that is unplanned. An *elective Cesarean delivery* is planned and may be performed without a medical reason. While there are many reasons for doing a Cesarean, the main goal is to deliver a healthy baby and have a healthy mother. Particular reasons for performing a Cesarean include the following:

- a previous Cesarean delivery
- to avoid rupture of the uterus
- baby is too big to fit through the birth canal
- fetal stress
- pre-eclampsia
- woman has an active herpes sore
- compression of the umbilical cord
- baby is in a breech presentation
- placental abruption
- placenta previa
- multiple fetuses—twins, triplets or more
- nonmedical factors, including older maternal age, maternal choice, more conservative practice guidelines and legal pressures

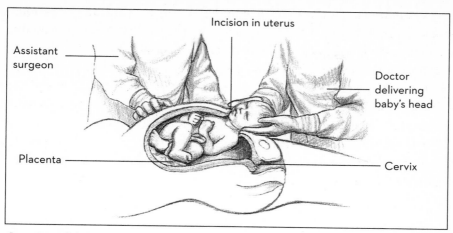

Cesarean delivery.

A Cesarean delivery for a first baby increases a woman's chances for placenta previa or placental abruption in her next pregnancies. A repeat Cesarean increases a woman's risk of placenta accreta in subsequent pregnancies, if the placenta implants low in the uterus and grows into the area of a previous Cesarean-delivery incision.

ACOG now recommends a Cesarean delivery not be scheduled any earlier than 39 weeks unless tests show the baby's lungs are mature. There is evidence indicating an elective Cesarean delivery before 39 weeks increases the risk of problems in the baby. When compared with babies delivered at 37 or 38 weeks, those delivered at 39 weeks or more had significantly *lower* rates of respiratory problems.

Babies born between 37 and 39 weeks of pregnancy have more respiratory problems than babies born vaginally or by emergency Cesarean. It is believed the hormones released during labor help baby deal with fluid in the lungs, and the compression of the baby's chest during labor and birth helps clear amniotic fluid from baby's lungs.

The rate of Cesarean deliveries performed in the United States in the last 50 years has risen. In 1965, only 4% of all deliveries were Cesarean. Today, it is 32% of all deliveries. For women over age 35, the rate is over 35%, and for women over 40, the rate is 40%.

If a woman has a Cesarean delivery, she is at greater risk for postpartum depression.

We can point to many reasons for the change. We believe it is related to better monitoring during labor and safer procedures for Cesarean delivery. Women are also having bigger babies. Another factor may be rising malpractice rates and healthcare providers' fears of litigation.

A woman often wants to know in advance if she will need a Cesarean delivery. A healthcare provider doesn't usually know the answer to this question before labor begins unless the woman had a previous Cesarean. We usually have to wait for labor contractions to begin before we can tell if the baby is stressed by them or if the baby fits through the birth canal.

A woman's weight may be an indicator of whether she will have a Cesarean delivery. Your body mass index (BMI) may be used to predict whether a Cesarean delivery may be necessary. One study showed women with a higher BMI had more Cesarean deliveries. It is important to determine whether risk of a Cesarean delivery is higher to help medical personnel prepare for an emergency Cesarean delivery. An epidural catheter for regional anesthesia is considered safer than general anesthesia for overweight women.

It's a good idea to discuss Cesarean delivery with your healthcare provider several weeks before your due date. Ask why you might need a Cesarean. Tell your healthcare provider your wishes and concerns in regard to having a Cesarean delivery.

How a Cesarean Is Performed

When you have a Cesarean delivery, first the anesthesiologist visits you to discuss pain-relief methods. After anesthesia is administered, the doctor begins by making a 5- to 6-inch incision in the area above your pubic bone. A cut is made through tissue down to the uterus, where a horizontal incision is made into the lower part of the uterus. The doctor reaches into the uterus and removes the baby, then removes the placenta. Each layer is stitched; the entire procedure takes a half hour to an hour.

A Cesarean delivery is major surgery and carries with it certain risks, including infection, bleeding, shock through blood loss, the possibility of blood clots and the possibility of injury to other organs, such as the bladder or rectum. A normal hospital stay after a Cesarean delivery is 2 to 4 days. Recovery is slower with a Cesarean than with a vaginal delivery. Full recovery normally takes up to 6 weeks.

If you want to start exercising after a Cesarean, discuss it with your doctor at your first postpartum visit, about 2 weeks after baby's birth. Before seeing the doctor, you can do some nonstrenuous walking, Kegel exercises and breathing exercises. You can lift things, as long as they aren't heavier than

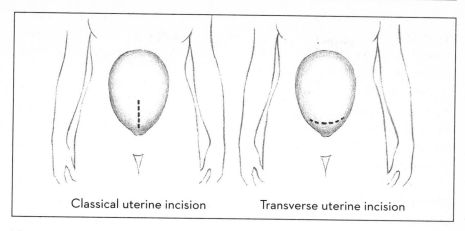

Classical uterine incision   Transverse uterine incision

The incision in the uterus for a Cesarean delivery is not always the same one made in the abdomen.

baby. At your 6-week checkup, talk to your doctor about more strenuous exercising, such as brisk walking, stretching and lifting light weights. Swimming can be very beneficial.

Vaginal Birth after Cesarean (VBAC)

Today, some women who have had a Cesarean with one pregnancy deliver vaginally with a later pregnancy. This is called *vaginal birth after Cesarean (VBAC).* Many of these deliveries are successful. However, research shows nine out of 10 women who had a previous Cesarean delivery choose a repeat Cesarean for the next birth.

A number of factors in your situation must be considered. Ask your healthcare provider for information before making this decision. Certain criteria must be met before you can have a VBAC, including the following.

- The type of uterine incision from a previous Cesarean delivery is important. (This incision may not be similar to the incision made in your abdomen.) With a classical incision, which goes high up on the uterus, labor is *not* permitted in subsequent pregnancies.
- The size of your pelvis is important. If you are small and your baby is large, it may cause problems.
- You have no medical complications, such as diabetes or high blood pressure.
- You are expecting only one baby.
- Your baby is entering the birth canal head first.

If you're considering a vaginal birth with this pregnancy, ACOG has made some recommendations about the birthing facility. It should offer the ability to perform an emergency Cesarean delivery within 30 minutes, the ability to monitor the fetus continuously and a fully equipped, 24-hour blood bank.

If you're interested in a vaginal birth, discuss VBAC with your healthcare provider well in advance of labor so plans can be made. Discuss the benefits and risks, and ask your healthcare provider for his or her opinion as to your chances of a successful vaginal delivery. He or she knows your health and pregnancy history. Include your partner in the decision-making process.

What Happens after Your Baby Is Born

Things happen quickly once your baby emerges into the world. First, baby's mouth and throat are suctioned. Then the healthcare provider clamps and cuts the umbilical cord (or your partner may cut the cord). If your partner wants to cut the umbilical cord after the baby is delivered, discuss it with your healthcare provider *before* you go into labor. What your partner may be allowed to do varies from place to place.

Lily had delivered 2 days earlier. She called me because she thought she should be feeling a lot better, and she was afraid something was wrong because she didn't. She said her breasts were sore and ached, it felt as though her uterus were still contracting (especially when she breastfed) and sitting down was an ordeal because her episiotomy was sore. I told her all these things were normal, and we talked about what she could do to help make things better. In the hospital, she had taken some pain medicine but didn't want to take any more because she was nursing. I told her the prescription she had been given was safe and would probably help a lot. Breastfeeding stimulated her uterus to contract to help it get smaller so it wouldn't bleed. We talked about Sitz baths for her episiotomy, and I reminded her the pain medicine would also help with that discomfort. When I saw her a few weeks later, she said my suggestions had made her life a lot easier.

• •

Once the initial evaluation is complete, baby is returned to you. Later, the baby is placed in a heated bassinet for a period of time. See a more complete discussion of what happens to baby and to you after birth in Chapter 19.

Is Home Birth Safe?

Home births happen. Of the 25,000 home births that occur every year in the United States, 25% (a little over 6000) of them are unplanned. That means the other 75% (nearly 19,000) of home births are planned. But are home births safe?

You may talk with friends or acquaintances who had a home birth and everything went fine. Some women want to give birth at home because they feel it's more natural. Another factor may be the high cost of labor and delivery, especially if you don't have full insurance coverage.

But research shows that giving birth at home is an extremely risky undertaking. One study showed twice as many infant deaths and serious, dangerous complications when babies are delivered at home. What can be done at home if your baby has serious problems and needs immediate medical care that can only be provided at a hospital or birthing center staffed by professionals?

We know there are also dangers to mom. First-time pregnant women who deliver at home have nearly triple the risk of complications after baby's birth. In addition, the chance of serious problems increases when a woman suffers from various pregnancy problems. Even carrying more than one baby increases your risk.

The American College of Obstetricians and Gynecologists has firmly stated that home birthing is hazardous to a woman and her baby. Based on Dr. Curtis's own experiences with the aftermath of home births, we must concur. We advise any woman who is considering this option to talk to her healthcare provider about the safety and wisdom of delivering her baby at the hospital or a birthing center.

Chapter 19

After Baby's Birth

Your baby has been delivered. You have a new person in your life who needs your care and attention. But you also need care and attention as well as time to tend to your own needs. Soon after birth, you may start thinking about how to feel your best again. Keep in mind your body can't recover overnight from 9 months of pregnancy, so don't expect it to. Relax and take your time!

The recovery period following your baby's birth (the first 6 weeks) is called the *postpartum period*. Your body rapidly downsizes as it begins to recover after pregnancy. During this time, you go through many physical and emotional adjustments.

Because older women have a higher chance of having complications during pregnancy and delivery, you may not bounce back as quickly as a younger woman. This may make postpartum recovery a slower process. But take heart—you *will* return to normal! But it may be a new "normal" now.

You can help yourself during the postpartum period in many ways. Eat nutritiously, allow others to help you and accept the fact that you may have to take it easy for a while. Another way you can help yourself is to learn as much as you can about what may happen after delivery.

What Happens to Your Baby after Birth?

When your baby is delivered, the healthcare provider clamps and cuts the umbilical cord, and the baby's mouth and throat are suctioned out. Then baby is usually passed to a nurse or pediatrician for initial evaluation and attention. Apgar scores (see page 314) are recorded at 1 and 5 minutes after birth. An identification band is placed on the baby so there's no mix-up in the nursery.

It's important to keep the baby warm; the nurse will dry the baby and wrap him in warm blankets. This is done whether the baby is on your chest or attended by a nurse or healthcare provider.

If your labor is complicated, baby may need to be evaluated more thoroughly in the nursery. The baby's well-being and health are of primary concern. You'll be able to hold and to nurse him, but if your child is having trouble breathing or needs special attention, such as monitors, immediate evaluation is the most appropriate procedure at this time.

Your baby will be taken to the nursery where he is weighed, measured and footprinted (in many places). Drops to prevent infection are placed in the eyes. A vitamin-K shot is given to help with blood-clotting factors. Your baby may receive the hepatitis vaccine if you request it. Then he is put in a heated bassinet for 30 minutes to 2 hours.

Your pediatrician is notified immediately if there are problems or concerns. Otherwise, he or she will be notified soon after birth, and a physical exam will be performed within 24 hours.

After I deliver my baby, how long will I stay in the hospital?
After a vaginal delivery, you'll spend 1 to 2 days in the hospital. After a Cesarean delivery, it'll probably be 2 to 4 days. This varies, depending on several factors:

- your healthcare-insurance coverage
- problems during pregnancy, labor or delivery
- complications with your baby

Tests for Your Baby

A baby is examined and evaluated at 1 minute, 5 minutes and, sometimes, 10 minutes after birth. The system of evaluation is called the *Apgar score*. This scoring system is a method of evaluating the overall well-being of the newborn infant. In general, the higher the score, the better the infant's condition. Areas scored include the baby's heart rate, respiratory effort, muscle tone, reflex irritability and color.

A baby with a low 1-minute Apgar score may need to be resuscitated. This means a pediatrician or nurse must help stimulate the baby to breathe and to recover from the delivery. In most cases, the 5-minute Apgar score is higher than the 1-minute score, as baby becomes more active and more accustomed to being outside the uterus.

Blood is taken from baby's heel for a *blood screen*. Tests are done for anemia, sickle-cell disease, hypothyroidism and blood-glucose levels. Results often indicate whether baby needs further evaluation.

The *Coombs test* is administered if your blood is Rh-negative, type O or if you have not been tested for antibodies. It tests blood taken from the umbilical cord. Test results indicate whether you have formed Rh-antibodies.

The *reflex assessment* tests for several specific reflexes in baby, including the rooting and grasp reflexes. If a particular reflex is not observed, further evaluation will be done.

In the *neonatal maturity assessment*, various characteristics of baby are assessed to evaluate her neuromuscular and physical maturity. Each characteristic is assigned a score; the sum indicates baby's maturity.

The *Brazelton neonatal behavioral assessment scale* covers a broad range of newborn behavior. An observation test, it provides information about how a newborn responds to her environment. It is usually used when a problem is suspected, but some hospitals test all babies.

All 50 states and the District of Columbia require every newborn be screened for many life-threatening disorders. State laws and rules vary, but all states require screening for 21 or more of 29 serious genetic or functional disorders including:

- biotinidase—to determine if baby is deficient in biotinidase
- congenital adrenal hyperplasia—to learn if adrenal glands are functioning properly
- congenital hypothyroidism—to check thyroid levels
- cystic fibrosis—to determine if baby has cystic fibrosis
- hemoglobinopathies—to check for defects in the hemoglobin

- homocystinuria—to learn if baby has a B_{12} deficiency and will need a special diet
- galactosemia—to determine if baby can handle galactose efficiently
- maple-syrup urine disease—to determine if some amino acids must be restricted for baby
- PKU—to test for phenylketonuria

The state of New York requires hospitals to check every newborn for HIV. Results are reported to the mother or guardian.

For further information about baby after birth, read our book *Your Baby's First Year Week by Week.* It contains a lot of information you may find useful.

What Happens to *You* after Baby Is Born?

You will probably be discharged from the hospital a day or two after your baby is born if labor and delivery were normal and baby is doing well. Some women choose to go home 24 hours after the birth of their baby or even sooner. If you have a Cesarean delivery, you will probably need to stay a few days longer.

Your blood pressure and bleeding are checked regularly in the first hours after the birth. You will be offered medication for pain relief and encouraged to nurse your baby.

Changes in Your Uterus

Your uterus goes through great changes after baby is born and takes several weeks to return to its original size. The size of your uterus at birth is quite large. Immediately after delivery, you can feel the uterus around your navel; it should feel very hard. You are checked frequently to make sure it remains hard after delivery. If it feels soft, you or a nurse can massage it so it becomes firm.

The uterus shrinks about a finger's width every day; this is called *involution*. In the hospital, someone will check you daily; this exam can be a little uncomfortable.

Afterpains

Afterpains are just what they sound like—pains you experience after baby's birth. They are normal; you'll probably feel them for several days after birth as your uterus contracts. Contractions occur to prevent heavy bleeding and enable the uterus to return to its normal size. Cramps can be eased by lying on your stomach and by taking mild pain relievers. An empty bladder enables

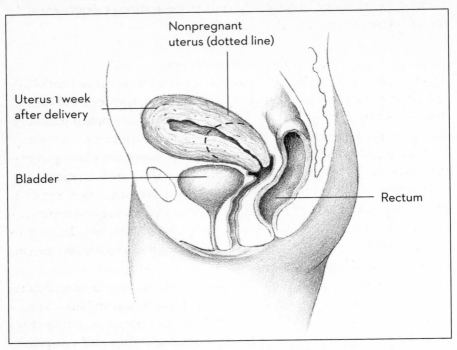

Nonpregnant
uterus (dotted line)

Uterus 1 week
after delivery

Bladder

Rectum

Your uterus shrinks a great deal after delivery. This illustration compares a nonpregnant uterus with a uterus 1 week after birth.

the uterus to work more efficiently, with less pain, so drink lots of fluids and urinate often.

Bleeding after Delivery

After you deliver your baby, the uterus shrinks from the size of a watermelon to the size of a volleyball. It's not unusual to lose blood during labor and delivery; however, heavy bleeding after birth can be serious. A loss of more than 17 ounces (500ml) in the first 24 hours after delivery, called *postpartum hemorrhage,* is significant. Bleeding is controlled by massaging the uterus (called *Credé*) and with medication. Bleeding lessens gradually over time, then stops.

A number of things may cause heavy bleeding after the birth, including a uterus that won't contract, lacerations or tearing of the vagina or cervix during birth, a large or bleeding episiotomy, a tear or rupture in the uterus, retained placental tissue, or clotting or coagulation problems. If you experience a significant change in bleeding after you go home, call your healthcare provider. Some bleeding is normal, but it's best to talk to your healthcare provider about it. He or she may want to see you, prescribe medication or determine if the amount of bleeding is normal.

Bowel Movements

It's not unusual to have sluggish bowels for a few days after your baby's birth. The digestive system slows down during labor, and pregnancy and delivery stress abdominal muscles. You may have had an enema or emptied your bowel during the pushing phase of labor. Pain medication can cause constipation. These all contribute to changing bowel habits. Don't worry about having a bowel movement for the first 4 or 5 days. Constipation at this time is acceptable.

To help your system work more efficiently, eat a diet high in fiber and drink lots of fluid. You might need a laxative. Prunes, prune juice and apple juice are natural laxatives. Over-the-counter stool softeners also help. If you don't have a bowel movement within a week after delivery or you become uncomfortable, call your healthcare provider.

An episiotomy or hemorrhoids can make a bowel movement more difficult or make you more apprehensive about having one. If you still have hemorrhoids after delivery, be assured they usually shrink on their own. If you have problems with them, a compress of witch hazel or commercial compresses can offer relief. Ice packs may also help them shrink.

Breast Changes

After delivery, breasts may be sore whether you breastfeed or bottlefeed. If you bottlefeed, your milk still comes in; healthcare providers don't give medication to stop it as they did in the past. Your breasts fill with milk, called *engorgement*. Engorgement lasts a few days and can be very uncomfortable. You can ease discomfort by wearing a support bra or binding your breasts with a towel or an Ace bandage. Ice packs also help milk dry up.

If you feed baby formula, don't empty your breasts unless you really have to because of pain—your body will replace the milk with more milk! Avoid nipple stimulation and running warm water over your breasts. These practices stimulate breasts to produce milk.

You may have a mild fever with engorgement. Acetaminophen can help reduce the fever and discomfort. See also the discussion of breastfeeding in Appendix B.

Headaches

Headaches can be a problem for some women after delivery, and they can make you miserable. A headache can be caused or influenced by many factors, such as a long labor, having to push for a while or not sleeping in 24 to 36 hours.

If you had pre-eclampsia or pregnancy-induced hypertension, either could cause a headache after delivery. An epidural or spinal anesthetic for labor or a Cesarean delivery can result in a headache called a *spinal headache*. It doesn't happen often—about once in every 100 deliveries—and is treated with bed rest and fluids.

Tell your healthcare provider if you have a headache that doesn't go away or doesn't get better, especially if a headache is severe or accompanied by blurred vision or nausea. He or she can recommend a course of treatment for you. Usually rest, fluids and mild pain medicine help.

Hyperemesis after Pregnancy?

It has been commonly believed symptoms associated with hyperemesis gravidarum (severe morning sickness, see Chapter 11) disappear after pregnancy. This is the case for the majority of women, but a few women continue to have problems even after baby's birth.

Studies show some women with severe hyperemesis gravidarum can experience symptoms well beyond delivery that can take months to overcome. Symptoms include food aversions, gastroesophageal reflux (GERD), digestive problems, nausea, gallbladder issues, fatigue and muscle weakness. Women who received I.V. feedings during pregnancy because they couldn't eat had the highest rate of symptoms.

Recovery can take a few months to as long as 2 years. Some believe it takes 1 to 2 months of recovery for *every month* you were ill during pregnancy. Women who have nausea and/or vomiting into late pregnancy usually find it takes several months to regain their energy and to restore nutritional reserves.

Talk to your healthcare provider if hyperemesis gravidarum persists after baby's birth. You may need to see a nutritionist. It is especially important to seek help before you plan another pregnancy.

Pain in the Perineum

You may feel pain in the *perineum,* the area between the vagina and anus. The area may have been stretched, cut or torn during delivery. Most of the soreness should be gone in 3 to 6 weeks.

Ice packs offer some pain relief in the first 24 hours after delivery. Ice numbs the area and helps reduce swelling. After 24 hours, a warm bath or a soak in a Sitz tub can offer relief. Do this several times a day. Other remedies for perineal pain include numbing sprays, walking (to stimulate circulation), witch-hazel compresses and Kegel exercises (see Chapter 13).

Urination may be painful; acidic urine can sting the cut area. You may want to urinate standing up in the shower with running water washing over the area. The pressure exerted on your urethra during delivery may also make it a bit more difficult to urinate after baby's birth. This will slowly clear up.

Vaginal Discharge

After delivering your baby, you will experience a vaginal discharge similar to a heavy menstrual flow. This discharge, called *lochia,* lasts from 2 to 4 weeks. The discharge is red for the first 3 or 4 days, then turns pink, then brown and finally white or colorless at around 10 days. You will also have lochia if you have a Cesarean delivery, although it may be less than occurs with a vaginal birth.

If the discharge is foul-smelling, remains heavy or is extremely light the first few days, tell your healthcare provider. He or she may want to examine you.

If you don't breastfeed, your first menstrual period occurs within 6 to 8 weeks after giving birth. If you breastfeed, you may not have a regular menstrual period until you wean your baby.

Postpartum Warning Signs

If you take care of yourself after delivery, you should not feel ill. Occasionally problems do occur. Refer to the list of symptoms and warning signs below. Call your healthcare provider immediately if you experience any of the following:

- unusually heavy or sudden increase in vaginal bleeding (more than your normal menstrual flow or soaking more than two sanitary pads in 30 minutes)
- vaginal discharge with strong, unpleasant odor
- a temperature of 101F (38.3C) or more, except in the first 24 hours after birth
- chills
- breasts that are painful or red
- loss of appetite for an extended period
- pain, tenderness, redness or swelling in the legs
- pain in the lower abdomen or in the back
- painful urination or an intense need to urinate
- severe pain in the vagina or perineum

Your Emotions

Temporary emotional changes are not uncommon during the postpartum period. You may have mood swings, mild distress or bouts of crying. See the discussion of postpartum distress that begins on page 328. Mood changes are often a result of birth-associated hormonal changes in your body.

Lack of sleep may play a part in how you feel. Many women are surprised by how tired they are emotionally and physically in the first few months after baby's birth. Take time for yourself, and allow yourself a period of adjustment.

Sleep and rest are essential after baby is born. To get the rest you need, go to bed early when possible. Take a nap or rest when your baby sleeps.

Bonding with Your Baby

Have you heard how important it is to "bond with your baby"? What is bonding? Is it really important in your life with baby? When does it happen? How does it happen?

Bonding is a process that usually takes longer than one instance for it to occur. It's the *process* of becoming emotionally attached to your child, and it deepens over time.

We once believed bonding was a purely emotional response, but today we believe there is also a physical aspect to bonding. Some researchers theorize bonding stimulates production of prolactin and oxytocin in you, which causes you to feel more motherly toward your baby.

Carrie was due to deliver soon and wanted to breastfeed, but she was scared she couldn't do it. She had read books, talked to friends and knew lots of information. I think her biggest fear was she would be left alone with this new baby and wouldn't know what to do. I told her it didn't work that way, and there would be lots of help available. One of the best places to learn to breastfeed is in the hospital after baby's birth. The nurses are experienced in helping new moms learn how to get started, and they're available to help after you go home. Women have told me after they went home, they called the hospital nursery and even went back for help.

The hour following birth is a prime bonding time for mom, dad and baby. However, you can bond with your baby in the delivery room, your hospital room or at home. Don't be afraid the bond will be weaker if you and baby cannot "meet in the delivery room." A mother and her infant are programmed to connect after baby's birth. Both need each other. The mother needs to see, touch, smell and hold this person she has carried for 9 months. The baby needs the comfort of his mother's touch after going through the stressful birth process.

Bonding often begins in the delivery room. Ask your healthcare provider if procedures normally done can safely be postponed for a little while so you can share this time together. If you can't hold your baby, ask your partner or a nurse to hold the baby up to your face, where you can nuzzle him with your cheek.

Bonding can continue in your hospital room if baby's in your room. You can respond to baby whenever he needs you. Breastfeeding is one of the best ways for a mom to bond with her baby, especially if baby is fed on demand.

If you don't breastfeed, you can still bond when you bottlefeed. Respond to your baby when he cries. Look at baby, talk to him and hold him close. Create as much skin-to-skin contact as possible.

As your infant begins to mature, the bonding process will be strengthened. Relax and let it happen. Dad also needs to bond with baby. Encourage your partner to hold baby close and make eye contact and skin contact. He can also respond when the baby cries. Let Dad feed him when you begin expressing your breast milk.

The key to bonding is to focus on the baby and the experiences you share. Include baby in your daily activities. For example, if you're ironing or doing the dishes, put him in his infant carrier and keep him close to you. Talk to him or sing silly songs.

Holding, cuddling and cooing are other great ways to bond. Your baby will connect with you both when he feels the love and security you each offer.

Tubal Ligation

Some women choose to have a form of surgical sterilization performed, called *tubal ligation, postpartum tubal ligation* or *BTL,* while they are in the hospital after baby's birth. Tubal ligation is the number-one birth control method in the United States. About 28% of women who use contraception have chosen tubal ligation—11 million women. Half of all tubal sterilization procedures are performed following delivery of a baby, while the woman is still in the hospital.

The surgery involves blocking a woman's Fallopian tubes to prevent further pregnancies. If you have decided before baby's birth to have tubal ligation, doing it after delivery while you're still in the hospital can make sense. If you received an epidural for your labor and delivery, you're already anesthetized. If you didn't have an epidural, the procedure may require general anesthesia.

The failure rate for tubal ligation is 1 to 2 in 1000 procedures. Failure rates are a little higher with tubal ligations performed immediately after delivery than they are when they are performed at other times.

If you have a postpartum tubal ligation, your healthcare provider may want to examine you 10 to 14 days after you leave the hospital. He or she will check the incision to see if it is healing properly and look for signs of infection.

Exercise after Pregnancy

Many women are eager to begin exercising after baby is born. Exercise helps you feel better physically and can lift your spirits. You can start by doing simple isometric exercises the day after delivery. Practice holding in stomach muscles, or start with mild Kegel exercises.

When you're up and about again, you can do other forms of exercise. Do something you enjoy, and do it on a regular basis. Walking and swimming are excellent exercises to help you get back in shape. Your aerobic capacity can increase as much as 20% in the 6 weeks following baby's birth. This is good news, especially if you're overly fatigued. As your hormones return to a normal level, you'll probably have more energy. Before you start any postpartum exercise program, check with your healthcare provider. He or she may have particular advice for you.

Be careful about beginning an exercise program too soon. Don't overtire yourself by choosing a program that is too ambitious. Always get enough rest.

After a Cesarean delivery, light activity is important. In the hospital, you may have to practice coughing or deep breathing to keep lungs clear. Wiggle toes to aid circulation. Walking may not be easy, but it helps minimize the chances of developing a blood clot in your lower extremities. Check with your healthcare provider before starting an exercise routine or exercise program of any kind.

Recovery from a Vaginal Birth

A source of discomfort after you deliver will be in the vagina and between the opening of the vagina and the rectum, called the *perineum*. Pain or discomfort should lessen every day. You will be given a prescription for mild pain medications if necessary. It's OK to take pain medicine, but it usually isn't needed as much once you're home. You may want to continue to take your prenatal vitamins or iron supplements.

It's normal to bleed after delivery; bleeding continues for several days up to a couple of weeks. In the hospital, nurses will check bleeding to be sure it isn't excessive. If bleeding after delivery was excessive, you may be prescribed vitamins and iron. When you leave the hospital, you will still be bleeding, but the amount of bloody discharge should be decreasing. Sometimes when you go home and are more active, bleeding may be a little heavier at first, but it shouldn't last more than a few hours before it slows down again.

If there is concern about infection, you may be given antibiotics. If you're Rh-negative, you may be given RhoGAM. Laxatives and stool softeners are often prescribed to help you avoid constipation.

When you go home, increase activities gradually. Walk around, eat more normally and become more active each day. You may need to rest frequently—that's normal. Pay attention to your body. Most healthcare providers recommend you wait until after your 6-week postpartum checkup before you begin any strenuous activity, exercise or become sexually active again.

If you take pain medicines or have problems, such as dizziness, don't drive. It's OK to use stairs, but plan ahead so you're not running up and down stairs all day.

Full recovery is different for every woman. If you had complications or problems, it may take longer. From 2 to 6 weeks, you should be feeling a little better every day. You probably won't be taking pain medicine any longer, and bleeding will decrease or it will have stopped.

Recovery from a Cesarean Delivery

Recovery from a Cesarean delivery is different from recovery from a vaginal birth. You have undergone major abdominal surgery, so be prepared to take it easy for a while. Although you have experienced many of the same situations as someone who had a vaginal birth, you face some additional restrictions.

Get up and out of bed as soon as possible after baby is born. Moving helps prevent blood clots in the legs, lung collapse and pneumonia. Walking helps body functions, such as relieving constipation and abdominal gas.

Be careful not to strain stomach muscles. Avoid lifting anything heavy. Once home, keep your incision clean and dry, and watch for infection. Infection of a Cesarean incision usually occurs 4 to 6 days after surgery. If any of the following signs appear, contact your healthcare provider immediately. Signs of infection include the following:

- redness that spreads from the edges of the incision
- fever
- hardness around the incision
- discharge from the incision site

Although you did not deliver vaginally, you will probably experience painful uterine contractions for several days after delivery. This is a sign your uterus is returning to its prepregnancy size. If you breastfeed, you may notice the pains when your baby nurses.

You will have lochia with a Cesarean delivery. However, your discharge may be lighter than lochia that follows a vaginal birth.

If you're interested in exercising after a Cesarean, you can usually begin light exercise about 4 weeks after birth. You can probably resume full activity between 4 and 6 weeks postpartum. Your healthcare provider can advise you.

Resuming Sexual Relations

One concern you and your partner may share after delivery is postpartum sex. Getting back into "the swing of things" after your baby is born can be difficult. Stress, hormonal changes, emotions, fatigue and other physical factors, such as bleeding, can affect your sex drive. Pain from an episiotomy or an incision can also be a factor.

We once advised women to wait at least 6 weeks before having intercourse. If you feel no pain or discomfort and your episiotomy has healed, you can resume sexual relations when you feel comfortable. Be sure bleeding has stopped. For most women, this will be at least a few weeks after delivery.

If you decide to have intercourse, you need to take precautions if you don't want to become pregnant again. *You can become pregnant before you have a menstrual period.* Discuss birth-control options with your healthcare provider.

Birth Control after Pregnancy

Contraception is something you and your partner may want to think about. You will probably begin ovulating 6 to 8 weeks after birth, and you could get pregnant again. If you do not want to have another baby very soon, discuss birth-control options with your healthcare provider in the hospital or at your postpartum checkup.

Birth-Control Methods

Method	Effectiveness	Reasons to Use It
Oral contraceptives (estrogen and progestin)	99%	Bottlefeeding, not breastfeeding
Oral contraceptives (progestin only)	98%	Can use while breastfeeding
Condoms	97%	Convenient and easy to use
Diaphragms	94%	Convenient to use; may need to be refitted at your 6-week checkup
IUD	98–99%	Don't have to think about birth control; can be inserted at your 6-week checkup
Depo-Provera	99%	Can use while breastfeeding
Implantable contraceptives	97%	Can use while breastfeeding (may not be widely available)
Once-a-month birth-control injection	99%	Can use while breastfeeding

Breastfeeding protects you against pregnancy to some degree, but breastfeeding is *not* an effective method of birth control. If you breastfeed, consider birth-control methods if you want to postpone pregnancy.

If you used a diaphragm or cervical cap for birth control in the past, you need to be refitted after delivery. The size of your cervix or vagina may have changed. You may consider condoms or spermicides if you breastfeed. Neither interferes with breastfeeding.

If you bottlefeed, you may decide on a method that can be started immediately after delivery. These methods include hormone implants, Depo-Provera injections, a progestin-only pill or an IUD. If you want to use a combination birth-control pill, which contains estrogen and progestin, wait at least 2 weeks after delivery to begin.

Introducing Baby to Brothers and Sisters

When your older children come to the hospital to see you and meet the new baby, greet them with open arms (that means *not* holding the baby). If a younger child sees you holding the baby right away, he or she may feel displaced. Give your children, especially toddlers, lots of attention. It's hard on kids to be displaced by a new baby, so your extra attention is welcome.

When you go home, let your children help with the new baby. Even a young child can get you a diaper or baby wipes.

Remind those who come to visit to recognize your older children *before* the baby. This helps the older child feel secure and provides him or her the opportunity to "show off" the new baby. If you have to let some household chores go for a while to provide your children with the attention they need, that's OK.

Get Dad Involved

To help ease the transition, get your partner involved with older children. Try making these changes *before* the baby is born so they become part of your family routine. A few things dad can do to make older children feel special include the following.

- Take over some chores, such as getting older children ready for bed or reading to them.
- Create some special time together with the kids. Go to the library together on Saturday mornings, or cook dinner together one night a week.
- Spend time together at home. Make one evening a "family" evening when you play games, listen to music or read together. No TV on these special nights!
- Dad can help children learn to do chores. Even young children can help empty the trash or clear the table. When everyone works together, more work gets done faster. And it's more fun, too!

Feeding Your Baby

You must decide if you want to breastfeed or bottlefeed. Even after you choose a method, you may have to make adjustments after your baby is born.

Early in life, most babies eat every 3 to 4 hours, although some babies feed as often as every 2 hours. It may help your baby get on a regular schedule if you time the feedings. Or let baby set the schedule; some babies need to feed more often than others.

Sometimes a baby needs to feed more often than she normally does. See how often your baby wants to feed and whether she is growing properly. A baby usually waits longer between feedings and feeds longer at each feeding as she grows older.

A baby is usually the best judge of how much to take at each feeding. Usually she will turn away from the nipple when she's full.

••

At her 37-week visit, Lily wanted to talk about breastfeeding and bot-tlefeeding. With her first child, she had tried breastfeeding and had a miserable experience, giving up after 2 weeks. This time she planned to bottlefeed from the start and wanted to know if this was OK. Friends and family had been giving her a hard time about it. I reassured her bottlefeeding was fine and not to feel guilty. I told her breastfeeding wasn't for everyone; it's an individual decision. Lily left my office feeling better. Giving birth to, caring for and raising a baby requires making a lot of decisions. Some aren't easy to make.

••

Breast milk contains all the nutrients a baby needs, and it's easy for baby to digest. Breastfed babies have lower rates of infection because of the immunological content of breast milk. Breastfeeding can also give baby a sense of security and the mother a sense of self-esteem. However, if there are reasons you cannot or choose not to breastfeed, baby will do well if you bottlefeed her formula.

See the discussion of bottlefeeding and breastfeeding in Appendix B that begins on page 349.

After-Pregnancy Changes

After the birth of your baby, you may notice lots of changes in your body—it's only natural. You may see changes in your abdominal shape and skin. Breasts may also be affected.

Abdominal-Skin Changes

After they give birth, some women find their abdomen returns to normal naturally. For others, it never quite returns to its prepregnancy state. Abdominal skin is not like muscle, so it can't be strengthened by exercise. Perhaps the most important element affecting your skin's ability to return to its prepregnancy tightness is connective tissue, which provides suppleness and elasticity. As you get older, your skin loses connective tissue and elasticity. Other factors include your fitness level before pregnancy, heredity and how much your skin stretched during pregnancy.

Breast Changes

After giving birth, most women's breasts return to their prepregnancy size or even decrease a little in size. If you breastfeed, it takes longer for your breasts to return to normal. This is a result of the change in the connective tissue that forms the support system of your breasts. Exercise *cannot* make breasts firmer, but it can improve the chest area underneath so breasts have better support.

Weight Changes

Don't get anxious about losing pregnancy weight after your baby's birth. Regaining your prepregnancy figure may take longer if you're older. It's normal to lose 10 to 15 pounds immediately after baby is born. An additional 5 pounds of fluid may wash out of your system within a few days.

Extra weight may be harder to lose. Your body stored 7 to 10 pounds of fat as energy for the first few months after birth. If you eat properly and get enough exercise, these pounds will slowly come off.

If you breastfeed, all the nutrients your baby receives depend on the quality of the food you eat. Breastfeeding places more demands on your body than pregnancy. Your body burns up to 1000 calories a day to produce milk. When breastfeeding, you need to eat an extra 500 calories a day. Be sure they are nutritious calories (eat fruits, vegetables and breads—stay away from junk food). And keep up fluid levels.

Postpartum Distress Syndrome (PPDS)

You may experience many emotional changes after baby is born. Mood swings, mild distress or bouts of crying are not uncommon. Changes in moods are often a result of hormonal changes you experience after birth, just as they were when you were pregnant.

Many women are surprised by how tired they are emotionally *and* physically in the first few months after baby's birth. Make sure you take time for yourself. Sleep and rest can help you deal with mood shifts, which seem to occur more often when a woman is exhausted.

After pregnancy, many women experience some degree of depression. This is called *postpartum distress syndrome (PPDS)*. Some experts believe postpartum depression may begin *during* pregnancy, but symptoms may not appear until several months *after* delivery. They may occur when a woman starts getting her period again and experiences hormonal changes.

Postpartum distress syndrome can resolve on its own, but it can often take as long as a year. With more severe problems, treatment may relieve symptoms in a matter of weeks, and improvement should be significant within 6 to 8 months. Often medication is necessary for complete recovery.

If your baby blues don't get better in a few weeks or if you feel extremely depressed, call your healthcare provider. You may need medication to help deal with the problem.

Different Degrees of Depression

There are different degrees of depression. The mildest form is *baby blues*. Up to 80% of all women have "baby blues." They usually appear between 2 days and 2 weeks after the baby is born. They are temporary and usually leave as quickly as they come. This situation lasts only a couple of weeks, and symptoms do not worsen.

A more serious version of postpartum distress is called *postpartum depression (PPD)*. It affects about 10% of all new mothers. The difference between baby blues and postpartum depression lies in the frequency, intensity and duration of symptoms.

PPD can occur from 2 weeks to 1 year after the birth. A mother may have feelings of anger, confusion, panic and hopelessness. She may experience changes in her eating and sleeping patterns. She may fear she will hurt her baby or feel as if she is going crazy. Anxiety is one of the major symptoms of PPD.

The most serious form of postpartum distress is *postpartum psychosis (PPP)*. The woman may have hallucinations, think about suicide or try to harm the baby. Many women who develop postpartum psychosis also exhibit

---

Your Appearance

After your baby's birth, you may be concerned about your appearance. Although you won't immediately regain your prepregnancy figure, there are a few things you can do to look and feel better.

- Buy and wear a well-fitting, supportive nursing bra.
- Oversized shirts (your partner's may do the trick) offer you variety. Stay away from your maternity clothes, which you probably want to burn anyway.
- Wear tops untucked—wait a little while for tummy muscles to tighten up before tucking tops in.
- Wear comfortable drawstring pants, elastic-waist or stretch pants.
- A loose-fitting dress can be flattering because it doesn't hug your curves.
- Don't wear sloppy clothes, such as sweatshirts and sweat pants, very often; sometimes when you wear sloppy clothes, you feel sloppy.

signs of bipolar mood disorder, which is unrelated to childbirth. Discuss this situation with your healthcare provider if you are concerned.

After you give birth, if you believe you are suffering from some form of postpartum distress syndrome, contact your healthcare provider. Every postpartum reaction, whether mild or severe, is usually temporary and treatable.

It's normal to feel extremely tired, especially after the hard work of labor and delivery and adjusting to the demands of being a new mom. However, if after 2 weeks of motherhood you're just as exhausted as you were shortly after you delivered, you may be at risk of developing postpartum depression.

Causes of Postpartum Distress Syndrome

Researchers aren't sure what causes postpartum distress; not all women experience it. A woman's individual sensitivity to hormonal changes may be part of the cause; the drop in estrogen and progesterone after delivery may contribute to PPDS.

A new mother must make many adjustments, and many demands are placed on her; either or both of these situations may cause distress. If you had a Cesarean delivery, you may also be at greater risk for postpartum depression.

Other possible factors include a family history of depression, lack of familial support after the birth, isolation and chronic fatigue. You may also be at higher risk of suffering from PPDS if:

- your mother or sister suffered from the problem—it seems to run in families
- you suffered from PPDS with a previous pregnancy—chances are you'll have the problem again
- you had fertility treatments to achieve this pregnancy—hormone fluctuations may be more severe, which may cause PPDS
- you suffered extreme PMS before the pregnancy—hormonal imbalances may be greater after the birth
- you have a personal history of depression or you suffered from untreated depression before pregnancy
- you have experienced any major life changes recently—you may experience a hormonal drop as a result
- you are anxious or have low self-esteem
- you have a struggling relationship with baby's father
- your access to finances and health care is limited
- you experience little social support

- you had more than one baby
- you have a colicky or high-maintenance baby
- you experienced a lack of sleep during pregnancy, you sleep less than 6 hours in a 24-hour period or you wake 3 or more times a night

In addition, if you answer "most of the time" or "some of the time" to any of the following questions, you may be at increased risk.

- I blame myself when things go wrong (even if you have nothing to do with them).
- I often feel scared or panicked without good reason.
- I am anxious or worried without good reason.

Handling the Baby Blues

One of the most important ways you can help yourself handle baby blues is to have a good support system near at hand. Ask family members and friends to help. Ask your mother or mother-in-law to stay for a while. Ask your partner to take some work leave, or hire someone to come in and help each day.

Rest when your baby sleeps. Find other mothers who are in the same situation; it helps to share your feelings and experiences. Don't try to be perfect. Pamper yourself.

Do some form of moderate exercise every day, even if it's just going for a walk. Eat nutritiously, and drink plenty of fluids. Get out of the house every day. Eating more complex carbohydrates may help raise your mood. And giving baby a massage may help *you* because it helps you connect with your baby.

Talk to your healthcare provider about temporarily using antidepressants if the above steps don't work for you. Many women who suffer from postpartum depression require medication for up to 1 year.

Dealing with More Serious Forms of PPDS

Beyond the relatively minor symptoms of baby blues, postpartum distress syndrome can appear in two ways. Some women experience acute depression that can last for weeks or months; they cannot sleep or eat, they feel worthless and isolated, they are sad and they cry a great deal. For other women, they are extremely anxious, restless and agitated. Their heart rate increases. Some unfortunate women experience both sets of symptoms at the same time.

If you experience any symptoms, call your healthcare provider immediately. He or she will probably see you in the office, then prescribe a course of treatment. Do it for yourself and your family.

Your Distress Can Affect Your Partner

If you experience baby blues or PPD, it can also affect your partner. Prepare him for this situation before baby is born. Explain to him that if it happens to you, it's only temporary.

There are some things you might suggest to your partner that he can do for himself if you get blue or depressed. Tell him not to take the situation personally. Suggest he talk to friends, family members, other fathers or a professional. He should eat well, get enough rest and exercise. Ask him to be patient with you, and ask him to provide his love and support to you during this difficult time.

The Postpartum Checkup

Your body changes a lot in the 4 to 6 weeks following delivery. By the time you visit your healthcare provider for your 6-week postpartum checkup, your uterus will be about the size of a grapefruit. That's an incredible feat, considering it was the size of a small watermelon only a few weeks before!

At your visit, tell your healthcare provider if you have had headaches or experienced increased irritability or fatigue; you may be prescribed an iron supplement. You will have a physical exam, similar to the one at your first prenatal exam. Your healthcare provider will probably check your weight and blood pressure. The average weight loss after giving birth is about 12 pounds.

Your healthcare provider checks any incision you have. Your breasts are examined, and your uterus, ovaries and cervix are checked—yes, that means another pelvic exam. Your healthcare provider may discuss postpartum depression with you; you may undergo screening for the condition.

If you had a vaginal birth, your healthcare provider will examine any tears or incisions. If you had a Cesarean delivery, your incision will be examined. If you developed hemorrhoids or varicose veins during pregnancy, your healthcare provider will also check those.

If you took any medication before or during pregnancy, ask about continuing it or resuming it now. If you have any questions about your recovery, address them at this time. It's a good time to discuss birth-control options if you don't want to become pregnant again immediately.

Your 6-week postpartum checkup is also a good time to ask questions about future pregnancies. Discuss concerns about, and complications from, your recent delivery. This information can be helpful if you move or deliver with a different healthcare provider or hospital in the future.

Chapter 20

Back to Work?

After your baby is born, it seems as if the hard work is done—and most of it is. But if you are like many women and work outside the home, you must address issues related to your working life—from the type of childcare arrangement you choose to whether you will go back to work full-time.

Whether to continue working outside the home after baby's birth is a decision some mothers wish they didn't have to make. Others look forward to returning to jobs and careers they enjoy, even if that day comes sooner than they would prefer. Whatever the reason, returning to work after having a baby is as typical these days as staying home used to be. More than half of all mothers with preschool-age children work outside the home. For almost all of them, finding adequate childcare is an important issue.

Can I be a good mother if I go back to work?
Absolutely! Millions of women prove this every day. Many believe you can be an even better mother if you work outside the home. Happy mothers raise happy children. It may take some effort, planning and sacrifice by you and your partner, but you can do it!

Childcare Decisions

Arranging childcare for your new baby can be one of the most important tasks you face before returning to work. The best way to choose the right setting and best care provider is to know your options.

You do have choices. Any of a number of situations could be right for you; examine your needs and those of your child before you decide which to pursue. Let's examine some of the most common childcare arrangements.

In-Home Care

In-home care is the easiest option for you and your baby. You don't have to get baby ready before you leave in the morning or take her out in bad weather. You save commuting time in the morning and evening.

Care in your home is an excellent choice for a baby or small child because the environment is familiar. It provides your child with a great deal of attention. A relative or nonrelative may provide this care. A potential drawback to in-house care during the toddler years may be that the child won't have the chance to play with others her age.

When the caregiver is a relative, such as a grandparent or an aunt, you may find the situation challenging. Can you maintain your relationship with the relative caregiver while asking or telling him or her to do things the way you want them done?

If the caregiver is not a relative, the arrangement may be expensive. In addition, you are bringing someone you do not know into your home to tend your child. Ask for references, and check them thoroughly. Don't rush into an arrangement with a caregiver you haven't checked out thoroughly or you aren't completely confident about.

Care in a Caregiver's Home

Many parents take their children to someone else's home for care. Often these homes offer small group sizes and scheduling flexibility (for example, you may be allowed to leave your child a little longer occasionally). They offer a home-like atmosphere, and your child may receive lots of attention.

Home care is not regulated in every state, so check each situation carefully. Contact your state's Department of Social Services, and ask about its requirements. Sometimes local agencies oversee caregivers. Care providers must abide by certain standards or rules, such as the maximum number of children (including their own) allowed in the home. They may also have to obtain certification in first aid and CPR (cardiopulmonary resuscitation).

Your Responsibilities to Your Caregiver

Just as your caregiver has certain responsibilities to you, you have responsibilities to your caregiver. Be on time when you drop off your child or pick her up. Call if you're going to be late, even if the care is in your own home. Pay the caregiver on time. Provide diapers, formula or expressed breast milk, extra clothes and personal items for baby when they are needed.

Taxes

You must pay federal-withholding, state and local taxes for your care provider, including Social Security and Medicare taxes. If the person works in your home, you may also need to pay workers' compensation and unemployment insurance taxes. These taxes must be paid on a rigid schedule. Failure to pay on time can put you in a serious legal and financial predicament. Contact the Internal Revenue Service and your state Department of Economic Security for further information.

Childcare Centers

A childcare center is a larger setting in which children receive care. Centers vary widely in the facilities and activities they provide, the amount of attention they give each child, group sizes and childcare philosophy.

Ask about the training required for each childcare provider or teacher. Some facilities expect more from a care provider than others.

You may find some childcare centers do not accept infants. Often centers focus on older children because infants take more time and attention. If the center accepts infants, the ratio of caregivers to children should be about one adult to every three or four children (up to age 2). One adult for every four to six 2-year-olds and one adult for every seven to eight 3-year-olds is considered acceptable.

Don't be fooled by facilities; even the cleanest, brightest place is useless without the right kind of care provider. Visit it by appointment, then stop by unannounced a few times. Meet the person in charge and the people who will care for your child. Ask for references of parents whose children are cared for there. Talk to these parents before you make a final decision.

Infant Care

Babies have special needs; be sure the place you choose for your infant meets those needs. A baby must be changed and fed but also must be held and interacted with, must rest at regular times each day and be comforted when she is afraid.

When searching for childcare, keep in mind what is required for your child. Evaluate every situation in terms of how it responds to your baby's needs.

Special-Care Needs

If your baby has special needs and requires one-on-one care, expect to spend extra time finding qualified childcare. A child with special needs may be best cared for by someone who comes to your home. Ask for a referral from baby's healthcare provider or the hospital where your child has received care.

Caring for a Sick Child

All children come down with colds, the flu or diarrhea at some time. If you can't take time off from work to stay home with a sick child, you may have other care options.

In many places, "sick-child" day-care centers are available. They are usually attached to a regular day-care facility, although some are connected with hospitals. A center provides a comfortable place where an ill child can rest or participate in quiet activities, such as story time. Often a registered nurse heads the facility; this person can administer medication when necessary.

Some cities have on-call in-home care providers who come to your home when your child is too sick to be taken anywhere. The program is usually run by an agency that deals with childcare, and caregivers charge by the hour. This can be an excellent way to care for a child who is ill.

Hiring a Caregiver

Where do you start the search for the right day care for your child? Start with the following ideas.

- Ask friends, family and co-workers for referrals.
- Talk to people in your neighborhood.
- Ask at your church about programs it may sponsor.
- Call a local referral agency.
- Advertise in local newspapers, online resources and church bulletins to find interview candidates.

Talk to people over the phone first to determine whether you want to interview them. Ask about their experience, qualifications, childcare philosophy and what they seek in a position. Then decide if you want to pursue the contact with an in-person interview. Make a list of what to discuss, including days and hours the person is needed, duties, need for a driver's license and a benefits policy.

Whomever you choose to provide care for your child, check references thoroughly before you make a final decision. Have a potential caregiver provide you with the names and phone numbers of people she has worked for in the past. Call each family, let them know you are considering this person as a caregiver and discuss their experience with the candidate. Ask direct, probing questions. Beware of references who only tell you wonderful things about the caregiver. They could be close friends who have never really used the caregiver you are checking on.

Keep checking. After you hire someone, check the situation occasionally by dropping in unannounced. Pay attention to how your child reacts each time you leave or arrive; this can give you a clue as to how he or she feels about the caregiver.

The Cost of Childcare

Childcare can be a big-budget item in your household expenses. The cost of infant and toddler care (through age 3) can be expensive, depending on the type of care you choose. In-home care can be the most costly, with placement fees and additional charges you negotiate based on extra tasks you want the care provider to perform.

Sometimes the monetary benefit you receive after returning to work may be negligible. You may want to calculate the actual costs involved with day care, and make your decisions about working based on those calculations.

Public funding is available for some limited-income families. Title EE is a program paid for with federal funds. Call your local Department of Social Services to see if you are eligible.

Other programs that can help some families with childcare costs include a federal tax-credit program, the dependent-care assistance program and earned-income tax credit. The federal government regulates these programs; contact the Internal Revenue Service for further information.

When to Start Looking for Childcare

Finding the best situation for your baby takes time. Start the process several months before you need it. For special situations, such as twins, you might want to start the process even earlier. This often means finding childcare *before* your baby is born.

You may find a shortage of quality childcare for children under age 2. You may have to get on a waiting list for some arrangements. If you find a care provider you're comfortable with, ask to put down a deposit and set a date on which childcare begins. Keep in touch with the care provider. Plan to meet again before you place your child in daily care.

Going Back to Work

You may be concerned about returning to work even after you have dealt with childcare issues satisfactorily. It's important to find ways to ease the transition from home to work. Some co-workers will be supportive; others may not be.

You may find some of your greatest challenges come after work, when you get home. Your baby and partner need your time and attention. Even when you feel tired, you may have household chores to do. Arrange with your partner before you return to work to share these responsibilities. That way, each of you can give your baby undivided attention for some part of the evening. Set aside time just for you and your partner!

Going back to work takes some planning. Not everything will go smoothly at first, but what adventure does? With the number of childcare options available today and perhaps some creative approaches to your work schedule, you will be able to find a truly happy medium—one that works for you, your partner, your employer and your baby.

Before You Return to Work

If you make the decision to return to work, there are some things you can do to make the transition from home to career easier and more successful. Set up a schedule to get back into your working routine. Be selfish about personal time—you'll need it. But realize your partner probably needs the same thing, so allow equal time for him.

Keep an open mind. You may decide to go back to work but be miserable when you return. Is there any way to change the situation? Explore all your options, then use what works for you in your particular situation.

2 Weeks Before You Return to Work

Experiment with various feeding techniques before you make any final decisions as to whether you will continue breastfeeding or switch to bottlefeeding. You may decide to continue breastfeeding. You can do this fairly easily if your work is close to baby's day-care situation or your job offers day-care services, allowing you to visit when it's time to feed baby. If visiting baby during the day is not an option, you will have to pump your breasts; using a dual-action pump gets the job done twice as fast.

If you decide to switch to formula, eliminate one nursing every couple days, beginning with the early evening feeding. Switch to formula for day feedings. Eliminate the first and last feedings of the day as your final switch to formula.

Examine your wardrobe, and try clothes on! You may be larger in size (it's natural), or your body shape may have changed somewhat, making some clothes fit differently. If you intend to breastfeed or to pump your breasts during working hours, you may need clothes that allow you to do this easily. Pack some extra things to keep at work.

Try on shoes you may not have worn for a while. Shoe size can increase ½ to 1 full size during pregnancy. Often this increase is permanent, and your feet will remain larger, even after baby's birth.

Finalize day-care arrangements. Visit the place you have planned to leave your baby to check it out again and make sure they have enrolled your child.

It's also a good idea to have "sick-baby" arrangements made in case your child gets sick and you can't take him or her to day care. If you use a babysitter, you may need an alternate sitter in case *she* gets sick.

Evaluate your needs at home. Will you be able to eliminate certain chores or adapt yourself to accept different standards? You may not realize how valuable your time will be when you're at home—you probably don't want to spend time keeping everything sparkling. See if you can do chores more efficiently, such as cooking ahead for the week or shopping only once a week. Maybe you can hire someone to do some cleaning for you.

1 Week Before You Return to Work

Begin your work routine *this week*. Get up at the same time you would normally rise if you were going to work. Feed baby on the new schedule. Make and eat your own breakfast. Allow time to pack a lunch and fill baby's diaper bag.

Make a list of all the supplies you will need for the baby at home and at day care. Consider diapers, formula, baby clothes, extra bottles, a second car seat and anything else you may need for your baby's care and comfort.

Take baby to day care, then do errands or take care of other tasks. It's all part of getting ready to go back to work next week.

Choose your clothes, and lay them out the night before you go back to work. Be sure everything is OK to wear. Pack your baby's diaper bag with baby's things to take to day care. Eat a good meal, and go to bed early to get a good night's sleep.

The Day You Return to Work

If possible, choose a Wednesday or Thursday to return to work. It helps you get into the routine of working,

Time-Saving, Energy-Saving Tip

Others may watch your children at your home or come in to clean for you, and you need to give them a key to your house. Yet you want to keep your house secure. One way to do this is to have two different locks for your door. When the person needs to get into the house, lock only the lock they have a key for. At other times, use both locks.

but you'll only work a short week. This allows you to replenish your energy for the following 5-day work week.

If you can start back with fewer hours, that also helps. Five hours a day for a week is a good plan, gradually increasing to 8 hours a day.

Plan easy-to-fix meals for the first few weeks after you start working. Or prepare and freeze some dishes so you don't have to cook. You might even want to get take-home food a couple of times.

Don't get upset if you feel a great loss when you return to work. It's OK to grieve and feel some guilt when you leave your baby. Or you may feel some relief to get back to work. That's OK, too.

If you continue to breastfeed, take extra clothing to work with you in case you experience leakage of breast milk. Be sure you also have a good supply of breast pads.

Managing Your Time

Time is a limited resource; learning to manage your time well is the secret to relishing this busy time in your life. Make a daily plan and stick to it. Do what you can and delegate some responsibilities to others. Change your expectations if you need to. After that, concentrate on the baby, your partner and other important people in your life. Let less important things go. Enjoy the moment!

Can You Modify Your Work Situation?

After having a baby, some women decide to continue working outside the home but not full-time or not at their old schedule. You may be happier if you can find a way to work part-time or if you can adapt your schedule in some other way. There may be ways to modify your current work situation so everyone is happy—you, your boss, your partner and your baby.

If you want to work part-time, you may be able to share a job with someone else in the company who would also like to work part-time. Ask your employer.

Find out if flextime programs are available at your workplace. You may be allowed to modify your work schedule (for example, work four 10-hour days instead of five 8-hour days). Or you may come in early and leave early, or arrive and leave later. You may be able to set your own schedule, as long as you get your work done.

You might be able to work at home part-time or full-time. Many companies allow some employees to work at home.

If you work part-time or flextime, childcare may be harder to find. With some centers, you pay by the week, whether your child is there or not. An in-home care provider may need the money that only full-time work offers. But some centers are more flexible than others, and some in-home care providers may be delighted at the prospect of a lighter schedule.

Breastfeeding and Work

You don't have to stop breastfeeding when you return to work, but you may need to make adjustments. If you breastfeed exclusively, you will need to pump your breasts or arrange to see your baby during the day. You may nurse your baby at home and provide expressed breast milk or formula for your care provider to give baby when you're away.

One way to smooth the back-to-work transition for you and baby is to begin storing breast milk a couple of weeks before you return to work. Use an electric breast pump to express milk between feedings for about 2 weeks before you return to work. Don't start sooner—you may produce too much milk. A breast pump with a double-pumping feature empties both breasts at once.

Freeze expressed milk in a variety of quantities from 1 to 4 ounces. This gives the caregiver options as to how much to thaw for a particular feeding.

You might also pump and store breast milk while you're at work. You may be uncomfortable if you don't pump your breasts because your milk continues

to come in. Take a breast pump with you, and refrigerate or freeze breast milk after you pump it.

If you remain at home until your baby is between 4 and 6 months old, baby may be able to skip the bottle and start drinking from a cup. Earlier than 4 months, your baby will need to learn to drink from a bottle.

If You Stay Home

You may decide to stay home with your baby. If you do, the change from leaving the house each day to staying at home can be dramatic. You may find being at home isn't as easy as you thought it would be. Staying home may mean less companionship, less money and the loss of routine.

Try to anticipate some of these changes and meet them halfway. Don't bury yourself in motherhood and exclude all other activities. Make an effort to get out, meet people and get involved in new experiences with your baby. Consider joining an exercise class designed for new mothers and babies; the YWCA and similar organizations frequently offer classes.

If you have worked full-time, you may not have met many people in your neighborhood. Once you're home full-time, you'll have an opportunity to make friends. If other new mothers are in the neighborhood, you might start an infant play group that meets once or twice a week. Take turns hosting. Babies play, and moms talk!

Stay in touch with your colleagues at work. Drop in to see them, or go out to lunch with a group. See what they are up to, and stay on top of what is happening in your field.

Chapter 21

Looking Ahead

More couples choose to delay childbearing, and predictions are that more women will become pregnant and deliver babies in their 30s and 40s in the years to come. We believe there is reason for optimism for these pregnancies. Pregnancy at any age is an adventure full of physical and emotional challenges, and highs and lows.

People are more aware of the importance of taking care of their health. Fewer people smoke. They drink less alcohol, and they are more aware of the dangers of drug use. Regular exercise and better eating habits are more often the rule, not the exception. All of these activities help everyone involved prepare for a pregnancy, and the result is healthier pregnancies resulting in healthier babies and moms.

Is my next pregnancy likely to be the same as this one was?
Every pregnancy is different, but there are often similarities from one pregnancy to another. Complications or problems during a pregnancy may not repeat, but it's good to know about them. Discuss them with your healthcare provider before your next pregnancy.

Medical advances are made every year. Two of the greatest areas of growth have been in technology for pregnancy and in care of the premature infant. In the past, babies born before 32 weeks seldom survived; if they did, they had major problems. Today, babies born as early as 25 weeks survive, and there are even cases of babies born earlier than this surviving and doing well.

In this book we have discussed many technologies—ultrasound, amniocentesis, chorionic villus sampling, fetoscopy—genetic counseling and other advances in obstetrics. All promise more advances in the goal of a healthy baby and a healthy mother.

Researchers have found it's important for a man also to take good care of himself before a pregnancy so he can contribute healthy sperm. Healthy sperm along with the woman's good health help ensure a healthy baby.

Each individual (or couple) is different. A healthy 38-year-old woman who eats right, exercises and takes good care of herself will probably do better during pregnancy than a 23-year-old woman who eats poorly, doesn't exercise and lets herself go. Every pregnancy is different.

There is much reason for optimism and encouragement in pregnancy for the older woman. We have come a long way in our care of the pregnant woman and her developing baby.

In the past, many doctors frowned on pregnancy after age 35, but women decided they were going to have babies anyway. And it looks as if this trend is going to continue.

If You Experience Secondary Infertility

Sometimes a couple has no trouble conceiving; however, when they try to get pregnant again, they have difficulty and cannot get pregnant. This is called *secondary infertility*, and it's more common than you may believe. Many couples experience it.

If you and your partner have difficulty becoming pregnant a second time, examine your lifestyle. Each of you should look at your food intake, alcohol consumption, smoking practices and any medications (prescription and over-the-counter) you may be taking. Explore situations and issues that might be affecting your fertility, then take steps to correct any problems. If you still cannot conceive, see your healthcare provider, have any tests he or she recommends, and make necessary changes to help increase your chances of conceiving another child.

It's Up to You!

Be an active participant in your pregnancy; you are vital to its success. The birth of your baby is a significant and wonderful event in your life. Despite the possible problems that might occur during a pregnancy, it's more likely you and your baby will do well. The best things you can do are to plan ahead for pregnancy, exercise regularly, eat right, take care of medical problems before getting pregnant and seek prenatal care early. Remember—it's for the good of you *and* your baby!

Appendix A:
Cord-Blood Banking

You may have heard about storing blood from your baby's umbilical cord after birth. *Cord blood* is found in the umbilical cord and placenta, which in the past was usually thrown away after delivery. Stem cells have proved useful in treating some diseases. Treatment corrects and/or replaces diseased or damaged cells.

Stem cells are present in cord blood. They are the forerunner of cells that make all blood cells. In cord blood, these special cells are undeveloped and can become many different kinds of blood cells. Cord blood doesn't need to be matched as closely for a transplant. This feature can be important for members of ethnic groups or people with rare blood types, who often have more difficulty finding acceptable donor matches.

How Cord Blood Is Used

Cord blood has been used since about 1990 and has been used in over 10,000 procedures. Umbilical-cord blood (UCB) is good for treating diseases that affect the blood and immune systems.

UCB-derived stem cells are being studied as therapy for many disorders. To date, umbilical-cord blood has been used to treat over 75 life-threatening diseases, and more uses are likely to be found in the future.

If you or your partner have a family history of some specific diseases, you may want to consider saving and banking your child's umbilical-cord blood in case it's needed for treatment in the future. Siblings or parents can use the blood; in fact, the most common use for stem cells from cord blood is between siblings. However, stored blood can't be used to treat a genetic disease in the child from whom the blood was collected. Those stem cells have the same genetic problems.

If you're interested, discuss this situation with your healthcare provider at a prenatal appointment. To date, over 600,000 family cord-blood units have been stored. However, you only have *one chance* to collect and save your baby's umbilical-cord blood.

Before making a decision, ask about how and where blood is stored and the cost of storing it. This is a decision you need to make together as a couple. But first you need good information, such as cost, because insurance may not cover blood storage.

In many hospitals, expecting mothers learn about cord-blood donation when they are admitted to the hospital. Donating cord blood is free.

Collecting and Storing Blood

If you decide to save and store your child's umbilical-cord blood, the cord-blood storage bank you choose sends you a collection kit, which is used to collect blood after delivery. It's collected within 9 minutes after birth, before you deliver the placenta. It's taken directly from the umbilical cord; there's no risk or pain to mom or baby. You can also bank the blood if you have a Cesarean delivery.

After cord blood is collected, it's usually picked up by a courier and taken to a banking facility where it is frozen and stored. At this time, we don't know how long frozen cells will last. Cord blood has been banked only since 1990; however, storage at this time is better than it was when freezing and storing blood first began.

It's expensive to collect and to store umbilical-cord blood. Collection and storage can run between $1000 and $2000. A year's storage can cost around $100.

There are two types of banks—*private blood banking* and *public blood banking*. You may be advised to use private blood banking if you have a history of some illnesses. With private banking, access is guaranteed to your own or a relative's stored blood. Cord blood is available for you or a family member if you need it in the future.

Public UCB banks provide donor cells to those who need stem cells from cord blood. However, donors can't be guaranteed their own or a relative's cord blood. Anyone needing the cord-blood products may get the blood. In some areas, needs-based help is available.

If you donate your child's cord blood to a public bank, his or her name is added to a national registry. If the child ever needs cord blood, he or she is guaranteed it.

Most banks require the mother to be tested for various infections before blood is accepted. This can add to the cost of saving the blood. Your insurance company may pay for this testing if you have a family history of a disease that might be treated with umbilical-cord blood. Call and ask them if you're interested.

Some health-insurance companies pay the collection and storage fees for families at high risk of cancer or genetically based diseases. Cord-blood banking services may waive fees for at-risk families who are unable to afford them.

The blood bank you choose should be accredited by the American Association of Blood Banks. They have established procedures for collecting and storing umbilical-cord blood.

Donating Cord Blood

If you don't think you'll need the blood, you may want to donate it. If cord blood isn't used for patients, it may be used by researchers.

There are 20 public cord-blood banks in the United States at this time. They work with hospitals that ask women if they are willing to donate their baby's cord blood.

This is an expensive procedure, so not all hospitals participate in the program. In addition to increasing the amount of blood a public bank receives, many are attempting to increase their range of ethnic backgrounds and diversity by asking women of color to donate their baby's blood. If you're interested, ask your healthcare provider for information about cord-blood banking services and cord-blood donation in your area. In some states, the law requires information on UCB banking to be provided to you.

Appendix B: Feeding Your Baby

The Bottlefeeding Option

Many women choose to bottlefeed baby—studies show more women bottle-feed than breastfeed. In fact, many new moms begin by breastfeeding, but by 3 months, over 65% of all babies are bottlefed exclusively. By the age of 6 months, only 12% of all babies receive only breast milk.

Don't feel guilty if you decide to bottlefeed—it's a personal decision you're entitled to make. You won't be considered a "terrible mother" because you choose not to or cannot breastfeed. Baby will be OK if you bottlefeed him.

We don't want any mother to feel guilty if she chooses bottlefeeding. Some-times a woman cannot breastfeed because of a physical condition or problem. You may be unable to breastfeed if you are extremely underweight or have some medical conditions, such as a prolactin deficiency, heart disease, kidney disease, tuberculosis or HIV. Some infants have problems breastfeeding, or they are unable to breastfeed if they have a cleft palate or cleft lip. Lactose in-tolerance can also cause breastfeeding problems.

Occasionally a woman just doesn't have the time or energy to breastfeed if she has many other demands on her. Some women want to breastfeed and try to, but it doesn't work out. If breastfeeding doesn't work for you, please don't worry about it.

Bottlefeeding doesn't always mean feeding baby formula. You can also bot-tlefeed expressed breast milk. There may be many reasons you may choose to introduce your baby to the bottle. One is so dad can feed baby. Another is so mom can get a bit of rest. This is especially important if the new mother is ill or suffers from postpartum distress syndrome.

For a more complete discussion of bottlefeeding baby, read our book *Your Baby's First Year Week by Week*.

It's an Individual Choice

Your baby can receive good nutrition if you bottlefeed him iron-fortified for-mula. Some women enjoy the freedom bottlefeeding provides. It can make it easier for someone else to help care for the baby. You can determine exactly how much formula your baby is taking in at each feeding. There are also other advantages to bottlefeeding.

- Bottlefeeding is easy to learn; it never hurts if it's done incorrectly.
- Dad can be more involved in caring for baby.
- Bottlefed babies may go longer between feedings because formula is usually digested more slowly than breast milk.
- A day's supply of formula can be mixed at one time, saving time and effort.
- You don't have to be concerned about feeding baby in front of other people.
- It may be easier to bottlefeed if you plan to return to work soon after baby's birth.
- If you feed iron-fortified formula, baby won't need iron supplements.
- If you use fluoridated tap water to mix formula, you may not have to give baby fluoride supplements.
- Premeasured formula containers are great when you're on the go.

Most parents want to establish a strong bond with baby. However, some fear bottlefeeding won't encourage closeness with their child. They fear bonding won't happen between parent and baby. It's not true that a woman must breastfeed her baby to bond with him.

You *can* make bottlefeeding a bonding experience. When feeding baby, choose a quiet place—this helps baby concentrate on eating. Skin-to-skin contact while feeding helps bring mom (or anyone else feeding baby) and baby closer.

If you make formula from tap water, use cold water. Many pipes contain lead; heated tap water releases lead from pipes. If you want to warm up the formula, use hot water on the *outside* of the bottle.

It takes about 10 to 15 days for your milk production to decline and stop if you don't breastfeed. The greatest discomfort is usually experienced between the third and fifth day after delivery. To help ease soreness, wear a sports bra day *and* night, take acetaminophen or ibuprofen, and use cold packs.

Your Nutrition If You Bottlefeed

Even if you bottlefeed, it's important to follow a nutritious eating plan, such as the one you followed during pregnancy. Continue to eat foods high in complex carbohydrates, such as grain products, fruits and vegetables. Lean meats, chicken and fish are good sources of protein. For your dairy products, choose the low-fat or skim types.

You need fewer calories than you would if you were breastfeeding. But don't drastically cut your calories in the hopes of losing weight quickly. You still need to eat nutritiously to maintain good energy levels. Be sure the calories you eat are not from junk foods.

Here is a list of the types and quantities of foods you should try to eat each day. Choose 6 servings from the bread/cereal/pasta/rice group. Eat 3 servings of fruit and 3 servings of vegetables. From the dairy group, choose 2 servings. Eat about 6 ounces of protein each day. We still advise caution with fats, oils and sugars; limit intake to 3 teaspoons. And keep up your fluid intake.

Formulas to Consider

Commercial formula first became available in the 1930s. Today, we have many types and brands of formula available to feed baby. Ask your pediatrician about the type of formula you should use. The American Academy of Pediatrics recommends a baby be fed iron-fortified formula for the first year of his life. Feeding for this length of time helps maintain adequate iron intake.

When choosing formula, there isn't much difference among the brands of regular formula available. Most babies do well on milk-based formula. Basic infant formula comes from cow's milk and is modified to make it more similar to breast milk. It's also easier to digest than regular cow's milk. Most formulas are iron fortified. A baby needs iron for normal growth; one study showed too little iron can lead to problems.

Formulas are packaged in powder form, concentrated liquid and ready-to-feed. The end product is the same. Powdered formula is the least expensive. When choosing formula, go for the powdered type in cans. Cans containing liquid formula often are lined with plastic containing BPA. To help you avoid BPA, many companies sell products in glass or BPA-free containers.

All formulas sold in the United States must meet the same minimum standards set by the FDA, so they are all nutritionally complete. You don't need to worry about contaminated formula. Formula production is strictly controlled, so the risk of contamination is very low. It's illegal to import formula from other countries. If you know of any store selling foreign formula, don't buy it!

Many formulas on the market include two nutrients found in breast milk—DHA and ARA. DHA (docosahexaenoic acid) contributes to baby's eye development. ARA (arachidonic acid) is important in baby's brain development. Studies show babies fed with formula supplemented with DHA and ARA do better on cognitive tests than do babies fed formula without them. They also have better visual sharpness.

Bottlefeeding isn't cheap—you'll spend $1500 to $2000 to feed baby formula for the first year.

Feeding Equipment to Use

Don't buy plastic bottles or containers with the number 7 on the label or bottom. This helps avoid exposing baby to BPA. When you feed baby with a bottle, you may want to use a slanted one. Research shows this design keeps the nipple full of milk, which means baby takes in less air. A slanted bottle also helps ensure baby is sitting up to drink. When a baby drinks lying down, milk can pool in the eustachian tube, which may lead to ear infections.

You'll also have to choose a nipple for baby's bottle. A wide, round, soft flexible nipple helps baby latch on with his mouth opened wide, similar to nursing. Another type of nipple allows formula or pumped breast milk to be released at the same rate as breast milk flows during nursing. A twist adjusts the nipple to a flow that is slow, medium or fast. In this way, you can find the flow that works best for your baby. The nipple fits on most bottles. Check local stores or the Internet if you're interested.

Bottlefeeding Pointers

Bottlefed babies take from 2 to 5 ounces of formula at a feeding. They feed about every 3 to 4 hours for the first month (6 to 8 times a day). If baby fusses when his bottle is empty, it's OK to give him a little more.

If baby pulls away from the bottle, it's usually a sign he's finished feeding. However, you may want to try burping him before ending the feeding.

You know baby's getting enough formula if he has 6 to 8 wet diapers a day. He may also have 1 or 2 bowel movements. Stools of a bottlefed baby are more solid and greener in color than a breastfed baby's.

If your baby poops after a feeding, it's caused by the *gastrocolic reflex*. This reflex causes squeezing of the intestines when the stomach is stretched, as with feeding. It's very pronounced in newborns and usually decreases after 2 or 3 months of age.

After baby drinks 2 ounces, burp him. Burp baby after every feeding to help him get rid of excess air. If baby doesn't want a feeding, don't force it. Try again in a couple of hours. But if he refuses two feedings in a row, contact your pediatrician. Baby may be sick.

The Breastfeeding Option

Until the 1940s, babies were breastfed almost exclusively. Today, about 70% of all new moms start out breastfeeding their babies; however, most have stopped by the time baby is 6 months old.

Breastfeeding is the healthiest way to feed baby. For many women, it's also a wonderful, loving time and may complete the birth experience.

All babies receive some protection from mom against disease before birth. During pregnancy, antibodies pass from mother to baby through the placenta. They circulate through baby's blood for a few months after birth. Breastfed babies receive continued protection in breast milk.

Breastfed babies contract fewer infections than bottlefed babies because breast milk is bacteria-free and actively helps newborns avoid disease. One

Breastfeeding Counselors and Lactation Consultants

If you have problems breastfeeding after baby's birth, people are available to help you. Contact your local La Leche League to be put in contact with a breastfeeding counselor who can offer support and share experiences, usually for no fee. She may be available by telephone to answer questions, or she may visit you at home.

When a *breastfeeding counselor* comes across a problem beyond her scope, she can refer you to a *lactation consultant*. Breastfeeding counselors and lactation consultants often work closely together. A lactation consultant is a qualified professional who may work in hospitals, home-care services, health agencies and private practice. She can help with basic breastfeeding issues, assess and observe you and your baby, develop a care plan, inform healthcare providers of the situation and follow up with you as needed. You can even contact a lactation consultant before baby's birth.

Contact the International Lactation Consultant Association for further information; their website is www.ilca.org.

study showed breastfed babies are less likely to develop ear infections than bottlefed babies. Good news for mom as well! Studies show breastfeeding releases oxytocin, a hormone that can lower blood pressure. You may find you cope a little better with stress if you breastfeed.

Breastfed babies are less likely to develop allergies and asthma. Breastfeeding for as short as 3 months may reduce baby's risk of developing allergies and infections. Studies show babies fed only breast milk for 6 months had fewer instances of asthma, food allergies and eczema into their teenage years. Breastfeeding for the first 6 months also helps reduce the risks of juvenile diabetes, childhood leukemia, stomach viruses, ear infections and SIDS. Studies show you may lower your child's risk of SIDS by as much as 50%!

Breast milk is easy to digest; for a preemie, it is often the best nourishment. It cannot become contaminated, be mixed incorrectly or served at the wrong temperature. There are also benefits for you—breastfeeding helps metabolize fat deposits your body laid down during pregnancy.

Choline and docosahexaenoic acid (DHA) can help build baby's brain cells during breastfeeding. Choline can be found in milk, eggs, whole-wheat bread and beef. DHA is found in fish, egg yolks, poultry, meat, canola oil, walnuts and wheat germ. If you eat these foods while you're breastfeeding, you help your baby obtain these important supplements.

Breastfed babies need extra vitamin D because breast milk doesn't contain enough of this important vitamin. Talk to your pediatrician about giving baby 400IU of a liquid vitamin-D supplement every day, beginning at birth.

You can usually begin breastfeeding your baby within hours after birth. If you breastfeed within 1 hour of birth, you begin to establish your milk supply; you can also take advantage of baby's natural sucking instinct. When you breastfeed soon after birth, it provides your baby with *colostrum,* the first milk your breasts produce. Colostrum contains important factors that help boost her immune system. Breastfeeding also causes your pituitary gland to release oxytocin, which helps the uterus contract and decrease bleeding. Breast milk comes in 12 to 48 hours after birth.

Breastfeeding is an excellent way to bond with your baby. Closeness between mother and child can be established during the feeding process. Don't be discouraged if breastfeeding doesn't feel natural to you at first. It takes some time to find out what works best for you and your baby. Hold her so she can easily reach the breast while nursing; hold her across your chest or lie in bed. She should take your nipple into her mouth fully, so her gums cover the areola. She can't suck effectively if your nipple is only slightly drawn into her mouth.

For the first few weeks, feed your baby eight to ten times a day for 20 to 30 minutes at each feeding. Take more time if your baby needs it.

For a more-complete discussion of breastfeeding baby, read our book *Your Baby's First Year Week by Week*.

How Breastfeeding Affects You

Breastfeeding your baby will definitely have some effects on you. It may help you lose weight, but studies show you need to breastfeed baby for at least 3 months to get any benefit. Breastfeeding your baby may also reduce *your* risks of diabetes, high blood pressure and heart disease in later life.

If there's a history of breast cancer in your family, especially your mother or sisters, breastfeeding may protect you against developing breast cancer. One study recommends women with a family history of breast cancer should be strongly encouraged to breastfeed. New research shows it may cut your breast-cancer risk by nearly 60%!

Keep drinking lots of fluids. Staying hydrated can help increase your milk production and energy levels. After your milk supply is well-established (about 6 weeks), strenuous exercise shouldn't impact your milk supply.

When you breastfeed, you may not be getting enough zinc, vitamin D, vitamin E, calcium or folate. Lack of these vitamins and minerals may leave you feeling irritable and tired. Ask your healthcare provider about continuing your prenatal vitamins while breastfeeding because they contain many of the vitamins and minerals you need.

While breastfeeding, you may not have menstrual periods and you may not ovulate, meaning you won't get pregnant. However, don't rely on breastfeeding alone if you don't want another pregnancy right away. Take precautions.

Be careful with oral contraceptives; hormones can get into your milk and pass to your baby. Choose some other form of birth control until you're finished breastfeeding. You may choose a "minipill" (a progesterone-only birth-control pill), condoms, a diaphragm or an IUD. Implantable contraception, Depo-Provera and a once-a-month birth-control injection are safe to use if you nurse.

Most substances you eat or drink (or take orally, as medication) can pass to baby in your breast milk. Your baby may react to spicy foods, chocolate and caffeine when you ingest them. Researchers suggest a breastfeeding mother avoid peanuts because of a possible peanut allergy in her baby. Be careful about what you eat and drink when you breastfeed.

Other interesting facts about breastfeeding and you.

- Sleep loss can affect your milk supply.
- Breastfeeding depletes *your* supply of choline. You need 550mg a day to replace it.
- Mothers who are breastfeeding can continue to nurse their babies while being treated for the flu.
- Breastfeeding does *not* make your breasts sag. Your age, weight before pregnancy, your breast size and whether you smoke are greater factors in determining whether your breasts will sag after baby's arrival.

Watch your alcohol consumption. When you do have a drink, don't have more than one, and make it wine or beer because the percentage of alcohol in beer and wine is lower than that in hard liquor. Beer and wine pass from your body in about 3 hours. Studies show it takes up to 13 hours for hard liquor to leave the body.

Is Your Baby Getting Enough Milk?

You may be concerned about how much breast milk your baby gets at a feeding. There are clues to look for. Watch her jaws and ears while she eats—is she actively sucking? At the end of a feeding, does she fall asleep or settle down easily? Can she go 1½ hours between feedings? You'll know your baby is getting enough to eat if she nurses frequently, such as every 2 to 3 hours or eight to twelve times in 24 hours; gains 4 to 7 ounces (120 to 210ml) a week or at least 1 pound (0.46kg) a month; and appears healthy, has good muscles and is alert and active.

There are some warning signs to watch for. There may be a problem if:

- your breasts show little or no change during pregnancy
- you experience no engorgement after your baby's birth
- there is no breast milk by day 5 postpartum
- you can't hear your baby gulping while she breastfeeds
- your baby loses more than 10% of her birth weight
- your baby wets fewer than six diapers and has fewer than three stools a day
- your baby never seems satisfied

Other Breastfeeding Facts

Many women are surprised when they experience *milk letdown*. Soon after a baby begins to nurse, a woman feels a tingling or cramping in her breasts; this means milk is flowing into the breast ducts. It occurs several times during feeding; sometimes a baby chokes a bit when the rush of milk comes too quickly. You may also experience this letdown when it's time for your baby to nurse or when you hear a baby crying—your own or any other baby!

There is some controversy about when to introduce a bottle to a breastfed baby. Talk to your pediatrician about it. If you're going to try giving baby a bottle, give her expressed breast milk because she's familiar with the taste. In addition, feed a bottle an hour or two *after* breastfeeding—it's easier to get her to try a bottle when she's not starving.

If your baby is sick or premature and you want to breastfeed, pump your breasts and store the milk or take it to the NICU to feed her until you can nurse her. This helps establish your milk production, and you'll have a good supply of breast milk on hand when baby comes home. If you have enough breast milk stored, you may want to consider donating your extra breast milk to a breast-milk bank. Call your local La Leche League for information.

Women who have had breast-enlargement surgery with silicone implants are often able to breastfeed successfully; ask your healthcare provider about it if this concerns you. You should also be able to breastfeed after a breast reduction. Milk production may be less after such surgery, but it is usually enough to satisfy a baby.

If you need help with breastfeeding your baby, ask friends and family members. They may have solutions. Call your healthcare provider's office—office

If your baby is a boy, your breast milk contains 25% more calories than if your baby is a girl.

personnel may be able to refer you to someone knowledgeable. You can also look on the Internet or in the telephone book for the La Leche League, an organization that promotes breastfeeding. Someone from a local affiliate can give you advice and encouragement.

Disadvantages of Breastfeeding

Let's be honest—there are disadvantages to breastfeeding. Breastfeeding ties you completely to baby because you must be available when she is hungry. Other family members may feel left out.

Because breast milk empties rapidly from baby's stomach, most newborns need to feed every couple of hours. You may spend more time feeding baby than you anticipated. Pay careful attention to your diet.

In addition, you may experience physical problems. Below is a discussion of some of the more common problems many breastfeeding moms face.

Engorgement

A common breastfeeding problem for some women is *breast engorgement*. Breasts become swollen, tender and filled with breast milk. What can you do to relieve this problem?

- The best cure is to drain the breasts, if possible, as you do when breast-feeding. Some women take a hot shower and empty their breasts in the warm water.
- Ice packs may help.
- Feed your baby from both breasts *each time* you feed. Don't feed only on one side.
- When you're away from baby, try to express some breast milk to keep your milk flowing and breast ducts open. You'll also feel more comfortable.
- Mild pain medicines, such as acetaminophen, are often useful in relieving the pain of engorgement. Acetaminophen is recommended by the American Academy of Pediatrics (AAP) as safe to use while breastfeeding.

If you have a cold or other virus, it's all right to breastfeed. It's OK to breastfeed if you're taking most antibiotics as long as you know the drug is compatible with nursing. Ask your healthcare provider or pharmacist if any medication prescribed for you should not be taken while breastfeeding. Ask *before* you begin taking it; some antibiotics should be avoided.

- You might need to use stronger medications, such as acetaminophen with codeine, a prescription medication.
- Call your healthcare provider if engorgement is especially painful. He or she will decide on treatment.

Sore Nipples

When you breastfeed your baby, you may get sore nipples, which occur for various reasons. If your baby doesn't take your nipple fully into her mouth during breastfeeding, her jaws can compress the nipple and make it sore. Your clothing can also irritate tender nipples.

Nipple shields, worn inside your bra between the nipple and fabric, provide some relief. A mild cream can also provide soothing relief. Ask your pharmacist or healthcare provider for the names of products that are approved for use during nursing. Take heart—sore nipples rarely last longer than a couple of days. Continue breastfeeding while your breasts are sore.

> If you're having problems with breastfeeding, keep a log of the time and length of each feeding and which side you nursed on. This may help you evaluate the situation more clearly.

Plugged Milk Ducts

Sometimes milk ducts in the breast become plugged. A plugged duct prevents milk from flowing freely and makes some parts of the breast feel tender or firm. These become more painful after breastfeeding.

A plugged duct usually takes care of itself if you continue to nurse frequently. If it doesn't resolve on its own, apply a warm compress to the affected area or soak the breast in warm water. Then express milk or breastfeed while massaging the tender area. You may take acetaminophen. If problems continue, contact your healthcare provider.

Breast Infections

Large red streaks that extend up the breast toward the armpit or a breast that becomes firm or hard usually indicates a breast infection. Call your healthcare provider immediately. A fever may develop within 4 to 8 hours of appearance of the red streaks. Your healthcare provider will want to start antibiotic treatment quickly because antibiotics work best in the first 12 to 16 hours of infection.

Microwaving breast milk can kill antibodies that help protect baby from illness and disease.

To help prevent an infection, eat healthfully and get enough rest to reduce stress and to keep your immune system in top fighting form. Don't wear tight-fitting bras, especially underwire bras, because they may block milk flow. This may cause an infection. Empty your breasts on a regular schedule to avoid engorgement. After each feeding or pumping, let nipples air dry for a few minutes.

Don't stop nursing if you have a breast infection or think you have one; continue breastfeeding. If you stop, the infection may get worse. You won't pass the infection to the baby.

Feeding More Than One Baby

One of the greatest challenges for parents of multiples is deciding how to feed them. Some mothers want to breastfeed exclusively. (It's an added bonus for multiples because they are usually smaller than single-birth babies, and breast milk is extremely beneficial for them.) Some moms say bottlefeeding is the only way to go. Others try to combine the two and breastfeed *and* bottlefeed their babies.

Supplementing with formula allows your partner and others to help you feed the babies. You can breastfeed one while someone else bottlefeeds the other. Or you can nurse each one for a time, then finish the feeding with formula. In either case, someone else can help you feed the babies.

Switch babies from one breast to the other at different feedings. This ensures each baby gets visual stimulation on both sides. It also helps prevent problems in you, such as engorgement in one breast if one baby isn't feeding as well as the other. By switching breasts, the demand for milk remains about the same for each breast, so breasts tend to remain equal in size.

Breastfeeding babies for one or two feedings a day gives them the protection from infection that breast milk provides. Research has shown that even the smallest dose of breast milk gives baby an advantage over babies only fed formula.

One of the best things you can do is to consult a lactation specialist—you're going to need some sound advice. You might want to do this *before* babies are born so you can make a plan. If babies are early and you can't nurse them, begin pumping! Pump from day one, and store your breast milk for the time babies are able to receive it. In addition, pumping tells the body to produce breast milk—pump and the milk will come. It just takes some time.

Be sure to take good care of yourself. Your attempts at breastfeeding may make you feel like a 24-hour fast-food restaurant, but you'll be giving your babies the best start in life.

One goal to work toward is getting both babies on the same schedule. But that's not always easy to do. One baby may be more interested in feeding than the other, but try to feed them both at the same time when possible.

Breastfeeding multiples is a challenge. If you decide to try it, experiment with various situations and positions to find what works best for you. Some mothers nurse both babies at the same time. There are special cushions on the market designed to help you hold and nurse two babies at once.

Milk Banking

For over 100 years, breast-milk banking has been practiced in the United States. With milk banking, a woman donates screened expressed breast milk for babies at risk. A physician's prescription is required to purchase milk from a bank.

Babies with special medical needs are usually first in line for breast milk and its immunity-boosting benefits. Women with low milk production or those families with an adopted baby often have a difficult time getting this milk for their babies.

It's expensive to purchase milk from a milk bank. It can cost as much as $5 per ounce to buy banked breast milk. Some insurance plans cover a portion of the expense; others do not cover anything at all.

If you want to gift your milk to infants in need, contact the Human Milk Banking Association of North America (hmbana.org). They will give you the name of a milk bank near you. You will be screened, along with your milk, for safety.

Milk Sharing?

Milk sharing is becoming more common across the country. Some women and their babies engage in *cross nursing*, which involves splitting breastfeeding duties with another woman and her baby. Women say they like the flexibility it provides, and the babies get to bond with other people.

However, the medical community generally warns against milk sharing. You must know the health status of the mom who is sharing her breast milk with you. Does she smoke or drink alcohol? What kinds of foods does she eat? How much water does she drink?

You must also match your baby's age to the baby's age of the donor mother. Breast milk is specific for a baby and changes as the baby grows. A newborn infant needs milk that contains particular nutrients. If the milk-sharing mother has a baby that is quite a bit older, her milk will not contain many of the nutrients your newborn needs. If you're interested in milk sharing, keep the following in mind.

- Be sure the donor mother lives healthfully. Ask about the foods she eats, medications she takes, smoking and drinking habits, and exposure to any toxic substances.
- Insist on testing for you both. Exchange test results for cytomegalovirus, HIV, hepatitis, herpes, strep, staph, syphilis and tuberculosis.
- Never buy milk online. You don't know if it's safe.
- Be sure your baby's age is very close to the age of the baby you are sharing mother's milk with.

Your Nutrition if You Breastfeed

You need to think about your nutrition when you breastfeed. It's important in making breast milk. You will probably be advised to eat about 500 extra calories each day during this time because you secrete 500 to 1000 calories into your breast milk every day! The extra calories help you maintain good health, so they should be nutritious, like the ones you ate during pregnancy. Choose 9 servings from the bread/cereal/pasta/rice group and 3 servings from the dairy group. Fruit servings should number 4, and vegetable servings should number 5. The amount of protein in your diet should be 8 (237ml) ounces a day during breastfeeding. Be careful with fats, oils and sugars; limit intake to 4 teaspoons (20ml).

Some foods can pass into breast milk and cause baby stomach distress. You may want to avoid chocolate, foods that produce gas in you, highly spiced foods and any other foods you have problems with. Discuss the situation with your healthcare provider and your pediatrician if you have questions.

You need to continue to drink lots of fluids. Keeping hydrated can help increase your milk production and energy levels. Drink at least *3 quarts* (3L) of

Breastfed babies need extra vitamin D because breast milk doesn't contain enough of this important vitamin. Talk to your pediatrician about giving baby 400IU of a liquid vitamin-D supplement every day, beginning at birth.

fluid every day. You'll need more in hot weather. Be careful with caffeine-containing foods and drinks—they can act as diuretics.

Keep up your calcium intake. Ask about the kind of vitamin supplement you should take. Some mothers take a prenatal vitamin as long as they breastfeed. Some new moms take lactation supplements that contain higher doses of some vitamins and minerals and lower doses of iron than prenatal vitamins.

Tips to Get Started

You may have some problems when you begin breastfeeding. Don't be discouraged if you do. It takes some time to discover what works for you and baby. There are things to do to help make breastfeeding a success. Below are some things to keep in mind as you begin nursing.

It takes practice! Although breastfeeding is a natural way to feed baby, it takes time and practice to get the hang of it.

Feed baby on demand—this could be as many as 8 to 10 times a day or more! A baby usually cuts back to eating 4 to 6 times a day by age 4 months. A breastfed baby will take in only as much breast milk as she needs, so your milk production will usually adjust to her needs.

Hold baby so she can easily reach your breast while nursing. Hold her across your chest, or lie in bed. Her tummy should touch you; tuck her lower arm between your arm and your side.

Help her latch on to your breast. Brush your nipple across her lips. When she opens her mouth, place your nipple and as much of the areola as possible in her mouth. You should feel her pull the breast while sucking, but it shouldn't hurt.

Nurse baby 5 to 10 minutes on each breast; she gets most of her milk at the beginning of the feeding. Don't rush her—it can take as long as 30 minutes for her to finish. Baby may not need burping. As you begin, burp between feedings at each breast and when baby finishes. If she doesn't burp, don't force it. She may not need to.

Some experts believe you can start feeding baby a bottle almost as soon as you get home from the hospital. Discuss it with your pediatrician.

Medications during Breastfeeding

Be very careful with *any* medicine you take if you breastfeed. If you take codeine for pain after delivery, watch baby for signs of difficulty breathing, limpness and extreme drowsiness.

Take a medication *only* when you need it, and take it *only* as prescribed. Ask for the smallest dose possible. Ask about possible effects on the baby so you can be alert for them. Wait to get treatment, if possible. Consider taking medication immediately after nursing; it may have less of an effect on baby.

Many new mothers are worried about taking antibiotics while breastfeeding. Most fears are unfounded because most of the commonly used antibiotics are safe for breastfeeding moms.

There is some concern about metronidazole (Flagyl). The AAP suggests a woman shouldn't breastfeed while taking it. She should also throw out milk for 24 hours after finishing the medicine before she begins breastfeeding again.

If a medicine could have serious effects on your baby, you may decide to bottlefeed while you take the medication. You can maintain your milk supply by pumping (then throwing away) expressed milk.

> Don't believe the old wives' tale that drinking beer will help increase your milk supply.

Appendix C:
If Your Baby Is Premature

Over 475,000 babies are born prematurely in the United States every year. In the past 30 years, the number of preterm births has increased by 30%. Research shows about 25% of preterm births are a result of a pregnancy problem. However, for nearly 50% of all premature births, the cause is unknown.

A baby born prematurely is often called a *preemie;* the type of care he receives depends on how early he was born. Some babies are not extremely early and won't require extensive care. Other babies need long-term care and won't go home for weeks or months. The rule of thumb is the earlier a baby is born, the longer he'll need care.

All premature babies are individuals. Your baby will be evaluated and tended to based on his unique needs. For a more complete discussion of your premature baby, read our book *Your Baby's First Year Week by Week.*

Immediate Care for Your Newborn

When a baby is born early, many things can happen very quickly. A preemie needs more care because her body can't take over and perform some normal body functions. If baby has difficulty breathing, the nursing staff will help her, which can be done in many ways. After baby is tended to in the delivery room, she will be moved to the infant-care nursery or to a special unit for treatment, evaluation and care.

If baby needs wide-ranging, in-depth care, she will be moved to the neonatal intensive-care unit, also called the NICU (pronounced *NICK-U*). The nurses and physicians who work in these units have received specialized education and training so they may care for preemies.

The first time you see baby for any length of time may be after she has been moved to the NICU. You may be amazed by her size. The earlier she was born, the smaller she will be.

As time passes and baby grows, you'll probably be able to hold her. You will also be encouraged to care for her, such as giving her a bath, changing her and feeding her. Kangaroo care (skin-to-skin contact) for 1 hour a day, several times a week provides many health benefits for a preemie.

You'll see many pieces of equipment and machines in the unit. They are there to help provide the best care possible for your baby. Monitors record various information, ventilators help baby breathe, lights warm baby or help treat jaundice. Even baby's bed may be unique.

Feeding Your Preemie

Feeding is very important in a premature baby. In fact, a baby being able to feed on his own for all of his feedings may be one of the milestones the doctor looks for when considering when to release him. Breastfeeding or bottlefeeding for every feeding is a major accomplishment.

For the first few days or weeks after birth, a premature baby is often fed intravenously. When a baby is premature, he may not have the ability to suck and to swallow, so he can't breastfeed or bottlefeed. His gastrointestinal system is too immature to absorb nutrients. Feeding him by I.V. gives him the nutrition he needs in a form he can digest. In addition, premature babies often have digestive problems. They need to be fed small amounts at each feeding, so they must be fed often.

If you're going to breastfeed baby, you'll need to supply your breast milk. Pumping may be the answer. Studies have shown that any amount of breast milk is good for a preemie, so seriously consider this important task.

DHA and ARA are two nutrients present in breast milk that can really help a preemie. If you can't breastfeed, ask the NICU nurses if baby will be fed a special preemie formula that contains these nutrients.

The composition of your breast milk when baby is born prematurely is different from the breast milk when baby is full-term. Because of this difference, baby may also be supplemented with formula.

Choosing a Pediatrician for Your Preemie

The care your baby receives after leaving the hospital is very important. Try to find a pediatrician who has had experience caring for premature babies. You'll probably be seeing this doctor quite frequently during the first year, so it's important to feel comfortable with him or her.

Problems Some Preemies May Have

When a baby is born prematurely, she hasn't had time to finish growing and developing inside the womb. Being born too early can impact baby's health in many ways. Today, with all the medical and technological advances medicine has made in the care of premature babies, we are fortunate that many children have few long-term difficulties.

Some immediate problems your baby may have are listed below. Some are short term; others may need to be dealt with for the rest of the child's life:

- jaundice
- apnea
- respiratory distress syndrome (RDS)
- broncho-pulmonary dysplasia (BPD)
- undescended testicles
- patent ductus arteriosus
- intracranial hemorrhage (ICH)
- retinopathy of prematurity (ROP)
- respiratory syncytial virus (RSV)

Taking Baby Home

At some point, you'll be able to take baby home. Your baby will be ready to go home when he has no medical problems that require him to be in the hospital, can maintain a stable body temperature, takes all of his feedings on his own (no tube feeding) and is gaining weight.

People in the NICU will help you prepare for this important event. They can help you plan for any special-care needs before you take baby home. Once home, most preemies do well.

Your premature baby may be at an increased risk for SIDS. To help protect him, follow established guidelines for reducing SIDS for the entire *first year* of your baby's life. It's important to put baby *on his back* every time you put him in his crib or bassinet!

Mental and Physical Development of Your Baby

As baby grows and develops, you must always keep in mind that she was born early. For as long as the first 2 years of her life, development may be slower than the development of children who were born close to their due date. Your baby will have two ages—her *chronological age* (when she was born) and her *developmental age,* which is based on the date she was due. Developmental age is also called *adjusted age.*

Experts believe children born early may need help well beyond the early years. As parents, you'll want to be involved in measuring your child's learning and behavior activities. Discuss this with your physician so you can work together as a team to help your child.

When a baby is born early, it may take her longer to reach an event marking a new development or stage. These are called *milestones* and help you determine how baby is advancing. It really doesn't matter *when* your child reaches a milestone as long as she eventually reaches it!

When you evaluate how your child is developing, correct her age for the weeks of prematurity. Consider her developmental age from her due date, not her actual date of birth! For example, if baby was born on April 18th but her due date was actually June 6th, begin measuring her development from June 6th. Consider this her "developmental birthday."

Glossary

Abortion. Termination or end of pregnancy; giving birth to an embryo or fetus before it can live outside the womb, usually defined as before 20 weeks of gestation. May be spontaneous, often called a *miscarriage,* or induced, as a medical procedure to terminate a pregnancy.

Acquired immune deficiency syndrome (AIDS). Debilitating illness that affects the body's ability to respond to infection. Caused by the human immune deficiency virus (HIV).

Aerobic exercise. Exercise that increases your heart rate and oxygen intake.

Afterbirth. Placenta and membranes expelled after baby is delivered. See *placenta.*

Alpha-fetoprotein (AFP). Substance produced by unborn baby as it grows inside the uterus. Large amounts of AFP are found in amniotic fluid. Larger-than-normal amounts are found in maternal bloodstream if neural-tube defects are present in the fetus.

Amino acids. Substances that act as building blocks in developing embryo and fetus.

Amniocentesis. Removal of amniotic fluid from amniotic sac; fluid is tested for some genetic defects or fetal lung maturity.

Amniotic fluid. Fluid surrounding baby inside the amniotic sac.

Amniotic sac. Membrane that surrounds baby inside the uterus. It contains baby, placenta and amniotic fluid.

Anemia. Any condition in which the number of red blood cells is less than normal. Term usually applies to the concentration of the oxygen-transporting material in the blood.

Anencephaly. Defective brain development combined with absence of bones normally surrounding the brain.

Angioma. Tumor, usually benign, or swelling composed of lymph and blood vessels.

Antigen. Substance formed in the body or introduced into the body that causes formation of antibodies, which interact specifically with the substance.

Anti-inflammatory medications. Drugs to relieve pain or inflammation.

Apgar score. Measurement of baby's response to birth and life on its own. Taken 1 and 5 minutes after birth.

Areola. Pigmented or colored ring surrounding nipple of the breast.

Arrhythmia. Irregular or missed heartbeat.

Aspiration. Swallowing or sucking foreign body or fluid, such as vomit, into an airway.

Asthma. Disease marked by recurrent attacks of shortness of breath and difficulty breathing. Often caused by an allergic reaction.

Atonic uterus. Uterus that is flaccid or relaxed; lacks tone.

Baby blues. Mild depression in woman after delivery.

Back labor. Pain of labor is felt in lower back.

Bilirubin. Breakdown product of pigment formed in the liver from hemoglobin during destruction of red blood cells.

Biophysical profile. Method of evaluating fetus before birth.

Biopsy. Removal of small piece of tissue for microscopic study.

Birthing center. Facility in which a woman labors, delivers and recovers in the same room. May be part of a hospital or a freestanding unit. Sometimes called *LDRP,* for *labor, delivery, recovery* and *postpartum.*

Blood pressure. Push of blood against walls of arteries, which carry blood away from the heart.

Bloody show. Small amount of vaginal bleeding late in pregnancy; often precedes labor.

Board certification. Doctor has had additional training and testing in a particular specialty. In the area of obstetrics, the American Board of Obstetrics and Gynecology offers this certification. Certification requires expertise in care of women.

Braxton-Hicks contractions. Irregular, painless tightening of uterus during pregnancy.

Breech presentation. Abnormal position of fetus. Buttocks or legs come into the birth canal before the head.

Carcinogen. Any cancer-producing substance.

Cervix. Opening of the uterus.

Cesarean section (delivery). Delivery of baby through an abdominal incision rather than through the vagina.

Chadwick's sign. Dark blue or purple discoloration of mucosa of vagina and cervix during pregnancy.

Chemotherapy. Treatment of disease by chemical substances or drugs.

Chlamydia. Sexually transmitted venereal infection.

Chloasma. Extensive brown patches of irregular shape and size on face or other parts of the body.

Chorionic villus sampling (CVS). Diagnostic test done early in pregnancy. Biopsy of tissue is taken from inside the uterus through the abdomen or cervical opening to determine abnormalities of pregnancy.

Chromosomal abnormality. Abnormal number or abnormal makeup of chromosomes.

Chromosomes. Thread in cell's nucleus that contains DNA, which transmits genetic information.

Clomiphene-challenge test. Way of testing for ovulation using drug that stimulates ovaries.

Colostrum. Thin, yellow fluid that is the first milk to come from breasts. Most often seen toward the end of pregnancy. It is different in content from milk produced later during nursing.

Condyloma acuminatum. Sexually transmitted skin tags or warts caused by human papilloma virus (HPV). Also called *venereal warts.*

Congenital problem. Problem present at birth.

Consanguinity. Being related by blood to the person you are married to.

Constipation. Infrequent or incomplete bowel movements.

Contraction stress test. Test of response of fetus to uterine contractions to evaluate fetal well-being.

Contractions. Squeezing or tightening of uterus, which pushes baby out of the uterus during birth.

Cord-blood banking. Saving or preserving umbilical-cord blood following delivery.

Corpus-luteum cyst. Normal cyst on ovary after ovulation.

Cystitis. Inflammation of the bladder.

Cytomegalovirus (CMV) infection. Group of viruses from herpes virus family.

D&C (dilatation and curettage). Surgical procedure in which cervix is dilated and uterine lining is scraped.

Developmental delay. Condition in which baby's development is slower than normal.

Diastasis recti. Separation of abdominal muscles.

Differentiating. Changing, especially because of growth.

Dilatation. Opening or stretching of cervix during baby's birth or surgery, such as a *D&C.*

Dizygotic twins. Twins derived from two different eggs. Also called *fraternal twins.*

Due date. Date baby is expected to be born. Most babies are born near this date, but only 1 of 20 are born on the actual date.

Dysplasia. Abnormal, precancerous changes in cells of the cervix.

Dysuria. Difficulty or pain urinating.

Eclampsia. Convulsions and coma in woman with pre-eclampsia. Not related to epilepsy. See *pre-eclampsia.*

Ectopic pregnancy. Pregnancy that occurs outside the uterine cavity.

EDC (estimated date of confinement). Baby's anticipated due date. Calculated from first day of the last menstrual period, counting forward 280 days.

Edwards' syndrome. See *trisomy 18*.

Effacement. Thinning of cervix.

Electronic fetal monitoring. Use of electronic instruments to record the fetal heartbeat.

Embryo. Organism in the early stages of development.

Embryonic period. First 10 weeks of gestation.

Endometrium. Mucous membrane that lines inside of uterine wall.

Enema. Fluid injected into the rectum for the purpose of clearing the bowel.

Engorgement. Congestion, as filled with fluid.

Epidural block. Type of anesthesia injected around spinal cord during labor or some types of surgery.

Episiotomy. Surgical incision of the perineum (area behind the vagina, above the rectum). Used during delivery to avoid tearing of the vaginal opening and rectum.

Estimated date of confinement. See *EDC*.

Expressing breast milk. Manually forcing milk out of the breast.

External cephalic version (ECV). Procedure done late in pregnancy in which healthcare provider manually attempts to move baby in a breech position into the normal head-down position.

Face presentation. Baby comes into the birth canal face first.

Fallopian tube. Tube that leads from uterine cavity to area of the ovary. Also called *uterine tube*.

False labor. Tightening of uterus without dilatation of the cervix.

False-negative test result. Result indicates test is negative, but it is actually positive.

False-positive test result. Result indicates test is positive, but it is actually negative.

Fasting blood-sugar test. Blood test to evaluate amount of sugar in blood following period of fasting.

Ferrous gluconate. Iron supplement.

Ferrous sulfate. Iron supplement.

Fertilization. Joining of sperm and egg.

Fertilization age. Dating pregnancy from time of fertilization; 2 weeks earlier than gestational age. Also called *ovulatory age*.

Fetal anomaly. Fetal malformation or abnormal development.

Fetal arrhythmia. See *arrhythmia*.

Fetal-growth restriction. See *intrauterine-growth restriction*.

Fetal monitor. Device used before or during labor to listen to and to record fetal heartbeat. Monitoring baby inside the uterus can be external (through maternal abdomen) or internal (through maternal vagina).

Fetal period. Time period following embryonic period (first 10 weeks of gestation) until birth.

Fetal stress. Problems with baby that occur before birth or during labor, requiring immediate delivery.

Fetus. Refers to unborn baby after 10 weeks of gestation until birth.

Forceps. Special instrument placed around baby's head, inside birth canal, to help guide baby out of the birth canal during delivery.

Fragile-X syndrome. Abnormal X chromosome.

Frank breech. Baby presenting buttocks first; legs are flexed and knees extended.

Fraternal twins. See *dizygotic twins.*

Full-term infant. Baby born between 38 and 42 weeks of pregnancy.

Gene regulator. Gene that regulates operation of another gene.

Genetic counseling. Consultation between a couple and specialists about genetic defects and the possibility of presence or recurrence of genetic problems in pregnancy.

Genital herpes simplex. Herpes simplex infection involving genital area. It can be significant during pregnancy because of danger to a newborn infected with herpes simplex.

Gestation. Pregnancy.

Gestational age. Dating pregnancy from first day of last menstrual period; 2 weeks longer than fertilization age. Also called *menstrual age.*

Gestational diabetes. Occurrence of diabetes during pregnancy.

Globulin. Family of proteins from plasma or serum of the blood.

Glucose-tolerance test. Blood test done to evaluate body's response to sugar. Blood is drawn at intervals following ingestion of a sugary substance.

Glucosuria. Sugar in the urine.

Gonorrhea. Contagious venereal infection, transmitted primarily by intercourse. Caused by bacteria *Neisseria gonorrhoeae.*

Group-B streptococcal infection. Serious infection occurring in mother's vagina and throat.

Habitual miscarriage. Occurrence of three or more spontaneous miscarriages in a row.

Heartburn. Discomfort or pain that occurs in the chest, often after eating.

Hematocrit. Determines proportion of blood cells to plasma. Important in diagnosing anemia.

Hemoglobin. Pigment in red blood cell that carries oxygen to body tissues.

Hemolytic disease. Destruction of red blood cells. See *anemia*.

Hemorrhoids. Dilated blood vessels in rectum or rectal canal.

Heparin. Medication used to prevent excessive clotting of the blood.

High-risk pregnancy. Solvable problems may occur during pregnancy and should be expected. Woman may need special medical attention, often from a specialist. See *perinatologist*.

HIV. Human immunodeficiency virus. Debilitating illness that affects the body's ability to respond to infection. Precursor to AIDS.

Human chorionic gonadotropin. Hormone produced in early pregnancy. Measured in a pregnancy test.

Hydramnios. Increased amniotic fluid.

Hydrocephalus. Excessive accumulation of fluid around baby's brain. Sometimes called *water on the brain*.

Hyperbilirubinemia. Extremely high level of bilirubin in blood.

Hyperemesis gravidarum. Severe nausea, dehydration and vomiting during pregnancy. Occurs most frequently during first trimester.

Hyperglycemia. High blood-sugar levels.

Hyperkeratosis. Increase in size of the horny layer of the skin.

Hypertension, pregnancy-induced. High blood pressure that occurs during pregnancy. Defined by an increase in the diastolic or systolic blood pressure.

Hyperthyroidism. Elevation of thyroid hormone in the bloodstream.

Hypoglycemia. Low blood-sugar levels.

Hypoplasia. Defective or incomplete development or formation of tissue.

Hypotension. Low blood pressure.

Hypothyroidism. Low or inadequate levels of thyroid hormone in the bloodstream.

Identical twins. See *monozygotic twins*.

Immune globulin preparation. Substance used to protect against infection from certain diseases, such as hepatitis or measles.

In utero. Within the uterus.

In vitro. Outside the body.

Incompetent cervix. Cervix that dilates painlessly without contractions.

Incomplete miscarriage. Miscarriage in which part, but not all, of uterine contents are expelled.

Induced labor. Labor started or speeded up using a medication.

Inevitable miscarriage. Pregnancy complicated by bleeding and cramping. Usually results in miscarriage.

Insulin. Peptide hormone made by the pancreas. It promotes body's use of glucose.

Intrauterine-growth restriction (IUGR). Inadequate fetal growth during pregnancy.

Iron-deficiency anemia. Anemia produced by lack of iron in the diet; often seen in pregnancy. See *anemia.*

Isoimmunization. Development of specific antibody directed at red blood cells of another individual, such as baby in utero. Occurs when Rh-negative woman's blood mixes with Rh-positive blood, such as with blood transfusion or during amniocentesis or an accident.

Jaundice. Yellow staining of skin, sclera (eyes) and deeper tissues of the body. Caused by excessive amounts of bilirubin.

Ketones. Breakdown product of metabolism found in the blood, particularly in conditions of starvation or uncontrolled diabetes.

Kidney stones. Small mass or lesion found in kidney or urinary tract that can block flow of urine.

Klinefelter's syndrome. Abnormal number of sex chromosomes (XXY).

Labor. Process of expelling fetus from the uterus.

Laparoscopy. Surgical procedure performed for tubal ligation, diagnosis of pelvic pain, diagnosis of ectopic pregnancy or for other diagnoses.

Leukorrhea. Vaginal discharge characterized by white or yellowish color; primarily composed of mucus.

Lightening. Change in shape of pregnant uterus a few weeks before labor. Often described as baby "dropping."

Linea nigra. Line of increased pigmentation running down abdomen from bellybutton to pubic area during pregnancy.

Lochia. Vaginal discharge that occurs after delivery of baby and placenta.

Mammogram. X-ray study of breasts to identify normal and abnormal breast tissue.

Mask of pregnancy. Increased pigmentation over the area of the face under each eye. Commonly has the appearance of a butterfly.

Meconium. First intestinal discharge of newborn; green or yellow in color. Consists of epithelial or surface cells, mucus and bile. Discharge may occur before or during labor or soon after birth.

Melanoma. Pigmented mole or tumor that may or may not be cancerous.

Meningomyelocele. Congenital defect of central nervous system of baby. Membranes and spinal cord protrude through an opening or defect in vertebral column (spine).

Menstrual age. See *gestational age.*

Menstruation. Regular or periodic discharge of bloody fluid from the uterus.

Microcephaly. Abnormally small development of head in developing fetus.

Miscarriage. See *abortion.*

Missed miscarriage. Failed pregnancy, without bleeding or cramping. Often diagnosed by ultrasound weeks after a pregnancy fails.

Monilial vulvovaginitis. Infection caused by yeast or monilia. Usually affects vagina and vulva.

Monozygotic twins. Twins conceived from one egg. Often called *identical twins*.

Morning sickness. Nausea and vomiting experienced primarily during first trimester of pregnancy. Also see *hyperemesis gravidarum*.

MRSA. Methicillin-resistant Staphylococcus aureus.

Mucus plug. Secretions in cervix; often released just before labor.

Natural childbirth. Labor and delivery in which no medication is used; mother remains awake to help deliver baby. Woman may have taken classes to prepare her for labor and delivery.

Neural-tube defects. Abnormalities in development of the spinal cord and brain in fetus. See *anencephaly; hydrocephalus; spina bifida*.

Nonstress test. Test in which baby's movements are noted, along with changes in fetal heart rate.

Nurse-midwife. Nurse who has received extra training in care of pregnant women and delivery of babies.

Obstetrician. Physician who specializes in care of pregnant women and delivery of babies.

Oligohydramnios. Lack or deficiency of amniotic fluid.

Omphalocele. Congenital hernia at the bellybutton.

Osteopathic physician. Physician trained in osteopathic medicine, a system of treating medical ailments based on belief that ailments generally result from pressure of displaced bones on nerves and are curable with manipulation. Osteopaths rely on physical, medicinal and surgical methods, much as their medical-doctor counterparts.

Ovarian cycle. Regular production of ovarian hormones in response to hormonal messages from the brain. The ovarian cycle governs the endometrial cycle.

Ovulation. Cyclic production of an egg from the ovary.

Ovulatory age. See *fertilization age*.

Oxytocin. Medication that causes uterine contractions; used to induce labor. Also the hormone produced by pituitary glands.

Palmar erythema. Redness of palms of the hands.

Pap smear. Routine screening test that evaluates presence of premalignant or cancerous conditions of the cervix.

Paracervical block. Local anesthetic for cervical dilatation.

Patau's syndrome. See *trisomy 13*.

Pediatrician. Physician who specializes in care of babies and children.

Percutaneous umbilical blood sampling (PUBS). Removal of blood from umbilical cord while baby is still inside the uterus.

Perinatal death. Death of baby around the time of delivery.

Perinatologist. Physician who specializes in care of high-risk pregnancies.

Perineum. Area between rectum and vagina.

Phenylketonuria (PKU). Hereditary disease that prevents oxidation of phenylananine (an amino acid) into tyrosine. Left untreated, brain damage may occur.

Phospholipids. Fat-containing phosphorous. Most important are lecithins and sphingomyelin; they are important in maturation of fetal lungs before birth.

Physiologic anemia of pregnancy. Anemia during pregnancy caused by increase in the amount of plasma (fluid) in blood compared to the number of cells in blood. See *anemia*.

PIH. See *hypertension, pregnancy-induced*.

PKU. See *phenylketonuria*.

Placenta. Organ inside the uterus attached to baby by the umbilical cord. Essential during pregnancy for growth and development of embryo and fetus.

Placenta previa. Low attachment of placenta, very close to or covering the cervix.

Placental abruption. Premature separation of placenta from the uterus.

Pneumonitis. Inflammation of the lungs.

Polyhydramnios. See *hydramnios*.

Postmature baby. Pregnancy of 42 or more weeks.

Postpartum blues. See *baby blues*.

Postpartum depression. Depression after delivery.

Postpartum hemorrhage. Bleeding more than 15 ounces (450 ml) at or after delivery.

Postterm baby. Baby born 2 weeks or more past its due date.

PPROM. Preterm premature rupture of membranes.

Pre-eclampsia. Combination of symptoms significant to pregnancy, including high blood pressure, edema, swelling and changes in reflexes.

Pregnancy-induced diabetes. See *gestational diabetes*.

Premature delivery. Delivery before 38 weeks of pregnancy.

Prenatal care. Program of care for pregnant woman before birth of her baby.

Prepared childbirth. Woman has taken classes about what will occur during labor and delivery. She may request pain medication if she feels she needs it.

Presentation. Describes which part of the baby comes into the birth canal first.

Preterm birth. Baby born before 38 weeks of pregnancy.

Products of conception. Tissue passed with a miscarriage.

PROM. Premature rupture of membranes.

Proteinuria. Protein in urine.

Pruritis gravidarum. Itching during pregnancy.

Pubic symphysis. Bony prominence of pelvic bone. Landmark from which healthcare provider may measure during pregnancy to follow growth of the uterus.

Pudendal block. Local anesthesia during labor.

Pulmonary embolism. Blood clot from another part of the body that travels to the lungs. Can close passages in the lungs and decrease oxygen exchange.

Pyelonephritis. Serious kidney infection.

Quad-screen test. Measurement of four blood tests to determine fetal well-being.

Quickening. Feeling baby move inside the uterus.

RDA. Recommended dietary allowance; amount of a substance as established by the Food and Drug Administration.

Rh-negative. Absence of rhesus antibody in the blood.

RhoGAM. Medication given during pregnancy and after delivery to prevent isoimmunization. Also see *isoimmunization.*

Rh-sensitivity. See *isoimmunization.*

Round-ligament pain. Pain caused by stretching ligament on sides of the uterus during pregnancy.

Rupture of membranes. Loss of fluid from the amniotic sac. Also called *breaking of waters.*

Seizure. Sudden onset of a convulsion.

Sexually transmitted disease (STD). Infection transmitted through sexual intercourse or other sexual activity.

Sickle-cell disease. Disease caused by abnormal red blood cells shaped like sickles or cylinders.

Sickle-cell trait. Presence of trait for sickle-cell disease. Not sickle-cell disease itself.

Sickle crisis. Painful episode caused by sickle-cell disease.

Skin tag. Flap or extra buildup of skin.

Sodium. Element found in many foods, particularly salt. Ingestion of too much sodium may cause fluid retention.

Spina bifida. Congenital abnormality characterized by defect in vertebral column. Spinal cord and membranes of the spinal cord protrude outside the protective bony canal of the spine.

Spinal anesthesia. Anesthesia given in the spinal canal.

Spontaneous miscarriage. Loss of pregnancy during the first 20 weeks of gestation.

Stasis. Decreased flow.

Station. Estimation of baby's descent in the uterus in preparation for birth.

Steroids. Group of hormone-based medications. Often used to treat diseases. Includes estrogen, testosterone, progesterone, prednisone.

Stillborn. When baby is born, it is not alive.

Stress test. Test in which mild contractions of mother's uterus are induced; fetal heart rate in response to the contractions is noted. Also called *contraction stress test* or *CST.*

Stretch marks. Areas of skin are stretched and become scarred. Often found on abdomen, breasts, buttocks and legs.

Surfactant. Phospholipid present in the lungs that controls surface tension of lungs. Premature babies often lack sufficient amounts of surfactant to breathe without assistance.

Syphilis. Sexually transmitted venereal infection caused by *Treponema pallidum.*

Systemic lupus erythematosus (SLE). Connective-tissue disorder common in women in the reproductive ages. Antibodies made by the person act against person's own tissues.

Tay-Sachs disease. Inherited disease characterized by mental and physical retardation, convulsions, enlargement of head and, eventually, death. Trait usually carried by Ashkenazi Jews.

Telangiectasis. Dilatation or swelling of a small blood vessel; sometimes called an *angioma* or *spider angioma.*

Teratogenic. Causes abnormal development.

Teratology. Branch of science that deals with teratogens.

Term. Baby is considered "term" when it is born between 38 and 40 weeks. Also called *full term.*

Thalassemia. Group of inherited disorders of hemoglobin metabolism; results in decrease in the amount of hemoglobin formed. Most commonly found in people of Mediterranean descent.

Threatened miscarriage. Bleeding during first trimester of pregnancy without cramping or contractions.

Thrombosis. Formation of blood clot (thrombus).

Thrush. Monilial or yeast infection occurring in the mouth or mucous membranes of newborn infant.

Thyroid disease. Abnormality of thyroid gland and its production of thyroid hormone. See *hyperthyroidism; hypothyroidism.*

Tocolytic agents. Medications to stop labor.

Toxemia. See *pre-eclampsia.*

Toxic shock syndrome. Overwhelming reaction to poisons made by bacteria.

Toxic strep-A. Bacterial infection that can cause severe damage to anyone infected with it; usually starts in a cut on the skin, not as a sore throat, and spreads very quickly. It can involve the entire body.

Toxoplasmosis. Infection caused by *Toxoplasma gondii.*

Transverse lie. Fetus is turned sideways in uterus.

Trichomonal vaginitis. Venereal infection caused by trichomonas.

Trimester. A 13-week period of pregnancy.

Triple-screen test. Measurement of three blood tests to determine fetal well-being.

Trisomy. Extra chromosome.

Trisomy 13. Extra chromosome 13.

Trisomy 18. Extra chromosome 18.

Turner's syndrome. Missing chromosome 45X.

Twin-to-twin transfusion syndrome. Blood flow to twins is not equal; one twin gets more blood than the other twin during pregnancy.

Umbilical cord. Cord connecting placenta to developing baby. It removes waste products and carbon dioxide from baby and brings oxygenated blood and nutrients from mother through the placenta to baby.

Ureters. Tubes from the kidneys to the bladder that drain urine.

Urinalysis. Urine test; healthcare provider tests urine during pregnancy to check for signs of disease or infection.

Uterus. Organ an embryo/fetus grows in. Also called the *womb.*

Vaccine. Mild infection given to cause production of antibodies to protect against subsequent infections of the same type.

Vacuum extractor. Device used to help deliver baby.

Vagina. Birth canal.

Varicose veins. Dilated or enlarged blood vessels (veins).

Vascular spiders. See *telangiectasis.*

Vena cava. Major vein that empties into the right atrium of heart. It returns unoxygenated blood to the heart for transport to lungs.

Venereal warts. See *condyloma acuminatum.*

Womb. See *uterus.*

Yeast infection. See *monilial vulvovaginitis; thrush.*

Zygote. Early embryo that develops from a fertilized egg.

Index

Working, during pregnancy
  at a computer, 16
  exercises, 17
  Family and Medical Leave Act
    (1993), 26–27
  parental leave laws, 27
  part time, 18(B)
  precautions, 15
  Pregnancy Discrimination Act of
    1978, 25–26
  preparation to leave, 28–29
  safety issues, 15–16
  stress relief, 18

X-rays, 80, 81, 120, 141, 256, 273, 274

Yoga, 153, 201, 202, 204, 205
Your Baby's First Year Week by Week
  (Curtis and Schuler), 233, 315,
  349, 355, 365
Your Pregnancy for the Father-to-Be
  (Curtis and Schuler), 231, 232(B)

Zinc, 191, 224, 355
Zyban, 54(B)
Zyrtec, 218